Race and Diplomacy in Zimbabwe

The "Rhodesian crisis" of the 1960s and 1970s, and the early 1980s crisis of independent Zimbabwe, can be understood against the background of Cold War historical transformations brought on by, among other things, African decolonization in the 1960s; the failure of American power in Vietnam and the rise of Third World political power at the UN and elsewhere.

In this African history of the diplomacy of decolonization in Zimbabwe, Timothy Lewis Scarnecchia examines the relationship and rivalry between Joshua Nkomo and Robert Mugabe over many years of diplomacy, and how both leaders took advantage of Cold War racialized thinking about what Zimbabwe should be, including Anglo-American preoccupations with keeping whites from leaving after Independence. Based on a wealth of archival source materials, including materials that have recently become available through thirty-year rules in Britain and South Africa, this book uncovers how foreign relations bureaucracies in the United States, Britain, and South Africa created a Cold War "race state" notion of Zimbabwe that permitted them to rationalize Mugabe's state crimes in return for Cold War loyalty to Western powers. This title is also available as Open Access on Cambridge Core.

Timothy Lewis Scarnecchia is an associate professor of African History and Kent State University in Ohio. He is the author of *Urban Roots of Democracy and Political Violence in Zimbabwe: Harare and Highfield, 1940–1964* (2008) and numerous articles on Zimbabwean political history. His research for this book has brought him to work in archives in the United States, Britain, South Africa, and Zimbabwe.

T0382239

African Studies Series

The African Studies series, founded in 1968, is a prestigious series of monographs, general surveys, and textbooks on Africa covering history, political science, anthropology, economics, and ecological and environmental issues. The series seeks to publish work by senior scholars as well as the best new research.

Other titles in the series are listed at the back of the book.

Race and Diplomacy in Zimbabwe

The Cold War and Decolonization, 1960–1984

TIMOTHY LEWIS SCARNECCHIA
Kent State University

CAMBRIDGE
UNIVERSITY PRESS

CAMBRIDGE
UNIVERSITY PRESS

Shaftesbury Road, Cambridge CB2 8EA, United Kingdom

One Liberty Plaza, 20th Floor, New York, NY 10006, USA

477 Williamstown Road, Port Melbourne, VIC 3207, Australia

314–321, 3rd Floor, Plot 3, Splendor Forum, Jasola District Centre,
New Delhi – 110025, India

103 Penang Road, #05–06/07, Visioncrest Commercial, Singapore 238467

Cambridge University Press is part of the Cambridge University Press & Assessment

It furthers the University's mission by disseminating knowledge in the pursuit of
education, learning, and research at the highest international levels of excellence.

www.cambridge.org
Information on this title: www.cambridge.org/9781009281706
DOI: 10.1017/9781009281683

© Timothy Lewis Scarnecchia 2023
Reissued as Open Access, 2023

First published 2023

A catalogue record for this publication is available from the British Library.

Library of Congress Cataloging-in-Publication Data
Names: Scarnecchia, Timothy, author.
Title: Race and diplomacy in Zimbabwe : the Cold War and decolonization, 1960–1984 / Timothy
Lewis Scarnecchia.
Description: Cambridge ; New York, NY : Cambridge University Press, 2020. | Series: African studies
series | Includes bibliographical references and index.
Identifiers: LCCN 2021025393 (print) | LCCN 2021025394 (ebook) |
ISBN 9781316511794 (hardback) | ISBN 9781009054614 (paperback) |
ISBN 9781009053860 (ebook)
Subjects: LCSH: Decolonization – Zimbabwe. | Cold War. | Zimbabwe – History – 1965–1980. |
Zimbabwe – History – 1980– | Zimbabwe – Foreign relations – 1965–1980. | Zimbabwe – Foreign
relations – 1980– | Zimbabwe – History – Autonomy and independence movements. | Zimbabwe – Race
relations – History – 20th century. | BISAC: HISTORY / Africa / General
Classification: LCC DT2981 .S33 2020 (print) | LCC DT2981 (ebook) |
DDC 968.91/04–dc23
LC record available at https://lccn.loc.gov/2021025393
LC ebook record available at https://lccn.loc.gov/2021025394

ISBN 978-1-009-28170-6 Paperback

Contents

Figures

Acknowledgments

I would like to thank Kent State University, in particular the College of Arts and Sciences, the Department of History, and the University Research Council for their support of my research trips over the years. I would in particular like to thank the Dean's Office of the College of Arts and Sciences, Cathy Lowe, who administered my internal grants, and Kay Dennis and Carla Weber in the history department, who processed my travel funds through the Department and College. I am grateful to the Gerald R. Ford Presidential Library and Museum for a travel grant to visit the Ford Library, and, more recently, archivist Elizabeth Druga for her assistance with photographs from the Ford Library used in this book.

On the subject of thanking archivists and archives, I would like to thank the archivists in the United States at the National Archives II in College Park, MD, and the Jimmy Carter Presidential Library and Museum. The same is true for the South African archives, including the National Archives, the Department of Foreign Affairs archives archivist Neels Muller, and the SADF Archives, where I received excellent assistance from archivist and military historian Evert Kleynhans. I would like to thank Peter Limb for letting me know about the George Houser papers at Michigan State University Library before Peter retired from his archivist role there, as well as Jessica Achberger, who made it possible for me to view the Houser papers located at Michigan State University. I would also like to thank Josh Pritchard and Jim Brennan for their help with key files.

In terms of academic colleagues who have helped me think of how to approach this topic, I would like to thank Joss Alexander, Terri Barnes, Hazel Cameron, Andy DeRoche, Shari Eppel, JoAnn McGregor, Jamie Miller, Sue Onslow, Brian Raftopoulos, Vladimir Shubin, Wendy Urban-Mead, Luise White, and others who have commented on previous journal articles and conference papers that were part of this research. I would especially like to thank Arrigo Pallotti for his discussions on the role of Julius Nyerere in the diplomacy over Rhodesia. Further thanks go to Arrigo, along with Mario Zamponi, Corrado Tornimbeni, and Anna Maria Gentili, for their hospitality toward me during my visits to the University of Bologna. I would also like to thank Arrigo and Corrado for permission to use some materials in Chapter 3 from two book chapters I published in their edited collections.[1]

I would like to thank Kent State University graduate assistant Joe Bean for his professional editing help on an earlier draft. I would like to thank two very talented undergraduate honor students, David Austin and John Koleski, who spent much of their summer helping me make the text more readable and helping with footnotes. I am grateful to graduate student Sarah Zabic for providing me with materials from the archives of the former Yugoslavia that relate to ZANU and ZAPU. Thanks also to then graduate student Ben Allison for his help, especially in locating and translating two files from the Bukovsky Archives. In terms of my use of US and British FOIA sources, I have only cited US FOIA sources located in the US State Department's digital FOIA library or the Digital National Security Archive. I have not cited any British FOIA files that were previously shared with me, and I personally photographed all the files cited from the British National Archives used in this book, aside from a few Ministry of Defence files that Allison Shutt kindly shared with me from the British National Archives in 2018.

I would also like to thank David B. Moore for his hospitality in Johannesburg and our many conversations about Zimbabwean politics and history. I appreciate all that David has done for me, especially in introducing me to many of his students and a younger generation of Zimbabwean politicians and scholars. I would like to thank Ibbo Mandaza for always providing informative and interesting discussions at his SAPES Trust headquarters, as well as good meals. I also want to thank Wilson Nharingo for his hospitality and introducing me to his colleagues, and for their perspectives on the history in which they participated. I have not made use of these

[1] Timothy Scarnecchia, "Proposed Large-Scale Compensation for White Farmers as an Anglo-American Negotiating Strategy for Zimbabwe, 1976–1979," in Arrigo Pallotti and Corrado Tornimbeni, eds., *State, Land and Democracy in Southern Africa* (Burlington, VT: Ashgate, 2015), 105–26; Timothy Scarnecchia and David Moore, "South African Influences in Zimbabwe: From Destabilization in the 1980s to Liberation War Solidarity in the 2000s," in Arrigo Pallotti and Ulf Engel, eds., *South Africa after Apartheid: Policies and Challenges of the Democratic Transition* (Leiden: Brill, 2016), 175–202.

interviews in this book, but hopefully the next book I write will do so. Thanks as well to Gerald Mazarire for his conversations in Harare, where he always makes me realize how much there is to learn from him about Zimbabwe's war of liberation. I would like to thank Irene Stanton and Murray McCartney for their hospitality and accommodations while in Harare at their Weaver Cottages – always a peaceful place with great conversations. At the University of Zimbabwe, I would like to thank the Department of Economic History for their collegial hospitality, including Professors Pius Nyambara and Joseph Mtisi, who I have known for many years, and to the younger generation of professors for welcoming me there and allowing me to present some of my research to the department.

I would like to thank journal editors who have provided permissions to make use of some of the evidence and some sections from my previously published articles. These include the editors at *Kronos*,[2] the *African Journal on Conflict Resolution*,[3] *Acta Academia*,[4] the *Journal of Southern African Studies*,[5] and the *Journal of Commonwealth and Imperial History*.[6] I would like to thank Sabelo Ndlovu-Gatsheni for permissions to make use of some evidence and sections for the two book chapters I wrote for his edited volumes on Mugabe and Nkomo.[7] I would also like to thank the CIA Public Affairs Office for permitting

[2] Timothy Scarnecchia, "Rationalizing 'Gukurahundi': Cold War and South African Foreign Relations with Zimbabwe, 1981–1983," *Kronos* (November 2011), 87–103.
[3] Timothy Scarnecchia, "The Congo Crisis, the United Nations, and Zimbabwean Nationalism, 1960–1963," *African Journal on Conflict Resolution* 11, no. 1 (2011), 63–86.
[4] Timothy Scarnecchia, "Catholic Voices of the Voiceless: The Politics of Reporting Rhodesian and Zimbabwean State Violence in the 1970s and the Early 1980s," *Acta Academica* 47, no. 1 (2015), 182–207.
[5] Timothy Scarnecchia, "Front Line Diplomats: African Diplomatic Representations of the Zimbabwean Patriotic Front, 1976–1978," *Journal of Southern African Studies* 43, no. 1 (2017), 107–24.
[6] Timothy Scarnecchia, "The Anglo-American and Commonwealth Negotiations for a Zimbabwean Settlement between Geneva and Lancaster, 1977–1979," *The Journal of Imperial and Commonwealth History* 45, no. 5 (2017), 823–43.
[7] Timothy Scarnecchia, "Intransigent Diplomat: Robert Mugabe and His Western Diplomacy, 1963–1983," in Sabelo Ndlovu-Gatsheni, ed., *Mugabeism? History, Politics and Power in Zimbabwe* (New York: Palgrave Macmillan, 2015), 77–92; Timothy Scarnecchia, "Joshua Nkomo: Nationalist Diplomat: 'Father of the Nation' or 'Enemy of the State,'" in Sabelo Ndlovu-Gatsheni, ed., *Joshua Mqabuko Nkomo of Zimbabwe: Politics, Power, and Memory* (London: Palgrave Macmillan, 2017), 173–92.

me to reproduce CIA maps from the early 1980s. They only request that I add the following statement here: "The Central Intelligence Agency has not approved or endorsed the contents of this publication."

I would like to give an especially big thanks to Cambridge University Press editors Maria Marsh and Dan Brown for their hard work in helping to shepherd my book proposal and manuscript through to approval and then to production. I would also like to thank Atifa Jiwa and Natasha Whelan at Cambridge University Press for all of their work on the editing and production side of things. I would like to thank Joseph Shaw for his copyediting expertise, as well as the anonymous readers who helped me improve the book based on their insightful comments and suggestions.

Lastly, I would like to thank my family for their patience with me. Much thanks to Rita and Mira, and also to Sean for his help with editing and proofreading. I would also like to thank my father, Lewis Scarnecchia, for permitting me to use his montage artwork for the cover.

Abbreviations

AAP	Anglo-American proposal/Anglo-American plan
ANC	African National Congress (South Africa)
ANC	African National Council (Rhodesia)
BBC	British Broadcasting Corporation
BMATT	British Military Advisory and Training Team
EXCO	Executive Committee (Internal Settlement)
FCO	Foreign and Commonwealth Office (Britain)
FRELIMO	Front for the Liberation of Mozambique
FROLIZI	Front for the Liberation of Zimbabwe
GOZ	Government of Zimbabwe
LOMA	Law and Order Maintenance Act
MK	*Umkhonto we Sizwe* (Spear of the Nation) – the South African ANC's armed wing
MPLA	Popular Movement for the Liberation of Angola
NDP	National Democratic Party (Southern Rhodesia)
OAU	Organization of African Unity
PF	Patriotic Front
SADF	South African Defence Force
UANC	United African National Council
UDI	Unilateral Declaration of Independence
ZANLA	Zimbabwe African National Liberation Army
ZANU	Zimbabwe African National Union
ZANU-PF	Zimbabwe African National Union – Patriotic Front
ZAPU	Zimbabwe African People's Union
ZIPA	Zimbabwe People's Army
ZIPRA	Zimbabwe People's Revolutionary Army
ZNA	Zimbabwe National Army

This title is part of the Cambridge University Press *Flip it Open* Open Access Books program and has been "flipped" from a traditional book to an Open Access book through the program.

Flip it Open sells books through regular channels, treating them at the outset in the same way as any other book; they are part of our library collections for Cambridge Core, and sell as hardbacks and ebooks. The one crucial difference is that we make an upfront commitment that when each of these books meets a set revenue threshold we make them available to everyone Open Access via Cambridge Core.

This paperback edition has been released as part of our Open Access commitment and we would like to use this as an opportunity to thank the libraries and other buyers who have helped us flip this and the other titles in the program to Open Access.

To see the full list of libraries that we know have contributed to *Flip it Open*, as well as the other titles in the program please visit www.cambridge.org/fio-acknowledgements

Introduction

The history covered in this book focuses on the decolonization process that brought majority rule to the colony of Southern Rhodesia. The white minority settlers tried to delay decolonization, deciding to declare their own Unilateral Declaration of Independence in 1965, forming a republic in 1970, and then trying to create a new hybrid state called Zimbabwe-Rhodesia in 1979. They finally relinquished control back to the British in 1979, temporarily returning to the official status of a British colony. The British governor oversaw the return of liberation war armies and the first real majority universal election in February 1980, which led to the lowering of the British flag and raising of the Zimbabwean flag on April 18, 1980. Bob Marley was in Zimbabwe for the festivities, playing his hit song "Zimbabwe," which contained the prophetic lines:

> No more internal power struggle;
> We come together to overcome the little trouble.
> Soon we'll find out who is the real revolutionary,
> 'Cause I don't want my people to be contrary.

It seems, at times, that much of the writing and talking about Zimbabwean modern political history has revolved around defining "who is the real revolutionary." This "purity" test was at the heart of interparty rhetoric since the split between the Zimbabwe African People's Union (ZAPU) and the Zimbabwe African National Union (ZANU) in 1963, and it is still part of the larger questions about liberation war histories. This book's motivation has been to see what the archives can reveal through words used during the decolonization process. In addition to leading the nationalist movements, many of Zimbabwe's leaders also had to serve as diplomats, negotiating the terms by which Zimbabwe would become a sovereign nation. The goal of this book, written some forty years after the transition of power, is to provide readers access to the arguments used by the many different

1

diplomats and leaders who contributed to the diplomatic record of decolonization. I use these archives to examine a series of simultaneous struggles. The first is the struggle and competition between Joshua Nkomo's ZAPU and Robert Mugabe's ZANU. That competition is what originally brought me to research in diplomatic archives, wanting to test if I could write a history of this rivalry through mostly Western and African archives.

There are other struggles and competitions explored in this book as well. Among them was the competition among the presidents of the Frontline States – a loose coalition of African countries committed to ending apartheid in South Africa and white minority rule in Rhodesia – over who would be able to assist their preferred candidate to become the leader of the new Zimbabwe. Another struggle was between the Western powers and the Soviet Union/China over who would succeed in putting their sponsored liberation movement into power in Zimbabwe. The United States and Britain together went up against South Africa in deciding the fate of Zimbabwe's new leadership, while competing between themselves over who should be their "man in Zimbabwe." All of these different struggles are addressed in what follows, although the central focus throughout the book remains the competition between Nkomo and Mugabe.

Even though the interactions and diplomatic debates described in the following pages may have taken place in embassies and the halls of foreign offices and state departments, the consequences for the ongoing war were real, at times extending that violent conflict, and at times preparing the way to end the conflict. Given the importance of the liberation war itself in defining political rights in Zimbabwe over the last forty years, and the extensive debates over who was, and who still is, "the real revolutionary," this book is an attempt to let some of the historical evidence that is otherwise stuffed away in quiet archives do some of the talking in a pursuit of answers to the questions raised by Bob Marley in his song "Zimbabwe." Zimbabwe's principal "flaw" as a new nation was that it was created hastily and forced two competing liberation parties and armies to merge into a national army. The spilt between ZAPU and ZANU had happened seventeen years before independence and was permitted to continue because of the Cold War funding of both their militaries by numerous states. As the elected ruling party, ZANU would then go on to use the instruments of state coercion to punish the losing rival party, ZAPU. My research interests have also concerned the roles of the American and British diplomats through those years of terror for some Zimbabweans, otherwise known as the *Gukurahundi*, from 1983 to 1987. In researching this book, I deliberately wanted to move the chronology beyond the usual diplomatic history that ends or begins the story in 1980. This is also made possible given that archived documents from the early 1980s are now unclassified and shared by the US State Department's FOIA Library, or available in hard copy at the British National Archives.[1]

Cold War Race States

I have deployed an analytic framework throughout this book that examines Zimbabwe's late decolonization processes through the lens of what I call "Cold War race states." The analytical questions addressed in this book concern the role of race as a central category of action in the Cold War diplomacy regarding decolonization in southern Africa, and in particular Rhodesia and Zimbabwe. Much has been written about race and the Cold War, especially about the important nexus between American domestic racism and Cold War diplomacy. Three books, all published in 2001, dealt directly with American domestic race politics and international diplomacy over ending white minority rule in Rhodesia. Thomas Borstelmann's *The Cold War and the Color Line*, Gerald Horne's *From the Barrel of a Gun*, and Andrew DeRoche's *Black, White, and Chrome*, all firmly established the fundamental role of race and racism in US foreign policy related to the ending of one of the last white race states in southern Africa.[2] Since these important books were written in 2001, there have been a number of excellent books published that further utilize the diplomatic archives in the United States, Britain, South Africa, and the Commonwealth nations, particularly on the American side of the diplomatic history.[3]

---

[1] I have included links to the digital US State Department FOIA Reading Room in the notes for these items.

[2] Thomas Borstelmann, *The Cold War and the Color Line: American Race Relations in the Global Arena* (Cambridge, MA: Harvard University Press, 2001); Gerald Horne, *From the Barrel of a Gun: The United States and the War against Zimbabwe, 1965–1980* (Chapel Hill: University of North Carolina Press, 2001); Andrew DeRoche, *Black, White, and Chrome: The United States and Zimbabwe, 1953 to 1998* (Trenton, NJ: Africa World Press, 2001).

[3] See Nancy Mitchell, *Jimmy Carter in Africa: Race and the Cold War* (Washington, DC: Woodrow Wilson Center Press, 2016); Eddie Michel, *The*

The concept of race in "race state" is meant to specifically refer to the white settler state of Rhodesia, and its comparison to other white and black race states in Africa at that time. This concept needs to take into account the transformation of the race state comparison over almost a two decade-long delay in decolonization. Therefore, the race state concept and comparison reflected different meanings of race in a global Cold War context than it had for the earlier independence movements in the rest of sub-Saharan Africa. It also meant that world powers interpreted the potential success of a decolonized settler state against the backdrop of their own particular views of recently decolonized nation states elsewhere in Africa. While the concept does connect to American and British ideas of race and racism, the use of "race states" here is not meant in the same way that it usually deployed, as the influence of American or British racism in foreign policy – although the concept certainly builds on that important literature that mostly concerned the early Cold War.[4]

The challenge of applying a "Cold War race states" argument rests in its changing contexts and connotations in different periods over nearly

White House and White Africa: Presidential Policy Toward Rhodesia during the UDI Era, 1965–1979 (New York: Routledge, 2019); Filipe Ribeiro de Meneses and Robert McNamara, *The White Redoubt, the Great Powers and the Struggle for Southern Africa, 1960–1980* (London: Palgrave, 2018); Piero Gleijeses, *Visions of Freedom: Havana, Washington, Pretoria and the Struggle for Southern Africa, 1976–1991* (Chapel Hill: University of North Carolina Press, 2013); Jamie Miller, *An African Volk: The Apartheid Regime and Its Search for Survival* (Oxford University Press, 2016); Andy DeRoche, *Kenneth Kaunda, the United States and Southern Africa* (London: Bloomsbury, 2016); Stuart Doran, *Kingdom, Power, Glory: Mugabe, ZANU and the Quest for Supremacy, 1960–1987* (Midrand, South Africa: Sithatha Media, 2017); Sue Onslow, "South Africa and Zimbabwean Independence," in Sue Onslow, ed., *Cold War in Southern Africa: White Power, Black Liberation* (London: Routledge, 2009), 110–29; William Bishop, "Diplomacy in Black and White: America and the Search for Zimbabwean Independence, 1965–1980" (Unpublished PhD thesis, Vanderbilt University, 2012).

4   See Penny M. von Eshen, *Race against Empire: Black Americans and Anticolonialism, 1937–1957* (Ithaca, NY: Cornell University Press, 1997); Ryan M. Irwin, *Gordian Knot: Apartheid and the Unmaking of the Liberal World Order* (Oxford University Press, 2012); Brenda Gayle Plummer, *Rising Wind: Black Americans and U.S. Foreign Affairs, 1935–1960* (Chapel Hill: University of North Carolina Press, 1996); Thomas Noer, *Cold War and Black Liberation: the United States and White Rule in Africa, 1948–1967* (Columbia: University of Missouri Press, 1985); Philip Muehlenbeck, *Betting on the Africans: John F. Kennedy's Courting of African Nationalist Leaders* (Oxford University Press, 2014).

two decades of diplomacy. Starting in the early 1960s, Rhodesia was still part of the Central African Federation, and there were certainly some efforts by the British and other world powers to encourage Rhodesia toward a majority rule government at that time. After the 1965 Unilateral Declaration of Independence, however, Rhodesia lacked international recognition and remained a white minority-rule state. In 1979, the experiment of Zimbabwe-Rhodesia provided a short-lived and imperfect white-minority government with a black prime minister, one that failed to gain international recognition. A new and significant "race state" transformation came only after the election of Robert Mugabe and ZANU and the transfer of power from the original colonial power, Britain, to the new Zimbabwean state on April 18, 1980.

My argument in what follows is that the "Cold War race states" concept helps to better understand the opportunities various projections of racialized notions of a "white state" or "black state" created within negotiation and diplomacy. Inherent in this concept are the notions of what international actors presumed to be the characteristics of a black African state. The literature on this racialized relativism is large, particularly in the theoretical discussion over the limits of sovereignty in an unequal global system.[5] Zimbabwe's early years as a "black state" witnessed extreme forms of state-sponsored violence against those supporting ZAPU. Pre-independence diplomacy is not usually associated with explanations of this violence. I believe that it is important to examine closely how the debates and mechanisms of creating a majority-rule sovereign state in Zimbabwe may have contributed to the ways state crimes against thousands occurred in the early 1980s, and how these crimes were interpreted by those very same powers who had helped create Zimbabwe.

The bulk of this book discusses the evidence produced by numerous politicians, diplomats, contacts, journalists, and other odd informants.

[5] See, for example, Achille Mbembé and Libby Meintjes, "Necropolitics," *Public Culture* 15, no. 1 (Winter 2003), 11–40; Achille Mbembe, *Necropolitics* (Durham, NC: Duke University Press, 2019); Achille Mbembe, *Critique of Black Reason* (Durham, NC: Duke University Press, 2017); Paul Gilroy, *Against Race: Imagining Political Culture beyond the Color Line* (Cambridge, MA: Harvard University Press, 2002); Mahmood Mamdani, *Neither Settler nor Native: The Making and Unmaking of Permanent Minorities* (Cambridge, MA: Harvard University Press, 2020); Adom Getachew, *Worldmaking after Empire* (Princeton University Press, 2019).

This evidence in the written archives offers new ways to think and write about the intense diplomacy around solving "the Rhodesia Problem." For those looking for a more comprehensive perspective on the diplomacy of these years, there a number of books written on it. Political scientists like Stephan Stedman and Mordechai Tamarkin have produced extremely detailed studies of the diplomacy over Zimbabwe's decolonization.[6] These works show the complexity of multilateral and bilateral relations in the Zimbabwe case. I am not attempting to treat the evidence I have read in the archives to chronicle the negotiation process. I am more interested in the way information was communicated to, and processed by, different actors in this history. I believe memorandums of conversation, for example, can provide not only a sense of the discussions between key actors, but also offer perspectives on what different state and non-state actors thought of each other and how they predicted or anticipated moves by the other actors. I do think there is value to political scientists and students of diplomacy in having access to this sort of evidence when it comes to learning the art of diplomacy and negotiation. Most importantly, I feel that future generations of diplomats can ask how they would have performed in "real time" as part of a major negotiation. There is also an opportunity here to learn from the mistakes of the past. Not simply in the clichéd sense of not repeating mistakes, but in the sense of considering the banality of diplomatic work and how, over years, that routine performance of intelligence gathering, sharing, and interpreting creates a "group think" that reinforces institutional racism and prejudice toward others in negotiations.

The Zimbabwean decolonization process did, in fact, include very different types of actors. The racial element – not only the race of the actors, but the use of race as a major element in the negotiations – comes out more in the narrative when looking beyond descriptions of the key moments, the turning points, and so on. In that sense, the following narrative is not preoccupied with keeping track of the relative strengths and weaknesses of various bargaining positions. My interest is also in those moments when diplomats expressed sincere doubt about a possible resolution, or when otherwise marginalized

---

[6] Stephan Stedman, *Peacemaking in Civil War International Mediation in Zimbabwe, 1974–1980* (Boulder, CO: Lynne Rienner Publishers, 1991); Mordechai Tamarkin, *The Making of Zimbabwe: Decolonization in Regional and International Politics* (London: Frank Cass, 1990).

politicians voiced their own perspectives, usually making claims that their exclusion was unfair. I am also interested in what diplomats knew of the internal conflicts in Zimbabwe's nationalist movements, and how they explained these to their political higher-ups. The British Foreign and Commonwealth Office (FCO) archives have numerous files titled, for example, "The US Involvement with the Rhodesia Problem," or "Tanzania's Involvement with the Rhodesia Problem." Rhodesia was Britain's problem, so a lot of effort went into collecting intelligence to help shape policy.

Organization of the Book

The first section of the book (1960–75) explores the inability of the British and the international community to deliver majority rule and decolonization in Rhodesia in the 1960s, which in turn helped to further differentiate "white African" states such as Rhodesia, the Portuguese colonies in southern Africa, and most importantly South Africa itself. The second section of the race state argument begins in 1976, covered in Chapters 3 and 4, and occurs when then US secretary of state, Henry Kissinger, became obsessed with flipping the "race state" definition of Rhodesia into a black African state to avoid the unsavory prospect of having the United States defend a white minority-rule state against the Cubans and the Soviets. The 1976 Geneva conference was organized for this purpose, and although it failed to end the conflict and bring about majority rule, it enabled the two main liberation movements to gain more prominent positions at the negotiating table, with Mugabe benefiting the most from this recognition.

The remaining chapters in this section, Chapters 5 and 6, focus on the late 1970s and highlight the importance of a race state solution for Zimbabwe. The negotiations witnessed many different strategies by the Anglo-Americans and South Africans – some that failed and some that worked – to shape the future "black state" in ways that they thought would be to their benefit. The key African parties, outside of the Zimbabwean nationalists themselves, were the Frontline State presidents, of whom the three principal leaders were Zambia's Kenneth Kaunda, Tanzania's Julius Nyerere, and Mozambique's Samora Machel. Botswana's President Seretse Khama and Angola's Agostinho Neto played smaller but at times key roles in the negotiations.[7] Other actors in the negotiations were the South Africans, the Rhodesian Front government, and the Zimbabwean nationalists themselves. The Frontline State presidents, the Nigerians and other Commonwealth nations, and the leaders of Zimbabwean political parties themselves all did their best to make the most of the constellation of issues encapsulated in the "Rhodesian problem," one of the final decolonization processes to be negotiated in Africa. The outcome of this competition was not always one-sided and created a number of opportunities for the Zimbabwean nationalists.[8]

The third and final section of the book covers the 1980 elections, the transfer of power from the British to the Zimbabweans, and the post-1980 attempts by Mugabe's party to destroy Nkomo and his ZAPU political party. This third stage shows the Cold War powers consistently providing Mugabe and his military direct and tacit support to keep him on "their side" in the resurgent Cold War of the early 1980s.[9] In this situation, diplomats and leaders categorized newly independent Zimbabwe as a "black African state" to rationalize the high levels of violence which, in the Cold War calculus, were viewed as acceptable in different racialized states at the time.

To avoid anachronisms and stay away from overusing these tropes, it is important to point out that by invoking the use of "race" in

---

[7] Piero Gleijeses, *Visions of Freedom: Havana, Washington, Pretoria and the Struggle for Southern Africa, 1976–1991* (Chapel Hill: North Carolina Press, 2013); Jamie Miller, *An African Volk: The Apartheid Regime and Its Search for Survival* (*Oxford University Press, 2016*), Andy DeRoche, *Kenneth Kaunda, the United States and Southern Africa* (London: Bloomsbury, 2016); Arrigo Pallotti, *Nyerere e la decolonizzazione dell'Africa australe, 1961–1980* (Florence: Mondadori, in press)

[8] For the Frontline States' contributions to the creation of Zimbabwe, see Carol B. Thompson, *Challenge to Imperialism: The Frontline States in the Liberation of Zimbabwe* (Boulder, CO: Westview Press, 1986); and Gilbert Khadiagala, *Allies in Adversity: The Frontline States in Southern African Security, 1975–1993* (Athens, OH: Ohio University Press, 1994).

[9] See Catholic Commission for Justice and Peace and Legal Resources Foundation, *Breaking the Silence, Building True Peace: A Report on the Disturbances in Matabeleland and the Midlands, 1980–1988* (Harare: CCJPZ and LRF, 1999), reprinted in *Gukurahundi in Zimbabwe: A Report on the Disturbances in Matabeleland and the Midlands, 1980–1988* (London: Hurst and Company, 2007); Lloyd Sachikonye, *When a State Turns on Its Citizens: 60 Years of Institutionalised Violence in Zimbabwe* (Johannesburg: Jacana, 2011); Shari Eppel, "'Gukurahundi': The Need for Truth and Reparation," in Brian Raftopoulos and Tyrone Savage, eds., *Zimbabwe: Injustice and Political Reconciliation* (Harare: Weaver Press, 2005), 43–62.

diplomacy during these years, I am assuming that Rhodesia and Zimbabwe are two different race states, and I confront how all actors racialized negotiations. It is, of course, debatable to say that race was the only category of analysis separating Rhodesia from Zimbabwe, but from the perspective of international, regional, and domestic diplomacy and negotiations, race was *the* fundamental category of difference used to justify various positions in the negotiations. The reality of racial categories and essentializing in this diplomacy is quite stark. Representatives from all sides in the negotiations spoke instrumentally in terms of "the blacks" and "the whites." These were not simply anecdotal references: these racial categories were integral to the rhetoric and, more importantly, the power relations reflected in the peculiarities of race states during the Cold War.

One racialized theme throughout the negotiations to end the liberation war and to transition to majority rule was the commonly held notion that "black African states" were not equal to "European states" – a euphemism for white settler states – on a number of criteria. The most important for Western powers was the assumption that once whites left or were forced out of a former African colony, the economy would suffer severe shocks. Therefore, one of the main goals for Rhodesia, which was such a "late decolonizer," was to negotiate safeguards including large-scale financial compensations to keep whites in Zimbabwe after independence. Much work has been done on this topic, especially as it relates to the post-independence land issue in Zimbabwe, but the history of how this concern was racialized throughout the negotiations from 1976 to Lancaster House in 1979 is an important element of diplomacy to explore.[10]

Another major theme found in the following chapters is the ability of African states and liberation movements in the region to take advantage of Kissinger's attempts to force a settlement. This important intervention by Kissinger and the United States provided the Zimbabwean nationalists a new advantage in the otherwise stagnant regionally driven negotiations of the mid-1970s. Although Kissinger

---

[10] Sue Onslow, "Race and Policy: Britain, Zimbabwe and the Lancaster House Land Deal," *The Journal of Imperial and Commonwealth History* 45, no. 5 (2017), 844–67; Timothy Scarnecchia, "Proposed Large-Scale Compensation for White Farmers as an Anglo-American Negotiating Strategy for Zimbabwe, 1976–1979," in A. Pallotti and C. Tornimbeni, eds., *State, Land and Democracy in Southern Africa* (Burlington, VT: Ashgate, 2015), 105–26.

represented the most powerful nation on the world scene in these years, American power was open to numerous forms of manipulation by those leaders in the region, who suddenly found themselves receiving greater attention than usual from the Americans. When the Americans wanted help with solving the "Rhodesia Problem," opportunities for development aid and military aid opened up. This was very important for Zambia and Mozambique, the two countries bordering Rhodesia that would host the Zimbabwean liberation armies. Rather than seeing this period as one of imperial power being deployed in a region where it was otherwise lacking, it is useful to see American power in southern Africa as attempting to use economic leverage, military aid, and international prestige in ways that would help legitimate and even create national leaders and movements. This was especially the case for those nationalist leaders like Nkomo and Mugabe outside of Rhodesia, the Patriotic Front leaders, but also for the white leaders of South Africa and Rhodesia. Constantly wanting to avoid falling into what they viewed as imperialist traps, Nkomo and Mugabe had a great deal of room to maneuver. That space became much smaller in late 1979, however, when a combination of factors and pressures forced both of them to accept a fairly extreme version of a decolonization constitution that included safeguards for the white population of Rhodesia.[11]

The potential for a "race war" in Rhodesia had diverse meanings depending on who invoked the concept and in what context. It meant something different to Rhodesia, South Africa, Tanzania, Britain, and the United States. Nevertheless, all parties in the negotiations invoked the concept of a potential race war to help strengthen their own positions in negotiations. Some might ask whether or not the liberation war for Zimbabwe was itself a race war, but it is difficult to make this claim given denials of the racial intentions of the belligerents. Neither side was bent upon the destruction of the other based on race. The Rhodesian army certainly relied heavily on black Rhodesian soldiers to fight the war, as they tried to make the war about upholding "civilization" against communism. Such a view cannot overlook the oppressive

[11] See Luise White, *Unpopular Sovereignty: Rhodesian Independence and African Decolonization* (University of Chicago Press, 2015), 172–205. For valuable comprehensive Zimbabwean histories, see especially Alois. S. Mlambo, *A History of Zimbabwe* (Cambridge University Press, 2014); B. Raftopoulos, ed., *Becoming Zimbabwe: A History from the Pre-colonial Period to 2008* (Harare: Weaver Press, 2009).

racial order of Rhodesian society. Perhaps it is difficult to understand the nonracial elements of the liberation war: fundamentally, it was without a doubt ideologically and literally a war against a racist system, and not a "race war" in the way white settlers often referred to as the "ever present danger," as white settlers have done historically. Fundamentally, the liberation war, while shaped by racial divisions, can be characterized as a war fought against the white minority–ruled Rhodesian state bent upon maintaining white privilege enshrined in minority rule. The liberation forces were fighting to destroy this brutal and unequal system and create a majority rule sovereign state that would put an end to white privilege and all the inequalities that were associated with such a system. Whether or not such a goal was achieved is a different question. The liberation struggle also focused on historical land theft and appropriation by white settlers as a central element of white minority rule, so getting back the land was a major motivation for the war itself. As will be discussed, negotiations had a difficult time reconciling the liberation party's claims for the return of land with Western powers' preoccupation with keeping whites in Zimbabwe after the transition.

Mugabe versus Nkomo

A main question in what follows is the long and divisive competition between Joshua Nkomo of ZAPU and Robert Mugabe of ZANU. It may seem like this competition was simply a question of personal power, and that certainly is a large part of it. But the divisions between ZANU and ZAPU and Mugabe and Nkomo became a fundamental part of Zimbabwe's decolonization process and would have a major impact on post-independence Zimbabwe. The way in which this division was, and continues to be, explained as one of ethnic difference remains one of the most troubling legacies. This book attempts to offer a more nuanced history of this competition in order to move away from the predominance of an explanation of ethnic competition, or what was then referred to by diplomats and nationalists as "tribalism." Yet, the challenge to privilege the political rivalry is made difficult as much of the diplomatic discussion of differences between personalities and rivalries were made through references to this ethnopolitics. These narratives, or storytelling, created a conformation bias, which developed over years, of relaying ethnic rivalry as the primary explanation of the competition between Nkomo and Mugabe, ZAPU and ZANU, and many other politicians and political formations. These institutional "archives" were then used to rationalize violence after 1980 in ways that distanced the Anglo-Americans from responsibility for what happened in the "sovereign" state of Zimbabwe.

It would be fairly easy to invoke a "character is destiny" trope when analyzing the Nkomo–Mugabe rivalry. I am not interested in doing that here. By emphasizing the Nkomo–Mugabe competition during the decolonization phase and after independence, the narrative is not so much concerned with explanations based on "character" as to why they ultimately failed to integrate their military and political organizations, but more with the larger implications their rivalry would have on a series of important elements in diplomacy, as well as the culmination of their rivalry after independence. It is also true that there exist strong loyalties to Nkomo or Mugabe, so I am aware that by avoiding the "character is destiny" trope, I may be disappointing both audiences. A goal in writing this book is to avoid praising one side and demonizing the other; however, like with ethnicity, there is a large amount of "demonizing" to be found coming from both sides to be found in the sources cited in the following chapters. To draw a direct line to more recent events would be anachronistic, which is an easy trap to fall into when discussing Zimbabwean nationalist history. The act of writing history in Zimbabwe became even more politicized in the 2000s, especially with the call to write history that would serve the ruling party, the "patriotic history" that Terence Ranger described so well in his critical article of this development. Since then, a school of more critical writings about Zimbabwean political history has developed to counter patriotic history.[12]

---

[12] Terence Ranger, "Nationalist Historiography, Patriotic History and the History of the Nation: The Struggle over the Past in Zimbabwe," *Journal of Southern African Studies* 30, no. 2 (2005), 215–34; Sabelo Ndlovu-Gatsheni, "Rethinking Chimurenga and Gukurahundi in Zimbabwe: A Critique of Partisan National History," *African Studies Review* 55, no. 3 (2012), 1–26. Sabelo Ndlovu-Gatsheni, "Introduction: Mugabeism and Entanglements of History, Politics, and Power in the Making of Zimbabwe," in S. Ndlovu-Gatsheni, ed., *Mugabeism: History, Politics and Power in Zimbabwe* (New York: Palgrave Macmillan, 2015), 1–25; and S. Ndlovu-Gatsheni, "Introduction: Writing Joshua Nkomo into History and Narration of the Nation," in S. Ndlovu-Gatsheni, ed., *Joshua Mqabuko Nkomo of Zimbabwe: Politics, Power, and Memory* (New York: Palgrave Macmillan, 2017), 1–49;

One note on "truth" and evidence in diplomatic history. Readers may, or may not, be aware that an older-style diplomatic history was originally built on a functionalist foundation that assumed words in diplomatic archives and records could be used to construct a reliable narrative of events simply because they appear in an "official" archive. I am not suggesting that the location of the evidence in state archives makes it more truthful or objective than other forms of evidence. Rather, I am interested in revealing how this evidence, which was used to make decisions, helped create consensus within foreign relation bureaucracies, and among political leaders who received their information from these bureaucracies. What follows contains a great deal of direct quotes from the archives. At times, this evidence is used to demonstrate that not all of the intelligence used by governments was reliable or correct. All the same, the collecting, classifying, and dissemination of gathered intelligence at the diplomatic level was key to decision-making, however "untrue" the evidence, or descriptions of the evidence, may have been. Much of what is quoted from the archives is done to show the sort of arguments and theories that were considered as evidence by those making decisions, not as pure facts or truths. Luise White's work is especially influential to my methodology. Her work established that "truth claims" are better treated as competing texts and that it is not the historian's role to try and privilege one over the other, but rather to explore how conflicting truth claims can be viable parts of creating a plausible historical narrative.[13] This approach, of course, does not mean that I am somehow more "objective" in the narrative. The decisions made over what evidence may have been more significant than other evidence gets to the heart of the historian's skills. It can take years of reading thousands of documents to begin to

James Muzondidya and Sabelo Ndlovu-Gatsheni "'Echoing Silences': Ethnicity in Postcolonial Zimbabwe, 1980–2007," *African Journal on Conflict Resolution* 7, no. 2 (2010), 257–97; Blessing-Miles Tendi, *Making History in Mugabe's Zimbabwe Politics, Intellectuals and the Media* (Oxford: Peter Lang, 2010). For a critique of Ranger's formulation, and recognition of a more critical school of Zimbabwean history, see Ian Phimister, "Narrative of Progress: Zimbabwean Historiography and the End of History," *Journal of Contemporary African Studies* 30, no. 1 (2012), 27–34.

13 Most relevant to this book is Luise White, *The Assassination of Herbert Chitepo: Texts and Politics in Zimbabwe* (Bloomington: Indiana University Press, 2003); however much of her approach is articulated in Luise White, *Speaking with Vampires: Rumor and History in Colonial Africa* (Oakland: University of California Press, 2000).

understand what may or may not have been important in reconstructing how decisions were made as well as why some ideas and theories were discarded along the way.

Most importantly, the words diplomats and politicians said to each other are not meant to represent an objective truth because these words appear in the archive. All of the quotes in this book should be seen rather as an opinion or argument used to try and persuade another individual or state to act in a certain manner. It is this art of persuasion that is so fascinating to examine. Diplomatic historian David Painter once related to me an old adage about diplomacy: "that a soldier's job is to die for his/her country, while a diplomat's job is to lie for her/his country." That certainly holds true in what follows. In addition, the recorded words themselves are, of course, only part of the story, as diplomats were susceptible to numerous influences beyond the textual record left to be read by historians years later in archives. There were personal relationships, considerations of national interests, opinions of other foreign diplomats – all of these elements influenced the way diplomats chose to interpret the words and actions of ZANU and ZAPU leaders during these years. To say that what they related back to their governments represent an objective, sole, or a privileged truth is unrealistic. What the diplomatic record does help historians to do, however, is to present a particular system of knowledge, however incomplete, which was molded by local conditions, the quality of their information, and the personal prejudices and biases of those involved.[14]

There are limitations to a strictly archival approach, and some readers will undoubtedly feel that the narrative around key figures should have been given more attention. I decided, however, to base this book almost entirely on sources from the archives. Recent works on Zimbabwean decolonization have shown the value of extensive interviews with military and political leaders.[15] There are also very

---

[14] A very useful formulation of this process can be found in Charles Tilly, *Why? What Happens When People Give Reasons ... and Why* (Princeton University Press, 2008).

[15] Blessing-Miles Tendi, *Army and Politics in Zimbabwe: Mujuru, the Liberation Fighter and Kingmaker* (Cambridge University Press, 2020); Gerald Mazarire, "ZANU's External Networks 1963–1979: An Appraisal," *Journal of Southern African Studies* 43, no. 1 (2017), 83–106; David Moore, *Mugabe's Legacy: Coups, Conspiracies and the Conceits of Power in Zimbabwe* (London: Hurst, 2021); Doran, *Kingdom, Power, Glory*. See Jocelyn Alexander and

strong collections of interviews with diplomats who were part of these negotiations.[16] My approach here, however, is to work primarily with evidence left in archives, to the extent that this material helped to inform and shape policy and opinions of the multiple parties and states involved in the Zimbabwean negotiations.

In addition to official state archives, I have also used some evidence from the papers of the American activist George Houser. Houser's papers are based on his notes from his trips to southern Africa in the 1970s. George Houser was a significant figure among those Americans involved in solidarity work with African liberation struggles. He was the director of the American Committee on Africa (ACOA), an influential policy group committed to challenging American support for colonial and settler states in Africa. When Houser retired from this directorship, Tanzanian president Julius Nyerere and other African leaders wrote statements in honor of his service. Nyerere described Houser as one of those key figures in history who worked "quietly in the background of events, devoting their skill, their commitment, and their lives to causes they believe in." Nyerere wrote, "George Houser is such a man, and his service has been given whole-heartedly and without reserve to the cause of human freedom and human equality, with special reference to the struggle against colonialism and racialism in Africa."[17] This was very high praise coming from Nyerere, indicating the level of trust and respect anti-imperialist African nationalists had in and for Houser. Houser's personal notes on the conversations he had with Zimbabwean nationalists are therefore particularly helpful because African nationalists shared different information with

JoAnn McGregor, "*Adelante!* Military Imaginaries, the Cold War, and Southern Africa's Liberation Armies," *Comparative Studies in Society and History* 62, no. 3 (2020), 619–50.

[16] See especially Sue Onslow and Anna-Mart van Wyk, eds., *Southern Africa in the Cold War, Post-1974*, Critical Oral History Conference Series (Washington, DC: Woodrow Wilson International Center for Scholars, 2013); The Association for Diplomatic Studies and Training Foreign Affairs Oral History Project; Michael Kandiah and Sue Onslow, eds., *Britain and Rhodesia: The Route to Settlement* (London: Institute of Contemporary British History Oral History Programme, 2008).

[17] ACOA Tribute to George Houser, "Messages to George Houser," 8. Other messages came from Robert Mugabe, Kenneth Kaunda, Oliver Tambo, Sam Nujoma, and Henry Isaacs, African Activist Archive, http://kora .matrix.msu.edu/files/50/304/32-130-132B-84-GMH%20ACOA%20Tribute %20pro%20small.pdf.

Houser compared with what they said in conversations with official state diplomats.

As much as what follows may contain some controversial evidence, I would ask the reader to remember that I have included such materials, with citations, that may contain untruths, as well as characterizations of individuals that are harsh and unkind. I include this because it helps to better understand the atmosphere of multilateral negotiations. It is also possible that "bad intel" may have, at times, helped to shape the policy recommendations within the foreign relations bureaucracy, although such inconsistent reports rarely sustained major shifts in policy. As will hopefully become clear, my main argument about the evidence in this book is that as it continued to accumulate it came to define fairly narrow interpretations of possibilities. This led eventually to an interpretation that turned what should have been a recognizable political competition and subsequent political acts of revenge into something unrecognizable, something monstrous, that the foreign relations bureaucracies and political leaders were then able to rationalize into their own understandings of what was not only possible, but acceptable.

The historical narrative that follows will likely disappoint some readers, mainly because I have tried to avoid categorizing individuals in the story as either purely revolutionary or as "sell-outs," as is often the way this story has been told. As the reader will hopefully see, these commonly held biases do not reflect the full story of many years of diplomacy by Zimbabwean leaders. To paraphrase Fela Kuti, I would therefore ask for some patience from Zimbabwean readers, and an open mind from non-Zimbabwean readers, as I have tried my best to present the evidence through the eyes of the participants rather than through the culmination of events over the last forty years.

1 | *Historical Background 1960–1970*

The central focus of this book is on the complex, multiparty, and international diplomacy conducted primarily between 1976 and 1979 that resulted in Zimbabwean independence. However, to better understand the array of forces involved over time, the first two chapters explore the political rhetoric of Zimbabwean nationalists, and the history of internal politics in the main nationalist parties before 1976.

The politics of Zimbabwean nationalism was not only shaped as a response to Rhodesian politics. The global Cold War nature of the Congo crisis helped to develop and frame a regional language of African nationalism and white settlerism in the early 1960s. The rhetoric of anti-imperialism and decolonization in Southern Rhodesia was in many ways different from that of West and East Africa. Zimbabwean nationalists did participate in pan-African politics, but as the goal of a similar decolonization path became less and less achievable, the rhetoric and strategies used by the nationalists transformed into something uniquely southern African. It is important, therefore, to establish in this first chapter the rhetorical tropes and metaphors developed earlier in the 1960s, to help understand how they were deployed in the 1970s. One event in 1959 merits attention: In February of that year, the government of Prime Minister Edgar Whitehead in Southern Rhodesia began a campaign against African nationalists by instituting a state of emergency that banned the Southern Rhodesian African National Congress and resulted in the arrest and detentions of many of its key leaders. Throughout the period, global debates over race, liberation politics, and sovereignty that became operationalized in Cold War logics had an important impact on the political outcomes of decolonization and the rise of Mugabe and ZANU-PF in Zimbabwe in the 1980s. This chapter examines these issues chronologically in two five-year periods, 1960–65 and 1966–70. The first section, 1960–65, connects events in Southern Rhodesia, the first Congo crisis in the early 1960s, the diplomacy of an early Zimbabwean nationalist movement, and the recalcitrant diplomacy of the Rhodesian state.

1960–1965

Wider transformative events in Southern and Central Africa during 1960 must be considered in discussing "African nationalism" in Southern Rhodesia. One major intervention came in the form of British prime minister Harold Macmillan's famous "Wind of Change" speech on February 3, 1960 to a joint session of the South African parliament. Macmillan provided a challenge to both white politicians and African nationalist politicians, as he claimed that "[t]he wind of change is blowing through the continent, and, whether we like it or not, this growth of national consciousness is a political fact."[1] White minority governments in southern Africa were not willing to accept Macmillan's claim as a "political fact" as he intended; they preferred to see themselves during the rest of 1960 as exceptions to this African "wind of change." Only seven weeks after Macmillan's speech, the violence of South African apartheid became a global concern following the Sharpeville massacre on March 21, 1960. The Sharpeville massacre – where police officers overreacted and used deadly force out of proportion to the threat posed by the demonstration, killing sixty-nine people – was immediately followed by security campaigns against the leadership and operating structures of both the African National Congress (ANC) in South Africa and the Pan-African Congress in South Africa (PAC).[2]

On July 19, 1960, following a pattern similar to after Sharpeville in South Africa, the Whitehead government of Southern Rhodesia ordered a dawn sweep of African townships in Salisbury and Bulawayo to arrest and detain key leaders and activists in the National Democratic Party (NDP). The NDP had formed to continue the work of the banned Southern Rhodesian African National Congress. The government's arrests were followed by mass action on the part of the nationalists and their urban supporters, as large crowds marched into Salisbury from the township of Harare to demand a meeting with Whitehead. The Whitehead government refused to

[1] Harold Macmillan, *Pointing the Way: 1959–61* (London: Macmillan, 1971), 156; speech cited in full in Ritchie Ovendale, "Macmillan and the Wind of Change in Africa, 1957–1960," *The Historical Journal* 38, no. 2 (June 1995), 455–77.

[2] Philip Frankel, *An Ordinary Atrocity: Sharpeville and Its Massacre* (New Haven, CT: Yale University Press, 2001); Tom Lodge, *Sharpeville: An Apartheid Massacre and Its Consequences* (Oxford: Oxford University Press, 2011).

meet with the protestors and instead responded with tear gas and baton charges. Subsequent riots in Bulawayo and Gwelu resulted in the killing of unarmed Africans by the police, the first such police killings since the 1896–98 uprisings of the Shona and Ndebele against the British South Africa Company.[3] As in South Africa, the leaders of the Southern Rhodesian government were convinced that a strategy of direct confrontation and containment would be the most effective means to stop the development of mass political action from African nationalists.

The speed by which the Whitehead government produced legislation to back this strategy also corresponded with the politics of fear among the white electorate. Dr. Ahrn Palley, a vocal oppositional voice in parliament, suggested that the real reason for the successive waves of repressive legislation was because Southern Rhodesian African nationalists were now gaining a voice in London on the future of the Central African Federation. Like South Africa after Sharpeville, Palley charged, the Whitehead government hoped to use repression, arrests, and detentions to weaken African nationalism.[4] The popular responses to the arrests in 1959 and 1960, and the riots that followed, demonstrated that African residents in Southern Rhodesia's main urban areas, with or without formal leadership, were willing to challenge the oppressive system and face long jail sentences and fines.

In fact, this "state of emergency" approach had galvanized more of the educated and moderate African elites to take leadership roles in the nationalist movement.[5] After the arrest of the NDP leadership, a new group of politicians had emerged, including advocate Herbert Chitepo, Leopold Takawira, newspaper editor Nathan Shamuyarira, and Robert Mugabe, the latter a forty-one-year-old schoolteacher recently returned from Ghana. These intellectuals found themselves pushed into NDP leadership positions in 1960 following the arrests of other leaders. Such men had remained in multiracial organizations but the radicalization of the state and the quick pace toward recognition of African political rights in Northern Rhodesia (Zambia) and Nyasaland

---

[3] See Francis Nehwati, "The Social and Communal Background to 'Zhii': The African Riots in Bulawayo, Southern Rhodesia in 1960," *African Affairs* 69, no. 276 (July 1970), 250–66; and Terence Ranger, *Bulawayo Burning: The Social History of a Southern African City, 1893–1960* (London: James Currey, 2010), 221–40.

[4] Southern Rhodesia Legislative Assembly Debates, July 5, 1960, col. 181.

[5] Palley noted this in Parliament: Ibid.

(Malawi) convinced them of the possibility of an equally quick transition to majority rule in Southern Rhodesia, based on British support for the "wind of change" in Africa.[6] In 1956, Herbert Chitepo had written a prescient speech for a conference he was unable to attend. "Time is short and this is not only a unique opportunity for Africa, it is also the last," he wrote, "for if we cannot succeed together, Africans will be driven to adopt open racialist nationalism."[7] By 1960, the ability to continue to think in terms of a multiracial nationalism in Southern Rhodesia had all but evaporated. Later, living in exile in Lusaka, Zambia, Chitepo would become a key leader in the liberation war.

The new "fear" of African political participation that Palley decried was evident in the Whitehead government's swift introduction of repressive legislation intended to slow the momentum of African nationalist parties and mass participation in nonviolent protests. The legislation was rationalized to white voters as assurance that Southern Rhodesia's minority rule was not going to be challenged by moves from the British to break up the Central African Federation and to grant majority rule in all three territories. At the same time, the legislation was designed to convince the British that it was not discriminatory toward Africans in Southern Rhodesia. South Africa's high commissioner in Salisbury in 1960, H. T. Taswell, pointed out this dual strategy: "Sir Edgar Whitehead is playing a political game of give and take, of mixing liberalism with toughness." He predicted that Whitehead, who Taswell viewed as "more to the left than to the right," might learn in the next elections that "he has underestimated the hardening strength of forces of the right in this country."[8] In 1962, the victorious Rhodesian Front brought Winston Field into office as prime minister. Field would carry white-minority rule further down the road, later taken further still by Prime Minister Ian Smith, toward the

---

[6] On the transition of political moderate elites to nationalist politics, see Michael O. West, *The Rise of an African Middle Class: Colonial Zimbabwe, 1898–1965* (Bloomington: Indiana University Press, 2002), 177–235; Timothy Scarnecchia, *The Urban Roots of Democracy and Political Violence in Zimbabwe: Harare and Highfield, 1940–1964* (New York: Rochester University Press, 2008), 69–114.

[7] Richard Hughes, *Capricorn: David Stirling's Second African Campaign* (London: The Radcliffe Press, 2003), 126.

[8] H. T. Taswell to Secretary for External Affairs, Pretoria, November 12, 1960, External Affairs, 1/156/1 v3, Southern Rhodesia, Political Situation and Developments (11–10–60/30–1–61), South African National Archives, Pretoria.

1965 Unilateral Declaration of Independence (UDI) and direct violent confrontation with African nationalists.

Regional pressures on the Whitehead government were twofold. To the south, the South African apartheid government provided Whitehead with an example of how to respond against a restive urban township population with excessive police violence. To the north, Dr. Hastings Banda's negotiations with the British government had culminated in a Lancaster House agreement in August 1960 – leading to Nyasaland's (Malawi's) home rule and eventual majority rule. The agreement was seen by African nationalists in Southern Rhodesia as evidence that majority rule in a year's time was possible, just as many Rhodesian nationalists had optimistically predicted. The Whitehead government viewed the agreement as more justification for the use of state forces against African nationalists and their perceived supporters.[9] A London *Times* article from March 1961 commented that

Sir Edgar Whitehead found himself in office at a time when, to borrow Dr. Banda's words, the Nyasaland African not only kicked 'but taught the Southern Rhodesian African to kick too.' Any Prime Minister would therefore have been under the same necessity to tighten up the security legislation, though it certainly seems that some of the new regulations went much too far.[10]

Britain's responses to protests in Nyasaland and Northern Rhodesia had given hope and inspiration to the Southern Rhodesian African nationalists, who were confident that in the near future they too would repeat the transition from a nationalist leadership to leaders in a majority rule independent state.

Fear of Another Congo

Equally important to the decolonizing of most of British Africa in 1960 was the lesson taught by violent conflict in the Belgian Congo, following the transfer of power to African nationalists upon independence on June 30, 1960.[11] The violence drove a stream of white refugees from

[9] See John McCracken, "Labour in Nyasaland: An Assessment of the 1960 Railway Workers' Strike," *Journal of Southern African Studies* 14, no. 2 (January 1988), 279–90, esp. 281; Zoë Groves, *Malawian Migration to Zimbabwe, 1900–1965: Tracing Machona* (London: Palgrave Macmillan, 2020).

[10] "A Crucial Vote for Rhodesia," *Times* (London), March 7, 1961.

[11] For details on how the Congo crisis impacted the Central Africa Federation, see Mathew Hughes, "Fighting for White Rule in Africa: The Central African

the Congo into Northern and Southern Rhodesia in July 1960; many arrived with nothing but what they could carry with them, in a hurried exodus. This became tangible "proof" for many whites in Southern Rhodesia that the question of African independence could go "terribly wrong" for whites in the Federation.[12] To both whites and blacks in Rhodesia, the violence and political crises in the Congo served as a framework for discussing what could go wrong without proper planning. More critically, the discussions focused on the preparation of African political, civil, and military personnel capable of conducting a successful transfer. It also demonstrated how American and Soviet intervention into an African decolonization process could occur; an outcome not welcomed by either white or African politicians in Southern Rhodesia.

The editors of the *Rhodesian Herald*, for example, opined that the violence was proof of the claims that Whitehead, Sir Roy Welensky, the Federation's prime minister, and others, had been making for some time. In the weeks leading up to Congolese independence, Whitehead's speech to the Rhodesia National Affairs Association on June 14 had predicted that "the possibility of the army in the Congo taking over after independence was achieved at the end of the month." Whitehead criticized the Belgians for leaving the Congo without properly preparing the Congolese for independence, calling the decision to give independence in 1960 "the height of irresponsibility." Whitehead continued to build his case that the speed at which so many former European controlled colonies became independent would overtake the Western powers' ability to provide the needed aid and support, he believed. Such a deficiency would leave an opening for the communists, and what Whitehead saw as "the imminent danger of a backward slide to witchcraft and even slavery."[13] Welensky, with his usual penchant toward the hyperbolic, also warned of a communist takeover of the Congo one week before independence, warning "that the West is losing the battle for Africa." Welensky went on to say that "states granted independence but left with a crippled economy would have to sell

Federation, Katanga, and the Congo Crisis, 1958–1965," *International History Review* 25, no. 3 (2003), 596–615; John Kent, *America, the UN and Decolonisation: Cold War Conflict in the Congo* (London: Routledge, 2010).
[12]   "Congo Refugees Flee to Rhodesia; Hundreds Pour in by Ferry and Car – Americans Tell of Leopoldville Terror," *New York Times*, July 11, 1960, 2.
[13]   "Take-over by Army Possible – Sir Edgar," *Rhodesia Herald*, June 14, 1960.

themselves to the Communists as the price of their freedom."[14] He
predicted that "communist regimes" would fragment Africa and withhold from the West "resources of both manpower and minerals." This
point of view of decolonization was typical among white leaders in
Southern Rhodesia and the Federation.

As the Congolese crisis unfolded, the language became increasingly
strident. For many whites in southern Africa, the behavior of the
Belgians, including civilians who fled the violence immediately after independence, was interpreted as a sign of weakness. But it did not stop the
same voices from developing a sense of shared "victimhood" with white
settlers in the Congo. They were often portrayed as victims of American
and United Nations-inspired imperialism. The day following Congolese
independence, the *Rhodesian Herald* ran a short interview with the
former Governor-General of Mozambique, Senor Gabriel Teixeira. He
claimed the United States was to blame for black nationalism in Africa,
and that "to combat American adverse influences, Senor Teixeira said
white Africa will have to 'stand together and shoot together' to
combat the rising tide of black nationalism." Teixeira also had some
unsympathetic words for the white Belgians who fled the Congo for
the Federation and the Portuguese colonies. Teixeira charged that
"the spectacle of the Belgians running like frightened hares was dis-
graceful. They saw the flash of a blade and they broke all the Olympic
records running away."[15]

After the assassination of the Congo's first African leader, Patrice
Lumumba, became known publicly in early 1961, the incorporation of
the Congo crisis into Southern Rhodesian African nationalist rhetoric took
a more strident tone. The assumption that the United States and Western
powers had killed Lumumba to protect their interests in the mineral wealth
of the Congo became a motif for attacking the Cold War aspects of the
Congo crisis. By extension, the struggle for majority rule in Zimbabwe
began to be compared to either the pan-Africanism of Lumumba or the
"sell-out" of African interests by Moise Tshombe in Katanga. An article in
Zimbabwean African People's Union's publication *Radar* from April 5,
1961 began with a report about the Congo situation. Explaining the
agenda for the upcoming All-African People's Congress in Cairo, the

[14] "West Losing Battle for Africa, Welensky Warns," *Rhodesia Herald*, June 24,
1960, 1.
[15] "'Silly' U.S. Policy May Turn Black Africa Red," *Rhodesia Herald*, July 1, 1960.

article connected the Congo, South Africa, and the Southern Rhodesian situation: "Africa itself has urgent problems demanding the attention of her peoples. There is the Congo messed up by big power intrigues and subversion by imperialists." Referring to Rhodesia, the author noted that "[t]here is the Federation of Rhodesia and Nyasaland where Sir Roy Welenksy, leader of some of the 300,000 settlers who are resisting the liberation of 8,000,000 Africans, is introducing laws that will force Africans to accept Federation for fear of Welensky's white army." The *Radar* article criticized the British government for not standing up to Welensky and others, and for not challenging their "kith and kin" in the Rhodesias. The article ends with a call to "encourage those brave Africans" who would "break through the stone-wall of Salazar's dictators. Once Salazar has been blustered through and through, and Portuguese territories are won over to African Nationalism, Verwoerd's South Africa will crumble like a pack of cards at the flicker of a child's finger."[16]

Figure 1 Photo of, left to right, Robert Mugabe, George Silundika, and Joshua Nkomo. 1960. Getty Images.

---

[16] *Radar*, April 5, 1961, 1/156/1, vol. 4, BTS Southern Rhodesia, TS81, High Commissioner, Salisbury, 1960–63, National Archives of South Africa.

ZAPU and ZANU

The inability of the Zimbabwean nationalist movement to remain unified in the face of major state repression is writ large in the political history of the early 1960s. White politicians used the state, the judiciary in particular, to create a police state where arrests could be made on very little evidence. Individuals could be arrested if authorities believed they might do something against the state in the future. The Law and Order Maintenance Act (LOMA) from 1960 was targeted at African nationalists, and its passage was referred to by Chief Justice Tredgold as the "point of no return" for racial cooperation and liberal politics in Southern Rhodesia in 1960. In protest, Tredgold resigned as chief justice and tried unsuccessfully to start a new liberal political party. There is no doubt that LOMA was the most effective weapon white politicians used to suppress nationalist political activity inside Southern Rhodesia. As could be expected, LOMA helped exacerbate African nationalist hatred for the police state it created, and led many young men and women to commit themselves to leaving Southern Rhodesia to join the liberation war. Equally importantly, the LOMA detention policies meant that many nationalists spent ten years in detention camps and prisons, which became centers for education and political mobilization.[17]

Although the Rhodesian Front government had detained thousands of African nationalists by 1964 in anticipation of the UDI in 1965, the ability to arrest and detain nationalists was partly facilitated by the split in the nationalist movement that occurred officially in August 1963. The Zimbabwean African National Union (ZANU) broke away from the Zimbabwean African People's Union (ZAPU), and the ensuing political violence between their followers inside Rhodesia in 1963 and 1964 made it easier for the police to arrest individuals and to do so under the justification of "restoring peace." The rhetorical violence on the part of both parties, in their publications, show how irreconcilable the two groups of leaders became after having developed the nationalist movement together from the late 1950s into the early 1960s. The traditional narrative explaining the ZAPU–ZANU split

---

[17] See Munyaradzi Munochiveyi, *Prisoners of Rhodesia: Inmates and Detainees in the Struggle for Zimbabwean Liberation, 1960–1980* (New York: Palgrave Macmillan, 2014); Jocelyn Alexander "The Productivity of Political Imprisonment: Stories from Rhodesia," *The Journal of Imperial and Commonwealth History* 47, no. 2 (2019), 300–24.

revolves around a group of intellectuals in ZANU who became increasingly frustrated with the direction of the movement under the leadership of Nkomo by 1962–63. The main accusations against Nkomo's
leadership are assumed to be his initial support in London for the 1961
Southern Rhodesian Constitution, which he was later forced to reject;
his continual travel outside of the country in pursuit of international
solidarity for the nationalists; and his mishandling of the creation of
a government in exile in Tanzania.[18] While the latter issue is often seen
as the most contentious, it is instrumental to later relations of ZANU
and ZAPU with Julius Nyerere, the Tanzanian president. According to
Nkomo, he was originally given the go ahead to form a Zimbabwean
government in exile in Dar es Salaam, but by the time the rest of the
ZAPU leadership managed to reach Dar es Salaam, Nyerere had
changed his mind and told those leaders who were to form ZANU
that he was opposed to the idea to form such a government in exile.
After this, both Nkomo and his supporters, and those who would go on
to form ZANU, rushed back to Rhodesia to organize themselves.[19]
This led to major problems for those who had left Rhodesia, especially
for Robert Mugabe, who was out on bail at the time. In August 1963,
ZANU was eventually formed at the home of Enos Nkala in Highfield
Township in Salisbury. The Reverend Ndabaningi Sithole was chosen
to lead ZANU at that time. According to a quote in Martin Meredith's
biography of Mugabe, Enos Nkala was to have pronounced, "Now
I am going to see to it that Joshua Nkomo is crushed."[20] To compete

---

[18] For the NDP's own admission that their first major act of international
       diplomacy, participating in the constitutional talks in London in 1961, was
       a failure, see *Radar*, vol. 12, March 9, 1961, 1/156/1, vol. 4, BTS Southern
       Rhodesia, TS81, High Commissioner, Salisbury, 1960–63, National Archives of
       South Africa. "We make no bones about our part in the Southern Rhodesian
       Constitutional Conference, it was, to say the least, bad political performance."
       For a detailed discussion of the problems of this first act of major diplomacy by
       Nkomo, Reverend Sithole, Herbert Chitepo, and George Silundika, see
       John Day, "Southern Rhodesian African Nationalists and the 1961
       Constitution," *The Journal of Modern African Studies* 7, no. 2 (1969), 221–47.
[19] Joshua Nkomo, *Nkomo: The Story of My Life* (London: Methuen, 1984), 109–
       19; For the most detailed ZANU version of the split, see Maurice Nyagumbo,
       With the People: An Autobiography from the Zimbabwe Struggle (Salisbury:
       Graham Publishing, 1980), 162–94; for the impact of the split on political
       violence, see Scarnecchia, *Urban Roots*, 134–56.
[20] Martin Meredith, *Our Votes, Our Guns: Robert Mugabe and the Tragedy of
       Zimbabwe* (New York: Public Affairs, 2002), 32.

with the new ZANU party, ZAPU then formed the People's Caretaker Council as the ZAPU formation in Southern Rhodesia.

Examples of rhetorical violence in the publications of both ZANU and ZAPU at the time demonstrate the acrimonious nature of public discourse. An April 2, 1964 lead story in ZAPU publication *The Sun* claimed in its title, "Sithole runs into hiding as 6,000 people welcome Nkomo at Fort Victoria." Reverend Sithole and many of the ZANU leadership were from the Fort Victoria region, so the ZAPU perspective emphasized the popularity of Nkomo and the "tribalism" of ZANU: "While more than 6,000 singing, dancing, cheering and ululating sons and daughters of Mother Zimbabwe were giving the national president and lion of Zimbabwe, *Chibwechitedza* Joshua Nkomo, a hero's welcome into Fort Victoria, Ndabaningi Sithole, the self-styled leader of the insignificant, tribalistic and imperialistic ZANU ran into hiding with six non-Victorian mercenaries."[21] The reference to "non-Victorian" referred to the idea that Sithole, who was from the Fort Victoria [Masvingo] area, needed outsiders to defend him on his home turf. The reference to Nkomo as *Chibwechitedza*, is based on a chiShona name for someone who is like a "slippery rock," or an escape artist; someone who could escape dangerous situations.[22] In Nkomo's case, this label continued to apply as he would escape assassination attempts and arrests at many points in his political career. Not yet done, the author then goes on to disparage the other ZANU leaders, referring to them as "the Mugabes, Takawiras, Makombes, Mawemas, Zvobgos, Ziyambe, and a few other tribalistic stooges and power-hungry political rejects." Echoing a common insult used by both parties, the author described these leaders as "sell-outs" who had been "rejected by their own relatives who put national before tribal cause." The article ends by praising Nkomo "and his political policies of majority rule now under one man one vote and independence within this year."[23] As will be shown below, ZANU writers would be just as caustic in their criticisms of Nkomo and ZAPU.

---

[21] *The Zimbabwe Sun*, vol. 1, no. 6, April 2, 1964, RG 84, Foreign posts of the DOS, Entry number P 847, Rhodesia (Zimbabwe), File: U.S. Consulate General Subject files relating to labor matters, 1962–1969, Container 1, USNA.

[22] For an interesting analysis of the political meanings of *Chibwechitedza* as a political label, see Clapperton Mavhunga, *Transient Workspaces: Technologies of Everyday Innovation in Zimbabwe* (Cambridge, MA: MIT Press, 2011), 173–200.

[23] Ibid., n. 21.

Amendments to the Law and Order Maintenance Act by the Rhodesian Front Government, 1964–1965

In 1964, the Rhodesian minister of justice and law and order, Clifford Dupont, found a way around a constitutional challenge to the ongoing detentions of African nationalists, such as ZAPU leader Joshua Nkomo and ZANU leaders Ndabaningi Sithole and Robert Mugabe. Dupont combined restrictions in Section 44A of LOMA with provisions of the Protected Places Act of 1959. This allowed Dupont to restrict access to the detainees in the Wha Wha prison and Gonakudzingwa camps and to keep the media away from the African nationalist leadership by declaring their camps as "protected places." Dupont also included a "hanging clause" to LOMA, requiring the death penalty for those charged with the use of petrol bombs, and extended detentions without trials from 90 to 265 days. Describing these changes in the *Central African Examiner*, "Zhuwawo," a pen name for a nationalist leader, claims that all the amendments and restrictions eventually would fail. "But there is one thing which my colleague lawyer Dupont fails to realise: that there is a limit to repressive laws. You cannot go on indefinitely. Reaction breeds reaction; a repressive government would make its citizens react against it and the repressive laws become ineffective." The author goes on to say that "you cannot defeat a man's nationalist feelings by repressive measures. Nationalism is a religion. It is rooted in a man's heart and in his mind. Once a man decides to free himself from oppression it becomes a mental case." The writer concludes: "You can jail, restrict, hang, shoot, whip or burn him on the stake, but all the same he will continue. ... Repressive measures, instead of curbing him or deterring him, give him the sense of martyrdom if he suffers the punishment."[24]

Even before November 11, 1965, when the Rhodesian Front's UDI was issued, LOMA was the centerpiece of the Smith government's suppression of African nationalists, Desmond Lardner-Burke, the government's minister of justice and law and order, came to embody the injustices of LOMA, as he used the law to arrest and detain African leaders and the rank and file of the nationalist movement. Writing from the remote restriction area of Gonakudzingwa in March 1965, ZAPU's leader Nkomo commented on Lardner-Burke's new LOMA amendment

[24] "Zhuwawo's Bush Lawyer says ... Dupont is Wrong," *Central African Examiner*, May 1964, 15–16.

that allowed him to restrict or detain Africans for five years rather than one year without a new hearing.[25] Nkomo wrote, "I am surprised by people like Lardner-Burke who think that they can stop the sun from rising by the mere act of legislation." After repeating the claim that majority rule is the only possibility for the future, Nkomo declared, "Some of these laws may be used in reverse in the-not-too-distant future. Let that be clear to Mr. Lardner-Burke. Of course, as a majority Government we shall not need such stupid laws."[26] The ZAPU publication, *African Home News,* reported some of the "unbelievably severe sentences" under LOMA, citing the example of a Mr. Joseph Shasha, who "was sentenced to four years in prison for picking a stone and threatening to throw it at a police officer during a scuffle. He did not throw the stone, and no one was hurt." The same report described how Mr. Josiah Samuriwo was "sentenced to two-and-half years' hard labor when he was found guilty of 'assaulting, resisting and obstructing' two white policemen."[27] Samuriwo was charged with allegedly telling the constables "that they were 'white skinned pigs' who would go home bare footed." Samuriwo claimed that he was beaten and arrested at the police charge office when he went there to report police abuse.[28]

Diplomatic efforts around UDI were mostly limited to Commonwealth countries negotiating with Ian Smith and the Rhodesian Front government. There was not much hope at this stage that the African nationalists would have a meaningful say in the negotiations. In January 1965, American diplomats reported on a statement made by Ian Smith when he spoke to a crowd of 400 at Gwanda. He stated:

[25] Larry Bowman writes that the SR Government "detained 495 persons in 1959 and 1,791 from the beginning of 1964 to June 1965 .... Under the original LOMA, restriction orders were for three months, but they now can be for terms up to five years and they are always renewable." Larry Bowman, *Politics in Rhodesia* (Harvard University Press, 1973), 60.

[26] "Lardner-Burke Is a Desperate Man," *African Home News,* March 20, 1965, "From Gonakudzingwa, Restricted Area," Eileen Haddon Collection, Reel 2g, Center for Research Libraries, MF-2881, Reel 11.

[27] "Victims of 'Law and Order,'" *African Home News,* May 22, 1965, p. 1, Eileen Haddon Collection, Reel 2g, CRL MF-2881, Reel 11.

[28] Samuriwo was charged with assault and resisting, or obstructing, two white constables. "Josiah Samuriwo Jailed for Two and Half Years," in "Victims of 'Law and Order,'" *African Home News,* May 22, 1965, p. 1, Eileen Haddon Collection, Reel 2g, CRL MF-2881, Reel 11.

If the British Government's attitude was that Rhodesia could only have independence when it had an African majority, then there was no need for him to go to London. Also if the British Government was serious in suggesting a constitutional conference at which Joshua Nkomo and Ndabaningi Sithole would be present, such a conference would not take place in his lifetime.[29]

The road to the UDI on November 11, 1965 was therefore travelled without substantial interference from the nationalist movements, most of whose leaders had been arrested and detained. This suppression was not lost on African leaders in other countries, as particularly expressed at the Organization of African Unity (OAU) and the United Nations by Ghana's Kwame Nkrumah and Tanzania's Julius Nyerere. Kenya's Tom Mboya, a leading trade unionist and outspoken politician, issued a statement about the lack of British concern for Nkomo, who remained in detention in 1965. At the time of UDI, Mboya was Kenya's minister for justice and constitutional affairs and also the secretary general of KANU, Kenya's ruling party. Mboya chastised the British for accepting the Rhodesian government's illegal detention of Nkomo and other African leaders, declaring that "the present Rhodesian attitude . . . was a mockery of British justice and an attempt to undermine the judiciary." He went on: "It is significant that these are the actions of a British dependent territory. Had these same actions taken place in an independent African state, the world would have been told by the same minority European regime of Rhodesia how irresponsible and untrustworthy African leaders can be."[30] Stating this in November 1964, four years after most African colonies had gained their independence, and eleven months since Kenya's Independence, Mboya and others noted the hypocrisy in the different treatment of the new African "race state" versus the white, or European "race state" in southern Africa.

[29]   AmConGen Salisbury, "Deemphasis of UDI in Referendum Campaign,"
        November 2, 1964, A-365 POL 15–4, Rhod 1/1/6, USNA, General Records of
        the Department of State, Central Foreign Policy Files, 1964–66, Political and
        Defense: POL 14 RHOD to POL 16, Political Recognition RHOD, Box 2606,
        Declassified NND 959000.
[30]   From AmEmbassy Nairobi to Department of State, "Kenyan Reaction to the
        Rhodesia and Mozambique Political Situations," November 27, 1964, A-381
        POL 15–5 RHOD USNA RG 59, General Records of the Department of State,
        Central Foreign Policy Files, 1964–66, Political and Defense: POL 14 RHOD to
        POL 16, Political Recognition RHOD, Box 2606, Declassified NND 959000.

The Unilateral Declaration of Independence and Race States in Southern Africa, 1966–1970

A number of scholars have written detailed studies on the diplomacy around the UDI.[31] One thing to note is that Zimbabwean nationalists were, in large part, ignored during that diplomacy. That absence, and what was seen as an acquiescence on the part of the British to the Rhodesian Front, contributed to the strong animosity – or perhaps visceral hatred would be a better way of putting it – shared among Zimbabwean nationalists toward the British for allowing the UDI to occur. Many nationalist leaders were hopeful in 1963 and 1964, when they were arrested and put into prison or detention under the LOMA provisions, that they would not have to wait too long for a transfer to majority rule and would be asked to negotiate their roles in a transitional government. The notion of "PGs" or "prison graduates" had been the common experience of nationalists in British India, and then in Africa starting with Kwame Nkrumah in the Gold Coast in 1951 when he was released directly from prison to the state house to assume leadership of domestic policies. Many other leaders in former African colonies had experienced similar paths from prison to state house, however the leaders of ZANU and ZAPU were not to be as fortunate. Nkomo, Sithole, and Mugabe, along with many other leaders, would spend the first ten years of the illegal UDI government in detention. While in detention, the leadership of both organizations did their best to stay in contact with their allies and supporters inside and outside of Rhodesia. They hoped that international pressure could force the collapse of the Smith regime based on its illegality and the sanctions designed and implemented by the British and the United Nations.

The Rhodesian Front government, from its own perspective, grew in confidence after the British and international community failed to act beyond economic sanctions. Almost a year after the UDI, Ian Smith

---

[31] On the British response leading up to the UDI, see Carl P. Watts, *Rhodesia's Unilateral Declaration of Independence: A Study in International Crisis* (Basingstoke: Palgrave Macmillan, 2008); Anthony Verrier, *The Road to Zimbabwe: 1890–1980* (London: Jonathan Cape, 1986), 129–61; Kate Law, "Pattern, Puzzle, and Peculiarity: Rhodesia's UDI and Decolonisation in Southern Africa," *Journal of Imperial and Commonwealth History* 45, no. 5 (2017), 721–28; Zaki Laïdi, *The Super-Powers and Africa: The Constraints of a Rivalry: 1960–1990* (University of Chicago Press, 1990).

addressed the Rhodesian Front Congress in September 1966 with his usual "us against the world" rhetoric, suggesting that Rhodesia was building a wall between itself and its enemies: "Smith said that the seizure of independence had been 'the most important operation of all, building the new wall, a wall which was to hold back the flood waters."[32] Smith also criticized a recent Commonwealth prime minister's conference, which he described as the "most unpleasant, racial-conscious, color-conscious PM's conference ever held," which had "impertinence to discuss our Rhodesian problems in our absence, a violation of the most fundamental rights not only of democracy but of law."[33] Such statements characterized Smith's hyperbolic style that diplomats tended to ignore, but which had a ready audience in the white settler world, including a sympathetic community among powerful lobbies in the United States.

Understanding that the struggle was now going to be a long-term conflict, capable African nationalist leaders such as Herbert Chitepo – who would go on to lead ZANU's military efforts from outside Rhodesia while ZANU's executives remained in detention in Rhodesia – increasingly focused their disdain on the British for their role in allowing the UDI to happen and for allowing Rhodesia to continue to function. In a 1967 interview, Chitepo, as the National Chairman of ZANU, responded to a question about the role of Britain in the Zimbabwean struggle. Chitepo was asked what he thought of those who claimed that "freedom fighters in Zimbabwe are fighting in order to create a situation which would compel Britain to intervene militarily." "If that was the situation," Chitepo replied, "it would be quite easy." He emphasized that the British had said they would not intervene after the UDI "unless there was a breakdown of law and order." According to Chitepo, there had been many examples afterward of the breakdown of law in order, including the illegality "of anything that is being done by Ian Smith." His main point, however, was the racial element in what the British had in mind. What they meant, according to Chitepo, "was that they would consider it

---

[32] Ian Smith speech to Rhodesian Front Congress, September 23, 1966, Salisbury to Secretary of State, Control 262, September 24, 1966, POL 12 RF, POL 24 RF, Box RG 0084, Foreign Service Posts of the Department of State, Entry P 818, Rhodesia (Zimbabwe); US Consulate General, Salisbury, Unclassified Subject Files, 1966–70, 1966: CR to SP, Container 1.
[33] Ibid.

a breakdown of law and order the moment there are sufficient white necks or white throats cut. I think this is what they meant, and that they would intervene for that purpose." Chitepo then suggested that if ZANU's strategy had simply been to get the British to intervene, then "all we needed to do was to look for a few white throats to cut." He argued that racial violence was not part of ZANU's pattern, arguing that "[o]ur intention is a fairly simple and straight forward one – we want to establish in Zimbabwe an African Government, a government of the majority of the people who are by nature Africans. ... [W]e are not going to try and get it by asking for aid of the British. In fact we are at war with Britain herself." Chitepo concluded, "We are not regarding Britain as in any way different from Smith. They are two accomplices."[34] Chitepo's frustration with the British was shared among other nationalists. They felt that whatever claims the British could make to the universal ideals of justice and "fair play" were destroyed by the continued existence of an illegal Rhodesian government after the UDI. From the nationalists' position, the only way for the British to regain their respect would be to support their efforts to remove Smith from power and turn the government over to leaders elected by majority rule.

An example of the disdain with which Zimbabwean nationalists held the British was expressed in the *ZANU News* of September 7, 1965, which criticized the British for not sufficiently challenging Smith over the UDI. The editorial pointed to a potential "race war" that would have extensive repercussions. "The moral here is that Britain is looking for other countries to associate with a solution which she well knows contains ill-concealed seeds of a racial conflagration potentially capable of engulfing the whole world."[35] Such an argument pointed out that the "race war" concept was also very much on the minds of African nationalists, and the onus for such a war was placed on the

---

[34] Interview with Herbert Chitepo, *Zimbabwe News*, ZANU Lusaka, September 13, 1967 [no vol. or no. given on original], listed as "East Africa Edition," 1967, RG 0084, Entry# P 818: Rhodesia [Zimbabwe]: US Consulate General, Salisbury: Unclassified Subject Files, 1966–70, 1967: ACC to 1968: PER Container 2, USNA.

[35] "Editorial: Britain Unmasks Her Own Hypocrisy over the Political Deadlock in Zimbabwe," *ZANU News,* vol. 1, no. 6, September 7, 1965, p. 3, RG 0084, Entry P 818: Rhodesia [Zimbabwe]: US Consulate General, Salisbury: Unclassified Subject Files, 1966–70, 1967: ACC to 1968: PER, Container 2, USNA.

British in their acquiescence to Smith and the white settlers who had
seemed to have got away with the UDI.

A week after this publication and a month before the UDI, on
September 14, 1965, ZANU issued a "special bulletin" from Dar es
Salaam. The report celebrates the first "direct confrontation with the
enemy":

the Party's military wing the 'Crocodile Group' has with barely no sophisticated weapons but simply knives, bows and arrows, spears and axes and
above all the dire determination to dare fight a heavily armed enemy, had
implemented stage one of the Party's five-point master-plan – OPERATION
CONFRONTATION – commendably."[36]

These first attempts to infiltrate into Rhodesia by the first groups of
liberation soldiers were not exceptionally successful from a military
perspective, but these did have a major psychological and political
impact. The ability to send fighters into Rhodesia and to engage with
Rhodesian forces also permitted ZANU and ZAPU to claim a much
more important legitimacy within the OAU and at the United Nations,
for example. They were also in a better position to approach nations in
the Eastern bloc and in Africa for military training and weapons. The
Zimbabwe People's Revolutionary Army (ZIPRA) under ZAPU
received initial support from the Soviet Union and Egypt, and the
Zimbabwe African National Liberation Army (ZANLA) under
ZANU received aid from China and Tanzania. Both armies would
then receive significant assistance from Eastern European nations as
well, as will be discussed in the following chapters.

The first major incursion into Rhodesian territory by a joint ZAPU
and South African ANC group in July 1967 came under heavy criticism
in ZANU publications where it was viewed to be an opportunistic
alliance and mission designed to gain control of aid from the OAU's
Liberation Committee at the expense of ZANU's ZANLA. In ZANU's
Zimbabwe News, an article entitled "Down with the Alliance" lambasted ZAPU and South African ANC leaders for orchestrating the
mission. Calling ZAPU's James Chikerema and South African ANC
leader Oliver Tambo "careerists" and comparing them to the Katanga
leader Moise Tshombe, the author made the point: "There exists
within the Southern Africa nationalist movement a reactionary bunch

---

[36] Ibid.

whose ideas of revolution consists chiefly of sacrificing the precious blood of a few freedom fighters in order to create a favorable impression among their international backers."[37] The author states that this new ZAPU–ANC military alliance was a major tactical error: "Here was irresponsible clowning at its best: James Chikerema and Oliver Tambo unwittingly granting South Africa a perfect diplomatic excuse for military intervention in Rhodesia. We have never for a moment accused PCC [People's Caretaker Council] of being serious about anything, let alone about revolutionary affairs."[38] The author noted that since an OAU summit was near, "A PCC–ANC alliance was announced and a batch of ANC youths were hastily sent across the Zambezi, the aim of it all being to impress the Liberation Committee and get more cash." The article suggests that besides these issues, it was also the case that South African and Zimbabwean blacks had their differences, and it wasn't clear that either would be able to fight for the other's liberation. "The historical fact, if we must be honest with ourselves, does not allow us at this point to pretend that a Southern African, even though he may be black, can automatically find acceptance among the people of Zimbabwe." The ZANU author concluded, "To shed our blood for our country and liberate ourselves is an honor which we Zimbabweans would never want to share with anybody at this stage .... Publicity stunts staged for no better purpose than to impress an impending international conference are a complete sell-out."[39]

This increased cooperation between the South African and Rhodesian militaries points to the dilemma created by ZAPU and ZIPRA's cooperation with the South African ANC and its armed wing *Umkhonto we Sizwe* (Spear of the Nation). According to ZANU, the venture pointed out a potentially important problem confronting the liberation forces – the

[37] "Down with the Alliance," *Zimbabwe News*, vol. 2, no. 19, October 6, 1967 USNA, April 2013, Day 1, file 2, RG 0084, Entry P 818: Rhodesia [Zimbabwe]: US Consulate General, Salisbury: Unclassified Subject Files, 1966–70, 1967: ACC to 1968: PER, Container 2, NARA II. Stephen Davies refers to this failed joint operation as "the last time the Congress would attempt military action against the South African government in the 1960s." This failure was used by the South Africans as a rationale for supporting "white colonial buffer states." Stephen Davies, *Apartheid's Rebels: Inside South Africa's Hidden War* (New Haven, CT: Yale University Press, 1987), 22–23.

[38] Ibid. The People's Caretaker Council was what ZAPU was renamed within Rhodesia after being officially banned in Rhodesia, and after the 1963 split in ZAPU that led to the formation of ZANU.

[39] Ibid.

increased role of South African forces fighting to defend Rhodesia. After claiming that South Africa has added troops to "raise the strength of the fascist regular army in Rhodesia of 4,500 to nearly 10,000," the author suggested "by admitting publicly that Vorster was sending troops to Rhodesia, Smith had conceded that the war raging in Rhodesia was of a scale too large for his tiny army to cope with." But beyond this admission was a bigger potential danger that shaped much of the Cold War response to the Rhodesian military confrontation. There was always the possibility that Smith would try to use his forces to draw Zambia into a direct conflict and bring the South Africans and, more importantly, the Americans and their Western allies to support Smith against what would be "sold" as a communist-led invasion. The author argued that "Smith is now trying to blame the war of his own creation upon Zambia. . . . He has chosen to provoke Zambia in order to bolster up the fiction that Zambia is the source of his trouble and certain doom." The author suggests that for Smith, in the "back of his mind is the burning desire to be recognized in imperialist circles . . . . He looks forward to an international imperialist army fighting for the salvation of his fascist regime. He is hankering after another Vietnam in Zimbabwe."[40]

Domestically, Smith continued to present an overconfident public position by assuring his supporters there was little to worry about militarily. For example, he commented in 1967 that "terrorist infiltration over the past months had passed off with very little concern . . . and we grow in strength every day." He said he believed the guerrilla forces "have probably tried their strongest hand in the recent episode." He thought that this "first joint effort of South African and Rhodesian terrorists working together" had been done to influence possible talks between the Rhodesians and the British. "'Whenever these people feel there is a chance of Britain and Rhodesia coming to terms, they do this sort of thing because that is the last thing they want of course. Recognition of Rhodesia – this would be a serious blow to them."[41]

[40] "Courting Trouble," *Zimbabwe News*, vol. 2, no. 19, October 6, 1967, USNA, April 2013, Day 1, file 2, RG 0084, Entry# P 818: Rhodesia [Zimbabwe]: US Consulate General, Salisbury: Unclassified Subject Files, 1966–70, 1967: ACC to 1968: PER, Container 2, NARA II.

[41] AmConsul Salisbury to SecState, POL 23, quoting interview with Ian Smith in *Rhodesia Herald*, September 7, 1967, RG 0084, Entry# P 818: Rhodesia [Zimbabwe]: US Consulate General, Salisbury: Unclassified Subject Files, 1966–70, 1967: ACC to 1968: PER, Container 2, NARA II.

These arguments and attitudes would persist into the 1970s and become an important part of negotiations that made the Western powers, specifically the United Kingdom and the United States, suspicious of Rhodesian claims of outside communist interference in the liberation war. This was the case before 1975 and the end of the Portuguese colonies in Southern Africa. Before the rapid decolonization of these colonies, the threat of communist intervention in Rhodesia seemed more imagined than real.[42] As the next chapter will show, events in Angola and Mozambique quickly raised the stakes for a Cold War conflict in Rhodesia, and increased pressure for American and British diplomatic interventions with South Africa, the Frontline States, and Rhodesia itself. The next chapter will examine important trends in the period of 1970–75. The most important of these trends involve difficulties within ZANU and ZAPU to maintain unity within their individual organizations operating in Zambia and Tanzania and, later, in Mozambique. These internal troubles in ZAPU and ZANU would seriously impede the goal of unifying their military efforts to fight more effectively against the Rhodesian state in the early 1970s.

---

[42] See Filipe Ribeiro de Meneses and Robert McNamara, *The White Redoubt, the Great Powers and the Struggle for Southern Africa, 1960–1980* (London: Palgrave, 2018); Donal Lowry, "The Impact of Anti-communism on White Rhodesian Political Culture, ca. 1920s–1980," *Cold War History* 7, no. 2 (2007), 169–94.

2 | The Early 1970s

International pressure on the white settler UDI government of Rhodesia to accept majority rule as the condition for a decolonization and independence process acceptable to the British increased steadily during the first half of the 1970s. The concept of "No Independence before Majority Rule" (NIBMAR) had been somewhat dormant since the late 1960s, but it moved to the foreground again in the early 1970s as attention from the Afro-Asia bloc in the United Nations kept the issue alive in the General Assembly. There was also attention from Commonwealth member states who still believed Britain needed to take responsibility for fixing the problem they had punted down the road in 1965.[1] Following the passage in 1969 of yet another Rhodesian constitution, a 1970 referendum on whether or not to become a republic was successful among the limited franchise electorate. Confidence was high among whites in Rhodesia, as the campaign was run on a sense of optimism that the Rhodesian state had weathered the worst of the storm and was now moving toward normalization as a recognized sovereign state. This internal domestic "white citizen" optimism did not, however, match the international condemnation of a white settler republic.

In 1971, the Conservative Party in Britain attempted to reopen negotiations with Smith's UDI government, and British foreign secretary Alec Douglas-Home went to Salisbury in November where, as Bishop Abel Muzorewa describes it in his memoir, "he made a big show of consulting all shades of Rhodesian opinion."[2] The result of this visit was a "Proposal for a Settlement," which involved changes to the franchise requirements in the 1969 Constitution. These changes were meant to allow more black Rhodesians to vote, but the white

---

[1] Elaine Windrich, *Britain and the Politics of Rhodesian Independence* (New York: Africana Pub. Co, 1978), 162–85.

[2] Abel Muzorewa, *Rise Up and Walk: The Autobiography of Bishop Abel Tendekai Muzorewa* (London: Evans Brothers, 1978), 92.

minority would remain in control. In 1972, the official "Pearce Commission" was created to visit Rhodesia and obtain testimonies from rural and urban Africans to ascertain if they accepted the new constitution. Supporters of the still-detained executives of ZAPU and ZANU worked together with African religious leaders to organize a nationwide "No" campaign. In addition to testing internal opposition to the Smith regime, the campaign brought Muzorewa to the stage as an internal African nationalist leader. He gained national recognition for his leadership in the successful "No" campaign, and soon became an important addition to the leadership struggle within the larger Zimbabwean nationalist movement.[3] The failure to obtain British approval of the 1969 Constitution was a setback to the Rhodesian government's plans for greater international recognition. However, the ruling Rhodesian Front government continued to maintain confidence and popularity among its followers. It would not be until 1974–75 that Smith and his colleagues were confronted by British and South African pressure to seriously negotiate.

From a military perspective, the early 1970s presented an array of challenges to Zimbabwean nationalist forces. Primarily, self-inflicted leadership conflicts made recruiting, training, and supplying those who joined the liberation forces difficult. Rhodesian intelligence infiltrated the security of the military leadership in Lusaka and Dar es Salaam, and in the camps in Tanzania and Zambia. These leadership struggles are important to outline, as these internal battles would significantly handicap any real prospects for unity in the second half of the 1970s.

Both nationalist parties had continued to organize and train their recruits separately, thanks to the support of Zambia and Tanzania, as well as other external backers: the Soviets supported ZAPU's Zimbabwe People's Revolutionary Army (ZIPRA) and the People's Republic of China supported ZANU's Zimbabwe African National Liberation Army (ZANLA). With Joshua Nkomo, Ndabaningi Sithole, Robert Mugabe, and other political leaders detained in Rhodesia, the external leadership of political and military leaders worked from Lusaka and Dar es Salaam. For ZAPU, these included Jason Moyo, James Chikerema, George Nyandoro, and George Silundika. As historian

---

[3] Ibid., 92–137; Luise White, *Unpopular Sovereignty: Rhodesian Independence and African Decolonization* (Chicago: University of Chicago Press, 2015), 206–32.

Enocent Msindo describes this period in his study of Kalanga ethnic politics in Zimbabwe, the leaders began to blame each other for failures in executing the war. As with so many leadership conflicts in Zimbabwean history, the divisiveness likely started as personal issues but would soon be defined and explained by ethnic politics. Msindo points out that the divisions in ZAPU were primarily between those who were ethnic Kalangas, Ndebeles, and Shonas. The ZAPU leadership had a dramatic falling out after Moyo blamed Chikerema and other Shona leaders for failing to deliver necessary supplies to the military, and for the rise of "tribalism" in the party. Chikerema reacted violently to these accusations. The Kalanga leadership were kidnapped, only to be rescued by Zambian authorities.[4]

Leo Baron, Nkomo's long-time lawyer advocate, recounted his interpretation of the ZAPU leadership infighting in 1970, explaining that Chikerema and Nyandoro had "abducted the other three executive members of ZAPU, Moyo, Silundika, and [Edward] Ndlovu. As a matter of fact, it was touch and go." Baron said Zambia's minister of home affairs, Aaron Milner, had to negotiate with Chikerema and Nyandoro to eventually release the other three leaders.[5] The result was the formation of a new party, the Front for the Liberation of Zimbabwe (FROLIZI), which sought to forge a new, nonfactionalist military effort that would mend the split between ZAPU and ZANU. Former ZAPU leaders Chikerema and Nyandoro joined ZANU's Nathan Shamuyarira to make up FROLIZI's initial leadership. However, FROLIZI's relatively quick rise and fall demonstrated how intractable the ZAPU and ZANU sides were. The Frontline State presidents, and in particular Tanzania's Julius Nyerere, had hoped initially that FROLIZI offered the possibility of resolving the divide between ZAPU and ZANU by allowing a unified military command to emerge. In the process, the creation of yet another military command structure complicated the existing liberation armies' efforts to receive funding and training from the Organization of African Unity's Liberation Committee and from other sources.

---

[4] Enocent Msindo, *Ethnicity in Zimbabwe: Transformations in Kalanga and Ndebele Societies, 1860–1990* (New York: University of Rochester Press, 2012), 204–6.

[5] National Archives of Zimbabwe, "Interview with Leo Baron," Oral History Collection 239, 75–76.

Before addressing issues of disunity in ZANU, it is worth discussing the impact of the Carnation Revolution in Portugal of 1974, which intensified pressures on the Rhodesian crisis and hastened major diplomatic and military developments. Historian Jamie Miller has provided a careful reading of how this revolution, and the subsequent Portuguese-announced independence dates for Mozambique and Angola, caused a significant shift in South African diplomacy and military thinking about Rhodesia and southern Africa. Miller states, "If a rapprochement with black Africa was one part of Vorster's statecraft program, then a distancing of Pretoria from other forms of white rule on the continent was the other."[6] The decision by the new Portuguese government to announce the forthcoming independence of Mozambique (June 25, 1975) and Angola (November 11, 1975) created extremely favorable possibilities for the Zimbabwean liberation armies. Before exploring the global impact of this shift in Chapter 3, it is important to consider how the end of Portuguese colonialism in southern Africa also caused a détente between apartheid South Africa and the regional African-led governments. This was predominantly the case with Zambia, where President Kenneth Kaunda and his long-serving diplomat Mark Chona worked to negotiate with South Africa's prime minister, John Vorster, to pressure Smith's government into restarting negotiations with African nationalists in 1975.[7]

Direct talks between Smith and the nationalist leaders during the détente period would prove unsuccessful. This period did, however, lead to the release of the key leaders of ZANU and ZAPU from detention in Rhodesia. Nkomo of ZAPU and Sithole of ZANU were permitted to give public speeches in Rhodesia for the first time since 1964. This freedom of the "old guard" leaders had major implications for both parties, but the immediate crisis was in ZANU, where the leadership was already undergoing a major realignment that began in late November 1974 and would continue until after the assassination of their primary political and military leader in exile, Herbert Chitepo, on March 18, 1975.

[6] Jamie Miller, *An African Volk: The Apartheid Regime and Its Search for Survival* (Oxford: Oxford University Press, 2016).

[7] Andrew DeRoche, *Kenneth Kaunda, the United States and Southern Africa* (London: Bloomsbury Academic, 2016), 40–41; Miller, *An African Volk*, 141–52.

The Nhari Rebellion and ZANU's Leadership

It is helpful to consider the Nhari Rebellion of November–
December 1974 in the context of diplomacy and the internal politics
of ZANU and ZANLA. The Nhari Rebellion took its name from one its
chief instigators, Thomas Nhari, who along with Dakarai Badza,
attempted to confront the ZANLA and ZANU leadership about shortages on the war front – although some historians argue they were
motivated by the humiliation of their previous demotions. By the end
of 1974, the Nhari Rebellion revealed major fissures in the ZANU and
ZANLA situation. As historians have argued, while most contemporary analysts emphasized ethnic rivalry as its cause, the rebellion could
also be viewed as an attempt by some of the older members of ZANU's
executive to try and maintain control of the party and the war effort as
a younger generation began to exert its influence. As Wilf Mhanda
describes, a key element in the timing of the rebellion was the return
from China of a new group of commanders who pushed for a more
radical, intransigent position within ZANU.[8]

As the rebellion was put down, many of the rebellious ZANLA
soldiers were killed, and some older ZANU leaders accused of leading
the rebellion were quickly rounded up by ZANLA. John Mataure,
a long-time leader in ZANU, was summarily executed. Significantly,
the operation to put down the rebellion was called *Gukurahundi* and
involved soldiers brought from camps in Tanzania.[9] Zambian police
were involved in arresting some of the rebels, eventually turning them
over to ZANU and its military leader, Josiah Tongogara, who had been
a target in the rebellion. Failing to kill Tongogara, the rebels kidnapped

---

[8] See Wilfred Mhanda, *Dzino: Memories of a Freedom Fighter* (Harare: Weaver,
     2011), 48; Zvakanyorwa Wilbert Sadomba, *War Veterans in Zimbabwe's
     Revolution: Challenging Neo-colonialism and Settler and International Capital*
     (Oxford: Boydell & Brewer, 2011), 17; Luise White, *The Assassination of
     Herbert Chitepo: Texts and Politics in Zimbabwe* (Bloomington: Indiana
     University Press, 2003), 20–22; Blessing-Miles Tendi, *The Army and Politics in
     Zimbabwe: Mujuru, the Liberation Fighter and Kingmaker* (Cambridge:
     Cambridge University Press, 2020), 42–52; Fay Chung, *Re-living the Second
     Chimurenga: Memories from the Liberation Struggle in Zimbabwe* (Uppsala,
     Sweden: Nordic Africa Institute, 2006), 92–95.
[9] Tendi notes, from his 2015 interview with Rugare Gumbo, that Gumbo alleged it
     was Tongogara who went behind the backs of the ZANU leadership to have
     Nhari and Mataure executed before their trial was concluded. Tendi, *Army and
     Politics in Zimbabwe*, 47.

his wife for a short period. The subsequent killings of rebels and suppression of the rebellion by Tongogara and his loyal troops based in Tanzania showed how dissent was to be handled in ZANU and ZANLA. As historian Gerald Mazarire states, "The gun had thus not only triumphed over the party but a new form of punishment – execution by the gun – had been popularised, and was only to be curtailed by the arrest of members of the Dare and High Command after the assassination of Herbert Chitepo."[10]

The Nhari Rebellion would turn out to be a fortuitous event for Mugabe. He had tried to attend the Lusaka meeting where the new unity accord was signed by Nkomo, Sithole, Chikerema, and Muzorewa, but had been forbidden to attend the conference by President Nyerere and the other Frontline State presidents, who did not recognize his claim at that time to a ZANU leadership position. His absence from the unity negotiations, which ostensibly had placed ZANU and ZANLA under the joint command of the African National Council (referred to as the ANC) – an umbrella organization of four different movements – allowed him to further challenge Sithole's leadership. Most importantly, Mugabe gained support among the younger, more radical leaders and members of ZANU/ZANLA who opposed any unity accords and negotiations with the Smith regime. This would help his claim to the leadership role in late 1975, as described in Chapter 3.

George Houser Hears Conflicting Accounts of the Failed Lusaka Accords

The American activist George Houser visited Zambia in October 1975. Houser directed the American Committee on Africa and the Africa Fund, and had developed close relations with African nationalists and liberation war leaders over decades of involvement with the anticolonial struggles in Africa. As mentioned in the Introduction, Houser's detailed transcripts of his talks are an invaluable source of insights into what the Zimbabwean nationalists were saying about events at the time. Given that members of ZAPU and ZANU trusted Houser as a progressive ally to their cause, they tended to tell him different

---

[10] Gerald Mazarire, "Discipline and Punishment in ZANLA: 1964–1979," *Journal of Southern African Studies* 37, no. 3 (2011), 578.

information than they provided to the American and British diplomats in Lusaka, Dar es Salaam, and Maputo.

One of the first Zimbabwean nationalists Houser met with during his 1975 trip to Lusaka was Enoch Dumbutshena. Dumbutshena was, like Chitepo, one of the first black advocates in Rhodesia. He had been a member of ZAPU, and was their London representative for ten years before coming home and taking up a position in Lusaka, where he was a successful lawyer. He got involved in politics again and joined FROLIZI, but by the time he spoke with Houser he was a supporter of Muzorewa's African National Council.[11] Houser met with Dumbutshena on October 20, 1975, at Dumbutshena's law office on the third floor of the Woodgate building, "across Cairo Road from the Lusaka Hotel." Dumbutshena described the internal politics of the ZANU leadership prior to the Nhari Rebellion. He said the "external committee" of ZANU had "voted 3 to 2 to depose Sithole" before Sithole was released from detention and before he arrived in Lusaka. Dumbutshena said it was Nyerere who insisted that Sithole be recognized as the leader of ZANU at the Lusaka talks because he could not be deposed by a committee, and such action would have to be taken at a ZANU congress. Dumbutshena related how Mugabe remained in detention, so he "was not involved in what took place." He then described a "power struggle" in ZANU that was based on "tribal subdivisions within the Shona." Houser notes that such subdivisions had not been a factor in the "internal policies of Zimbabwe," but had become important for reasons Dumbutshena "doesn't completely understand in the external politics."[12]

Based on Houser's summary of Dumbutshena's account, it appears that Chitepo was at the center of the conflict. Dumbutshena told Houser that "the Manyikas, led by Chitepo, seemed to think of themselves as more sophisticated than the other sub groups of the Shona. The Karanga rebelled against this." Houser speculates that this was never made a public position. "Nevertheless the Karangas felt that Chitepo was favoring the Manyikas in the positions of authority within the organization. It was the military leadership of the ZANU forces that

---

[11] Robert Cary and Diana Mitchell, "African Nationalist Leaders – Rhodesia to Zimbabwe: The Web Version of the 1977–1980 Who's Who," www.colonialrelic.com/biographies/enoch-dumbutshena.

[12] George Houser, "Lusaka and Mozambique Trip Notes 1975," MSS 294, Houser Papers, Special Collections, MSU Library.

took the lead in what happened." According to Dumbutshena, a "death list was drawn up which included Chitepo, who ironically enough as the chairman of Zanu was the one who had to sign the death warrants." Houser writes how "Enoch wondered what kind of blackmail was put on Chitepo to make him sign these warrants. . . . Enoch says that most of those killed were Zezuru and Kore Kore."[13]

According to Dumbutshena, the recent disunity in ZANU was related to the Lusaka Agreement and the decision to work with the African National Council. Once again, the division was described through Shona subethnicities. Dumbutshena described Sithole's support as coming from the Manyika, who wanted to work with the African National Council, whereas "the Karangas did not." Dumbutshena also claimed that Chitepo had spoken with Nyerere and told him that "he hoped that Sithole wouldn't be released from detention in Rhodesia too soon because he wanted to consolidate his own leadership position." Houser noted that "ZANU is very definitely divided" and that, on the day he was writing up his notes, the *Zambia Daily Mail* had reported that "Zimbabwe freedom fighters based in Tanzania at the Mgagao military camp came out in the strong statement opposing the ZLC [Zimbabwe Liberation Council – a short-lived external affairs wing of the African National Council] and Muzorewa, Sithole, and Chikerema. . . . They indicated that the only executive member of the ANC who they were prepared to follow was Robert Mugabe. This is a Karanga faction in Tanzania." This key development will be discussed further in Chapter 3.

Dumbutshena was not particularly optimistic about Nkomo and ZAPU. He recognized that Kaunda, the Zambian president, favored Nkomo, but added, "At the present moment Zambia is not interested in having military from [sic] its own bases." He also noted "Nkomo's position is weakened by the possibility of a sell-out which he does not

[13] Ibid. Similar arguments about the motivations of factions in the ZANU leadership were presented as the basic argument in the Zambian case against the detained ZANU leaders allegedly responsible for Chitepo's death. See Republic of Zambia, *Report of the Special International Commission on the Assassination of Herbert Wiltshire Chitepo* (Lusaka: Lusaka Government Printers, 1976). There is scholarly intervention on this theme in Masipula Sithole, *Struggles within the Struggle* (Salisbury: Rujecko Publishers, 1979). Professor Sithole details the personal reasons for internal splits and the politics of division within the leadership of ZANU and ZAPU.

think the Zimbabwe people are prepared to accept."[14] This is a reference to the possibility that Nkomo would enter into a compromise made possible by South African and Zambian cooperation during the détente. However, this comment points again to the persistent characterization of Nkomo by his rivals as a leader always on the verge of a "sell-out" of the Zimbabwean people. As the next chapters explore, as much as Nkomo would entertain any possibility for a negotiated settlement that would make him the leader in a new Zimbabwe, he was also never willing to accept a role short of complete control of the new Zimbabwean state. As will be shown, this would remain the main problem for Nkomo in his competition with Mugabe. As described in following chapters, Nkomo would often explain that he could convince, or have others convince, Mugabe to take on a secondary role to him.

Houser also had a conversation with President Kaunda while in Lusaka. Kaunda explained that the détente with South Africa was not meant to bring about change in South Africa but to try and resolve the independence of Namibia and Rhodesia. He did not think that Vorster was going to cooperate with the African presidents, but he did think he wanted a settlement in Rhodesia and Namibia. Kaunda stressed how costly the closed border with Rhodesia was for his own country's economy. He also emphasized the importance of negotiating with Smith to try and avoid future war, telling Houser that he "feels very strongly that there will be civil war in Zimbabwe if there is not some kind of agreement between the two sides there. He indicated that the killings within ZANU would be child's play compared to what would happen if the situation continued to deteriorate there."[15]

Houser also took the opportunity to speak with Muzorewa for about two hours after a chance meeting at the Kilimanjaro Hotel in Dar es Salaam, Tanzania, on November 4, 1975.[16] Houser said he wanted to hear Muzorewa's views about why the African National Council coalition had broken down, given that relations had been good between it and ZAPU when Nkomo had been in detention. Muzorewa explained that the "real issue has been the struggle for power and for leadership in the ANC." Muzorewa explained that problems arose when he, Sithole,

---

[14] George Houser, "Lusaka and Mozambique Trip Notes 1975," MSS 294, Houser Papers, Special Collections, MSU Library.
[15] Ibid.   [16] Ibid.

and Nkomo were in Lusaka discussing the new arrangements for the African National Council. One of the Frontline State presidents had suggested Nkomo be the leader but this was not accepted, as it "would have broken up the unity plans." It was a last-minute decision to install Muzorewa as president. The compromise was the decision to arrange a congress "in order for the people to decide who should be leaders and the executive of the united organization." But according to Muzorewa, "it became clear very soon that the holding of such a congress would be divisive." At this stage, "Muzorewa, Sithole, and Chikerema argued that the first thing to do was to win the country. Then the question of leadership could be decided." Nkomo did not agree with this view, and this started the split between Nkomo and Muzorewa.[17]

Muzorewa also blamed Nkomo for walking out of one of the meetings intended to organize the new Zimbabwe Liberation Committee. "The Bishop said at one of these meetings Nkomo was accused of making a secret deal with Smith. At this point Nkomo angrily walked out of the meeting." Houser asked Muzorewa if he believed there really was such a deal, to which Muzorewa replied, "Time will tell." Nkomo explains what he saw as the reason for the fall-out after the Lusaka agreement in his autobiography. He blames ZANU and FROLIZI for lacking "any organs or structures."[18] Once again, Houser was being told by one of Nkomo's rivals that Nkomo was in a position to potentially "sell out" the liberation movement.

British Interpretations of ZANU Infighting

In late 1974 and early 1975, as the pace of developments in southern Africa was starting to speed up with the announcement of independence in Mozambique and Angola, the British had embassy and high commission contacts in the Frontline States with both ZANU and ZAPU and relied on the local and foreign journalists for much of their information about internal developments. The information they were receiving about the end of the Nhari rebellion tended to confirm "tribal" or "ethnic" explanations of the leadership battle in ZANU. A story from the Gemini News Service in early March 1975, entitled

---

[17] Ibid.

[18] Joshua Nkomo, *Nkomo: The Story of My Life* (London: Methuen, 1984), 152. The Lusaka Agreement, dated December 7, 1974, is reproduced as an appendix in Nkomo's autobiography, after p. 252.

"45 of Sithole's Men Die in Secret Battle," argued that the internal violence was negatively impacting the war effort by ZANLA, as well as challenging Sithole's leadership role in ZANU. The author, who is not named, claims that the "problem" inside ZANU was "essentially tribal." The author concludes that the "Karangas hope the peace moves will fail and the intensification of guerrilla warfare will allow them to maintain their power and consolidate their rise from relative political obscurity."[19]

Views expressed in the Gemini News Service article were further supported among the British Foreign and Commonwealth Office (FCO) Rhodesia experts based on a conversation with Albert Mvula on March 6, 1975. Mvula, a Zimbabwean by birth, was a senior journalist at the *Zambia Daily Mail*. Mvula had two pieces of information to share with the British about developments in ZANU. The first involved Ian Smith's decision to rearrest Reverend Sithole in Salisbury after having released him and others for the détente talks. The report was being used by some in ZANU to spread rumors that it was done because Smith had a secret deal with ZAPU's Nkomo to bring him into constitutional talks without ZANU. Mvula explained that "he was sure ZANU would exploit this to the full and had already been spreading a story that Nkomo was prepared to make a deal and had met privately with Smith. He [Mvula] said that they were also capable of producing false evidence to support their allegations."[20]

The second piece of intel from Mvula, who reportedly had been a student of Mugabe's in Zimbabwe and said he had contacts in both ZANU and ZAPU, updated the FCO on the handling of the Nhari rebellion leadership in ZANU. Mvula claimed that when Sithole had come to Lusaka, he had demanded the release of all of the suspected plotters "held by the Karanga faction." The conclusion reached at the "trial" of the leaders, according to Mvula's sources, was that Noel Mukono had been the leader of the rebellion. Mukono was described as the member of the ZANU executive "who originally organized the north eastern front in Rhodesia and ... thus became somewhat out of touch with the developments in Lusaka." While fighting in Rhodesia, Mukono was demoted within the ZANU executive and given "an

---

[19] Gemini News Service, Special Correspondent, "45 of Sithole's Men Die in Secret Battle," p. 3, FCO 36/1728 1975, BNA.

[20] M. L. Croll, "Visit of Mr. Albert Mvula," March 6, 1975, FCO 36/1728, BNA.

unimportant external affairs job instead." Mvula then explained the motivations of the rebellion in ethnic terms. Mvula stated that Mukono's response to his demotion was to "obtain Manyika support against the dominance of the Karanga on the executive, arguing that the Karanga were sitting happily in Lusaka while the Manyika were suffering hardship in the north east." Mvula claimed that Mataure supported Mukono and had helped to organize "the attempted kidnapping of Tongogagara [sic] which set off the subsequent killings." Mvula's account helped confirm for the British the notion that the internal leadership issues in ZANU could be described best as ethnic competition. However, the Rhodesia department's Peter Barlow was not convinced that ethnicity was the defining factor. Barlow, who would have an important role as an FCO expert on Rhodesia, wrote "I do not think you need bother with Mr Mvula's revelations on the Karanga/Manyika infighting."[21] However, the assassination of ZANU leader Herbert Chitepo by a car bomb on March 18, 1975 would once again help to focus the "tribalism" lens used by the British FCO and others to try and make sense of the internal violence in ZANU and ZANLA.

The Chitepo Assassination on March 18, 1975

The news of Herbert Chitepo's assassination in Lusaka came as a shock to many, although it was widely known that his leadership

Figure 2 Herbert Chitepo. July 1973. Getty Images.

[21] "P. J. Barlow to Mr. Byatt," March 13, 1975, item 5, FCO 36/1728, BNA.

was under threat and he was in physical danger given the divisions within ZANU at the time. Chitepo was viewed as the most respected of the ZANU leaders and would have been on more familiar terms with diplomats in Lusaka. The British high commissioner in Lusaka, Stephen Miles, wrote to the FCO the day after the assassination to assess the reasons and motives for Chitepo's death. He explained that "ZANU lost no time in issuing a statement directly blaming Rhodesia regime for the assassination." However, Miles reported, "On the other hand, all our freedom fighter contacts have without exception declared their view that Chitepo's assassination was the work of elements within ZANU opposed to him personally." The rationale for this was further explained in relation to the situation Chitepo faced just prior to his death. According to Miles, one of his "freedom fighter contacts" described how "Chitepo had to an increasing extent been taking all important decisions into his own hands and that his talk with President Kaunda on March 16, which he had insisted on attending alone, may well have been the final straw for those who were considering his elimination." Miles added that it was "perhaps ironic that Chitepo, who was aware that his life was at risk, was advised directly by Mark Chona on March 16 to allow the Zambians to provide him with extra protection. Chitepo said that he would ask for such protection when he required it." Miles also reported how, one day after Chitepo's death, ethnicity remained the main motive given to him by his sources, and that Tongogara was the alleged main suspect: "Within the Zimbabwe liberation movements the main finger of suspicion is pointed at Tongogara, ZANU's military commander who has now gone into hiding." Miles concluded, "Further mayhem is not ruled out. Manyika elements may well seek to take revenge against what they consider to be the latest, if worst, example of extreme Karanga militancy."[22]

Reports in the days and weeks that followed would solidify these conclusions. On March 25, Miles met with Zambia's foreign minister, Vernon Mwaanga, who had informed him of the arrests of many "ZANU extremists" by the Zambian government. The arrests had

---

[22] Miles Writing from Lusaka (telno 611), March 19, 1975, "Chitepo's Assassination," item 9, FCO 36/1728, BNA. For details on Chitepo's assassination, and the competing claims of responsibility for the murder, see White, *Assassination of Herbert Chitepo*; Chung, *Re-living the Second Chimurenga*.

not yet been publicly acknowledged, but those arrested included "ZANU extremists Kangai, Hamadziripi, Mudzi and Gumbo," and they were searching for Tongogara. Mwaanga, according to Miles, had "hinted to me last night 24 March, even if he did not precisely say so, that extremist ZANU elements were responsible for [the] murder of Chitepo." Mwaanga had told Miles that Chitepo "had become a virtual prisoner of this group and was never allowed to go anywhere without one of them." Miles described how at the last meeting he had with Chitepo, just a few days before his death, Chitepo had been accompanied by Kangai.[23] The significance of this sort of explanation is that it helps to better explain how the British would later interpret Mugabe's role as leader of ZANU once he successfully assumed that role in 1976. The Rhodesian analysts at the FCO tended to fall into a similar reading where, more often than not, Mugabe would be seen as "hedged about by militant Karangas," similar to the conclusions reached about Chitepo. Chitepo was seen by the British, therefore, as a victim of circumstances and as a leader who fell victim to his more radical comrades, who saw him as a liability.

British high commissioner Miles also reported a conversation in Lusaka, about a week after the Chitepo assassination, with the leaders of ZAPU's war effort, Jason Moyo and Dumiso Dabengwa. They confirmed what Miles had heard from Mwaanga and others about Chitepo's murder: "they said evidence suggested it was an inside job and the perpetrators either enjoyed Chitepo's confidence or acted with the connivance of his guards." The ZAPU leaders were mostly worried about the impact of the arrest of the ZANU extremists by the Zambians in two areas: the future of the unity accord under the new African National Council umbrella, and the future of ZANLA's ability to effectively carry out the war effort. The ZAPU leaders, according to Miles, found it "ironical that Moyo and Chitepo, at [the] time of latter's death, had been cooperating more closely than at any time since [the] Lusaka agreement, whereas now ZANU personnel were likely to be, after their release, doubly embittered with both Zambians and other nationalists."

Given the political impact on the morale of ZANLA troops, they both hoped that the "Zambians had detained people merely for

[23] Miles Lusaka to FCO (telno 656), "Details on the Arrests of ZANU Leaders for Chitepo Assassination by Zambian Govt," March 25, 1975, FCO 36/1728, BNA.

screening and interrogation following Chitepo's murder and that they would shortly be released, but they did not seem too confident about this." Miles reports that Dabengwa was "particularly critical of the timing of Zambian action fearing that Smith might be encouraged by this move to estimate that guerrilla threat would be reduced and that he could therefore safely continue to hold Sithole and avoid further talks."[24] On March 29, Zambia's home affairs minister, Aaron Milner, made a public announcement about the arrests and the planned International Commission of Enquiry into Chitepo's death. Miles notes that, in making the announcement, Milner emphasized that "the Zambian Government would proceed with their investigations regardless of 'squeals' from some quarters outside of Zambia," and that "freedom fighters, like Zambians, were expected to abide by the country's laws. Zambia had suffered enough."[25] Responding to strong criticisms from ZANU voices in Tanzania, that it was Zambia alone who wanted to imprison and try the arrested ZANU and ZANLA leaders, President Kaunda indicated that it would be a Pan-African commission, made up of "a team selected from the Central Committee and Cabinet, Members of the OAU Liberation Committee and its Executive Secretary, as well as representatives of Botswana, Zaire, Congo Republic, Malawi, Tanzania, and FRELIMO [Front for the Liberation of Mozambique]." In addition, "Kaunda criticised Rhodesian nationalist leaders for their apparent lack of concern for the assassination of Chitepo. They had made no call for the killers to be tracked down while 'others' had demanded that Zambia must stop the investigation altogether."[26]

President Kaunda's personal anger at the ZANU leadership over the death of Chitepo, and also the Nhari rebellion before the assassination, led him and others in Zambia to speak openly about their frustrations at the Zimbabwean liberation movements that Zambia had been hosting since the early 1960s. In addition, the Zambian government further announced it was formally closing the offices of ZAPU, ZANU, and FROLIZI in Lusaka "and their registration cancelled until the

---

[24] Miles from Lusaka to FCO (telno 688), March 27, 1975, "Rhodesia," item 23, FCO 36/1728, BNA.
[25] Miles from Lusaka to FCO (telno 696), April 1, 1975, "Rhodesia," item 24, FCO 36/1728, BNA.
[26] Miles from Lusaka to FCO (telno 688), March 27, 1975, "Rhodesia," item 23, FCO 36/1728, BNA.

Rhodesian nationalists honoured the recent Lusaka agreement."[27] Chitepo's assassination appeared to have been the last straw for Kaunda and the Zambians when it came to cooperating and supporting ZANU and ZANLA in Zambia.

There were reports of public protests against the ZANU infighting in Zambia organized by Kaunda's ruling UNIP party, and the description of these rallies and speeches reveal the frustrations with the Zimbabwean nationalists. Press reports from protests held on April 3 indicated that somewhere between 5,000 and 20,000 people protested in Ndola, "where angry placard carrying party members marched through the city center chanting anti-Zimbabwean nationalist slogans including: 'Rhodesians must go home' and 'the government should stop supporting freedom struggle.'" The reporting described a speech at the Ndola Civic Center by "Mr Axon Chalikulima, Minister of the Copperbelt." Chalikulima thanked the crowd for supporting Kaunda and then lambasted the Zimbabwean liberation movements: "He told the demonstrators that Zimbabwe was not yet free because the freedom fighters were 'cowards, loved money and were corrupt,' 'their Independence would not come about by shouting from Lusaka, Cairo, Moscow, London, New York or anywhere else but by going to fight inside Rhodesia.'" He then mentioned the role Zambia had played up to this point: "Zambia had sacrificed too much for the Independence struggle for Rhodesia . . . . But even after everything we have done for them the stupid idiots can still not appreciate our help." Chalikulima then "called on Zambians not to molest ordinary Rhodesians living here."[28] That it was important for Chalikulima to warn against xenophobic attacks against "ordinary Rhodesians" in Zambia, shows the level of disdain some Zambians may have had for continuing to host the Zimbabwean liberation movement in early 1975. With hindsight, it is safe to say the situation would get much worse with increased incursions into Zambia by Rhodesian and South African troops over the next four years. But at this moment, after the loss of a major Zimbabwean nationalist with Chitepo's assassination, a new phase of the war was about to begin.

The arrest of ZANLA's leader Tongogara and most of the ZANU executive was a blow to ZANU, although it also gave space for

---

[27] Miles from Lusaka, "Our Telno 696," April 2, 1975, FCO 36/1728, BNA.
[28] Miles to FCO (telno 729), April 4, 1975, "My tel 696: Rhodesia," FCO 36/1728, BNA.

a younger group of fighters to organize as the Zimbabwe People's Army (ZIPA) in Tanzania and Mozambique after Mozambique became an independent nation in June 1975. The long process of the Chitepo Inquiry, and the lack of interest on Kaunda's part in releasing the ZANU leaders to Mozambique, demonstrated the resolve of both Kaunda and Nyerere in their desire to unify the Zimbabwean liberation movement. Unfortunately, Nyerere and Kaunda often differed on tactics even when they shared the same goal. Almost a year after the arrests, Jeremy Varcoe, the new British high commissioner in Lusaka, wrote to Peter Barlow in the Rhodesia department at the FCO about the Chitepo Inquiry. On March 9, 1976, Varcoe explained that Kaunda still maintained that Chitepo's murderers would be "exposed and punished." "This has surprised some people since it had, at one time, been hinted that no-one would actually be charged." Varcoe also related that Rhodesian lawyer, Enoch Dumbutshena, had told Varcoe that "when he had visited Mudzi, one of the ZANU hard-liners still held in prison, the latter had told him that only one or two people had been involved in the actual assassination."[29] This is a revealing response coming from Dumbutshena.

Varcoe stipulated what would happen to these political prisoners since the report had been released. He offered his own views: "I would have thought they [the Zambians] would only be too pleased to ship them out to Mozambique to join their colleagues in the camps and rid themselves of the embarrassment and accusations that they were hindering the freedom struggle and that the continued presence of Tongogara and the rest was beginning to give rise to."[30] This would remain a tension throughout much of 1976 but would be resolved by an unlikely source, as discussed in the following chapters. The release of these "ZANU extremists" by the Zambians to attend the Geneva conference was a major factor in the realignment of ZANU's executive under Mugabe's leadership.

US and Frontline State Policy toward Cubans in Southern Africa, 1975–1976

The policy of the United States toward southern Africa would make a sharp pivot after the Popular Movement for the Liberation of Angola

---

[29] Varcoe, British High Commissioner, Lusaka to P. J. Barlow, Rhodesia Department, FCO, March 9, 1976, "Rhodesia: The Chitepo Enquiry," FCO 36/1855, BNA.

[30] Ibid.

(MPLA) came out the winner in the Cold War contest for power in
Angola. In early 1975, however, all the coalition parties of the anti-
Soviet and anti-Cuban forces – including the United States, China,
South Africa, Mozambique, Zaire, Tanzania, and Zambia – believed
they could defeat the MPLA in Angola before the planned independ-
ence date of November 11, 1975. President Kaunda's lead diplomat,
Mark Chona, told the American embassy in Lusaka on April 11, 1975,
that all parties were confident of an MPLA defeat.[31] The rapid victory
of the Cuban- and Soviet-backed MPLA forces in Angola created an
immediate fear among the Americans in particular that the Soviet
Union and Cuba would attempt to repeat their Angolan success in
Rhodesia. Training and supply links were well known between the
Soviets and Nkomo's ZIPRA, and the urgent need to act quickly to
deter Nkomo from accepting further Soviet help, and especially new
Cuban support, became a priority. One key lesson learned from the
Angolan debacle, from the perspective of the Western powers, was that
the lack of unity between the movements they supported had seriously
damaged the anti-MPLA campaign. The Americans and their southern
African allies were determined not to repeat the same mistake in
Rhodesia, leading to pressure in 1976 to combine Nkomo's ZIPRA
army with ZANU's ZANLA forces. Confrontations between South
African troops and Cuban troops in Angola added to the Cold War
urgency to fast-track negotiations between Ian Smith's government and
the Zimbabwean liberation armies before the Soviets and Cubans had
a chance to gain a foothold in the struggle.[32] At the same time, the
South Africans had felt abandoned by the Americans in Angola, as the

---

[31] Lusaka to State, "Southern Africa: Zambian Views Following Kananga and Dar
Meetings," April 11, 1975, Document Number: 1976LUSAKA00665, Central
Foreign Policy Files, 1973–76, RG 59, General Records of the Department of
State, USNA.

[32] The Portuguese coup of April 25, 1974 against Prime Minister Marcello Caetano
was, according to Piero Gleijeses, caused by the unpopularity of colonial wars in
Guinea-Bissau, Angola, and Mozambique. Gleijeses asserts that it was more the
fighting in Guinea-Bissau than in Angola and Mozambique that led to the coup.
For Cuba's role in Angola, see Piero Gleijeses, *Conflicting Missions: Havana,
Washington, and Africa, 1959–1976* (Chapel Hill: University of North Carolina
Press, 2002), 229; Piero Gleijeses "Cuba and the Cold War, 1959–1980," in
Melvyn. P. Leffler and Odd Arne Westad, *The Cambridge History of the Cold
War. Volume 2: Crises and Détente* (Cambridge University Press, 2010), 327–45;
and John Hatch, *Two African Statesmen: Kaunda of Zambia and Nyerere of
Tanzania* (Chicago: Henry Regnery, 1976), 255–57.

US Congress had cut off covert aid in the post-Vietnam context that had been promised to assist South Africa's support for UNITA in Angola.[33]

In February 1976, it was clear that Smith was not cooperating in the talks with Nkomo. The British foreign secretary, James Callaghan, told German chancellor Helmut Schimdt what Nkomo had told him in London. According to Callaghan, "Mr. Nkomo feared that there was a real risk of break-down because Mr. Smith was not prepared to concede the basic principle of majority rule." Nkomo had painted a bleak future of what would happen next. He told Callaghan, "If the talks broke down the guerillas would take over. There would be early financial and material aid from the Eastern European countries and the Soviet Union and the Cubans would take every opening to make trouble." Interestingly, Nkomo then said that he, "Nkomo, would be one of the first casualties and within a year Rhodesia would be engulfed in chaos." Callaghan told Schmidt that Nkomo was asking for another month of negotiations. He also said, after hearing this dire projection, that he sent emissaries to the South African prime minister, John Vorster, and the US secretary of state, Henry Kissinger, to assist in trying to get Smith back into negotiations.[34]

The British were also warning Smith to negotiate in earnest with the African National Council in order to stave off communist intervention. Callaghan wrote a strongly worded letter to Smith on February 17 to not let the negotiations fail, or else once fighting began again, it would be difficult to avoid communist influence. "I daresay you see the danger but I am not at all sure how far the white community as a whole appreciates its full starkness. Such developments cannot but have the gravest consequences for you." Callaghan tried to leverage future British participation with the threat of outside intervention. "I and my colleagues would be more disposed to intervene if we were convinced that you were willing to act on the full implications of the situation. I am bound to say that in our view, there is little prospect

---

[33] On the Congressional politics of cutting covert aid at the end of 1975 and early 1976, see Robert David Johnson, *Congress and the Cold War* (Cambridge University Press, 2005), 222–28. See also Richard J. Payne, "The Soviet/Cuban Factor in the New United States Policy toward Southern Africa," *Africa Today* 25, no. 2 (1978), 7–26.

[34] "Note of Meeting between PM and Chancellor Schmidt," February 7, 1976, Item 11, PREM 16/1090, BNA.

of avoiding a disastrous outcome unless you go much further to meet the current African proposals."[35]

The United Kingdom's deputy under-secretary for the Middle East and Africa, Anthony Duff, presented Callaghan's alarmist call to Vorster in a meeting on February 10, 1976. Vorster suggested that Smith would not reach an agreement with Nkomo's basic demand for majority rule, as "such a demand would entail not a settlement but a surrender." Vorster asked Duff what would then happen, to which Duff replied, "The result would certainly be racial war and one in which South Africa could not but get embroiled." Pointing to events in Angola and "the confiscation of the property of Europeans in Mozambique," Vorster argued that "the Whites would not accept any assurances about their position in an independent Black Rhodesia." Duff asked Vorster how he would talk to Smith. Vorster said he wouldn't pressure Smith to "'hand over tomorrow." Instead, he would recommend that there should be a "gradual, orderly take-over by the Africans," saying perhaps "a transition period of 10 years would be not unrealistic." Vorster concluded, "The trouble was that when the Africans said they wanted immediate majority rule they meant it. They would want an election this year."[36]

President Kaunda of Zambia had advised Kissinger in February 1976 on how to best approach the stalemate in Rhodesia to avoid further Cuban involvement there after the Angolan experience. Kaunda's key diplomat, Mark Chona, met with Kissinger in Washington, DC, and according to Kissinger's account, warned the United States of the continued role of the Soviet Union and Cuba in southern Africa following the MPLA victory in Angola. Chona emphasized that the United States needed to take a proactive role in Rhodesia immediately to avoid another Soviet and Cuban victory. He advised Kissinger not to be content with containing Angola and urged him to "anticipate Soviet and Cuban involvement in other places and make their presence unnecessary." Kissinger replied that the United States "will not tolerate another massive Cuban move."[37]

[35] "Message to Ian Smith from Mr James Callaghan," 1976, item 13A, PREM 16/1090, BNA.

[36] "Record of a Meeting between Sir A. Duff and South Africa Prime Minister Held in Mr. Vorster's Office in Pretoria," February 10, 1976, item 11, PREM 16/1090, BNA.

[37] Secretary of State to American Embassy Lusaka, "Chona Meeting with Secretary," February 7, 1976, 1976STATE030916, Central Foreign Policy Files, 1973–76, RG 59, General Records of the Department of State, USNA.

After having laid out a new strategy for the United States, most of which would be incorporated into Kissinger's April 27 speech in Lusaka, Chona also made an appeal for American support of Nkomo over other Zimbabwean nationalist leaders. Chona made a strong case for American support of Nkomo, arguing that Nkomo was the "only Rhodesian working for peaceful solution," that while "Nkomo has been supported by USSR, he will never be Soviet man," that "Mozambique has traditionally supported Nkomo," and that if Smith accepts a deal with Nkomo, Mozambique and Zambia will stop guerrillas from attacking." Chona concluded that "if U.S. values peaceful strategy, it should show more direct interest in Nkomo's efforts."[38]

The Tanzanian president, Julius Nyerere, also weighed in on the topic of a possible "Angola" in Rhodesia in February, suggesting that the comparison was overdone. Expressing his opinions to the British diplomats in Dar es Salaam, Nyerere was critical of "the tendency to assume that events in the Rhodesia would follow the Angolan pattern, with Russian and Cuban involvement provoking American and South African retaliation." He believed that such a view could be "a matter of tactics for bringing pressure to bear on Smith but there should be no serious assumption that this would occur." He stated that other countries in southern Africa had become independent "without reliance on Cuba and Rhodesia could do the same."[39]

In terms of the leadership crisis among the Rhodesian nationalists, Nyerere "wondered whether it was fully realized in London that it was too late for a negotiated constitutional settlement." After the split in the African National Council, he said he had "advised Nkomo, Muzorewa and Sithole to build strong links with the freedom fighters in the camps but they had failed to do so and as a result they had all been rejected by the guerrillas and were not taken seriously by Smith." Given this failure, Nyerere and Machel were organizing "contingents of freedom fighters" to send into action. This new "Third Force" would have to be considered in any future negotiations, and therefore any deals made with Smith and the older nationalist leaders would not be valid. Nyerere told the British in February, "If by some miracle an agreement

---

[38] Ibid.
[39] Strong from Dar es Salaam to FCO (telno 54), February 25, 1976, "Rhodesia," item no. 4, FCO 36/1851, BNA.

were reached between Nkomo and Smith, it would be valueless unless it was acceptable to the guerrillas." Nyerere emphasized that it was necessary to realize that "the freedom fighters were a third force whose acceptance of the terms of any agreement was fundamental." To make his point even clearer, Nyerere asserted that should the British support "an agreement between Smith and Nkomo (and perhaps Muzorewa) ... he was very concerned that Britain should not find herself on the wrong side, facing the guerrillas" and he feared "some clever fellow in London" might decide to ignore the guerrillas if a settlement could be reached quickly. By stressing to the British that "the old leaders were now 'irrelevant' and had no influence whatever with the freedom fighters," Nyerere sought to emphasize how once fighting increased under the new Third Force, Smith would be "forced to negotiate (just as the Portuguese had been driven to negotiate with Machel)." Nyerere reassured the British that the Third Force would get its training and supplies from the Chinese and that "no one would call in the Russians because 'we do not trust them.' It was true that Nkomo received Russian support but it was inconceivable that 'his old friend' would let them in, much less the Cubans."[40] At this stage, Nyerere's skepticism over Russian and Cuban involvement on a scale approaching that of Angola in 1975 was shared by the British. This would be in stark contrast to Kissinger's point of view, who came to his southern African shuttle diplomacy determined to act quickly and decisively to avert "another Angola" in Rhodesia. President Kaunda and his lead diplomat, Mark Chona, perceptively understood this difference and hoped to make the most of it by obtaining American aid and support for their work on the diplomatic front.[41]

Mozambican FRELIMO diplomats understood how American fears of "another Angola" in Rhodesia could be leveraged to obtain much needed foreign aid. Mozambique's foreign minister, Joaquim Chissano, approached the American chargé in order to establish that

[40] Strong from Dar es Salaam to FCO (telno 54), February 25, 1976, "Rhodesia," item 4, FCO 36/1851, BNA.

[41] For the details of Kaunda's and Chona's negotiations for greater US military and development aid, see DeRoche, *Kenneth Kaunda*, 61–65. DeRoche notes that when Kissinger discussed increases in Zambia's military assistance, and a $10 million increase was suggested, "Kissinger joked that '10 million isn't a program, 10 million is a tip.'" Ibid., 64. Original Kissinger quote from "Memo of Kissinger Staff Meeting, March 5, 1976," 11–13, National Security Archives, Kissinger Transcripts. DeRoche, *Kenneth Kaunda*, n. 14, 244.

the Mozambican government was willing to make sacrifices to achieve majority rule in Rhodesia and that economic sanctions were being planned. Chissano told the Americans that "there are no foreign troops fighting in Rhodesia"; that "he expects there will be none in the future"; and that Mozambique "does not want another Angola in Africa." In return, Chissano asked for "meaningful and significant" American assistance via the United Nations to alleviate some of the economic problems brought on by its sanctions against Rhodesia. Chissano also suggested that if the United States wanted to propose more direct aid, it might be acceptable to Mozambique.[42]

A moderating voice on the topic came from Joan Wicken, who served as President Nyerere's personal assistant, as well as a lobbyist with many British politicians by supporting Nyerere's and Tanzania's views on Rhodesia. In a letter dated March 3, 1976, addressed to Tom McNally, an important Labour Party advisor to James Callaghan – then the foreign minister but soon to become prime minister a month later on April 5, 1976 – Wicken reiterated the general skepticism in Dar es Salaam over the saber-rattling coming from Washington and to a lesser extent London. She argued that although Tanzanians understood a Labour government should not be as susceptible to such claims, and therefore should have "an understanding that this is really a struggle about Liberation and is not a 'communist plot,' yet still people worry about the emphasis which is given to the Russians and Cubans in Angola ... and the fact that the 'danger of Cuban/Russian intervention' is used so often in the 'responsible' press." Wicken presented Nyerere's position that the Third Force now needs to be reckoned with in any future negotiations, and to leave them out of negotiations would be a big problem from the Tanzanian point of view.[43] As the pressure continued to build for some sort of diplomatic action on Rhodesia, the Americans acted based on countering the Cuban and Soviet victory in Angola.

Kissinger presented his ideas for a new South African policy at a Washington Special Actions Group meeting in the White House Situation Room on March 24, 1976. The topic was Cuba and Lebanon, and Kissinger began by saying, "We want to get planning

[42] These points were included in an NSC memo from Hal Horan to Brent Scowcroft on the US position on Rhodesia, National Security Council Memorandum, "U.S. Position on Rhodesia," March 8, 1976, Ford Library, USNSC Institutional Files, 1974–77, Box 20.
[43] Joan E. Wicken to Tom McNally, March 3, 1976, item 18, FCO36/1851, BNA.

started in the political, economic and military fields so that we can see what we can do if we want to move against Cuba."[44] William Clements, the US deputy secretary of defense, said, "I am appalled at the way Cuban military forces are being used overseas. Are we just going to sit here and do nothing?" Kissinger replied, "Rhodesia is a lousy case but it is not the only problem of its kind in southern Africa. If the Cubans destroy Rhodesia then Namibia is next and then there is South Africa." Kissinger noted his own respect for the perceived exceptionalism of apartheid South Africa:

It might take only five years and the South Africans just won't yield. They are stubborn like the Israelis. The problem is that no matter how we build our policy in southern Africa anything that happens will appear to have resulted from Cuban pressure. We could make it a proposition that it is unacceptable to us to have the Cubans as the shock troops of the revolution.[45]

Donald Rumsfeld then asked, "How do you prevent Cuba from doing that?" Kissinger replied, "You deter them from even trying it. We must get it into the heads of the leaders of African countries that they can't have it both ways. They can't have both the Cubans in Africa and our support." Kissinger added, "It was the same situation we had in Egypt a few years ago. I told them they could not have both the Soviet presence and our support and now the Soviets have left."[46] The briefing concluded that although the Rhodesian situation appeared to be less advantageous to the Cubans, quick actions on the diplomatic front were needed, as "over the next few months, however, these attitudes will probably change."[47] Kissinger's immediate public response was to issue warnings to the Cubans against their further involvement beyond Angola in southern Africa.

---

[44] At the time, the Washington Special Actions Group consisted of Robert Ingersoll from the State Department, Donald Rumsfeld and William Clements from the Department of Defense, Gen. George S. Brown from the JCS, Lt. Gen. Vernon Walters from the CIA, and Lt. Gen. Brent Scowcroft from the NSC. Washington Special Actions Group Meeting, Minutes, "Cuba and Lebanon," 3/24/76, Ford Library, USNSC Institutional Files, 1974–77, Box 20.

[45] Washington Special Actions Group Meeting, Minutes, "Cuba and Lebanon," 3/24/76, Ford Library, USNSC Institutional Files, 1974–77, Box 20.

[46] Ibid.

[47] DDCI Briefing for March 24 WASG meeting that detailed "Cuban policy toward revolutionary movements," Ford Library, USNSC Institutional Files 1974–77, Box 20, 7–8.

Figure 3 Henry Kissinger and Zambian president Kenneth Kaunda. Lusaka, Zambia, April 27, 1976. Courtesy Gerald R. Ford Presidential Library.

The Ford administration's new southern Africa policy was announced by Kissinger in a speech in Zambia on April 27, 1976. According to historian Tom Noer, the speech directly challenged the older American strategy of supporting Smith. "Not only did he [Kissinger] give the standard American defense of 'self-determination, majority rule, equal rights, and human dignity for all peoples of southern Africa,' but he also made it clear that Washington would no longer offer any support to the Smith Government."[48] In order to convince the Zimbabwean nationalists that the United States was indeed turning against Smith's UDI regime, Kissinger warned that the "Salisbury Regime," as he referred to the Rhodesian Front government in his April 27 speech, "cannot expect United States support either in diplomacy or in material help at any stage in its conflict with African states or African liberation movements. On the contrary, it will face our

[48] Tom Noer, *Cold War and Black Liberation: The United States and White Rule in Africa, 1948–1968* (Columbia: University of Missouri Press, 1985), 244.

unrelenting opposition until a negotiated settlement is achieved."[49] The pressure was now put on the Frontline State presidents, from the American perspective, to produce a unified Zimbabwean guerrilla force free of Cuban and, to a lesser extent, Soviet influence.

Kissinger's true intentions, however, were still in support of the whites in southern Africa. In a conversation with President Ford on April 21, 1976, just before he left for his Africa shuttle diplomacy, Kissinger explained his strategy to support majority rule, while also telling President Ford, "Basically I am with the whites in Southern Africa. I think it is no better for the majority to oppress the minority than vice versa. But in my comments I will support majority rule in Rhodesia." Kissinger concluded that he would " say the same about South Africa, but softer." After explaining his line of action, he concluded, "It will be something of a sensation."[50]

---

[49] Department of State, "Address by the Honorable Henry A. Kissinger, Secretary of State at a Luncheon in the Secretary's Honor Hosted by His Excellency Kenneth Kaunda, President of Zambia, the State House, Lusaka, Zambia," April 27, 1976, p. 3. Ford Library, Kissinger Trip to Africa File Box, "Election Campaign Papers: David Gergen," Box 16.

[50] Memorandum of Conversation, President Ford, Dr Henry A. Kissinger, Brent Scowcroft, Oval Office, April 21, 1976, www.fordlibrarymuseum.gov/library/document/0314/1553439.pdf. For detailed coverage of this transition in US strategy, see Eddie Michel, *The White House and White Africa: Presidential Policy Toward Rhodesia during the UDI Era, 1965–1979* (New York: Routledge, 2019), 156–71.

3 | Liberation Struggles in Southern Africa 1975–1976

From the perspective of the British and American diplomats in the region, prospects of a more radical or "extremist" faction taking control of ZANU seemed more realistic after the assassination of Herbert Chitepo on March 18, 1975. Chitepo's death and the rearrest of ZANU leader Reverend Sithole by the Smith regime in Salisbury on March 4, 1975 offered little hope that the Lusaka agreement would channel the liberation movement under the newly formed African National Council coalition. The British were interested in locating Robert Mugabe. Although Mugabe had been released from detention in 1974, his whereabouts were unknown to the British in April 1975. He had been scheduled to attend an OAU meeting in Dar es Salaam as part of the African National Council group, but Bishop Muzorewa informed the British that Mugabe had not attended and had gone to Mozambique, where he was under house arrest.

The British high commissioner to Zambia, Stephen Miles, suggested that Mugabe would have difficulties if he were sent to Lusaka, because he had accused the Zambian government of involvement in Chitepo's death. Miles added that "provided he [Mugabe] gave assurance of working within ANC and abandoning ZANU he might be released."[1] A few days later, Peter Barlow, a leading Rhodesia expert in the FCO, wrote a brief summary on Mugabe at the request of the prime minister's office. Barlow explained how Mugabe had been the "second in rank" in ZANU but reportedly had taken over from Sithole during their time in detention. Mugabe had gone to the Lusaka talks in November 1974, but the four Presidents "insisted on the reinstatement of Sithole." Barlow indicated that Sithole had done well in regaining his supporters in Rhodesia, under the African National Council, since that time. Barlow was also under the impression that Mugabe had left Rhodesia

---

[1] Miles from Lusaka to FCO, "Your Telno 38 to Lourenço Marques: Robert Mugabe," April 15, 1975, FCO 36/1728, BNA.

on April 4 with Edgar Tekere because of the rearrest of Sithole. Mugabe had apparently told the Amnesty International representative in Salisbury, when they spoke at Sithole's trial, that "they expected more redetentions." Barlow also speculated that the Rhodesian authorities had possibly tipped off Mugabe about his possible redetention, "so that he would remove himself without causing the regime embarrassment of a new martyr."[2]

Robin Byatt, an important British diplomat in the Rhodesian department in the mid-1970s, who would later become the first British high commissioner to Zimbabwe in 1980, recommended caution over supporting Mugabe in 1975. Byatt warned against reaching assumptions about why Mugabe was arrested by the Mozambicans. "I am not confident that we know the whole story. The convolutions of the feuding which has been going on within the ZANU faction of the ANC are complex and obscure, involving personal, tribal, and some political differences." For the moment, Byatt recommended that "it would be unwise to make any intervention on his behalf vis-à-vis the Zambians or FRELIMO, even though we have some degree of consular responsibility for him as a Rhodesian citizen."[3] It would take another three or four months for the British and Americans to sort out what had happened to Mugabe and why he had gone to Mozambique. Before continuing that narrative, it is important to first establish how events in Angola and Mozambique heightened the Cold War elements of the Rhodesian conflict and drew the Americans into a more direct role in the crisis.

Delivering a Unified Liberation Movement for Zimbabwe, 1976

Given the poor record of cooperation both within and between ZANU and ZAPU during the 1970s, it was no small task for Julius Nyerere and the other Frontline State presidents to try to push ZANU and ZAPU into some sort of unified movement. While the "old guard" of ZAPU and ZANU were attempting to reassert their control of the liberation war, a younger generation of military leaders met at the Mgagao ZANLA camp in Tanzania after Chitepo's death. During this crucial meeting in October 1975, they produced one of the key

---

[2] R. A. C. Byatt, "Robert Mugabe," April 18, 1975, FCO 36/1776, BNA.
[3] Ibid.

documents in the Zimbabwean liberation war, the Mgagao Declaration, which included a statement distancing the younger leaders from the old guard leaders (such as Nkomo and Sithole) and claimed it was time for the younger leaders to push forward with a united command of ZANLA and ZIPRA. Wilf Mhanda maintains that it was the Mgagao Declaration that made it possible to form the ZIPA, because it denounced Sithole's role as leader of ZANU and distanced the military leaders from the old guard political leaders.[4] As mentioned earlier, the Mgagao Declaration did, however, recognize Robert Mugabe as the only political leader who could act as a spokesperson for this new military force.[5] The new organization, ZIPA, took effective control of the liberation war with the support of Nyerere and Samora Machel. In terms of future diplomacy, it is important to note that Nyerere insisted that ZIPA receive all military assistance through the OAU's Liberation Committee. Agreement was reached a few weeks after the Mgagao declaration with Nyerere to restart OAU's Liberation Committee's military assistance as long as both ZIPRA and ZANLA leaders agreed to work together within ZIPA. As Wilbert Sadomba recalls, this "rapprochement of ZIPRA and ZANLA boosted military aid in the form of supplies from foreign allies, especially to the near-starving, Chinese-backed, ZANLA forces."[6]

Nyerere had insisted on this channeling of military supplies through the OAU's Liberation Committee to force a unity between the two factions. Nyerere explained in an April 1976 meeting with the US secretary of state, Henry Kissinger, that this was to avoid another Angola, where a Chinese-supported faction had confronted a Soviet-supported faction. Nyerere claimed that Nkomo had complained about the arrangement, because the Soviets would likely reduce their support for ZIPRA if it had to go through the OAU's Liberation Committee. Nyerere told Kissinger that he had rebutted Nkomo's complaint by saying "We will tell the Russians that if they cannot accept channeling aid through a third organization, then they are only interested in

---

[4] Wilfred Mhanda, *Dzino: Memories of a Freedom Fighter* (Harare: Weaver, 2011), 90.
[5] Gerald Mazarire, "ZANU's External Networks 1963–1979: An Appraisal," *Journal of Southern African Studies* 43, no. 1 (2017), 96.
[6] Zvakanyorwa Wilbert Sadomba, *War Veterans in Zimbabwe's Revolution: Challenging Neo-colonialism and Settler and International Capital* (Oxford: Boydell & Brewer, 2011), 20; Mhanda, *Dzino*, 91.

creating factions."[7] Kissinger replied to Nyerere "We support your policy. It's a good idea." He then asked how the aid was apportioned. "We don't," Nyerere said. "One army is being built. The freedom fighters have come under a joint leadership." At this point the new leadership was not identified, but Nyerere added that they refused to work with Muzorewa. Later in the conversation, Nyerere said military aid for FRELIMO had been channeled through Tanzania and the OAU's Liberation Committee. Kissinger responded, "Even previously we never opposed FRELIMO because it was a unified movement. Its ideologies are not our own, but we deal with it. The question of ideology is not an obstacle for state relations."[8]

The stage was set, therefore, for a leader of a unified liberation movement to emerge, and Kissinger had given his support to Nyerere, in particular, and all the Frontlne State presidents more generally, to produce the new unified leadership. In April, during Kissinger's first Africa trip, the British and the Zambians were confident that Joshua Nkomo was the right man for the job. It would appear even Nyerere, who would become a strong supporter of Mugabe after Geneva, still believed Nkomo was the frontrunner in March 1976. According to details provided to the British by journalist David Martin, after Martin met with Nyerere in early March 1976, Nyerere was not yet a strong supporter of Mugabe. Martin related Nyerere's impressions of the Zimbabwean leaders: "Despite his insistence that freedom fighters were now primarily loyal to [the] new military leadership, i.e. 'Third Force', Nyerere still backed Nkomo as [the] best of the Zimbabwean political leaders." Nyerere went further, as he "dismissed Muzorewa, Sithole and Chikerema with one-word epithets: to these [he] now added Mugabe." According to Martin's story, Mugabe "apparently has, contrary to Karanga claims, little or no influence among freedom fighters and at most limited access to the camps."[9]

In late February 1976, after the ZIPA commanders had demonstrated their ability to wage war against the Rhodesians, Nyerere and Machel signaled to the British that their support for the African

[7] NSC, "Memorandum of Conversation, Nyerere and Kissinger," Monday April 26, 1976, Dar es Salaam, Document 01933, Digital National Security Archives, 6.
[8] Ibid., 7.
[9] Miles from Lusaka to FCO, "Rhodesia," March 8, 1976, item 14, FCO 36/1851, BNA.

National Council group was waning. A British diplomat who met with Nyerere in Dar es Salaam reported that Nyerere now held the view that talks between Smith and the African National Council could "come to nothing" because the factions were "dealing from weakness." Nyerere reportedly said, "Nkomo won't fight, the Bishop wants to preach, and Sithole is a write off." Nyerere had told a visiting Norwegian Labour Party leader that "a new and more dynamic leadership is forming."[10]

In May 1976, Nyerere was even more adamant that time was running out for the African National Council leaders, and for Nkomo. British diplomat and key FCO advisor on Rhodesia, Dennis Grennan, reports of a meeting he had with Nyerere's confidant, Joan Wicken, in Dar es Salaam on May 10, 1976. Wicken passed a message from Nyerere to then prime minister James Callaghan: "He [Nyerere] felt that that if the ANC political leadership remained split then the events of the next few months would pass them by, and a new leadership would emerge from the ranks of the Third Force." Wicken said it was an urgent matter, according to Nyerere, "as events in Rhodesia were likely to hot up very quickly and that this really was the last chance for the Nkomo's and the Muzorewa's [sic]." Wicken relayed Nyerere's request to the prime minister that it would be good for Callaghan to "put as much pressure as possible on Nkomo to get him back into a united ANC."[11] Wicken emphasized that the power behind Nyerere's "last chance" remark was his confidence in the newly realigned "Third Force" under ZIPA. Nyerere "did not think that even the South Africans would get Smith to negotiate" and thought that the Frontline State presidents were convinced they needed to "get the war under way as quickly as possible." To do this, Wicken described their plan to concentrate the fighting forces in Mozambique "and as far as possible in the same camp." She added that it was hoped this move "should help to get over tribal divisions and create a sense of unity on the basis of common objectives, training and experience."[12]

It was into this precarious situation that the Americans suddenly arrived on the scene, prompted by Kissinger's attempt to score a Cold War diplomatic victory in southern Africa before the end of President

---

[10] Strong from Dar es Salaam to FCO, "Rhodesia," February 25, 1976, item 4, FCO 36/1851, BNA.

[11] D. J. Grennan, "Notes for the Record, Rhodesia," May 10, 1976, item 50, FCO 36/1851, BNA.

[12] Ibid.

Gerald R. Ford's brief term in office. All of this required the cooperation of the Frontline State presidents to bring a unified Zimbabwean nationalist movement to the negotiating table, along with South Africa's help to bring Smith and his Rhodesian Front to meaningful negotiations. As the next chapter will explore, the resulting Geneva conference in late 1976 brought all the key actors together, but few of them were capable of accepting any meaningful shifts away from their original positions. The Geneva conference is important, however, because it very much assisted Mugabe's claims as the political leader of ZANU and helped him to start on the road toward establishing his alliance with ZANLA leaders as well.

Mugabe's Diplomatic Efforts

As will be argued in the next chapter, Mugabe's ability to present himself at Geneva as the leader most capable of unifying and leading the guerrilla movement based in Tanzania and Mozambique, and to present himself as a moderate to the Americans, was part of a larger effort by him to externalize, or "internationalize," ZANU's nationalism – a lesson he learned in the early 1960s.[13] Nkomo assumed that he himself was the logical leader of the Zimbabwean liberation movement, based on his longstanding role as the "father" of Zimbabwean nationalism. He was put forward as such by the British and the Zambians, but the Americans were not as willing to accept Nkomo for a number of reasons. Firstly, Nkomo received funds from the Soviets and therefore was perceived externally as more likely to receive aid from the Soviets and Cubans after coming to power. Secondly, even though Nyerere would persuade the Americans in 1976 that the fighting forces would decide (as in FRELIMO's case) their future leaders, none of the old guard leaders, except for Nkomo, were sufficiently in command of the fighting forces to claim sole leadership. Nkomo, however, did not have the advantage of successes on the battlefield as ZIPA was having in 1975–76. Lastly, there was the issue of ethnicity, with Nkomo a Kalanga, but associated with the larger minority SiNdebele speakers, which meant he was a minority leader against the chiShona-speaking population in Zimbabwe. The

---

[13] See William C. Reed, "International Politics and National Liberation: ZANU and the Politics of Contested Sovereignty in Zimbabwe," *African Studies Review* 36, no. 2 (September 1993), 31–59.

wildcard in all of this was Mugabe, who had played his cards well by establishing himself in Mozambique.

A key step in Mugabe's rise to the leadership of ZANU and ZIPRA was the Mgagao Declaration, which, after Chitepo's death, recognized Mugabe as the leader of ZANU who the ZANLA/ZIPA forces trusted to negotiate on their behalf. Mugabe might have been put under house arrest in Mozambique by Machel to keep him from interfering with the newly formed "Third Force," ZIPA. Nyerere and Machel were concerned ZIPA would repeat the murderous factionalism experienced in previous attempts at cooperation between ZANLA and ZIPRA. As Zimbabwean historian Wilbert Sadomba argues, this did not stop Mugabe from using the text of the Mgagao Declaration as justification for his leadership role. To Sadomba and others, that was not the document's intention. The ZIPA fighters "expressed sympathy for Robert Mugabe 'for defying the rigours of guerrilla life' and chose him to be their 'middle man' (i.e. power broker)" but this did not mean that they recognized him as their leader.[14] Mugabe would, however, make the most of the opportunities offered by American and international attention in 1976 to better position himself as the key leader in a coalition of liberation forces.

Given his lack of international recognition, Mugabe began a diplomatic campaign to establish his role as both the leader of ZANU and ZIPA by July 1976.[15] He met with British diplomats in Maputo for the first time on July 20, 1976. The account of the meeting characterized Mugabe as a politician wanting to impress upon the

---

[14] Sadomba, *War Veterans in Zimbabwe's Revolution*, 21. For the struggle between ZIPA leaders and Mugabe, see David Moore, "The ZIPA Moment in Zimbabwean History, 1975–1977: Mugabe's Rise and Democracy's Demise," in Carolyn Basset and Marlea Clarke, eds., *Legacies of Liberation: Post-colonial Struggles for a Democratic Southern Africa* (Toronto and Cape Town: Fernwood and HSRC, 2011), 302–18. For the full text of the Mgagao Declaration, see Appendix C in Mhanda, *Dzino*, 278–83. The key passage reads: "An Executive Member who has been outstanding is Robert Mugabe. He has demonstrated this by defying the rigours of guerrilla life in the jungles of Mozambique. Since we respect him most, in all our dealings with the ANC leadership, he is the only person who can act as a middle man."

[15] Mugabe met with US congressional representative Steven Solarz in July 1976. Mugabe told Solarz that "today the Third Force high command was composed entirely of ZANU military leaders who were loyal to him." Maputo to State, "Solarz: Meeting between Congressman Solarz and ZANU leader Edward [sic] Mugabe," July 9, 1976, 1976MAPUTO00785, Central Foreign Policy Files, 1973–76, RG 59, General Records of the Department of State, USNA.

British that he was not a radical in the FRELIMO mold. For example, he emphasized his Catholic background, and hence,

on human grounds, if no other, [he] does not wish for a protracted guerilla war. He pointed out that unlike FRELIMO, who have come to politics from guerilla war, he (and the other Zimbabwe leaders) were politicians and have only taken to armed struggle in despair of a political settlement. He does not therefore share the outlook of the FRELIMO leaders.[16]

Further in the report, Mugabe indicated that "he gathered that the US and UK wanted to see Nkomo as the leader of the future independent government." Charles de Chassiron, an FCO diplomat stationed in Mozambique at the time, summarized his reply to Mugabe: "I assured him that this was not so. The leader or leaders would be those who gained sufficient support from the people of Zimbabwe to form a government, and we should have to accept them." De Chassiron relayed Mugabe's skepticism of the US role, stating, "Mugabe said that he had been quite willing to talk to U.S. Congressman [Stephen Solarz] who had visited him, but he remained suspicious of American motives as far as Rhodesia was concerned. He had not forgotten that the U.S. cast its first Security Council veto in 1970 over Rhodesian sanctions." De Chassiron concluded, "This was the first time I had met him. I found him quite an impressive and likeable man, but rather mild and modest with nothing of the swagger or the ruthlessness of Machel."[17]

At the time of these first encounters with Mugabe by a new generation of British diplomats, the leadership question in ZANU and ZANLA was still unsettled. Wilf Mhanda has argued that he and other ZIPA military commanders were in the process of developing ZIPA into a political organization in its own right after 1975, but Nyerere and Machel were working to unify the existing ZANU and ZAPU leaders with ZIPA to work as a unified force at the Geneva conference. ZIPA's political aspirations and their challenge to Mugabe's and Tongogara's leadership of ZANU and ZANLA were to be brought to an abrupt halt after the Geneva talks.[18]

A report sent by the British Head of Chancery in Lusaka, Jeremy Varcoe, in mid-July 1976 indicates how important the approval of the

---

[16] Charles de Chassiron to Laver, "Rhodesia Department," July 26, 1976, Maputo, pp. 1 and 2, FCO 36/1853, BNA.
[17] Ibid.   [18] See Mhanda, *Dzino*, 135–97.

Frontline State presidents was for the Zimbabwean nationalists. Varcoe described, second-hand, a meeting between a Zambian journalist and Nkomo. The journalist told Varcoe that Nkomo "had been understandably depressed and had conceded that if things went on as they were the man likely to emerge as the first leader of Zimbabwe was Robert Mugabe." In this situation, just a few months before the forced unity of the Patriotic Front, Nkomo was pessimistic about his chances to emerge on top of the Zimbabwean nationalist leadership struggle. This was a rhetorical style Nkomo was well known for, however. He was willing to express the worst-case scenario to see what options others might recommend. In this case, it would appear his reason for pessimism was the decision by the OAU's Liberation Committee "to authorize all arms and equipment to be channeled to the freedom fighters through the governments of Mozambique and Tanzania." Nkomo felt that his ZIPRA troops were being marginalized by this decision, because it helped "the former ZANLA guerrillas" who were seen as "now the sole recipients of outside support." According to this source, "Nkomo further admitted that Mugabe had a considerable following amongst those in the camps."[19] Nkomo and his generals would find ways to continue to supply ZIPRA from the Soviets and Eastern bloc allies via Angola, so his pessimism on this point would not be supported as the war intensified.

Varcoe had met with Stephen Solarz, a US congressional representative, on July 11 in Maputo. Solarz had just returned from the port town of Quelimane, Mozambique, where he had met with Mugabe. According to Varcoe, Solarz's impression confirmed Nkomo's concern about ZANLA's position in 1976: "Obviously Mugabe made a big impression on Solarz who shares Nkomo's view that unless there is some dramatic new development ZANLA will be the force which effectively wrests power from the whites." Varcoe added, however, that it appeared that "Mugabe is still under FRELIMO control to the extent that he is not allowed free access to the ZANLA camps but he claims (and we have some corroboration for this) that he is in close contract with the freedom fighters."[20] Solarz's contact with Mugabe had shown that some American politicians were trying to make sense of

---

[19] J. R. Varcoe to Barlow, "Rhodesia," July 13, 1976, item 94, FCO 36/1825, BNA.
[20] Ibid.

Figure 4 Edward Ndlovu, Joshua Nkomo, Clement Muchachi, and Henry Kissinger. Lusaka, Zambia, April 27, 1976. Courtesy Gerald R. Ford Presidential Library.

where the leadership would come from should progress be made in the talks. Before the Geneva talks, Mugabe was only just beginning his campaign to prove that he was the right man for the position.

Still, Nkomo had a strong ally in President Kaunda of Zambia. During Kissinger's first Africa trip in April 1976, Kaunda had arranged for Kissinger to meet directly with Nkomo in Lusaka. Nkomo was clearly Kaunda's choice; he reasoned that Nkomo was the most moderate of the leaders, and that if the United States would get behind him, he would quickly drop his ties to the Soviets and the Cubans and guarantee a Zimbabwe favorable to Zambia and the United States.[21] In July 1976, this plan was apparently acceptable to Kissinger, as he expressed in a breakfast meeting with then CIA director George Bush. Bush summarized Kissinger's prediction of how the Rhodesia plan would progress: "the UK would be out front, the UK would put forward a guarantee

---

[21] Vladimir Shubin, *The Hot "Cold War": The USSR in Southern Africa* (London: Pluto Press, 2008), 170.

scheme, some land would be distributed. Smith would turn over the reins of government to Nkomo, the UK would be back in Rhodesia for two years." Bush concluded, "The British want credit for the plan. The whites would stay. Apparently, Kaunda, Khama, and Nyerere all agree Vorster is on the program. The program must be kept quiet, otherwise if the Soviets find out about it they would try to blow it sky-high."[22]

Kissinger never met directly with Mugabe during his 1976 shuttle diplomacy, something that Mugabe would criticize him for later when discussing the issue with American diplomats. However, other senior level American diplomats met with Mugabe during the Geneva talks. These conversations gave Mugabe an opportunity to introduce himself to a new cadre of American diplomats. As he had done in the early 1960s, he gained influence by presenting himself as willing to work with the United States.[23] By the mid-1970s, there had been little continuity among American diplomatic personnel in Southern Rhodesia. The Americans had closed the Consulate General's office in Salisbury in 1970 as a response to British demands for diplomatic isolation of Ian Smith's UDI government.

Indicative of this lack of continuity were the views of Ambassador Edward Mulcahy, who had served as the consulate general in Salisbury from 1959–63. Since then, he had been promoted to new roles in the state department, serving as Kissinger's deputy assistant secretary of state in 1972, then as US ambassador to Chad, before being appointed ambassador to Tunisia in 1976. In April 1976, Mulcahy was asked to comment on a document circulating in London that suggested he had signed off on the notion of supporting Mugabe "as a compromise leader," as a better choice over Nkomo and Bishop Muzorewa. The letter had been shown to Tanzanian president Julius Nyerere by journalist David Martin, and therefore came to the attention of the American diplomats in Dar es Salaam. Ambassador Mulcahy vehemently denied any involvement with the document and called it a forgery. He went on to call Mugabe a "has been" with little chance of surfacing as a contender for the leadership role

[22] George Bush, "Notes on Breakfast with Secretary Kissinger, 13 July," July 14, 1976, CIA Electronic Reading Room, FOIA DOC_0000496841.

[23] Mugabe had been particularly close to the American Consul General, Paul Geren, in the early 1960s. When ZANU was forming in Dar es Salaam in August 1963, Geren quickly traveled there from Salisbury to assess what Mugabe and Sithole might need in terms of assistance from the Americans. See Timothy Scarnecchia, *The Urban Roots of Democracy and Political Violence in Zimbabwe: Harare and Highfield, 1940–1964* (Rochester, NY: University of Rochester Press, 2008), 135–36.

among the Zimbabwean nationalists.[24] Given the years that had passed since Mulcahy had left Salisbury in 1963, it isn't so surprising then for him to reach this erroneous conclusion about his "old" Zimbabwean contact.

Kissinger and Nyerere Meet in Dar es Salaam, April 1976

Nyerere certainly viewed the trajectory of the Mozambican liberation struggle as a potential template for the Rhodesian struggle. After an hour of private talks on Sunday April 25, Kissinger and Nyerere met with their colleagues and drank a toast at the presidential residence. Kissinger did not take any wine and Nyerere called him a "teetotaler." Nyerere then explained his own attitude toward drinking: "I was a teetotaler. Until the victory in Mozambique. I never dealt with Portugal. I never knew Portuguese wine." Nyerere went on, telling Kissinger:

Figure 5 Henry Kissinger and Tanzanian president Julius Nyerere. Dar es Salaam, April 26, 1976. Courtesy Gerald R. Ford Presidential Library.

[24] "Secret U.S. Policy document on Rhodesia," April 23, 1976, 1976LONDON098848, Central Foreign Policy Files, 1973–376, RG 59, General Records of the Department of State, USNA.

Then Samora [Machel] discovered stacks and stacks of wine in cellars there. He sent it to me. So they'll serve it to you. [Laughter] Since Samora sent it to me, I call it 'Samora' [Laughter] I always say: 'Bring me Samora.' [Laughter].[25]

Kissinger followed up this banter by asking Nyerere to tell him about the origins of FRELIMO. Nyerere explained the history of Mozambican resistance, starting from 1962 and Eduardo Mondlane's work at the United Nations, Mondlane's formation of the "front for the liberation of Mozambique," and the fight against the Portuguese, "a year after the formation of the OAU." Kissinger asked about Machel's trajectory to the leadership role, and Nyerere's response serves as a model for what he and others likely wanted to see happen with the Zimbabwean nationalists.

Nyerere said Machel was "one of the freedom fighters" who worked as a hospital assistant before leaving Mozambique and then went to Tanzania where he joined the army. When Mondlane was assassinated in 1969, Machel was selected as leader. Kissinger, in a display of his lack of knowledge about the region, inquired, "Oh, Mondlane was assassinated?" Nyerere's explanation serves as an outline of what he likely envisioned for the new "Third Force," ZIPA, and his hopes for new, unified Zimbabwe liberation forces: "It was planned by the Portuguese, with infiltrators. When he was assassinated, they came together to find a new leader. They were divided, as the politicians now fighting in Rhodesia . . . . But at the Congress, the fighters came, so they chose Machel." Kissinger replied that Charles Percy, a US senator, had been impressed with Machel and that the United States was "not interested in pitting one faction against another." He reiterated that when he met with Nkomo in Lusaka, it was "just to show the symbolism of meeting with someone from the Liberation Movement" and that he would be "interested in meeting Sithole as well."[26] Kissinger was still, apparently, unaware of Mugabe's campaign to be the main leader of ZANU.

Kissinger and Nyerere met again the next day, Monday April 26, at the Tanzanian State House. Nyerere took the opportunity to criticize

---

[25] Memorandum of Conversation, Nyerere and Kissinger, Msasani (The President's Residence), Dar es Salaam, April 25, 1976, Nyerere and Kissinger, Msasani, Document 01932, Digital National Security Archive [DNSA], 10.

[26] Ibid., 11.

Bishop Muzorewa for his inability to provide financial assistance to the freedom fighters. Nyerere told Kissinger that the new ZIPA forces "refused to see Muzorewa because they didn't want to identify with one faction. They are still ready to meet with a united political leadership." Nyerere went on to criticize Muzorewa for withholding funds he raised from Scandinavian countries: "The Bishop collected one million dollars in Scandinavia, but he hasn't given any to the freedom fighters!"[27]

An interesting counter narrative to Nyerere's criticisms of Muzorewa had come a month earlier, when Muzorewa had sent a long and detailed complaint to Nyerere, written in March of 1976. He accused the OAU's Liberation Committee and the Mozambican and Tanzanian governments of keeping the African National Council from supplying and training their troops. Muzorewa wrote that both he and Reverend Sithole were kept from meeting with the liberation forces in the camps of Mozambique and Tanzania. A copy of Muzorewa's complaint, addressed to Nyerere as "Chairman of the O.A.U. sub-committee of four Frontline States," is in the archives of the former Yugoslavia.[28] The accusations are detailed and sharp, describing how different teams of the African National Council leadership had, on multiple occasions, travelled to Tanzania and Mozambique to address the liberation forces, but were kept from doing so by the leader of the OAU's Liberation Committee, Tanzanian Colonel Hashim Mbita. According to the document, Mbita was in the process of forming ZIPA, the "Third Force" that Nyerere and Machel had wanted to replace the factionalist groups in ZIPRA and ZANLA. The document attempts to refute claims that the leaders of the African National Council had not been willing to travel to Tanzania to meet the fighters in their camps: "The story going around that the leadership has 4 times refused to go to the camps to explain things to the cadres and give them direction and guidance is not true. Rather, the African National Council leadership has been refused access to the camps."

---

[27] NSC, Memorandum of Conversation, Nyerere and Kissinger, Monday April 26, 1976, Dar es Salaam, Document 01933, DNSA, 6.

[28] "Memorandum to the Chairman of the O.A.U. sub-committee of four Frontline States His Excellency President Julius Nyerere, from the African National Council of Zimbabwe (A.N.C-Z)," *Arhiv, Centralnog Komiteta Seveza Komunista Jugolsavije*, A CK SKJ, IX, 140/47, Br. Listova 10, datum 24, IV, 1976. Thanks to Sarah Zabic for sharing this and other Zimbabwean related files with me.

Muzorewa describes how after a Frontline State presidents' summit in Lusaka in September 1975, the African National Council leaders had been "assured by President Machel that we could come to Mozambique and embark on concrete preparations for waging armed struggle." Two members of the African National Council's defense council went to Mozambique to "put forward a program of action." However, they were told that "the time was not yet ripe for the ANC leadership to go into the camps" and they should return to Lusaka. Further attempts to go to Tanzania and Mozambique are detailed, describing how each of these was turned back because "the spirit in the camps is sour," allegedly according to Colonel Mbita whilst he was establishing the "'Third Force' high command with dissident elements." The document goes on to name these dissident elements, and to associate them with Herbert Chitepo's assassination. The "ringleaders" are described as those who had stood "against unity as constituted on December 7, 1974."[29] This was the date when the Lusaka Agreement was signed, which had placed Muzorewa, at least on paper, as the official leader of the merged ZAPU, ZANU, FROLIZI, and the African National Council. Muzorewa would make similar complaints again in 1978, as is discussed further in Chapter 6, but it shows the extent to which Nyerere and Machel, along with the OAU's Liberation Committee under Mbita's command, were heavily involved in shaping the "Third Force" and limiting Muzorewa's and Sithole's contact with the liberation forces. That Nyerere would go on to complain to Kissinger about the ineptitude and lack of interest on the African National Council leaders' part in supporting the war effort raises some interesting questions about how both sides made accusations and counter accusations. It would also show Nyerere's lack of patience with Muzorewa and Sithole.

From the perspective of Kissinger and the South Africans, Nkomo and Muzorewa seemed the most likely candidates to take over the leadership from Smith before the Geneva conference. Meeting with Prime Minister Callaghan at 10 Downing Street on August 5, 1976, Kissinger presented his view of the Zimbabwean leadership. "The black Rhodesian leaders would need to be brought in and this might best be done through an approach to Nkomo: to the extent that he was losing support he would want to grasp at this initiative." Kissinger

---

[29] Ibid.

added that "once it was moving it was thought that Muzorewa would not want to be left behind." No mention was made of Mugabe at all.[30] Kissinger made it clear to the British that the United States planned to "use" Smith to get a settlement. He argued that Smith was necessary for the transition to avoid "confusion" that Machel could exploit. "He [Kissinger] concluded therefore that we should use Smith in this sense and then move brutally against him when it was right to do so." Callaghan asked Kissinger "what kind of 'brutal move' could be made against Smith? Could Vorster in fact deliver on this?" Kissinger replied that "he [Kissinger] had warned Vorster that the U.S. Government would turn against South Africa if he backed down." Kissinger suggested that his leverage with Vorster would be for the United States "to adopt a policy of resisting commercial investment in South Africa on the grounds of its apartheid policy, and this would certainly be popular domestically in the U.S." Kissinger, was "convinced that Vorster would come along," and added his personal view of the South African prime minister: "he was not a maneuverer and he wants a move on the situation."[31]

Records from the Rhodesians in July 1976 indicated that European allies were also pressuring the South Africans to, in turn, put pressure on the Rhodesians to work out a deal with Nkomo. The Rhodesians discussed the Kissinger initiative with a South African diplomat, a Mr. Short. After telling Short that "it seemed obscene to discuss our proposed fate without our participation," the Rhodesian diplomat asked Short "If they did not see through Russian/Machel grand design" of communist aggression toward Rhodesia. Short replied that "they did but it made little difference. They claimed that they had learned to live with communism and could outwit it and beat it." Short explained how German leader Helmut Schmidt had made it clear to the Rhodesians that "Europe would only physically intervene to stop further penetration by Russians and allies in Southern Africa if Kissinger's initiative got rolling." Schmidt had warned, however, that if Rhodesian intransigence attracted "external intervention," there should be no doubt that "neither America nor Europe would come to our side." Short also warned that France's President Valéry Giscard d'Estaing was

---

[30] "Meeting with Dr. Kissinger on 5 August 1976 at No. 10 Downing Street," item 111, FCO36/1829, BNA, 6.
[31] Ibid.

"wobbling badly over the supply of sophisticated arms" to South Africa. After these warnings from Short, the Rhodesian diplomat was told that "Nkomo was still regarded as the man we should talk to. This would be [the] only hope for [a] settlement [of] our own making." The indication here being that Mugabe and ZANLA were assumed to be too closely allied with Machel and Nyerere. "He [Short] thought Kaunda could still be won if we could come to saleable agreement with Nkomo and non-Marxist groupings."[32]

During a September 11, 1976, meeting between Kissinger and then South African Ambassador to the United States, R. F. "Pik" Botha, Kissinger reassured Botha that he trusted Vorster and not Smith, and that "the reports from Rhodesia are scary. Because they [the Smith regime] look weaker. Our bargaining position will erode." Botha wanted Kissinger to tell Nyerere that the South Africans had removed "a couple of thousand" South African police from Rhodesia," to show that the South Africans were serious about removing their support for the Smith regime in order to hasten a negotiated settlement. Kissinger then stated, "The big problem now is whether the blacks can organize themselves, to respond to our initiative." Botha replied, "If they can't you'll have Muzorewa and Nkomo. The man who first establishes himself in Salisbury is the man who will rule Rhodesia and be recognized by the OAU, even if he initially isn't the strongest." Kissinger agreed, adding "We have information that Nkomo is gaining strength." Once again, Mugabe was not mentioned in this meeting.[33]

Kissinger reassured Botha that the British would not pressure the South Africans. But as Ambassador Botha had told Kissinger earlier in August, there was an urgency for reaching a settlement from South Africa's point of view. "If Smith starts attacking Zambia, Botswana, and Mozambique, we'll be involved in a maelstrom. This is the first public warning ... We have to figure out a way to stop it. It's our security and safety that are at stake here." Botha added, "We won't let the British lord it over us while Russian tanks come in. We'll impose it."[34] Kissinger

---

[32] For Gaylard from ADR, "Discussion with Short," Pretoria, July 8, 1976, item 288, File: "Detente: Official Communications with South Africa," vol. 4, Rhodesian Government, Prime Minister Department, 51/39/7, Smith Papers.

[33] Memorandum of Conversation, Henry Kissinger and R. F. Botha, September 11, 1976, Washington, DC, Document 02057, DNSA.

[34] Memorandum of Conversation, Amb R. F. Botha and Henry Kissinger, August 12, 1976, Secretary's Office, Department of State, Document 02015, DNSA, 9.

responded, "They won't. It'll be settled by the middle of September. ... Once there is a British plan on the table, we can impose it or you can. But if it's your plan, the world will howl that it's you. Callaghan thinks he's clever saying it's his plan and our leverage." Botha replied, "Incredible." Kissinger continued, "It's personally infuriating, but it's useful. I've been trying to get someone to step forward. If he's stupid enough to do it ... It's a lot better than if I just thrust myself into it."[35] It is possible to think that Botha's "incredible" response to Kissinger's comments had to do with Kissinger's portrayal of Callaghan's belief that the British should take the lead, or it could also have been a way of expressing his respect for Kissinger's backhanded strategy to get Callaghan and Britain committed to taking the leading role.

Meeting with Kissinger and others in London on September 4, 1976, the British foreign secretary, Anthony Crosland, started by presenting an overview of the Frontline State presidents' position. "They felt passionately that it would be necessary to get Ian Smith out of the picture. They would not accept an interim government dominated by Nkomo; they wanted a government more broadly based." In addition, Crosland added, "Presidents Nyerere and Machel were strongly opposed to Britain's assuming a colonial role in Rhodesia." Crosland then asked Ted Rowlands, the under-secretary of state for foreign and commonwealth affairs, to describe to Kissinger his impressions of Samora Machel's position on negotiations. Rowlands described how impressed they were with Machel, how they found him "unexpectedly pragmatic and un-ideological." Rowlands interpreted Machel's view of negotiations: "He [Machel] thought he would be able to get a Frelimo-style regime installed in Salisbury through negotiation because 'his men' would come out on top." Rowlands also added that Machel "suspected that it was our intention to promote the emergence of a government sympathetic to the West." To which Kissinger replied, "'He is right!'"[36]

This was followed by a discussion of the British position on negotiations. Kissinger asked "whether it would be correct to summarise the British view as being that: (i) Ian Smith would first have to go; (ii) there would be a genuine negotiation between the European caretaker

---

[35] Ibid.
[36] "Record of a Meeting between the Foreign and Commonwealth Secretary and the American Secretary of State, Dr. Kissinger, at FCO Office," September 4, 1976, item 337, FCO36/1832, BNA.

government and the Rhodesian nationalist team; (iii) the two sides would then agree on composition of a provisional government." Crosland did not object to this summary, but said he thought the Americans "seemed to be concerned that negotiations between a caretaker government and the ANC would be tantamount to a surrender and hence that they would be giving unconditional support to a black government not dominated by Nkomo." This is an interesting suggestion that helps substantiate that Nkomo was the first choice of the British and Americans, at least in September 1976. Kissinger replied with his usual doom and gloom scenario: "that the worst case he could envisage was one in which a caretaker government was formed and then invited to surrender: the new African government would then split and there would be a civil war." This echoed his fear of "another Angola," but it also foreshadows a constant theme over the next four years: the need to try and avoid a civil war between ZANU and ZAPU, or at least while the Anglo-Americans were involved in the transition to majority rule. As time would show, Kissinger was not too far off with his "worse-case scenario," but it was still a scenario that he believed was worth the risk to gain a Cold War advantage for the United States.

Kissinger then stated something quite curious: "He felt that American public opinion would prefer to see the whites defeated in battle rather than pressured into surrender." Crosland didn't believe this to be a possibility, suggesting that if "the whites were asked to surrender, the Rhodesian armed forces would fight." Kissinger's comment about American public opinion came from his own experience after the April Lusaka speech. He was fond of relating how that speech had aroused public disapproval, saying that the speech "had provoked 1,800 letters, of which a mere 23 had been in favour of his policies." The note taker indicated that at this point, Kissinger described to Crosland the "extent of anti-black feeling in the U.S.," although there was no further elaboration in the notes. This was likely a reference to the American public preferring a war in which the Rhodesians were defeated on the battleground to a surrender, which had more to do with the way Americans racialized the conflict into their own racial history and identities.[37] In Kissinger's calculation of American domestic

---

[37] For domestic pressures on Kissinger and Ford, see Gerald Horne, *From the Barrel of a Gun: The United States and the War against Zimbabwe, 1965–1980* (Chapel

opinion, it was the case that white racial solidarity with white Rhodesians meant that it would be best to make sure any settlement did not look like "a surrender" of white settlerism. This notion of not making the Rhodesian whites surrender appears often in Kissinger's discussions on Rhodesia.

Kissinger must also have been concerned about the implications of the Rhodesian talks on the US presidential elections in November, but he would later play down this concern in a conversation with Crosland almost a month before the election. Kissinger related his interpretation of the Frontline State presidents' view of his motive vis-à-vis the US presidential elections:

They believed that the U.S. needed their support for electoral reasons. But they were wrong. The blacks in America would always vote democrat; the liberal whites, to whom his plan would appeal, would also vote democrat; those to whom his plan would not appeal were Republicans and they might be encouraged to stay away from the polls. In electoral terms, therefore, his present initiative could be a net liability.[38]

After Kissinger's boastful remarks to Ambassador Botha a few weeks earlier, it is interesting to read his discussion with Prime Minister Callaghan on September 24. Given that Kissinger already felt Callaghan had put himself and Britain at the front of the Anglo-American initiative, Kissinger kept pushing Callaghan toward committing to this leading role. Discussing British responsibility for the conference, Kissinger gave reasons why the Americans could not lead it: "First, we have no legal responsibility; second, the constitutional forms in which this is couched are foreign to us. For an American diplomat to be doing it would be strange." Callaghan replied, "You are doing all right!" to which Kissinger retorted, "Stealing your ideas." Kissinger's third point was that a more prominent US role would get them in a "Cold War competition with the Soviet Union." His final point would be the real stickler for the British in terms of the shape of the Geneva conference and their role in it. Kissinger

Hill, NC: University of North Carolina Press, 2001), 149–59. Andrew DeRoche, *Black, White, and Chrome: The United States and Zimbabwe, 1953–1998* (Trenton, NJ: Africa World Press, 2001), 211–28; Eddie Michel, *The White House and White Africa: Presidential Policy Toward Rhodesia during the UDI Era, 1965–1979* (New York: Routledge, 2019), 144–46.

[38] "Record of a Meeting between the Foreign and Commonwealth Secretary and the American Secretary of State, Dr. Kissinger, at FCO Office," September 4, 1976, item 337, FCO36/1832, BNA.

stated, "You have a legal responsibility to create a framework for an interim government." This is something the British remained steadfastly opposed to accepting. Later in the meeting, Callaghan encouraged Kissinger to work with Nyerere and Kaunda. Kissinger, however, again pushed Callaghan to take the lead. "But it is a lot easier for them to work with the British, and it avoids problems. Because for us to get actively involved would work against all our theories that superpowers shouldn't be in Africa. It is not an attempt to evade. As we discussed, the objective should be to create as close to a Kenya situation as possible. You are in the best position to do it."[39] Such exchanges showed Kissinger doing his best to manipulate the British into taking the lead and responsibility for future negotiations, using Kenya's decolonization process as a model.

A few weeks later, Kissinger further bonded with Zambian president Kaunda over their mutual mistrust of the British for their failure to take responsibility for Rhodesia. When Kissinger met with President Kaunda in Lusaka on September 20, 1976, he reiterated his mistrust of the British by presenting his and the American view as more enlightened from an African nationalist perspective than the British view. Kaunda told Kissinger, "I would generally rather deal with the Labour party in the UK. But over Rhodesia we have differed. They did not do the right thing at the very outset. They should have acted firmly at the outset, and if they had, this thing would not have happened." Kissinger said, "I am struck in dealing with the UK, that they have a funny image of Africa. I really don't think they understand." Kaunda replied, "I always said that the United States should not see Africa through British eyes. Since the end of empire they have been insular." Kissinger added, "And they are both jealous and bureaucratic, which has been our problem on this negotiation," to which Kaunda responded, "The loss of empire influenced their thinking." Kissinger concluded, "And it is a pity, because their top personnel are able, but they are such a petty mentality."[40] President Kaunda asked

[39] Memorandum of Conversation, Prime Minister James Callaghan and Henry A. Kissinger Cabinet Room, Number 10 Downing Street London, "Southern Africa," September 23, 1976, Document 0208, DNSA, 3. See also "Note of a Meeting between the Prime Minister and Dr. Kissinger at 10 Downing Street on Thursday, 23 September 1976," FCO 36/1835, BNA; and "Note of Meeting between the FCO Secretary and the U.S. Secretary of State, Dr. Kissinger … FCO Office," September 24, 1976, FCO 36/1835, BNA.

[40] Memorandum of Conversation, President Kaunda, Mr. Nkomo, Mr. Mark Chona, Secretary Kissinger, State House, Lusaka, Zambia, September 20, 1976,

Kissinger for a copy of the "Rhodesia points" that he would give to
Vorster and Smith. Kissinger stated, "I will give you a copy of the
Rhodesia points, but this is not an official version, it is a series of
notes, and I would have to disavow them if they are published." "I
assure you they will not be," replied Kaunda. Kissinger said, "My
giving you these is a mark of my confidence in you. But I cannot give
them in Dar. Could you talk with Nyerere about it?" "This is a sensitive
issue," Kaunda replied.[41] As it turned out, Kissinger was involved in
some of his trademark subterfuge here, as he would in fact give Smith
more bait in terms of guarantees for "the whites" when they met. This
lack of clarity on the documents shared with Smith would later end up
causing problems for Kissinger, and for all parties at the Geneva
Conference later in 1976.

Before Kissinger's second trip to Africa, the basis for a constitutional
conference was proposed by Tanzanian president Julius Nyerere.
Writing to Crosland on September 12, 1976, Nyerere explained his
decision to back the idea of a constitutional conference, now that the
Americans were involved, but he warned that such a conference would
be difficult. The lack of unity of the Zimbabwean leaders was one
reason. But Nyerere was hopeful that the task of negotiating independence would bring them together. Nyerere also offered Crosland an
outline of how independence could be achieved, including an agenda
for a future constitutional conference. Nyerere's proposal is worth
examining in full, because in many ways it became a blueprint for
what eventually transpired. Nyerere emphasized that his proposed
steps needed to follow a specific order: first, a "Constitutional
Conference is held in London, between Britain and the Rhodesian
Nationalists." This conference, according to Nyerere, "should seek to
reach agreement on: (a) an independence constitution; (b) the setting up
of a Provisional Government; (c) the date for independence."
The second step would be removal of the Smith regime to create "an
African majority Provisional Government – similar to that of the
'Chissano Government' in Mozambique from September 1974 to
June 1975." This would lead to the "ending of the war and the lifting
of sanctions simultaneously with the assumption of effective power by

RG 59, General Records of the Department of State, Records of Henry
Kissinger, 1973–77, Box 18, Memcons, September 76, folder 4, NARA II, 9.
Also Document 02075, DNSA.
[41] Ibid.

the Provisional Government." In turn, that would lead to "preparations for elections to be held before independence," and finally to independence.[42]

As had been clear from Nyerere's April meeting with Kissinger, Nyerere had Mozambique's recent transition to independence as his working model for the Zimbabwean process. At the Geneva conference, Britain's Ambassador to the United Nations, Ivor Richards, who would run the conference, would make an important deviation from Nyerere's suggestions by setting the date of independence as the first substantive agenda item. This effectively permitted a great deal of posturing that led to stalemates between the negotiating parties. Interestingly, the Lancaster House conference in 1979 would start with the constitutional negotiations first, which helped guarantee a successful negotiation. But in September and October 1976, all parties were very far from such a successful outcome.

Kissinger's Pre-Geneva Shuttle Diplomacy

Kissinger and South African prime minister John Vorster met for dinner on September 4, 1976, at the Dolder Grand Hotel in Zurich accompanied by a large entourage of their own. Kissinger asked Vorster for his views of Kaunda.[43] Vorster said he and Kaunda "got on very well," and that there were "two Kaundas – the one addressing his people, and the other doing business." Kissinger asked which of these the real Kaunda was, and Vorster said he didn't know, "because the African is the most natural actor ever created." Kissinger went along with this by saying Vorster had "disillusioned him" because Kaunda "was in tears after my Lusaka speech." Vorster then said Kaunda found his Idi Amin joke very funny when the two met for the first time. Vorster retold the joke to Kissinger, a play on words in which Amin ordered that the country be renamed Idi after him, and one of his advisors, "a wise man – one the few wise men left" – said,

---

[42] Brown from Dar es Salaam to FCO (telno 322), September 12, 1976, "Letter from Nyerere to Secretary of State Crosland," September 12, 1976, item 376, FCO36/1832, BNA.

[43] Memcon Vorster, Muller, Fourie, van den Bergh, Amb. R. F. Botha and Henry A. Kissinger, September 4, 1976, Dolder Grand Hotel Zurich, Switzerland, RG 59, General Records of the Department of State, Records of Henry Kissinger, 1973–77, Box 18, Memcons, September 1976, folder 1, USNA II, 1.

"Mr. President, you shouldn't do it." Amin asked, "Why not?" and, the wise man said, "There is nothing wrong with Idi. But it has just come to my attention that there is a country called Cyprus, and the people who live there are called Cypriots." Vorster added that when Kaunda heard this joke, "I've never seen a man laugh so hard in all my life." Kissinger responded, "But they're all great actors. It comes natural to them," which was met with laughter. The rapport between the two men was now firmly set, and the internationally besieged South African prime minister could trust the US secretary of state. The two had built a bond around a racist trope about Africans, one they were willing to make at the expense of President Kaunda – the leader who had worked so hard to bring Vorster and Kissinger together to pressure Smith and the Rhodesians in the first place.

The meeting finally began to discuss Rhodesia. The leaders were briefed on the Frontline State presidents concerns over the ability of the Zimbabwean nationalists to unify for talks and were told that the "boys with guns" would not cooperate with the political leadership's position in any future negotiations. Kissinger interjected to say that the "boys with guns" phrase was his. He had used it in his testimony before the Senate Foreign Relations Committee and claimed that President Nyerere had taken it from that testimony and was now using it. The briefing suggested that all the Frontline State presidents were of the opinion that further conflict was likely more realistic than peaceful negotiations at this point. Kissinger asked William Rogers, the undersecretary for economic affairs, to brief the South Africans on American ideas regarding plans to keep whites who could help in Rhodesia. Rogers summarized what was called an "international scheme for support for the transition in all its dimensions." This meant that the fund would provide support for "improving the lot of the blacks, and training the blacks for management." It also meant lifting sanctions and encouraging the World Bank to become involved in finding investors, and lastly, providing "assurances for the whites who can make a constructive contribution to the future of the country."[44]

Vorster asked if "they think they can run a sophisticated economy like Rhodesia, or do they realize they need the whites?" Rogers said the Frontline State presidents agreed with the American position that "whites have a role and should stay," and described a plan developed

[44] Ibid., 6.

with the British to offer "compensation in the case of expropriation" with "assurances in four areas: Pensions ... Housing, ... farms, [and] ... some right to transfer and liquidate assets." All such "guarantees would one way or another be underwritten by an international effort led by the British." Kissinger interjected to say that it was "paradoxically ... easier for us to get money from Congress for a fund organized by Britain than for one organized by the United States Government." [45] Kissinger added that perhaps Rhodesian industry could set up an "international consortium" that would contribute to this fund, with the United States and Britain acting as "guarantors of this fund, instead of us putting money in." This was thought as a way of incentivizing the plan from the perspective of white industry and an African government. Kissinger mentioned an amount that, as will be seen in further discussions on compensation in Geneva and at Lancaster House in 1979, would remain remarkably consistent. Speaking of the plan, Kissinger concluded, "Our obligation is the same in either case. But if we have to earmark $500 million now to Rhodesia, it will lead to endless debate. If we only commit ourselves to the fund, with no amount because some will be generated locally ... [sic]"[46] After Kissinger finished describing the plan, Botha compared it to "an insurance policy" and Kissinger agreed. "We'd like to handle it like an insurance policy rather than as a cash payment. It is better for our public than buying out the whites." "And for Africa," Muller added, and Vorster commented that "the Rhodesians would take exception if it were worded that way." Kissinger asked if they would accept it. Vorster said they would. "It would be regarded as a challenge to both black and white Rhodesians." Fourie asked, "But if the GNP doesn't go up ...," " to which Botha answered " ... there would be the insurance."

Kissinger continued to describe the plan. "And it doesn't cost the black government unless they start kicking whites out. As they force the whites out, they lose some. If there is a mass exodus, the guarantee fund would pay directly, and they would lose the investment. It is designed to create maximum incentive." South African Minister of Foreign Affairs, Hilgard Muller, interjected that "It seems to be very cleverly devised," and Kissinger said, "We pay money into a fund that either goes to the white settlers or the black government." This concept of "safeguarding" of whites by forcing a future black government from forcing the whites out is a clear example of "race states" in the Cold War. The rationale

[45] Ibid., 7.   [46] Ibid., 7.

behind it was that the Americans and British wanted to devise a scheme that could use development aid as a way to ensure the continued influence of whites in the economy, government, and military aspects of Zimbabwe. The reasons for even contemplating such a move had to do both with bringing Smith and the whites to the negotiating table, but also in a sort of imaginary of what black African states were capable of, or not capable of, based on what the western powers had observed elsewhere, particularly in Mozambique and Angola.

Vorster then commented, "The first question the Rhodesians will ask is: 'Is the money just a promise, or is it really there?'" Kissinger hedged a bit and then added, "I'll be honest. I don't think money will be really there until the next session of the Congress." Vorster pressed a bit further to know what amount the Americans were discussing so he can tell the Rhodesians. Rogers tried to hedge a bit more and Kissinger interjects: "You [Rogers] said $1.3 billion. This is considered low by our people." Muller said that the Rhodesians have also made calculations, and Kissinger stated "Theirs are higher." "For God's sake let's accept the higher," Vorster replied to laughter. After a discussion of how it may be easier to get contributions from other allies, Vorster told the Americans, "You understand there won't be a contribution from us." Here Kissinger challenged Vorster a bit, saying that the British had hoped the South Africans would do it symbolically. Vorster replied emphatically, "My answer is a decided no. It is impossible – for psychological, economic and political reasons. It will be seen as literally selling out and buying out." From Vorster's perspective, he thought that the position was "becoming very embarrassing and even self-defeating to some extent," and that the Rhodesians were saying "everyone talks about them and no one talks to them" and "getting very touchy." Vorster told Kissinger that South Africa " cannot be seen to be deposing Ian Smith," and that "the Rhodesians can depose him but not us." The US assistant secretary of state for African affairs, William E. Schaufele, Jr., along with Kissinger, then proposed the idea that South Africa's main role would be to guarantee that Smith could not spin out of any agreed "caretaker" or "interim" government, to which Vorster replied, "That's a horse of a different color."[47]

Kissinger emphasized to Vorster and to the other South Africans present that his main priority in this diplomacy was to change the

[47] Ibid., 13.

direction of negotiations so that should the Cubans and Soviets become directly involved in Rhodesia, the United States would not find themselves defending Smith. Kissinger suggested that the financial guarantees had another motivation: "I hate to say ... What we're doing is preventing Communist foreign penetration into Rhodesia." Kissinger said, "We might be terribly lucky; I'm not doing it with illusions." He argued that even if the Rhodesian were to win the war, that could also bring the risk of "foreign intervention," which they wouldn't be able to resist, given their "domestic situation." He then made the case that once he is out of the picture, the Carter Administration may advocate for defending the region. "I personally think, even in defense of the whites, that foreign intervention must be resisted. But I must tell you I am the only senior official who feels that way – even in this Administration. I can't even get the Pentagon to do contingency planning." He then put forward that "a Carter Administration would not resist." Implying that they would not make a stand against the Cubans and Soviets in Rhodesia. Rogers, however, interjected, "He might." Kissinger ignored Rogers' dose of realism and concluded, "I believe Cuban and Soviet intervention has strategic consequences that must be resisted, on behalf of everybody. If we do this and the blacks reject it, the moral situation is different."[48] In a move that was typical of Kissinger's negotiation style, he wanted the South Africans to know that he and the United States government did not care about Rhodesia per se, as long as the diplomacy could help put the United States in a better position vis-à-vis the Soviets and Cubans on the issue of supporting black rule. In terms of his hardball style, he wanted the South Africans to know that the United States would be fine if all they obtained was a commitment to majority rule that appeared to be brokered by Kissinger.

In terms of financial incentives, Vorster suggested that "if money was available to buy out land owned by whites, it will make a tremendous difference." Kissinger, understanding that there was opposition to this as a plan to pay whites to leave, said, "But it would be a mistake to present the plan as a plan to buy out the whites and send them out of Rhodesia." Rogers added, "It's bad politics and bad economics." South Africa's ambassador to the United States and permanent representative to the United Nations, Pik Botha, replied, "Make it

[48] Ibid., 21.

available but don't force it." Kissinger ended by saying, "It would be the ultimate irony if all of it is done but it's rejected because the blacks can't get organized." Botha agreed. Kissinger concluded, 'But still it must be presented. Because if it is rejected, we're in a much different position with respect to foreign intervention because it's not a fight against majority rule but against imperialism." Vorster replied, "Precisely."[49]

Kissinger would discuss the theme of the economic incentives with the Rhodesian team when they met in Pretoria on September 19. Rhodesia's deputy prime minister and minister of finance, David Smith, first broached the topic of financial compensation, stating that these should be designed "[n]ot to buy people out" – an idea he'd like to get away from – but to "inject development capital." Kissinger agreed. "That is our idea. We have the assurances of the British, French probably, and Germany. Probably Canada." Ian Smith added, "This is important, because the last thing we want to do is force people out." Kissinger replied, "No, we want to keep people in, and it's morally important to us too." Kissinger was obviously playing to Smith's need for reassurances before he made a speech accepting majority rule in two years' time. Smith responded: "Young people will want to know what kind of life they have before them, or else they'll leave." Smith then related one of his consistent themes: "If we're asked to commit suicide, people will pack up and go." Kissinger joked: "Are you going to tell the Rhodesians the U.S. asked you to commit suicide?" After some laughter, Ian Smith retorted, "I hope I'll be more tactful than that."[50]

From the American perspective, progress was made, as Vorster agreed to help corner Smith into accepting responsibility for promoting what Kissinger called "a proposal like this [Annex C], with an early timetable and outside guarantees, and a fund." Vorster made one more

---

[49] Ibid., 24.
[50] "Memorandum of Conversation, Kissinger, Ian Smith, et al.," RG 59, General Records of the Department of State, Records of Henry Kissinger, 1973–77, Box 18, Memcons, September 76, Folder 4, NARA II, College Park. For further details on the financial compensation plans, see Sue Onslow, "Race and Policy: Britain, Zimbabwe and the Lancaster House Land Deal," *The Journal of Imperial and Commonwealth History*, 45, no. 5 (2017), 844–67; Timothy Scarnecchia, "Proposed Large-Scale Compensation for White Farmers as an Anglo-American Negotiating Strategy for Zimbabwe, 1976–1979" in Arrigo Pallotti and Corrado Tornimbeni, eds., *State, Land and Democracy in Southern Africa* (Burlington, VT: Ashgate, 2015), 105–26.

comment: "The final point for me is that it's immoral for me to do it." Presumably this was in the context of not wanting to be responsible for bringing Smith's government down. In the end, Kissinger had Vorster's assurance that he would help commit Smith to the following: "a new government in two years, moving to an interim government when the process is completed." The program included "the guarantees in Annex C, plus economic guarantees." They agreed that both the United States and South Africa "will guarantee that Smith will carry it out." Interestingly, after Kissinger first indicated he was willing to make this public, Schaufele stated, "It will be known that it is the proposal we have been talking about." Kissinger said, "It may not be desirable."[51] This is a small point, but one that would later become a larger issue between the Americans and the British in the crucial weeks before the Geneva conference. This will be discussed further in the next chapter.

Selling Kissinger's Initiative to the US Congress

A few days after Ian Smith had gone on Rhodesian television to announce he had accepted the Anglo-American invitation to negotiate toward majority rule in two years' time, based on guarantees from Kissinger to protect Rhodesian white interests, Kissinger still had to convince the US Congress that what he was trying to do was worth their support. On September 28, Kissinger, along with President Ford and then-CIA director George Bush, briefed a bipartisan group of congressional leaders on Kissinger's negotiations in southern Africa. Kissinger asked Bush to give the group an intelligence report before making his own comments. Bush explained, "Assuming nothing were done it was our assessment that it would be 1978, at the very maximum, when we would witness the end of white control of Rhodesia by force. The Black Governments which would emerge from the conflict would be more attuned to communist influences than governments brought through negotiation." Bush added, "The Rhodesian

---

[51] Memcon Vorster, Muller, Fourie, van den Bergh, Amb. R. F. Botha and Kissinger, Eagleburger, Winston Lord (Director, Policy Planning Staff), Schaufele, Amb. William Bowdler, Peter Rodman, NSC Staff Meeting, September 4, 1976, Dolder Grand Hotel Zurich, Switzerland, RG 59, General Records of the Department of State, Records of Henry Kissinger, 1973–77, Box 18, Memcons, September 1976, Folder 1, 15.

Government was already under siege and the radical governments which we saw emerging from the violence would be beholden to outside communists."[52] This bleak Cold War prognosis was seconded by Kissinger, who argued, "The whites in Rhodesia will be overthrown within two years. There is also the risk that South Africa would be forced into the conflict by public opinion. It is our view that communist intervention would then be certain." He also predicted that the "only way Rhodesia can defend itself is through incursions along neighboring borders" and that "these countries will respond by asking for communist aid." Kissinger argued that these cross-border conflicts "will tend to radicalize their countries," and these increasingly radicalized countries "would then surround Zaire and could lead to an entire bloc in southern Africa hostile to the United States." Doing his best to prove the importance of his shuttle diplomacy to US interests, Kissinger concluded that "a successful resolution of the situation of southern Africa by force will not be lost on the countries" of the Middle East. Kissinger then commented on the complexity of the southern African negotiations compared with his Middle East shuttle diplomacy. "The difference between the negotiations here and the Middle East is that in Middle East there were two parties who had an agreement in principle. In southern Africa we have four front line states plus Angola. Among these five there is considerable distrust amongst each other. We also have four liberation movements which are severely divided."[53] This conversation also conveyed Kissinger's overriding concerns before Geneva. He wanted to push forward with a negotiated settlement to avoid a possible scenario where the United States would be forced to be on the side of Smith in fighting against the Cubans and Soviets, or a situation where a war would radicalize Zambia and allow the Soviets and Cubans to defend Zambia from Rhodesian attacks.

In contrast to the confidence the Americans had in their plan, Ian Smith was beginning to show his characteristic signs of "wiggling off the hook." A week after Smith's September 24 speech accepting the concept of majority rule, he sent a message to Kissinger, Crosland, and Vorster conveying his deep concern about the way the Frontline State

---

[52] Memcon, President Ford, Henry A. Kissinger, William E. Simon, George Bush, Bipartisan Congressional leadership, September 28, 1976, Cabinet Room, White House, NSA Memoranda of Conversation Collection at the Gerald R. Ford President Library, 2–3

[53] Ibid., 3–4.

presidents were promoting Mugabe as a potential leader for negotiations. Smith warned that since his speech, there had been a "marked change" in public opinion. This has been caused mainly by the militant and the intransigent attitude of certain black presidents and by the statements of nationalists such as Mugabe of which you are no doubt aware." Smith also warned that the lack of unity among the nationalists was a "forewarning of coming power struggles." He warned that should the Frontline State presidents promote Mugabe "as a leader of the African nationalists, the effect on public opinion, both among whites and among blacks, will be extremely serious." Referring to Mugabe's "long record of Communist affiliation" and recognizing Mugabe as "now emerging as the apparent spokesman of the terrorists based in Mozambique," Smith claimed that the intentions of the Frontline State presidents was "to establish a Marxist-type military dictatorship in Rhodesia on the model of that of Mozambique." "It appears that in this aim they have the full support of President Machel." His message ends with a warning: "Unless steps are taken urgently to reverse the current trend of loss of confidence among white Rhodesians, the position will deteriorate and there will be a real danger of a collapse of the economy and of the whole complex structure of government and of the security forces. If this should happen the Western powers who have forced Rhodesia into this situation will bear a heavy responsibility."[54] Smith's warnings came as the stage was set for the Geneva talks between Smith, the African National Council factions led by Muzorewa and Sithole, Nkomo's ZAPU, and Mugabe as the tentative political leader of ZANU.

From Kissinger's perspective, after two visits to Africa, he was confident that if all went well in the proposed negotiations, Nkomo would likely be the first leader of Zimbabwe. Even Nyerere seemed to have left Kissinger with this impression when they had met on September 15 in Dar es Salaam. Nyerere had briefed Kissinger on the difficulties of bringing Nkomo and Mugabe into a united front, but he was optimistic that the two movements could be unified. Discussing possible scenarios, Nyerere described to Kissinger a two-part solution: "(a) the present government should go in favor of an African government,

[54] Telegram from the Embassy of South Africa to the Department of State, Pretoria, September 30, 1976, 1629Z, *Foreign Relations of the United States. Volume XXVIII 1969–1976 Southern Africa*, item 213, p. 638.

and (b) a constitutional framework for the white minority and majority rule in 18 months to two years." Nyerere let Kissinger know that he had already discussed this possibility with Nkomo and Mugabe. "I explained this to Joshua and his colleagues, and to Mugabe – though I was not so specific as with Joshua. I asked 'supposing we can get this, would they be ready?' They obviously were excited. Their problem is to get together."[55]

By the time Kissinger met with Nkomo in September, however, Kissinger began to refer to Mugabe as a possible rival to Nkomo for nationalist movement leadership. In their second meeting on September 17, Kissinger, who greeted Nkomo with "Hello Mr. President!," asked Nkomo about the potential for continued fighting after independence. "When the black majority government is formed, will the other groups continue fighting?" Nkomo asked, "Which other groups?," to which Kissinger replied, "ZANU." Nkomo explained that he and Mugabe were fighting together. "We are fighting in alliance with ZANU. When we form a majority government, we expect the FLS [Frontline State] Presidents to support that government. Whoever fights them isn't fighting for majority rule, but for personal reasons. The black Presidents won't support a personal war." Kissinger then asked Nkomo, "Speaking candidly, do you think it will be you?" Nkomo replied, "I am the leader of Zimbabwe." Kissinger's reply to Nkomo must have been emphatic to warrant an exclamation point in the transcript: "That settles that problem! We have always worked on that assumption."[56]

---

[55] Memorandum of Conversations, Henry Kissinger and President Julius Nyerere, September 15, 1976. State House, Dar es Salaam, Memcons, September 1976, Folder 2. RG 59, NARA II.

[56] Memorandum of Conversation, Henry Kissinger and Joshua Nkomo, September 17, 1976, File: NODIS Memcoms, September 1976, Folder 2, RG 59, NARA II.

4 | "We Don't Give a Damn about Rhodesia"
The Geneva Talks, 1976

The Geneva talks on Rhodesia were a fairly elaborate undertaking pushed by the Americans and rather reluctantly hosted by the British.[1] The timing of the conference during the US presidential elections would mean that Kissinger and his team were not in a position to really push beyond what Kissinger managed to establish in his pre-conference shuttle diplomacy. From Kissinger's perspective, he had achieved his goal when Ian Smith made his September 24, 1976 speech on national television in Rhodesia, stating that he agreed with the Americans to accept majority rule in two years' time in exchange for a number of safeguards for white Rhodesians. For Kissinger, getting Smith and the Frontline State presidents to agree on the parameters of a conference was the key goal. As he told many of the parties in bilateral talks, the goal was to show the world that the United States was no longer supporting a white settler state in the context of the new Cold War race state logic created by events in Angola and Mozambique. As the Kissinger quote in this chapter title suggests, Kissinger was not interested in keeping up the pretense that he was even interested in the political outcome in Rhodesia. What was paramount to him was the need to avoid confronting the Soviet Union's arms and Cuban troops in Rhodesia.

As described in Chapter 3, Kissinger managed to obtain South African assistance to help sell the Anglo-American plans to Smith. This chapter examines how Kissinger's efforts were interpreted by the Frontline State presidents, the Patriotic Front (PF) leaders, the British, and the Rhodesians. The problems caused by Kissinger having offered Smith more than the Frontline State presidents and Joshua Nkomo and Robert Mugabe could accept quickly became evident at the Geneva

---

[1] The quote in the chapter title is from Henry Kissinger, taken from the Memorandum of Conversation, Washington, DC, December 21, 1976, in *Foreign Relations of the United States, 1969–1976*, Volume xxviii, Southern Africa, 235.

conference. In a certain sense, the impasse caused by Smith's insistence that Kissinger had offered him the five points as guarantees rather than a starting point helped to sink the Geneva talks. Even further, Kissinger had hoped that by offering Smith the insurance packages for whites contained in Annex C, Smith himself would have made these a bigger deal at Geneva. Kissinger had hoped that if Smith and the British managed to get the language of Annex C tabled during the talks, it would help move the negotiations in ways that would guarantee protections of land and pensions to whites, making them more accepting of a transition to majority rule. Kissinger, who did not attend the Geneva talks, was later disappointed that Annex C was not tabled by Smith.

The British, however, were more than happy to not have Annex C brought into the negotiations at Geneva. They had been incensed when they found out Kissinger had presented Annex C to the South Africans and Rhodesians as an Anglo-American position. They told Kissinger that since the document had not received Cabinet approval, they were not able to support it. The main reason for their objection was that Annex C went too far, in their opinion, in terms of Britain's responsibility for the transitional government. What will be shown in this chapter is that the Callaghan government was trying its best to avoid any commitment to a traditional decolonization role in Rhodesia. Kissinger and Nyerere, for their part, wanted the British to accept that role in terms of hosting a Lancaster House constitutional conference and appointing a British governor with powers to oversee the transition and election. This was the main tension between Nyerere and the British, and Kissinger and the British.

While all of these bilateral disagreements added to the failure of the Geneva talks, this chapter will also look at the major swing in the Zimbabwean nationalist leadership momentum caused by the Geneva talks. As the last chapter showed, Kissinger and others were depending on Nyerere and Kaunda to present a unified Zimbabwean leadership at the Geneva conference. This was again thought to be a safeguard against the problems with split loyalties in the Angolan conflict. The British and Kaunda were more than willing to push for Nkomo as the leader of this new united front. However, Nyerere and Machel were not convinced that Nkomo's Soviet-supported military wing was capable of taking the leading role in the fighting, given Nyerere's and Machel's support for the Chinese-backed ZANLA military. The problem was the uncertain relationship between the military and political leadership in ZANLA and ZANU. The destructiveness of the Nhari rebellion, especially the killing of many accused plotters, and Chitepo's assassination, meant that there was no clear ZANU leader in early 1976.

Into this leadership void entered Robert Mugabe, who had done what he could to show that he was distant from Ndabaningi Sithole and Abel Muzorewa, the two leaders who had tried to work within the Lusaka Accords' new umbrella African National Council. The ZANU leadership problem was further complicated by Nyerere's and Machel's attempt to reduce the internal violence and schisms in ZANLA by forming the "Third Force," the ZIPA, led by younger military leaders such as Wilfred Mhanda (whose war name was Dzino Machingura) and others. The problem for Nyerere was that while he was impressed with the military achievements of ZIPA, he was not so confident about the ability of this younger generation in ZIPA to represent themselves diplomatically at Geneva. Nyerere was interested in finding a way to check Nkomo's ability to negotiate directly with Smith and the British. The failures of the détente negotiations in 1974–75 had left Nyerere with the impression that Nkomo would break with the others and negotiate a direct path to majority rule with Smith. He also knew that Kenneth Kaunda in Zambia was pushing this scenario on the British and Americans, and so he needed a strong partner in the PF. This chapter will therefore explore how Mugabe took full advantage of the opportunities the Geneva talks presented him.

Before looking at Geneva, it is worth considering an interesting encounter between Kissinger and China's foreign minister, Chiao Kuan-hua [Qiao Guanhua], on October 8, 1976, at the office of the People's Republic of China's mission to the United Nations. The two discussed a number of topics, including US policy toward Angola and Rhodesia. Chiao stated his reservations about the future success of US policy in Rhodesia: "We have our doubts that you will reach your objective." Kissinger responded by stating that the United States had "two objectives in Africa. One is the liberation of black Africa. The other is to prevent Soviet intervention of a direct or indirect kind." Chiao replied, "Just not opposing liberation movements is not enough," to which Kissinger responded, "We are supporting them." "I have doubts that you are. You are not thoroughgoing, speaking quite frankly," Chiao countered. Kissinger asked what would constitute a more "thoroughgoing" strategy, and Chiao replied, "You should support the demands of the blacks." Kissinger pressed back, saying the United States was supporting their demands, but Chiao demurred, saying "the procedures you are adopting in Zimbabwe won't achieve their aim."

Kissinger then summarized US policy toward Rhodesia, which he described as a response to two different scenarios. "One is straight armed struggle which would bring in outside forces and add to the credit of those outside forces. If this were to occur, we could not resist those outside forces because we could not go to the support of white regimes against blacks." The alternative, which Kissinger said the United States was trying to achieve, was to "bring together the black forces of Mugabe, Muzorewa, and Nkomo in one black government that we can support to resist the intervention of outside forces. I consider Smith's position only the opening move."[2] Chiao again replied, "You can try, but we have our doubts." China's ambassador to the UN, Huang Hun, suggested Kissinger look carefully at the attitudes of the five Frontline States. "If you do not (satisfy them), they will be forced to accept Soviet assistance." Kissinger said the United States was doing this and believed the United States had the support of four of the five Frontline State presidents, with Angola being the only one that could not be counted on. Chiao again warned Kissinger that US efforts were "only half measures," and although the United States would "keep on trying ... you may find that the result is the opposite of what you expect. You may end up angering the blacks." Chiao and Kissinger went back and forth over the relative potential an interim government strategy might have for producing favorable results to keep the Soviets and Cubans out of Rhodesia. Kissinger reiterated that he was "hopeful that Mugabe, Muzorewa, and Nkomo are going to join forces." Chiao replied "We will have to see. We have our reservations." Kissinger responded "I see you have no better strategy," to which Chiao replied, "It is your problem." Kissinger went on to remind Chiao, "It is more than our problem. I remember in November 1973 when Premier Chou spoke to me regarding the need for global equilibrium to prevent Soviet expansion."[3]

What is interesting about this exchange, apart from Chiao's pessimistic view of US strategy in the region, is the extent to which Mugabe's name

---

[2] Memorandum of Conversation, Chiao Kuan-hua and Secretary Kissinger, October 8, 1976, PRC Mission to the United Nations, Document 00429, DNSA.
[3] Ibid.

had now entered Kissinger's vocabulary when discussing Rhodesia, even with the Chinese. In part, this may have been because of Chinese support for ZANLA, which could have led to Kissinger emphasizing Mugabe's importance. Chiao's diplomatic warning to Kissinger over his new southern African policy did express something Kissinger and the Anglo-Americans were not completely in touch with – that is, given Chinese support of ZANLA and Soviet support for ZIPRA, there was still not sufficient pressure on either Nkomo and Mugabe to negotiate seriously with the British and Rhodesians in 1976. Importantly, there were not sufficient ways to force the two militaries to cooperate given their outside sources of weapons. Nyerere and the other Frontline State presidents would try to squeeze the two in this way using the OAU Liberation Committee, but it was never enough to force unity.

Planning for Geneva

Once the invitations to attend the Geneva conference had been extended to Nkomo, Muzorewa, and Mugabe, questions arose regarding who else should attend, how many people the British would pay expenses for in each delegation, and the how long it would take to prepare and arrive for the conference. One issue – Mugabe's claim that he would not attend the Geneva conference if Sithole was invited – was resolved quickly. British diplomat Mervyn Brown talked with Nyerere on October 16 where he obtained Nyerere's assurance that Mugabe would attend and added that he still thought they should invite Sithole. Dennis Grennan, who was also in the meeting, asked Nyerere if "Mugabe's worry was that he would be disowned by ZIPA." Nyerere's response revealed the continued uncertainties over who was really representing ZIPA at the time: "Nyerere agreed that Mugabe did not control ZIPA, although he pretended that he did, and therefore we should not over-estimate him." Grennan reported that Nyerere "went on to imply that it would not matter greatly if ZIPA were not represented at Geneva. The Five Presidents would back a solution, not individual leaders. Africa would judge the conference by its results, and [if] these were satisfactory, i.e. achieving a genuine transfer of power, then ZIPA would be powerless to oppose it."[4]

---

[4] Brown from Dar es Salaam to FCO (telno 432), October 16, 1976, "YR Tel no 289: Rhodesia Conference," item 230, FCO36/1845, BNA.

Nyerere's comment revealed his frustrations with the Zimbabwean leadership over many years. He certainly knew enough of their history to remain apprehensive about their ability to deliver a united front at Geneva.

An important issue to resolve before the Geneva talks began was the status of those ZANU leaders arrested in Zambia over the assassination of Chitepo. Information from Botswana suggested that "the question of [the] release of detainees was a very serious one for Mugabe. According to Botswana Government's information ZIPA, who controlled him, would not let Mugabe attend [the] conference if certain of detainees were not released."[5] The leader who did the most to help free the ZANU leaders was apparently Nkomo, since Mugabe had little contact with the Zambians at this time and was, in any case, on bad terms with President Kaunda after criticizing his handling of the Chitepo murder investigation. Nkomo met with American Ambassador Stephen Low in Lusaka on October 14, 1976, where he gave the Americans and British the impression he was in control of the situation. Reportedly, Nkomo was optimistic that he and Mugabe would work as a team at Geneva, and that "he and Mugabe had decided to make two or three places available to Muzorewa within their delegations." Nkomo thought Bishop Muzorewa would accept, or face "essentially being frozen out of the meaningful conversation."

Nkomo spoke confidently of handling the issue of the ZANU prisoners still held in Zambia, telling Ambassador Low that he personally would "'take care' of the problem of the imprisoned Karanga," adding that "it would not be possible to get those released who had been formally charged (i.e. Tongogara), but four others whom Mugabe considered important would be made available." Nkomo planned to speak with the prisoners personally, "and he had informed Mugabe of this." Low was impressed by Nkomo's intervention on behalf of Mugabe's delegation and commented, "If Nkomo can indeed 'take care of' the Karanga problem, he will have established a basis for leadership of the nationalist movement beyond his own ZAPU organization."[6] That was likely Nkomo's desired impression, to

[5] Emery from Gaborone to FCO (telno 767), October 16, 1976, "Rhodesia Conference," item 241, FCO36/1845, BNA.

[6] Lusaka to Secretary of State, "Meeting with Nkomo," 1976Lusaka02781, October 15, 1976, Central Foreign Policy Files, 1973–1976, RG 59, General Records of the Department of State, USNA.

show he was in control, but as the Geneva conference unfolded, this initial act of leadership within the PF would eventually help Mugabe's prestige more than that of Nkomo.

Nyerere and Callaghan Debate the Race State Goals of Geneva

Tanzanian president Julius Nyerere wrote to James Callaghan, the British prime minister, on 31 October, explaining his concerns for the Geneva conference. The first point Nyerere made was to reiterate previous protests he and the Frontline State presidents had lodged with Prime Minister Callaghan about the Britain's selection of their UN ambassador, Ivor Richard, as chair of the Geneva conference. Nyerere stressed that they were not complaining about Richard personally, but that when Ian Smith first offered to host a conference in Rhodesia with himself as chairman, the Frontline State presidents had protested and refused, and then Britain had offered to host the conference. Nyerere explained: "The African states have all the time been emphasizing Britain's responsibility for decolonisation. Our desire that a British Minister should take the chair at the conference was a reflection of the same attitude: we wanted a Minister as a symbol of Britain's full commitment to getting the Rhodesian question finally solved."[7]

Nyerere's main point, however, was to emphasize that the Frontline State presidents "cannot support a white minority government which happens to have black faces in it." He wanted to make sure he and Callaghan were in "full agreement" over this point. Nyerere argued, "After the experiences of the last fifteen years or so, I am afraid race cannot be regarded as irrelevant: I wish it could. Unfortunately, we now have to go further and say that power in the transition has to be in the hands of an African-dominated government." Nyerere asked rhetorically if he and Callaghan agreed on this point.[8] Nyerere then closed his letter by challenging Callaghan's own statement that there is "no practical prospect of Britain assuming its colonial responsibility." Nyerere stated in his usual blunt style: "Jim, you have the responsibility, you can't run away from it. Rhodesia is not an independent

---

[7] Brown Dar es Salaam to FCO (telno 449), November 1, 1976, "Rhodesia Conference" ("Text of Further Letter to Prime Minister from President Nyerere, Delivered to Me [Brown] This Evening (31 Oct)"), item 437, FCO36/1848, BNA.
[8] Ibid.

country – Britain has herself been saying this in the United Nations and elsewhere ever since 1965." Nyerere's letter was received as the conference had begun, and his concerns about Britain's lack of commitment to taking the lead as the transitional power in Rhodesia would prove warranted.

Callaghan responded to Nyerere's letter on November 9, 1976. In his response, he continued his avoidance of committing his government to taking on the key role in the decolonization of Rhodesia. In doing so, he resorted to a common theme of British diplomacy in Rhodesia: racial fears of what a future African "race state" might hold. Callaghan identified the mutual goal of Britain and Tanzania, writing "it is common ground between us that members of the racist minority cannot be allowed, during the interim period, to frustrate the transition to independence under majority rule." However, Callaghan pushed back on the issue of race in terms of a lack of protection for those whites who would stay on. "It would be tragic if the African nationalists let him [Smith] off the hook by insisting on conditions which the sensible Europeans would regard as unacceptable and unworkable." He argued, "This would not prevent Zimbabwe eventually reaching majority rule, but it would be by the path of blood and economic destruction, rather than by the peaceful means that you and I wish to see." He also said, "I however, do not want to see, and I hope you would not either, a repetition of the mass exodus of the whites which occurred in Mozambique." Callaghan also skirted the issue of direct British involvement, saying that although there were a number of ways Britain could help, he was "deliberately confining [himself] to a broad statement of principle rather than enter into details." Callaghan concludes that such a strategy would help the Geneva talks proceed.[9] Nyerere wrote to Callaghan again on November 10, reiterating his main concern for the conference: "If there is no such transfer of effective power from the minority, we cannot be expected to support the new Government for it would still be a minority government with Black

---

[9] Fm Crosland FCO to Dar es Salaam, "Text of letter from the Prime Minister to President Nyerere," November 9, 1976, item 465, FCO36/1848, BNA. See also: Miles from Lusaka to FCO (telno 2678), November 9, 1976, "Rhodesia Conference," item 467, FCO36/1848, BNA; Brown from Dar es Salaam to FCO (telno 464), November 10, 1976 "Your Tel no 303: Rhodesia Conference," item 468, FCO36/1848, BNA.

African faces. Such a Government would not have the power to end the war, which would then continue with full O.A.U. support."[10]

Once the conference began, Mugabe and Nkomo worked as a team in the negotiations, while Bishop Muzorewa and Reverend Sithole were left on their own. The first major complaint from the PF was that Ivor Richard, as UN Ambassador for Britain, was not of ministerial status, and therefore did not have the legal authority to negotiate the decolonization process for Britain. This protest held up opening day ceremonies even further, and British foreign secretary Anthony Crosland was forced to send a message directly to the PF assuring them that Richard had authority to lead the conference. He was careful, however, to stop short of saying that Richard had authority to grant independence. Crosland's letter to Nkomo and Mugabe assured them that Richard was vested with authority by the Cabinet to "represent" the British government at the conference and to "speak for" that government. "The British government is the government which has constitutional responsibility for Rhodesia. In the name of the British Government I can tell you that we embark on this conference with the clear intention that it should be the beginning of the decolonization process."[11] Separately, Crosland also gave Richard specific instructions the day before the opening of the conference to avoid any commitment on the Britain's part to invest their authority in the process. "You should also take every opportunity, both in public and private, to re-iterate that Rhodesia is not a normal colony and the 'colonial power' does not have 'colonial responsibilities' in the traditional sense." Crosland instructed Richard to include this point in his opening statement.[12]

The debate over the independence date was the only substantive topic actually debated at Geneva, as talks between the principals broke down on this issue and precipitated Smith's departure from the talks. Given that Smith insisted on working from the five points he had agreed upon with Kissinger in September, the inability of Ambassador

[10] President Nyerere to Prime Minister Callaghan, October 14, 1976, attached to item 374, FCO36/1847, BNA.

[11] Bottomley from UKMIS Geneva to FCO (telno 368), October 28, 1976, "Following from Richard My Telno 366," item 44, FCO36/1802, BNA.

[12] Crosland to Richard (UKMIS Geneva) (telno 231) October 27, 1976 "Your Telnos 343 and (Not to all) 347: Rhodesia Conference," item 20, FCO36/1802, BNA.

Richard to support the five points as the basis of the Geneva talks allowed Smith an "out" from the conference. Smith left the conference and returned to Salisbury on November 4, 1976, two days after President Ford was defeated by Jimmy Carter in the US presidential election. As far as Smith was concerned, Kissinger's ability to guarantee the promises he had made in Pretoria were no longer viable.[13]

A good example of how the debate went at Geneva comes from a discussion among the heads of delegations on November 2. Richard called the meeting to have a "round-table discussion" about fixing the date of independence. The first of the "five points" that Smith insisted as the basis of negotiations stated that "Rhodesia agrees to majority rule within two years." Nkomo was the first to speak, making the point that "all the delegates at the conference agreed that their purpose was to work out ways to transfer power. Zimbabwe's independence had already been unduly delayed." He stressed that the PF "felt strongly that it was desirable to fix the date before going any further in discussion; and all Zimbabweans were waiting for a date to be fixed." Mugabe agreed with Nkomo, adding that "before discussing any proposals for the transfer of power it was necessary to have a date so they could be put into perspective and a programme drawn up."

Ian Smith's first comment demonstrated his frustrations, as he "pointed out that little progress had been made in the last two weeks." Sithole then gave a history lesson on the question of majority rule in Rhodesia, saying that "it was first raised in 1890." Ian Smith then interjected that the first of the five points had already fixed a date. "Independence should come two years hence." Sithole quickly corrected this, saying, "If he read the five points correctly independence should come within two years." Mugabe then questioned the authority of Smith's claim about the five points being an accepted document by all parties at the conference. Smith, speaking to Richard rather than Mugabe, asked "whether the Chairman had not communicated the five points to the leaders of the delegations." Richard claimed that he had,

---

[13] Smith would later tell political scientist Stephen Stedman, in a 1987 interview, that Kissinger had inferred to Smith "that if there was a new [US] government in November, Rhodesia's position would worsen." Stedman goes on to say that Ken Flower, an important Rhodesian intelligence officer, also interviewed by Stedman in 1987, "maintains that Kissinger's words were stronger: 'if the Republicans are not returned to office in November, the deal is off.'" Stephen J. Stedman, *Peacemaking in Civil War: International Mediation in Zimbabwe, 1974–1980* (Boulder, CO: Lynne Rienner Publishers, 1990), 98.

but Nkomo then "pointed out that the leaders had not come to the conference to discuss the five points." Muzorewa also said he did not take the five points as a "formal document but more like a note of conversation." Nkomo agreed and then suggested that "one year was surely 'within two years.'" Nkomo, Mugabe, and Muzorewa are all recorded as saying that "the period should be 12 months."[14]

At this point, Smith executed a pivot, a technique for which he was well known. He used the nationalists' refusal to accept the five points as the basis for the negotiations as his chance to evade and excused himself from the process. Historian Jamie Miller sums up Smith's trademark negotiating technique well: "redefining others' statements as categorical assurances and then tenaciously using these to allege betrayal on the other party's part regardless of context or subsequent events."[15] As the British and Frontline State presidents had warned Kissinger earlier in the year, Smith was "hard to pin down," and a day before the US election results were known, he was establishing the springboard for his exit. Smith responded to criticisms that the five points, and specifically point one on the timing of independence, "was taken from what he understood to be an Anglo/American agreement which had been put to him by Dr. Kissinger at their meeting." He went on to say that he would "in fact like to alter it.": "Two years was too short. But he was abiding by the contract that he had made. However, if there were to be a change from the agreed position of the two years, this would free him from his contract."[16] Immediately, Nkomo and Mugabe each asked what this contract was and with whom it had been agreed. The two PF leaders knew they could pressure Chairman Richard to distance his own position from what Kissinger had promised to Smith in September.

Smith and Richard then disagreed on the five points, with Richard asserting the familiar British response that "the [five] points were a basis for discussion at the conference." Mugabe jumped in, asking Richard "if he would confirm that the British Government was not a party to the agreement." According to the minutes of the meeting, the Chairman did so. Smith then stated that he "could not agree with what

---

[14] "Meeting of Heads of Delegations at the Palais des Nations on 2 November at 3:30 p.m.," November 2, 1976, item 88, FCO36/1803, BNA.

[15] Jamie Miller, *An African Volk: The Apartheid Regime and Its Search for Survival* (Oxford University Press, 2016) 152.

[16] "Meeting of Heads of Delegations at the Palais des Nations on 2 November at 3:30 p.m.," November 2, 1976, item 88, FCO36/1803, BNA.

the Chairman had said." Here, Smith summarized the conditions which others have identified as Kissinger's promises to Smith: "At his meeting with Dr. Kissinger he [Smith] had been satisfied that the latter was speaking on behalf of the American and British Governments and that he had consulted the four Black Presidents who had, in turn, cleared their lines with the Nationalist leaders." Here, Smith put the blame on Kissinger, telling Richard, "Perhaps he had been misled; but he himself had been clear and consistent throughout."[17]

Such interactions at Geneva demonstrate how well the nationalist leaders took advantage of both Smith's intransigence and his pattern of falling back on a position that presented him as a victim of another power's deceptiveness. Smith tried again to get Richard to accept his position as the starting point for negotiations, but once more Richard chose to agree with the nationalists. "The Chairman told Mr. Smith that he was asking too much for the delegates to be bound by an agreement on which they had not been consulted." The discussion then returned to a possible date of independence. Smith's party stuck to their original two years or more, while the nationalists were supportive of one year to eighteen months.[18]

Mugabe, Nkomo, and the Americans at Geneva

While the British were somewhat more familiar with Mugabe since the new generation of British diplomats first met with him in Mozambique in 1975, the Americans were much less familiar with him. The first American to meet with Mugabe at the Geneva conference was Frank Wisner Jr., a key American diplomat present in Geneva for the first month of the talks. Wisner reported he had gone to meet Mugabe in his hotel room on October 27 and that Mugabe, along with two of his aides "was tense and his approach both wary and intensive." Mugabe accused Wisner and the Americans of keeping Kissinger's plan a secret from him and sharing it only with Smith. This was a legitimate complaint. The Frontline State presidents had accused the Americans of a double standard in working out a plan first with Smith, and then presenting it as the basis for the negotiations at Geneva without the

---

[17] "Meeting of Heads of Delegations at the Palais des Nations on 2 November at 3:30 p.m.," November 2, 1976, item 88, FCO36/1803, BNA.

[18] Ibid.

African nationalist knowing exactly what Kissinger had offered Smith in exchange for Smith's September 24 speech accepting "majority rule." Wisner told Mugabe that the United States had given a copy to the British who would then make it available to conference participants.

Mugabe told Wisner that he was "suspicious of our motives" and asked why the United States "had never met with him" in preparation for the conference. Wisner explained that the United States relied on the Frontline State presidents, as designated by the OAU, to "find a Zimbabwe solution." Wisner then asked Mugabe to speak with him privately, and the two of them left Mugabe's advisors in the room and went to a corner to speak candidly. Wisner wrote: "During our conversation which was out of the earshot of his compatriots, Mugabe assured me that he had come to Geneva with a serious purpose and was intent on getting a settlement. Once we returned to the company of his colleagues he began his hard line again urging us to 'pressurize the British to pressurize Smith'."[19]

Mugabe had also impressed the US assistant secretary of state for African affairs, William E. Schaufele Jr., at a meeting on November 2, 1976. Schaufele's account of their encounter is reminiscent of the reports US diplomats sent back to Washington after meetings with Mugabe in the early 1960s. Schaufele related: "In what proved to be my most interesting and useful meeting with the nationalists, I spent almost an hour on Nov 2 with Robert Mugabe. Mugabe was relaxed and thoughtful. His questions were incisive." Schaufele believed the Americans were making progress with Mugabe, stating how, "[c]ompared to Wisner's meeting, Mugabe has overcome his initial reservations about the role we have played in the Rhodesian settlement."[20]

Mugabe had once again demonstrated his diplomatic skills. Schaufele had made it clear to Mugabe "that if the conference failed we [the United States] would not be able to continue in our role but if violence led to foreign intervention from outside Africa the U.S. could

---

[19] US Mission Geneva to Sec State Washington for Schaufele from Wisner "Rhodesian Conference; Meeting with Mugabe," 1976Geneva08443, Central Foreign Policy Files, 1973–1976, RG 59, General Records of the Department of State, USNA.

[20] Schaufele to State, "Rhodesian Conference: Nov 2 meeting with Robert Mugabe," 1976GENEVA064852, Central Foreign Policy Files, 1973–1976, RG 59, General Records of the Department of State, USNA.

not accept it." Mugabe replied by telling Schaufele how "gratifying" it was to have the United States involved after years in which "Britain had failed to assume its responsibilities as a colonial power and move effectively to 'decolonize Rhodesia'." Mugabe went on to assure Schaufele "that neither he nor his associates enjoyed military action. 'We are not a warlike people but nationalists were forced to take up arms because of Britain's failures and the inability of the West to do much more than pass 'pious resolutions'." Mugabe reassured Schaufele that the PF had no intention of creating Soviet or Chinese puppet states: "Of course the nationalists had accepted arms from Russia and China but 'we are not committed to their policies nor prepared to subject ourselves to them', he said."[21]

Schaufele asked Mugabe how cooperation was going among nationalists. Mugabe described his relationship with Nkomo as "particularly good and deepening." He said, "Muzorewa wishes to work with him and Mugabe can't ignore this request since much of internal ZANU is committed to Muzorewa's ANC." He also said that Muzorewa and Nkomo were unlikely to form an alliance because of "Muzorewa's personal difficulties with Nkomo." In closing, "Mugabe indicated he would like to stay in close touch" and urged that the United States "understand he and his ZANU allies were not tools of Soviet power."[22] The American diplomats were left with an impression of Mugabe as a leader grateful for US intervention into the diplomatic stalemate, which he blamed on the British.

A third meeting occurred on November 17 between Mugabe and John E. Reinhardt, an African-American diplomat who served as US Ambassador to Nigeria from 1971–75 and attended Geneva as US undersecretary for public affairs in the Ford Administration. Reinhardt reported that Mugabe's "comportment was much tougher than had been the case in his meetings with Schaufele and Wisner."[23] Reinhardt described Mugabe as "stubborn, argumentative and occasionally unpleasant." Mugabe was accompanied by his close adviser Mukudzei Mudzi and ZANU's US representative, Tapson Mawere. Mawere complained to Reinhardt about the lack of contact between

[21] Ibid.   [22] Ibid.
[23] From Geneva to State, "Rhodesia Conference: November 17 Meetings with Muzorewa, Sithole and Mugabe," November 17, 1976, 1976GENEVA0918, Central Foreign Policy Files, 1973–1976, RG 59, General Records of the Department of State, USNA.

Kissinger and Mugabe leading up to Geneva, given that Kissinger had met with Nkomo twice before the conference. He was upset that Kissinger reportedly had "never heard of Mugabe." Mawere complained that the United States was denying "ZANU students" scholarships to American universities, and Mugabe suggested that the United States "discriminated against ZANU."

Ambassador Reinhardt asked Mugabe, "How much room there was for compromise between the position he was advancing and those of the other parties at the conference?" Mugabe "laughed and indicated that he did not think there was much." Reinhardt reported that he "found the meeting with Mugabe most disappointing and was struck by his stern intransigence," adding that "[Ivor] Richard's term 'wild men' seemed today to fit comrade Mugabe and his group well."[24] Perhaps the chronology of these meetings helps explain why Mugabe became increasingly less diplomatic by mid-November. The US presidential elections had been decided. Kissinger was no longer relevant, and Ian Smith had left Geneva immediately after learning Ford had lost. Additionally, Mugabe was now on much firmer ground with the Frontline State presidents given his growing leadership role within ZANU and the PF by the end of the Geneva talks.

One reason for Mugabe's increased confidence was the legitimation he had received from the former ZANU military leaders who had been released from Zambian jails to come to Geneva. The reason for his continued intransigence, however, was in part the lack of confidence he had in his own leadership role over ZANLA and ZIPA. Unwittingly, the Frontline State presidents, the British, and the Americans, and even Joshua Nkomo, had played a role in asserting Mugabe's leadership role over ZIPA. After the conference began and Tongogara did, in fact, appear in Geneva to support Mugabe, Edward Ndlovu, Nkomo's confidant and member of the ZAPU Geneva delegation, would tell the Americans that it was Nkomo "and no one else – who convinced Kaunda to release Tongogara and his associates." Ndlovu also told the Americans, "Mugabe is not in charge. The ZANU central committee has only agreed to let him act as the conference spokesman."[25]

---

24 Ibid.
25 Geneva to Am Embassy London, "Rhodesia Conference: November 9 Meetings with the Nationalists," November 10, 1976, 1976Geneva276753, Central Foreign Policy Files, 1973–1976, RG 59, General Records of the Department of State, USNA. Luise White describes the intrigue and speculation as to why

Ambassador Reinhardt would also meet with the Rhodesian Front delegation on November 18 at the Hotel du Rhone. The account of the meeting prepared by the Rhodesians is an interesting example of an African-American diplomat meeting, along with Frank Wisner, with P. K. van der Byl, H. G. Squires, and J. F. Gaylard. All three of the Rhodesian representatives were Rhodesian Front hardliners left in Geneva by Smith after he had already returned to Salisbury. Predictably, the Rhodesian diplomats complained about Richard and the lengthy negotiations over the independence date. Van der Byl praised Kissinger's role, calling it "impeccable." The biggest complaint against the British was their acceptance of a future role in Rhodesia. Squires said that "Rhodesia had never been under British control and this was a source of considerable national pride." Van der Byl emphasized the importance of keeping the defense and security ministries under "white control." He argued this was "because of the crucial importance of the black policemen and soldiers." Van der Byl used the Congolese example to support his argument. "He reminded Mr. Reinhardt of the chaos that had occurred in the Congo when effective control of the *Force Publique* had been lost." Van der Byl asserted that if the Rhodesians were "pressurized into making further concessions," there would be a backlash from whites and also "there would be a major backlash from policemen, soldiers, and civil servants."[26]

Reinhardt also responded to questions from the Rhodesians about American domestic politics. Squires asked him for his view of a point of view, based on comments by the influential congressional representative Charles Diggs, who "had forecast a change of attitude on the part of the United States Government towards Africa because in several key

Nkomo assisted Mugabe in gaining the release of Tongogara and the others held for the murder of Chitepo. See Luise White, *The Assassination of Herbert Chitepo: Texts and Politics in Zimbabwe.* (Indiana University Press, 2003), 89–90. David Moore suggests that the British played a key role in convincing the Zambian courts to free these ZANU leaders, and Wilf Mhanda argues that ZIPA had been lobbying for the release of the ZANU/ZANLA leaders as well. See Wilfred Mhanda, *Dzino: Memories of a Freedom Fighter* (Harare: Weaver, 2011), 148–55.

[26] "Record of a Meeting at the Hotel du Rhone at 9:30 a.m. on Thursday, 18 November, 1976, Present: Mr. P. K. van der Byl, Mr. H. G. Squires, Mr. J. F Gaylard, Mr. Reinhardt, Mr. F. Wisner," Folder Geneva Conference Informal Meetings (American), Smith Papers, 4 005 (M).

states Carter had carried the day with the help of the negro vote." Ambassador Reinhardt replied that "he disagreed with this assessment but there were certain points beyond which any American administration could not go. He agreed that a political leader must take cognisance of trends in public opinion but he did not believe that the American policy would be very different after 20th January." That was the date when the Carter administration would come into power. Squires replied, "We would welcome the sort of down-to-earth assessment which the Americans made instead of the unrealistic thinking of the British."

At one point in the discussion, Reinhardt used the Cold war race state language by talking about "the blacks": "Mr. Reinhardt said that it should be clear to the blacks that this was their last opportunity. If they now deliberately chose the course of violence none of them would survive." This was a pretty harsh assessment of the situation. Squires agreed with Reinhardt, and then Gaylard continued by offering his view of Nkomo's political fortunes, describing how Nkomo's "stocks were high" when he was negotiating directly with Smith in 1975. "He was getting plenty of publicity and he appeared to be an effective leader." At Geneva, Gaylard added, Nkomo was "giving the impression of tagging along behind Mugabe and this was not enhancing his image among the Africans in Rhodesia."[27]

One question that troubled the Americans and British at Geneva was why Nkomo had partnered with Mugabe rather than Bishop Muzorewa. The previous chapters have shown why a Nkomo–Muzorewa alliance was a nonstarter, but still there were plenty of answers given to the Americans. Ian Smith had offered his own answer to this question, suggesting to Richard early in the Geneva Conference, on October 23, that Nkomo would not have wanted to partner with Mugabe, but thought Muzorewa was becoming too popular, so he needed to align with Mugabe to compete with Muzorewa's status inside Rhodesia.[28] Richard told Smith that "he hoped that one possible outcome would be a government led by Mr Nkomo and Bishop Muzorewa." Responding to this scenario, Smith "thought that the Bishop had greater popular

27   Ibid.
28   "Record of a Conversation between the Chairman of the Conference and the Rhodesian Prime Minister, Held at the Palais des Nations, Geneva, on 23 October at 11 a.m.," item 9, FCO36/1802, BNA.

support within Rhodesia than Mr Nkomo, though the latter was a more impressive personality with greater qualities of leadership."[29]

Post-Geneva International Diplomacy around Rhodesia and Zimbabwe

Summing up the Geneva conference in the January–February 1977 issue of the *Zimbabwe News*, ZANU's writers claimed that the calling of the conference by Britain was a "culmination of a series of behind-the-scenes imperialist maneuvers in their persistent bid to try and hijack the determined efforts and resolute prosecution of the armed struggle by the struggling masses of Zimbabwe, under, 'the leadership of their legitimate political movements which have formed the PF' of ZANU and ANC(Z)." The article continued: "Geneva was to be an internationally sponsored political fraud where the imperialists were to strip Smith and his racist thugs of only political power and reinvest this power in the hands of 'moderate and responsible' African puppets." The writers then offered ZANU as the only truly vanguard party who could defend the revolutionary character of the struggle. They claimed ZANU would avoid the problems that Lenin had predicted, that of the need to "smash the colonial institutions," as "[o]nly the PF delegation stood for the defence of the gains of the workers and peasants of Zimbabwe, and their determination to establish a truly free, democratic, socialist republic."[30]

Such revolutionary rhetoric somewhat failed to align with the practical experiences of the ZANU and ZIPA representatives at Geneva. Fay Chung has described the problems ZANU representatives encountered in their accommodation arrangements and living conditions.[31] From the beginning, both ZAPU and ZANU argued that the living expense stipends were insufficient given the high cost of hotels in Geneva. There were many offers to help the nationalists pay for their hotels, mostly from Tiny Rowland of Lonrho, the Swedish Government, and Zaire's Mobutu. In the end, the ZANU delegation was bailed out, not so much by these supportive capitalists and western

---

[29] Ibid.
[30] "Geneva Conference on Zimbabwe" and "Lessons of the Conference," *Zimbabwe News*, vol. 9, no. 2, January–February 1977, Maputo, 6–9.
[31] Fay Chung, *Re-living the Second Chimurenga: Memories from the Liberation Struggle in Zimbabwe* (Uppsala, Sweden: Nordic Africa Institute 2006), 165.

governments, but by the fire that destroyed Rex Nhongo's room and some adjacent rooms. Blessing-Miles Tendi, in his biography of Solomon Mujuru, indicates that both Tekere and Mugabe admit that they blamed the fire on the Rhodesians, "to make the Geneva talks even more intractable, but in actuality, Nhongo had started the fire."[32]

British diplomats in Geneva visited the hotel manager after the delegation had left to make sure everything was settled. The manager explained that the delegation had left the hotel an unpaid bar and room service bill of 36,000 Swiss francs. According to the hotel's manager, he wasn't too worried about the outstanding bills because the insurance payment for the fire had more than covered what was owed. He even asked the British when the ZANU delegation might be back as he wanted to host them again. Apparently, their vanguardist tastes were good for business.[33]

Bishop Muzorewa, in fact, complained in a letter to Richard about the lack of progress at the conference and the excesses of some of the delegates. Writing on November 26, Muzorewa asked Richard to "remember that we have now spent over a month in Geneva either discussing the question of fixing a date for the independence of Zimbabwe or literally doing nothing." Muzorewa complained that a whole week had passed without any information from Richard "about the prospects of holding either a plenary session or bilateral meetings." Muzorewa also commented on the morality of the situation, with the delay in independence by a month, "while some people are wining, dining, bickering and dithering in expensive, luxurious and posh hotels of Geneva, a city in a free and independent Switzerland."[34]

[32] Blessing-Miles Tendi, *The Army and Politics in Zimbabwe: Mujuru, the Liberation Fighter and Kingmaker* (Cambridge University Press, 2020), 91.

[33] 36,000 Swiss francs was the equivalent of $37,000 or £28,000 in 1976. See D. A. Martson to Mr. Harrison and Mr. Laver, "Lonrho and the Geneva Conference," November 4, 1976, item 470, FCO36/1848; Crosland to Oslo (telno 180), November 8, 1976, "Your telno 260 of 4 November," item 461, FCO36/1848, BNA; R. H. J. Ashton to J. N. Allan, "Mugabe Delegation and the Hotel Royal," December 29, 1976 item 490, FCO36/1848, BNA; J. N. Allan to M. O'D. B. Alexander, "Rhodesia Conference: Call on Swiss Mission on 17 December," December 21, 1976, item 491, FCO36/1848, BNA; Bottomley UK Mission Geneva to FCO (telno 521), December 26, 1976, "Fire in Hotel," item 282, FCO36/1808, BNA.

[34] R. J. Spencer, "Call on Bishop Muzorewa," November 26, 1976 (letter attached is addressed to Ivor Richard from Bishop Muzorewa), item 370, FCO36/1808, BNA.

Toward the end of the conference, Muzorewa and Sithole had reasons to be frustrated by some disturbing developments for their own positions as leaders. Some members of Muzorewa's United African National Council had joined the PF during the conference, and it was obvious to them that the British and Americans were more concerned with the PF's point of view than those of Muzorewa or Sithole. A memo from Robin Byatt indicated that Frank Wisner had reported to him a conversation between Botswana's Foreign Minister Archibald Mogwe and Bishop Muzorewa on November 26, where Mogwe "urged on the Bishop that the time had come when he must decide to let bygones be bygones and make his peace with Nkomo." According to Wisner, Muzorewa's reply to Mogwe was "that he had approached Nkomo for that purpose twice during the last ten days and had been rebuffed on each occasion. However, the Bishop indicated that he was prepared to turn a third cheek."[35]

While the hope of Muzorewa working with Nkomo failed to take root at Geneva, the Frontline State presidents and the PF had put forth serious claims that Smith would not move forward with realistic negotiations unless the British were willing to exert their authority into the process. Frank Wisner recounts a meeting on November 29 with Ambassador Richard, where Reinhardt recounted what he had heard from President Kaunda. "The latter [Kaunda] felt himself no longer bound by the five points. He had urged that Dr. Kissinger should persuade the British Government to appoint a Governor General." Richard still held out against the idea of the British taking a more direct role. "Richard said that it was just conceivable that Ministers might agree to our playing a balancing role, but we could not undertake executive responsibility in the traditional way."[36]

By the end of the conference, Zambia's Mark Chona was pushing for an agreement allowing the PF to take power before elections, which would have been to Nkomo's advantage. Britain's Robin Byatt wrote to the FCO that Frank Wisner had approached him at Geneva to see if he agreed with his recommendation to not accept Chona's proposal. According to Byatt, Chona had told Wisner that "the time had come for the Americans to decide that their own best interests lay in going along

[35] R. A. C. Byatt to Sir A. Duff, "Relations between Muzorewa and Nkomo," November 29, 1976, item 372, FCO36/1808, BNA.

[36] J. R. Young, "Note for the Record Call by Mr. Wisner," November 29, 1976, item 373, FCO36/1808, BNA.

with a PF dominated government, which might well endure beyond independence if one dispensed with elections, since this was the only basis on which the front-line Presidents could guarantee to deliver the freedom fighters." This is an interesting claim, and while it may have been Chona's opinion in late 1976, it would not be a unified position of the Frontline State presidents as the war continued. A particular stumbling block for them was that "Chona claims to see Nkomo as the senior partner and Mugabe as the junior partner in such a government." Byatt agreed with Wisner's view that he should not recommend what Chona had proposed to the State Department. Byatt added, "To indicate any interest in Chona's ideas at this juncture would tend to pull the rug from the under the conference." Byatt continued, "One of the conclusions Wisner draws from Chona's comments is that the Zambians attached prime importance to maintain the cohesion of the front-line Presidents. They and Botswana favour Nkomo, while Nyerere and Machel prefer Mugabe or ZIPA. Therefore the front-line alliance can only be maintained by keeping the PF together."[37]

British Views of Nkomo and Mugabe at Geneva

While the Americans enquired about the relative strengths of the possible leadership alliances, the FCO's Rhodesia Office's Rosemary Spencer delivered a substantive report on the topic in a paper dated November 22. Spencer and her colleagues provided an analysis of the motivations of the four main Zimbabwean nationalists. Her interpretation is guided by the typical fascination in the FCO with ethnic divisions, or what was then referred to as "tribalism," but the report offers useful insights into FCO thinking on the motivations of Nkomo, in particular, for entering into the PF alliance.[38] On Nkomo, Spencer's paper states: "He sees himself as the grand old man of Zimbabwe nationalist politics, with a presumptive right to the top political position in an independent Zimbabwe. He is leader of the best-run political

[37] R. A. C. Byatt to Rm Mansfield, "Chona's Discussions with Mr. Wisner," December 1, 1976, item 375, FCO36/1808, BNA.

[38] The report lists the tribal affiliations of the nationalist leaders as follows: "Joshua Nkomo, generally regarded as being Ndebele, but claimed by some to be Kalanga; Bishop Muzorewa, Shona/Manyika; Robert Mugabe, Shona/Zezeru; Ndabaningi Sithole, Shona/Ndau; Josiah Tongogara, Shona/Karanga; Rex Nhongo, Shona/probably Karanga." R. J. Spencer to J. C. Harrison, "The Nationalist Delegations," November 26, 1976, item 317, FCO 36/1807, BNA.

organisation inside Zimbabwe." The next point is that he is handi-capped by his ethnicity, in that "although his party executive are mainly Shona, his popular support is drawn from the Ndebele who make up 20 per cent of Rhodesia's population. (He has no Karanga following.)" The last point reflects the FCO's obsession with the Karanga. Spencer goes on to say that Nkomo's own guerrilla army only has "an estimated 200 trained cadres." She praises his delegation for being "solid and cohesive," and points out some "tough-minded" individuals, such as Jason Moyo, "who commands the respect of the all the guerrillas and is also known to have close links with the Russians."[39]

Spencer believed Nkomo wanted a settlement at Geneva, in part so he could "effectively neutralize the guerrillas based in Mozambique and Tanzania and could set up a transitional government which would give full rein to his superior political abilities – as he sees them – and his good party organisation."[40] She presumes Nkomo would like to be the leader of the transitional government, under the premise that he would then have an advantage in elections. Spencer labels the PF as "essen-tially a marriage of convenience which is privately opposed by many of his supporters." Although she recognizes that the PF was forced on Nkomo by the Frontline State presidents in order to facilitate the Geneva conference, Spencer also notes that the alliance presented "some opportunistic attraction for Nkomo himself, as it has given him a chance to demonstrate that he is prepared to take a tough line and thus to restore his credibility among the harder-line nationalists, which suffered as a result of his talks with Smith last year." Spencer also notes that Nkomo's image in the Western press as "a moderate" had added to the "widely" held perception that he has the backing of the British and the Americans. "He would no doubt like to believe that the alliance has brought the combined strength of the main guerrilla army and the ZAPU forces together behind himself and Mugabe." Spencer's report concludes by stating she did not believe Nkomo would be willing to split from Mugabe at the conference.

The report then turns to Mugabe, starting out with the ethnicity of his followers, who are identified as mostly Karanga, "though he himself

---

[39] R. J. Spencer to J. C. Harrison "The Nationalist Delegations," November 26, 1976, item 317, FCO36/1807, BNA.
[40] Ibid.

is half-Zezeru." The next point was hardly a ringing endorsement: "He has assumed the political representation of the guerrilla faction mainly because he is the only political figure to whom the majority of the guerrillas have not taken strong objection."[41] The report notes that Mugabe was not part of ZIPA, "and this indicates that he is not yet won the complete acceptance of the guerrillas." The pressure from the Frontline State presidents for Mugabe to join the PF was seen as an attempt to help Mugabe gain support inside Rhodesia, as he had very little at the time. "One of the aims of the front-line Presidents in promoting the formation of the PF was to combine Nkomo's political following with Mugabe's representation of the guerrillas, however tenuous." The new alliance was also recognized as helpful to Mugabe, because Nkomo was able to secure "the release of the ZANU detainees in Zambia and brought Zambian-based guerrillas under the joint control (at least nominally) of himself and Nkomo."[42]

The FCO's assessment of Mugabe's performance at the conference, echoing somewhat that of the Americans, saw Mugabe as "controlled" by his more radical advisors, and forced to take a more hard-line position. Spencer's report states: "But his [Mugabe's] performance at the conference does not indicate a man of depth or substance. He appears to be dominated by the wilder members of his delegation, notably Mudzi (who spent five years studying 'People's Law' in Leningrad) and Tekere." Spencer describes how, during the course of the conference, "Mugabe has shown himself increasingly shallow and little more than a prisoner of and spokesman for his group. He declines to attend any meetings unless at least some of his supporters are present." Spencer noted how "[o]n the rare occasions when we have seen him for a minute or two alone with Nkomo, he seemed agreeable and relaxed – quite different from the aggressively rude character he usually presents."[43] Spencer argued that at Geneva, ZANU seemed to want a settlement similar to the one FRELIMO achieved, where they could control the transitional government, the military, and the "disbanding of the Rhodesian army."[44] But if these conditions were not met, they were willing to return to the battlefield.

At this stage, in ethnic terms, the British saw Mugabe as the voice of the "Karanga," who, according to the report, "want an independent Zimbabwe with a Karanga-dominated Government which they feel

[41] Ibid.   [42] Ibid.   [43] Ibid.   [44] Ibid.

they have earned through their part in the guerrilla war."[45] Given this situation, the British were unsure what Mugabe would personally accept, suggesting that he "must have some doubts about his ability to continue to ride the Karanga tiger through the transitional period and into independence. His delegation is less disciplined, and his control of lieutenants less evident, than in the case of the other leaders."[46] By the end of November, the general assessment of the conference among the British was that there was little to no chance of getting all the nationalists to work together, and that the Mugabe faction of the PF was not interested in reaching an agreement that did not meet their demands for complete control of the transition.

African Leaders' Reading of Mugabe versus Nkomo

Commenting on a meeting with the Nigerian leadership in Lagos over Rhodesia in September 1976, American diplomats were a bit surprised that the new Nigerian leader, General Joseph Garba, couldn't remember Mugabe's name, and had to ask an aide, "Who's that third-force fellow we met?"[47] While the exchange points to the relative obscurity of Mugabe within some African diplomatic circles before the Geneva talks, it also shows that Mugabe had managed to circulate his case among key Commonwealth and OAU members prior to Geneva. As Wilf Mhanda remembered it, Nyerere used the term "Third Force" in order to avoid confusion about which faction was capable of receiving OAU Liberation Committee funding, and to stress the need for unity. ZIPA's military successes in early 1976, Mhanda argued, led to the acceptance of a merged ZANLA and ZIPRA command within ZIPA by mid-1976.[48] While ZIPA was making progress on the military front, Mugabe managed to consolidate his leadership over ZIPA through international meetings where he presented himself as the sole leader of ZIPA. But as Nyerere had indicated, Mugabe did not actually lead ZIPA at the Geneva conference, although the ZIPA leaders would

---

[45] Ibid.   [46] Ibid.

[47] Garba had only come to power three months earlier leading a coup against General Yakubu Gowan. American Embassy Lagos to American Embassy London, "Rowland-Duff Visit to Lagos," Document Number: 1976LAGOS10193, September 3, 1976, RG 59, USNA.

[48] Wilf Mhanda, "Chronological Developments Leading to the Geneva Conference," April 17, 2011. Personal communication with the author. See also Mhanda, *Dzino*.

endorse him as their political representative for the purposes of the conference.

Geneva also provided Mugabe the opportunity to meet with African leaders. On November 6, 1976, Mugabe travelled from Geneva to the resort town of Savigny to meet with Zaire's President Mobutu Sese Seko. Apparently, Mobutu had hoped to meet with all the Zimbabwean nationalist leaders and then send his views of each to the US secretary of state. Mobutu's opinion of Mugabe seemed to be fixated on his recognition of Mugabe's ambitions to use Nkomo in the PF. The account of this Mobutu–Mugabe meeting comes third hand to the Americans through Mobutu's liaison in Geneva. The unnamed liaison tells how "Mobutu had been unimpressed with Mugabe during their November 6 meeting in Savigny. He found, during the course of the conversation, that Mugabe skillfully advanced rhetorical arguments but was incapable of analyzing serious long-term problems."[49] Mobutu was also more interested in Mugabe's motives for exploiting his rivals, something at which Mobutu was obviously quite skilled.

According to this account, Mugabe explained to Mobutu how there had been attempts to unite all the nationalist leaders before Geneva, but that only Nkomo and Mugabe were able to agree. This was because the two of them had armies of their own, while Muzorewa and Sithole lacked their own armies. Mugabe then reportedly "promised that he and Nkomo would do everything possible to unite their armies." He also stated that while the unification "would permit Nkomo and Mugabe to control the situation ... the unification could not proceed without difficulties."[50] Mobutu, in his personal comments to the US State Department, saw through the veneer of cooperation in the PF position forwarded by Mugabe and Nkomo, and warned of trouble down the road: "We [Zaire] concluded from the meeting that Mugabe wishes to take advantage of Nkomo in order to penetrate the interior of Zimbabwe and install himself there ... . We have also observed that Mugabe has as his special mission the taming of Nkomo." Mobutu also

---

[49] Mobutu commented on Mugabe's dependence on others: "Mugabe appears to be dependent on his advisor Mukudzei Mudzi." Mudzi had been one of the detained ZANU leaders sent to Geneva from Zambia.

[50] For Schaufele from Wisner, "Rhodesia conference: Mobutu's November 6 Meeting with Mugabe," November 12, 1976, 1976GENEVA09022, Central Foreign Policy Files, 1973–1976, RG 59, General Records of the Department of State, USNA.

wanted to paint Mugabe as a communist: "We also noticed that Mugabe, by his language, is completely aligned with the communist cause. It is easy to see that he has been given careful ideological preparation by the leaders in Maputo."[51] Mobutu's reading of the situation, in retrospect, is much closer to how the actual situation would unfold, in terms of Mugabe's ambitions, than to the American diplomats' reading of Mugabe at Geneva. However, by the mid-1970s, Mobutu's opinions were taken with a large dose of cynicism back at the State Department. For example, on hearing reports from the Zairian foreign minister, Bernard Nguza, that there were Soviet weapons ("including some SAMS") in Dar es Salaam awaiting distribution to ZAPU forces in Zambia, the US embassy in Kinshasa commented that Zaire "obviously has its own reasons to bring to our attention any evidence of communist assistance in preparing for another armed conflict in Southern Africa."[52]

Regardless of their apparent ideological differences, Mugabe was not above asking Mobutu for financial assistance. At the end of the meeting, and after Nkomo had left, Mugabe "informed the president [Mobutu] that he could not carry out decisive action without the aid of Zaire. Mugabe requested immediate assistance, for his delegation in Geneva is suffering from financial difficulties." Mugabe explained how he and the ZANU delegation had been forced to check out of the Intercontinental Hotel in Geneva and move to the Royal Hotel because of lack of funds. Similarly to requests for funds from the Americans while in Dar es Salaam in the 1960s, Mugabe asked Mobutu's help in paying hotel bills. Mobutu "accepted the latter request and gave Mugabe $12,500 to help him with the stay of his delegation in Geneva."[53] While this $12,500 may seem to indicate American support for Mugabe via their intermediary, Mobutu, the record shows Mobutu saw Mugabe as a threat – not necessarily because he viewed him as a capable leader, but because if Mugabe were to come to power, Mobutu believed one of

---

[51] Ibid.

[52] Kinshasa to State, "GOZ Reports Arrival of Soviet Arms in Tanzania," November 24, 1976, 1976KINSHA09874, Central Foreign Policy Files, 1973–1976, RG 59, General Records of the Department of State, USNA.

[53] Mugabe also asked if he could come to Kinshasa to meet with Mobutu in order to "explain his problems in greater detail and spell out his requirements for assistance." For Schaufele from Wisner, "Rhodesia conference: Mobutu's November 6 Meeting with Mugabe," November 12, 1976, 1976GENEVA09022, Central Foreign Policy Files, 1973–1976, RG 59, General Records of the Department of State, USNA.

the more radical young leaders would carry out a coup against him. While at Geneva, Mobutu also gave $50,000 to Nkomo, $50,000 to Muzorewa, and $25,000 to Sithole.[54] In comparison, Mugabe's $12,500 for hotel bills seems less than a full endorsement.

Mobutu had also met with Nkomo and the other nationalist leaders. He even met with the Rhodesians. According to an account of Mobutu's meetings with Nkomo, it was said that "Nkomo asked Mobutu that African chiefs of State use their influence to help him reduce the power of ZANU which is directed by Nyerere and Machel." Mobutu's aide also described to the Americans Nkomo's alleged plan to marginalize Mugabe at Geneva. Mobutu cabled the Americans to say that Nkomo had told him "ZANU has no real leader" and that "Mugabe was imposed from the outside but is not popular and is not known within Rhodesia." According to the Zairian account, "Nkomo asked President Mobutu to give him the financial assistance necessary to recruit a man of confidence in Mugabe's camp in order to counterbalance Mugabe. This would permit Nkomo to defuse the threat which ZANU, Mugabe, and his masters pose." Mobutu told Nkomo, however, that Zaire could not help, and advised the Americans to "deal directly with Nkomo," as "[h]e is willing to act as an intermediary, if we so wish." According to Mobutu, Nkomo believed the issue of deciding on a date for independence – the issue that held up the conference for weeks – could be agreed on quickly, but "the only obstacle remaining in settling that issue is the intransigence of Mugabe who does not have the ability to make a decision alone."[55] Wisner, who sent this cable to William Schaufele, didn't agree with Mobutu's idea that the United States should help Nkomo with funds to basically "buy off" some of the ZANU leaders to move away from

---

[54] From Geneva for the Secretary from Schaufele, "Rhodesian Conference: Oct 30 Meeting With Richard," October 30, 1976, 1976GENEVA08557, Central Foreign Policy Files, 1973–1976, RG 59, General Records of the Department of State, USNA.

[55] N'Banda reportedly told Wisner: "Nkomo has not decided who within the Mugabe camp he can turn to his side but is certain that with money and the promise of a future position of influence he will be able to convince one or more important members of the ZANU delegation. Nkomo provided no specific plan to Mobutu nor did he tell Mobutu how much help he would require." From Geneva to State, "Rhodesia Conference: Mobutu Proposes That We Take Sides," November 15, 1976, 1976GENEVA09067, Central Foreign Policy Files, 1973–1976, RG 59, General Records of the Department of State, USNA.

Mugabe. Wisner held that Mobutu hadn't been at the conference, and nor was the conference even complete. He concluded, "I believe it is too early for us to be involved in selling an Nkomo dominated government." Wisner acknowledged Mobutu as a "skillful operator," but he thought it was "in our interest that he plays a quiet hand."[56]

Nkomo and Mugabe at Geneva

By December, Geneva's failures were clear. However, Nkomo was still reporting positively about the conference in interviews to the Rhodesian media. In an interview with Ross Fairbairn for the *Herald* newspaper in Salisbury, Nkomo explained that Ian Smith should return to Geneva and the talks should continue. He also sought to reassure whites in Rhodesia about his alliance with Mugabe in the PF. Nkomo sought to reassure people that he had not been changed by the formation of the PF, stating, "I am a realist. Mr Mugabe is the leader of Zanu and you cannot ignore the party or him. He has to be taken into account in solving the problems." Nkomo went on to say, "'We do not want fighting between Zapu and Zanu. We don't want our people to wage a war after finally getting the freedom they have strived to achieve for years.'"[57] Nkomo had voiced similar optimism about the Geneva conference in an interview with Denis Sargent from Geneva published in the *Herald* on the fourth of December. Nkomo explained that the opinion among whites that the leaders of the liberation movements "would like to see whites wiped out," was "completely mistaken." Nkomo stated how, "I have struggled almost 30 years to remove an evil, the separation of people by races." He further emphasized this point by saying, "We regard people as people, and white people as people like ourselves, with the emphasis on the people, not on the white."[58]

Problems at Geneva with Annex C and the Five Points

The importance of the Annex C issue at Geneva was that Kissinger had hoped that the provisions for a fund to help keep white Rhodesians

---

[56] Ibid.
[57] "Military Power is the Key Factor Says Nkomo," *The Rhodesian Herald,* December 6, 1976, 1.
[58] "Nkomo Hints That the PF Could Be Permanent," *The Rhodesia Herald,* December 4, 1976, 4.

from leaving the country upon independence was a significant "carrot" to gain Smith's cooperation. Kissinger had hoped that Smith would have "tabled" Annex C during the Geneva Conference in order to make the question of helping "the whites" the basis for future negotiations, particularly as Kissinger had agreed with Smith to include a revised five points that provided white control of a Council of State, the military, and "law and order" during the transition period. Annex C also promised more British assistance and protections of white-owned commercial farms and pensions for whites in Rhodesia. The British were therefore quite agitated when they found out that Kissinger had provided Annex C to the South Africans and Rhodesians as real position papers agreed to by the United States and Britain.[59]

Ambassador Richard had raised the issue with Smith at Geneva, asking him if he would table Annex C at the conference, but Smith refused to do so. To a certain extent Smith's refusal went against Kissinger's plan, leaving the Geneva talks all the more unproductive. When Kissinger asked Richard about what happened to the Anglo-American plan at a December 10 follow-up meeting in London, Richard told Kissinger, "Annex C as such is not a starter. It is very hard to see how if it was tabled as a conference document, or if Smith tabled it, it could bridge the gap." Richard told Kissinger that "[b]asically the nationalists all say there can be no Council of State or anything that smacks of it." What Richard meant here was that Nkomo and Mugabe refused to concede any role for Smith and his people in the transition. They wanted the British to be in charge of the transition, and they were not going to allow whites to remain in charge of the military or "law and order," or the proposed Council of State.[60]

Richard told Kissinger that he thought an adjournment until mid-January was in order. There was a brief joke made by Crosland that

---

[59] See items 11 to 27 of FCO 36/1802 for a number of telegrams between Washington, DC, London, and Geneva on ways to control the damage of Smith's mentioning of Annex C as the basis for white control of the Council of State in a press conference. The British wanted it to be stated that Crosland had stated in parliament on October 12 that Annex C was not an officially approved document for negotiations. Kissinger disagreed. The Americans were also adamant that this Anglo-American disagreement was not made public in the run up to the US presidential election.

[60] Memcon Kissinger and Crosland, December 10, 1976, FCO London, RG 59, General Records of the Department of State, Records of Henry Kissinger, 1973–1977, Box 19, NARA II.

they thought January 20 would be a good day, which was same day as President-elect Jimmy Carter's inauguration. Kissinger went along and said that "the only trouble is all the world press on that day would be filled with a picture of me being carried out in my chair." He said they should pick another day. They then continued to talk about why Annex C was not tabled by Smith. Kissinger suggested maybe he was told by the Anglo-Americans not to, and Wisner said it was Smith's own staff who had urged him not to, adding that Smith "is convinced that in the present mood it would be shot down." Kissinger pushed a bit harder and Richard read from his notes on why Smith refused to table it. "He felt in his view it would only create an explosion." Kissinger, who was usually the one to say things would "blow up," reflected on it and said "Then we better leave it as it is, because if we urge it we would be committed to back it."[61]

Having dropped the issue of Annex C, the British then briefed Kissinger on their new plans, which would replace the Council of State idea with the British Resident Commissioner, with a Council of Ministers chaired by the Resident Commissioner. Such a proposal was closer to what the Frontline State presidents and nationalists had asked for, and closer to the eventual decision made by the British to reinstate a Governor to oversee the transition and election in 1980. Crosland must have been made nervous by the proposal, because he interjected, "Just to clarify something. I've approved none of this. I just saw it an hour ago. But it is a promising approach." Kissinger, although having achieved in this plan what he had sought all along – greater British responsibility – also cautioned not to move too quickly. He described how he had written to Nyerere to let him know that "there was a possibility of a breakup, that there was a limit beyond which things couldn't be pushed." Kissinger described Nyerere's reply as conciliatory. Kissinger warned the British to not move too quickly for two reasons. First, he reminded them that "we got it to this point by combining our power with South African power." He warned, "If we don't bring the South Africans into it, what you work out with the blacks won't mean anything. I hate to see you and the blacks agree on something we couldn't deliver. He also warned that "this is a drastic change and the Rhodesians will possibly see it as total surrender to the

---

[61] Ibid.

blacks." Kissinger said he had instructed his people at Geneva "to talk about Annex C, not about getting rid of Smith."[62]

Kissinger wrapped up his experiences working on Rhodesia by saying that he thought if the conference were to end, "Nkomo is finished, and also Sithole and the Bishop." The British disagreed with this assessment, and Kissinger replied, "One thing that has impressed us is their highly developed instinct for their survival. There is no chance they'd survive a guerrilla war." The British under-secretary of state for foreign and Commonwealth affairs, Ted Rowlands, told Kissinger that "[p]arity is dead, so the question is how to give assurances and balances by other means than simply looking at the color of the faces around the table." Kissinger replied with the epitome of a race state assessment: "What the whites fear most is – they're not determined to prevent any action – but that the system after it's set up, will be overthrown, as all other systems in Africa." Crosland added, "This is what the blacks fear, too." The discussion went on a bit longer and in the end, Crosland thanked Kissinger for his official service, saying, "In spite of your insistence not to learn our constitutional structure, and your telegrams that you send from the worst places in cannibal-land, you've been a great friend of this country." The notetaker added "('Here, here', from the British side)."[63] So Crosland ended this chapter of the Anglo-American Rhodesia initiative on a racist note, signifying that the realities of Africa were still quite distant from his consciousness.

Kissinger would meet with Richard and other British diplomats in Washington, DC for a post-Geneva debriefing on December 21, 1976. Richard introduced new plans for moving the Rhodesian negotiations further. These will be discussed in the next chapter. What is important in this meeting, however, was the discussion of the strengths and weaknesses of the African nationalists' positions. Dennis Grennan, in particular, did not put much stock in ZIPA's ability to challenge the Rhodesian military at this time, stating that "ZIPA isn't such a problem." Grennan was doubtful that ZIPA was anywhere near as threatening a force at the time, saying, "I just don't believe Chona's analysis that they've got 4–5,000 well-trained men." Richard added, "They are school children and will go back to school." Grennan replied that they were not like the MPLA, "who have been fighting for ten years." Kissinger asked why Smith was negotiating if this were true.

[62] Ibid.   [63] Ibid.

William Squire, from the British Embassy, interjected that for the white Rhodesians, "like with the Israelis, casualties ... are serious." Kissinger retorted, "But the Israelis don't think they'll lose." Kissinger then addressed a key issue after the failure of Geneva, pointing out that it was the South Africans who got Smith to cooperate in September, "But they might decide this is a game they don't want to play again." Kissinger concluded, "*We don't give a damn about Rhodesia.* The only reason we got into it is to set a pattern for the rest of Africa."[64]

The discussion then turned to the strategies of the nationalists, particularly Nkomo. Kissinger asked why, if Kaunda supported Nkomo, did Nkomo work with Mugabe? He added one of his typical generalizations about African nationalists, "One thing I've learned is they usually know how to take care of their own survival." Grennan suggested that Nkomo was "misreading the situation." Later, when discussing the next steps, Kissinger said to the British that Kaunda "will produce Nkomo." Grennan suggested they should be careful to not go to Nkomo first, because "we don't want early on to give the impression we're trying to split him from Mugabe." Richard explained that he had talked with Nkomo alone, without Mugabe, about four times in Geneva. "On the whole, you're a lot better off seeing him alone; he's reasonable." Kissinger yet again interjected with one of his essentializing observations of African nationalists: "The Africans have impressed me with their cold-blooded appreciation of power." Getting back to Grennan's earlier point, he suggested that he "wouldn't assume" Nkomo had made a mistake. "I'd ask what it is that makes him think it's in his interest." Grennan stuck with his opinion, however, and added that Nkomo "assumes he can control Mugabe," which he viewed as Nkomo's mistake. Kissinger, agreeing with Grennan, conceded the point.[65]

When they met a few days later on December 24, 1976, Kissinger would tell South Africa's ambassador to the United States, Pik Botha, that he had tried to get Richard to introduce and table Annex C but Richard had told him it was impossible. Kissinger then told Botha, "I told Richard – contrary to the public mythology, I believe in telling everyone the same thing – that I was concerned about two things. One,

---

[64] Memorandum of Conversation, UK: Ivor Richard and Dr. Henry A. Kissinger, Washington, DC, December 21, 1976, *Foreign Relations of the United States, 1969–1976*, Volume xxviii, Southern Africa, 235.
[65] Ibid.

we had given our word on Annex C, and in eight years in public office I'd never broken my word. Second, we were afraid if it broke down, it would be an Angola-type situation."[66]

Conclusion

Kissinger would provide his own explanation for the failure of the Geneva talks in one of the volumes of his memoirs. He argues that because he and President Ford had become "lame ducks" almost immediately from the beginning of the talks – which began on October 28 shortly before Ford lost the election on November 2 – the talks were no longer taken seriously by the different parties. Ian Smith left Geneva the day after the US elections. Once this breakdown occurred, Kissinger argued that the British failed to take their own role seriously. Much of his description involved the infighting among British politicians over their roles in the talks. Kissinger agreed with a criticism by the Zimbabwean nationalists at the time. Placing Ivor Richard in charge of the talks was an indication of how little the British were willing to involve themselves in negotiations that might force them to play a larger role. Kissinger concluded by stating that the British intransigence and lack of urgency was partly responsible for Mugabe coming to power. "The price paid for the delay was that the radical factions of the guerrillas headed by Robert Mugabe assumed power under majority rule." Kissinger also reflected on the split among the Frontline State presidents: "The delay worked much as Nyerere had hoped and Kaunda had feared – though Nyerere was to derive little joy from the ascendance of Mugabe, who proved to be an intractable partner."[67] This is a convenient collapsing of the Geneva talks into the subsequent history of the liberation war, one that helps place Kissinger's diplomacy in a better light. Kissinger had at first hoped to work with Kaunda and the other Frontline State presidents to speed up the negotiations in order to forestall Cuban and Soviet influence and to

---

[66] Memorandum of Conversation, Washington, DC, December 24, 1976, Ambassador R. F. Botha, Secretary of State Henry A. Kissinger, Assistant Secretary of State for African Affairs, William E. Shaufele, National Security Staff, Peter W. Rodman, *Foreign Relations of The United States, 1969–1976*, Volume XXVIII, Southern Africa, 236. Italics added by author.

[67] Henry Kissinger, *Years of Renewal*, 1st ed. (New York: Simon & Schuster, 1999), 1015.

help Nkomo become the first Zimbabwean president; it was only after pressure from Nyerere that the Americans were introduced to Mugabe, who skillfully held out from accepting any form of negotiated settlement in order to secure his role as the political leader of ZANU, and the de facto political leader of ZIPA and ZANLA. The Geneva talks presented Mugabe an international stage to help solidify his reputation as a serious negotiator with the backing of the "boys with guns." The way Nyerere and Kaunda orchestrated the appearances of both the ZANLA leaders, such as Tongogara, and the younger ZIPA leaders, such as Wilf Mhanda, as part of Mugabe's delegation at Geneva would become Mugabe's biggest victory. After Geneva, Mugabe used this diplomatic victory in the Mozambican camps to consolidate power with the help of Samora Machel. Mhanda argues that the Geneva talks helped convert Machel from a strong supporter of the younger ZIPA leaders to a supporter of Mugabe – only because Machel had become convinced that Kissinger's diplomacy would transfer power to Zimbabweans within a matter of months. Mhanda writes of Machel: "[b]y forcing us [ZIPA commanders] to the conference as ZANU – essentially throwing his weight behind Mugabe's argument, the one we had resisted in Lusaka and which had also been rejected by Nyerere – Machel effectively put an end to ZIPA's existence."[68] Part of this was due to Mugabe's diplomatic skills and part of it had to do with the conflicting interests among the Frontline State presidents and within the Anglo-American camp. These differences would become more pronounced in the following three years of negotiations, and as argued in the following chapters, contributed to a failed attempt at a direct settlement between the PF and the Rhodesians in 1978, which prolonged the deadly war.

While Kissinger was making his farewell tour concerning his role in the Anglo-American negotiations, the young military leaders of ZIPA returned to Mozambique and began plans to integrate forces with ZIPRA. As Rugare Gumbo would later describe it, some in ZANLA and ZANU labelled the ZIPA leaders as "sell-outs" and created a situation where false claims were made against the ZIPA leaders. As Gumbo wrote in August 1979, "These genuine efforts of ZIPA were interpreted as efforts to usurp power or to engineer a coup." Gumbo claims that actions were taken against the ZIPA leaders, as "reports

[68] Wilf Mhanda, *Dzino*, 160.

furnished by Tongogara and Nhongo to the Central Committee in Maputo about activities of ZIPA in the camps, especially after the return of the central committee from the Geneva conference were that there was a state of war in the camps." Gumbo argues that these reports influenced "the central committee to take drastic measures against ZIPA." Gumbo describes how "forty five (45) ZIPA commanders including seven (7) leading members of the military committee and famile [sic] officer were placed under custody of the Mozambiqiuean [sic] government in January 1977." Gumbo adds that these arrests were "carried out unceremoniously without even charging or giving them any hearing." This supposedly temporary removal of ZIPA Commanders became "an indefinite isolation and expulsion."[69] When Gumbo wrote this in 1979, the ZIPA leaders had been in jail since January 1977, and he and other ZANU leaders had been held since January 1978. His arrest, and further consolidation of power by Mugabe and his allies in the military command of ZANLA is described in the following chapters.

Just a month before the arrest of the ZIPA leadership, Kissinger had joked with Ambassador Pik Botha about the nationalists post-Geneva. Kissinger asked Botha, to laughter, "Don't you think Nkomo, Sithole, Muzorewa and Mugabe would sit down together?" Pik Botha replied, "They'll be after each other, bribing and fighting. Kissinger replied, to more laughter, "Really? ... Don't they just want what is best for their people?"[70] Such jovial banter between Kissinger and Botha in December, when contrasted to what would happen in January to the ZIPA leaders who had helped legitimate Mugabe's leadership by backing him at Geneva, demonstrates the violence inherent in Cold War diplomacy, even when the principal actors are far removed from the scene of the crime.

---

[69] Rugare Gumbo, "The Truth about the Recurrent ZANU Crisis and the Emergence of a two line Struggle," letter signed, "By Detained ZANU Leaders, HIGH Command, ZIPA Military Committee, and other Senior Commanders in Mozambique" (no date; accompanying cover letter dated August 13, 1979), item 72, FCO 36/2496, BNA.

[70] Memorandum of Conversation, Washington, DC, December 24, 1976, Ambassador R. F. Botha, Secretary of State Henry A. Kissinger, Assistant Secretary of State for African Affairs, William E. Schaufele, National Security Staff, Peter W. Rodman, *Foreign Relations of the United States, 1969–1976*, vol. xxviii, Southern Africa, 236.

5 | *Negotiating Independence 1977–1978*

After the Geneva negotiations had unraveled in December 1976, all parties retreated from the negotiating table. The situation was further complicated by continuing tensions involving the United States over Cuban and Soviet influence; the inability of the PF to work together in executing the war; and, most importantly, Ian Smith's efforts to proceed with an "internal settlement" that would result in his own conceptualization of the "majority rule" he had agreed to in September 1976, without involving the PF. Regional power influences again became significant, as South Africa continued to invest heavily in Rhodesia's defense, and the Frontline State presidents continued to offer their national territories to the liberation movements. The Rhodesians continued to use their air force in cross-border raids to attack ZIPRA and ZANLA bases in Zambia and Mozambique, increasing the possibility that Cuban and Soviet forces would intervene. The Frontline State presidents were also aware that increased Cuban or Soviet assistance would generate more South African military assistance to Rhodesia and, as in Angola, bring even more overt participation by the South African Defence Force (SADF) into their countries.

These Cold War and regional tensions allowed Ian Smith enough space to move forward with what South African diplomats had suggested might happen after Geneva. By achieving an internal settlement with those African leaders not allied with the PF – Bishop Muzorewa, Reverend Sithole, and Chief Chirau, Smith could try to sell his settlement as "a majority rule" government. After such recognition, it was hoped international sanctions would be lifted and the Rhodesian economy could improve. It would then be possible to fight a "civil" war between an African-led government and what they hoped would be an increasingly marginalized minority radical position of the PF. As the next two chapters will argue, the process did not turn out as planned for the Rhodesians, and the South African regime would add its own twists to the equation late in the process. But at the outset of 1977, the idea of the internal settlement was not yet fully on the table. The immediate task for the British and Americans after the failure of Geneva was to regroup and attempt to concentrate their combined leverage toward moving the negotiations forward before the Cubans and Soviets became more involved in the war.

Before discussing the impact of the internal settlement talks on the negotiations, it is worth noting another significant assassination of a liberation war leader on January 22, 1977. This time it was ZAPU's Jason Moyo, the second vice president for external affairs, who was killed in Lusaka by a letter bomb addressed to him as "personal" from a friend in Botswana. Moyo opened the bomb himself and was killed immediately. Once again, an African nationalist leader was killed dishonorably in this war. In a period of a few years, both ZANLA and ZIPRA had lost key leaders by bombs in Lusaka. Joshua Nkomo returned from Yugoslavia and Robert Mugabe came to Lusaka for the funeral. The speeches by the two leaders are a revealing contrast. Nkomo thanked Mugabe for attending and made references to the differences between Moyo and Mugabe in Maputo when they had met to form the PF alliance before the Geneva conference. Nkomo also referred to Mugabe as "Robert," commenting, "I call him by his first name because I have worked with this young man, I know his heart."[1] This sort of public display of paternalism, in front of President Kaunda, must have annoyed Mugabe. In return, when it was time for Mugabe to speak, he only recognized Kaunda and had nothing to say to, or about, his elder Nkomo.

Mugabe, in his speech, praised Moyo as a personal friend to him and his wife, someone who had made his mark in Bulawayo trade union politics. Mugabe said that in September 1976, Moyo had come to Maputo to negotiate the PF. Mugabe told the mourners that Moyo "warned us all that we should not pretend to each other, but rather that we should recognize the difficulties in our way and the differences which could not be solved immediately." Although Mugabe went on to say that all Zimbabweans needed to carry on Moyo's fighting spirit, he never mentioned any need for ZANU and ZAPU unity. Instead, he

---

[1] "Speeches by J. Nkomo and R. Mugabe at the Burial of J. Moyo," Doc. 242, in Goswin Baumhögger, *The Struggle for Independence: Documents on the Recent Development of Zimbabwe (1975–1980)*, vol. 2 (Hamburg: Institute of African Studies Documentation Centre, 1984), 253–54.

criticized entering into any further negotiations with Smith and the Rhodesians. "How many times, since 1974, have we sat at negotiating tables and draw naught?" Invoking the objectives of Moyo, Mugabe asked everyone "to rededicate ourselves to an immediate intensification of our armed struggle as the only way to achieving our true independence."[2] Moyo had told a reporter from *Afrique* magazine earlier in January 1977 that there was no cooperation between ZIPRA an ZANU. In the interview, Moyo was asked if he was going "to continue the guerrilla [war] side by side with ZANU." He bluntly answered, "No." He said that ZANLA and ZIPRA had "battled together from November 1975 to April 1976." But then "problems arose in Mozambique and Tanzania and ended with the murder of fifty disarmed recruits." Moyo did not rule out future cooperation, saying they were doing all they could to overcome their differences.[3]

At the time of Moyo's murder, Nkomo had been in Belgrade once again making requests to the Yugoslavian Government for military assistance. A report from the Yugoslavian Department for International Relations describes Nkomo's talk with Stanet Dolanc, of the Executive Committee of the Presidency of the Central Committee of the Yugoslavian Communist League. The meeting was held on January 25, 1977. Nkomo thanked Dolanc for the continued support of the Zimbabwean liberation movements. The summary of Dolanc's reply suggests some impatience with the PF: Dolanc emphasized "that he has no intention of inferring or giving advice ... underlined the importance of unity, the need to overcome particularist interests." The Yugoslavian's were providing aid to both ZIPRA and ZANLA. The accounts from this time period showed that some care was given to provide equal amounts of weapons and cash to both parties and armies. Nkomo gave a history of the division between ZAPU and ZANU, blaming the breakoff of ZANU on "external influences." He argued that he was currently under pressure from external forces. "Someone [in the meeting] made it known that it was the USSR." Nkomo suggested that the non-aligned allies were more to his liking, "to whom we will belong when and if we become free." He argued that the non-alignment policy enabled them to "work together, think and create, but also to be our own."

---

[2] Ibid., 253–54.
[3] "Interview with Jason Moyo," *Afrique* Magazine, January 7, 1977.

Nkomo was careful, however, to make a distinction between his dependency on the Soviets and Mugabe's aid from the People's Republic of China. Acknowledging this fact of different sponsors, Nkomo added, "However, ZAPU managed to prevent the Soviets from penetrating their camps as instructors (they only accepted Africans as instructors) while ZANU did not prevent the Chinese." Nkomo argued that this Chinese influence "had a particularly negative effect on young people who did not know how to set boundaries and who succumbed to promises from outside." Interestingly, Nkomo then defended Mugabe, as suggested by the following from the notes of the meeting: "Mugabe, the leader of ZANU, understands the problem, and Nkomo believes that he will not succumb to pressure, especially from young people." He called ZANU an "undisciplined organization" but one that ZAPU "cannot ignore." Nkomo said he, along with Mugabe, "will manage to form the organization they want in Zimbabwe." Nkomo said there was no need to "go too fast … because of the situation in the movement and because of the dependence on the forces that help them." He also said they could not act without the support of the Frontline State presidents. Most importantly, he said there was no chance of a ZIPRA and ZANLA merger. "That is why now there are two organizations with joint leadership that will merge with one 'diplomatic' action, but there will be no parallel merger."[4] Even with this growing gulf between the two parties, Nkomo and Mugabe would continue to carry out international diplomacy with the Western powers as coleaders of the PF.

Nkomo visited Moscow from February 28 to March 7 to request further military aid and training for ZIPRA after the failure of Geneva. John Holmes, a British diplomat, reported what he could about Nkomo's visit from the Zambian diplomats in Moscow. The Zambians did not have much information to share, only that "the object of his visit was to ask for arms."[5] Holmes translated and summarized Nkomo's comments in the Soviet press, including a passage

[4] "Note of a conversation between Stanet Dolanc and Joshua Nkomo," Department of International Relations and Relations of the Presidency of the Central Committee of the Communist Yugoslavia, Part of 1406/86, Pov broj 109/1, Belgrade, February 3, 1977 *Arhiv, Centralnog Komiteta Seveza Komunista Jugolsavije.* (Thanks to Sarah Zabic for providing me this file and others related to Zimbabwe from the Archive.)

[5] Moscow to FCO, "Nkomo's visit and strong possibility of arms deals with ZAPU," February 28 to March 7, 1977, item 53, FCO36/1926, BNA. The

from *Pravda* on March 5, where Nkomo reportedly "claimed that Britain and the US, the creators of the Anglo-American Plan, had been concerned least of all about the fate of the Rhodesian people. The failure of the Geneva conference meant the end of Western plans for a settlement favourable to the West and harmful to the people of Zimbabwe." Nkomo then, according to Holmes, thanked the Soviets. "The Patriotic Front had decided on a broad campaign of military action against the racist regime. They were satisfied with the support they were receiving from the Soviet Union and the 'socialist' countries."[6]

Evidence from Soviet documents in the Bukovsky Archives includes a formal request, dated March 6, 1977, from Nkomo for weapons and supplies from the Soviets. Nkomo submitted a letter informing his Russian comrades that at that time ZAPU had "about 600 activists who have received military training who are awaiting transfer to Zimbabwe; 1,200 people who are undergoing training; 1,000 people who are starting training in a new camp, and 3,000 recruits who are in transitional camps in Zambia and Botswana." Nkomo remarked that they were planning to start new training in Angola. "Together with the governments of Angola and Cuba, we have reached an agreement to establish a ZAPU training camp. The Cuban comrades took over the logistical support of the camp at the initial stage for a period of 2 to 4 months." Nkomo reported how ZIPRA was "experiencing an acute shortage of some vital supplies" and asked for food item, tents, clothes, and blankets. Nkomo noted problems with sending supplies through Mozambique and Tanzania and said he would "discuss with President K. Kaunda the possibility of the Zambian government receiving the property intended for us through Mozambique or Tanzania." A statement was issued by the Communist Party's Central Committee approving the provisions for the training camp in Angola and sending 200 "activists for military training in the USSR at the end of 1977, including 20 people for training military pilots."[7]

"Anglo-American Plan" referred to by Nkomo is also known as the Anglo-American proposal.

[6] Ibid.
[7] Document CT50/131: "Joshua Nkomo to General Secretary of the Communist Party of the Soviet Union," March 6, 1977 and "On requests from the leadership of the African National Council of Zimbabwe," April 4, 1977, Bukovsky Archives, http://bukovsky-archives.net/pdfs/terr-wd/ct50-77.pdf. (Thanks to Ben Allison for locating and translating this document for me to use here.)

Internal Settlement Negotiations

An important theme for 1977 and most of 1978 is that the two PF
leaders did their best to keep their own differences out of their diplomacy, while emphasizing that the failure of the talks rested on the
shoulders of the British and Ian Smith. It was, of course, not difficult
for word to get around of the lack of unity between Mugabe and
Nkomo. Reports from diplomats in Nigeria and Egypt related
Nkomo's displeasure in Geneva with Mugabe's more prominent role
as a "partner" of the PF. One British diplomat was told by a Mr. Raid
how the Nigerian ambassador to Egypt had noted, "that in conversation with him, Mr Nkomo took a very hard and uncompromising line.
He seemed to be asking the other groups to dissolve themselves and
accept his leadership without any give and take."[8]

Mugabe's public views, based on an interview in the Tanzanian
Sunday News on January 2, 1977, were summarized by the British in
Dar es Salaam. From his perspective at Geneva, Mugabe explained,
"The PF's achievements were firstly, convincing [the British govern-
ment] of the seriousness of the Front's intention to secure a transfer of
power, and secondly exposing British and American intentions to
'establish a puppet government which they call moderate' and which
would 'forestall the armed struggle.'"[9] Asked about ZANU and ZAPU
unity, Mugabe explained that the Geneva conference had shown they
could "think and act as one," and that "if we are to unite, we have to
unite on the basis of the armed struggle." Geneva had "brought the
political leadership together, it had been agreed that 'we must look into
the possibility, if not the probability of bringing the two armies
together'."[10]

By late January 1977, after consolidating the support of the Frontline
State presidents and the OAU post-Geneva, and utilizing the assistance
of Tanzania and Mozambique to remove the ZIPA elements by arresting them in Mozambique, ZANU signaled to the British they were still
interested in continuing talks. At the end of January 1977, Varcoe met
in Lusaka with Rugare Gumbo, who Varcoe found "surprisingly

---

[8] Cairo to FCO, "Visit to Cairo of Joshua Nkomo," January 7, 1977, item 4,
    FCO36/1926, BNA.
[9] Dar es Salaam to FCO, "Sunday News Dar interviews Mugabe," January 2,
    1977, item 1, FCO36/1926, BNA.
[10] Ibid.

affable." They discussed what ZANU sought in future negotiations. Varcoe said Gumbo criticized the British at Geneva by stating that "it would be essential for the British Government to do more ground work first" in future negotiations. "By this he seemed to mean that we should first convince, persuade or pressurise Mr Smith into accepting that there must be an effective transfer of power to the black majority." Lewen replied to Gumbo by saying "that it was quite impossible for us to be able to 'sell' to Mr Smith (or to Mr Vorster) an immediate transfer of power." Varcoe stressed that the PF "must recognize that there is a point beyond which Mr Smith simply would not be pushed. To make concessions yes, to commit what he regarded as suicide no."[11] Gumbo asked Varcoe, "Why should we have struggled for 12 years to take power from Smith simply to hand it over to the British who would then in turn hand it over to us?" Varcoe concluded his report to the FCO: "I did not get the impression from our talk that the ZANU Executive have totally ruled out further negotiations. The difficulty is their insistence that they should be on their terms."[12]

The British were also debriefed by ZAPU after Geneva. Josiah Chinamano of ZAPU visited the FCO and had an interview with its assistant undersecretary for Africa, Philip Mansfield, in early February 1977. According to Mansfield, Chinamano explained that Smith and Bishop Muzorewa had begun negotiations on the "internal option."[13] Chinamano told Mansfield that there was a "consistent campaign in Rhodesia to brand Mugabe as a Marxist who would introduce extreme policies." Chinamano said that "[t]his campaign had also affected Nkomo by extension." Chinamano also suggested that if Smith held a referendum for an internal settlement, "the authorities would no doubt detain large numbers of people who were prominent in the PF." Chinamano was "in favour of reconvening the Geneva Conference without Smith." Mansfield also relayed, based on his conversation with Chinamano, "that the military situation was deteriorating from Smith's point of view. The number of guerrillas in the field was increasing steadily and they were able to enter villages when the security forces were elsewhere and to hold meetings with villagers to plan the

[11] J. R. Varcoe, "Note for the Record 'Rhodesia: PF,'" January 31, 1977, item 26, FCO36/1926, BNA.

[12] Ibid.

[13] P. R. A. Mansfield to Mr. Harrison, "PF," February 18, 1977, item 36, FCO36/1926, BNA.

future." Chinamano told Mansfield that "young white Rhodesians were leaving the country. Two had been on his flight to London. They had introduced themselves to him and explained that after five years of intermittent service they saw no future for themselves in Rhodesia and were going to Scotland to work on an oil rig."[14] Chinamano's pessimism about the future of the negotiations was perhaps tempered by the increasing capacity for ZAPU to recruit and train soldiers for the liberation war effort.

As the British weighed their options for restarting talks with the PF and Smith, they began receiving news at the end of February questioning Mugabe's control of the guerrilla forces, the same forces who had offered their endorsement of Mugabe as their political leader at the Geneva conference. Julian Marshall from the BBC reported to British diplomats in Maputo after meeting with ZIPA leaders at Geneva. He believed ZIPA would not survive the remainder of 1977, especially given the assassination of ZAPU's Jason Moyo, who had been a strong advocate of a combined military force. In the aftermath of Moyo's death, "no one could hold ZANU and ZAPU together for long." Marshall's assessment of Mugabe was also pessimistic. A British diplomat in Maputo, C. R. L. de Chassiron, described how "Marshall was quite adamant that Robert Mugabe would also be 'finished' in a few months. It was plain that Tongogara, Gumbo, and Hamadziripi had plans for ZANU which took no account of Mugabe's self-proclaimed leadership. ... Marshall felt that Tongogara definitely aims to replace Mugabe as ZANU's head."[15] De Chassiron noted that he had yet to meet with Mugabe, although he lived across the street from him when he was in Maputo. The British were dealing primarily with Edgar Tekere for the moment.[16]

In the early months of 1977, both ZANU and ZAPU were working to consolidate their competitive position with each other in the PF. Mugabe and his comrades were removing those in ZIPA who threatened the consolidation of ZANU and the leadership of ZANLA. Publicly, Mugabe repeated his commitment to the military cooperation of ZANLA and ZIPRA. The British high commissioner to Zambia, Stephen Miles, reported what Mugabe had said at a press conference in

---

[14] Ibid.
[15] Chassiron to Harrison, "Rhodesia Department, Maputo," February 28, 1977, item 50, FCO36/1926, BNA.
[16] Ibid.

Beira, Mozambique on March 15. The Zambian press indicated Mugabe had told reporters that "[t]here is a grave danger in having separate liberation armies which could erupt in a civil war in a free Zimbabwe. One of the main tasks of the coordinating committee of the PF is to reconstitute ZIPA so that we can bring our freedom fighters together to fight as one on all fronts."[17] The perception of unity among the PF was furthered at the FRELIMO conference in March 1977 where "Nkomo and Mugabe both read formal messages of greeting to the FRELIMO Congress on behalf of the PF and embraced on the rostrum."[18]

This orchestrated perception of greater unity in the PF may have created some optimism for the Anglo-American proposal post-Geneva, but the Smith government's initiative to negotiate the internal settlement with Bishop Muzorewa, Reverend Sithole, and Chief Chirau would throw a spanner into the works in 1977. Talks of an internal settlement rattled the confidence of Nkomo and Mugabe. At a press conference on March 18, 1977, Nkomo addressed the press about his socialist leanings, saying, "The people of Zimbabwe have decided to associate themselves with the masses of the socialist countries because they are more human and understand the problems facing the Zimbabwean in their just struggle. By contrast the West have lost direction." Nkomo added a humorous note, suggesting the West's concern that because they had "read the red book" they were Maoist was ridiculous. "We have been reading British history for a long time but we have not turned British." On a roll, Nkomo responded to a question about Bishop Muzorewa and Reverend Sithole forming a "possible alliance," by asking rhetorically, "What are they trying to form, another church?"[19] Nkomo's typical humor, however, glossed over the growing concern among the PF leadership and the Frontline State presidents that Smith could manage to create an internal settlement government that would be recognized internationally, resulting in the lifting of sanctions, and thus prolonging the war.

---

[17] Lusaka to FCO, "Rhodesia: Patriotic Front," March 16, 1977, item 59, FCO36/1926, BNA.
[18] Lewen to FCO, "Rhodesia: Nkomo Press Conference," February 7, 1977, item 29, FCO36/1926, BNA.
[19] Miles Lusaka to Priority FCO, "Rhodesia," March 18, 1977, item 56, FCO36/1926, BNA.

At the same time Mugabe and Nkomo were in Mozambique, ZAPU's Josiah Chinamano was in New York at the United Nations, briefing Britain's mission there. Chinamano told the British they were certain Bishop Muzorewa was secretly working with Smith to develop an internal settlement, with Smith hoping that "he would be able to demonstrate to the world that the internal option was massively supported by the African population." Chinamano told Britain's UN ambassador, Ivor Richard, who he knew from the Geneva talks, that ZAPU was willing to continue talks, "but not as a continuation of the existing Geneva exercise." Chinamano also said "ZAPU felt strongly that there was no longer need for the British to invite as many delegations as they had to Geneva. Now that the four [Frontline State presidents] and the OAU had decided that the liberation movement should be consolidated around the PF, it would be logical for Britain to avoid casting their net more widely." Chinamano hoped to make it clear that ZAPU and the PF were irrevocably opposed to allowing the Rhodesian-based nationalists to continue participating in negotiations. Richard was not willing to accept this second demand, stating that "the British Government had already indicated that it was not at present prepared to withdraw the existing invitations to Muzorewa and Sithole."[20]

Two days later, in an address to ZAPU members, according to High Commissioner Stephen Miles in Lusaka, "Nkomo made clear his opposition to any attempt at an internal solution to the Rhodesia problem." Nkomo called "Smith's overtures to the moderate Blacks as 'an attempt to usurp the rights of the people of Zimbabwe'." Miles quotes Nkomo further, on the internal settlement: "He also described it as – 'A challenge to the black people of the country and any others who will fight against an evil system even if it is in black hands'. 'The war is not against white people, it is against an evil system.' He warned that those who joined the system would be 'face to face with the Katusha' [Katyusha] (A type of Soviet Rocket)." Nkomo also indicated that the war was about destroying the racialized privilege of whites: "We don't want to build a state for a privileged few (i.e., whites)." He added, "When we talk about rights of people, we don't mean any particular group of people."[21]

---

20 UK Mission to the United Nations, A. D. Brighty, "Call by Josiah Chinamano to the UK Mission to the UN," March 18, 1977, item 58, FCO36/1926, BNA.
21 Miles Lusaka to Priority FCO, "Info Dar es Salam, Gaborone, Maputo, Cape Town, Washington, UK Mission New York," March 21, 1977, item 59, FCO36/1926, BNA.

Nkomo labelled those waiting to come to power through a referendum as "vultures" and accused the British of supporting the idea. Nkomo "questioned when in the history of colonialism a referendum had ever been held to choose a leader." Nkomo did not believe that any negotiations or conference would be successful unless it resulted in a transfer of power to the Zimbabwean people. "Until this happened it was pointless to hold a further conference, and that intensified armed struggle was the only way left to solve the problem."[22] This notion of a nationalist leader coming to power without an election would become problematic for Nkomo. Even though he talked about the need for an election, by 1978 and 1979 there were indications he would accept the idea of the transition to majority rule occurring with a transitional government led by himself, rather than having elections first.

This would be a central element of Nkomo's rivalry with Mugabe during the next three years – how to maintain a commitment to majority rule elections without splitting the PF into two parties where Mugabe would have an advantage in voting. The problem for Nkomo was that since the early 1960s, he and others were beholden to the notion of a majority rule election before independence. Nkomo could not go against this notion now, nor could the Frontline State presidents. Smith and Muzorewa's internal settlement, on the one hand, would create a crisis for the Frontline State presidents and the PF in negotiating, while adding more pressure to go beyond a partial manifestation of a majority rule government, given the restrictions on the franchise and the protection of whites built into the internal settlement.[23]

The prospects of an internal settlement also forced Nkomo and Mugabe to address white Rhodesians. Nkomo, as noted above, was careful to say the fight was against an "evil system" and not whites per se, but that black leaders would become enemies of the struggle once they joined Smith. Mugabe also reassured whites that ZANU was not a party fighting against whites but against the Smith regime. In an interview published in *Tempo* in Maputo, Mugabe stated that he would protect their rights in an Independent Zimbabwe: "We do not

[22] Ibid.
[23] Luise White, *Unpopular Sovereignty: Rhodesian Independence and African Decolonization* (University of Chicago Press, 2015), 233–54.

fight to defend individual interests. This is why in our contacts with the whites we have told them this, and it has also been necessary to tell them that we are not fighting to expel them from the country." Mugabe elaborated that ZANU sought "to construct a system where there is justice for all regardless of their colour or personal inclinations. This is the message which we have to constantly relay to them; because they think that we are carrying out a racial war and wish to expel them."[24]

In March of 1977, as the internal settlement talks were just getting underway, both PF leaders appeared to share the same public message. Both stressed the need to concentrate on the war effort. By contrast, the propaganda campaign inside Rhodesia made sure that those in Rhodesia were not given a chance to consider the nuances of Nkomo's and Mugabe's claims to universal rights, or to consider that the war was a liberation struggle to create rights for those left out of the minority, white-rule definitions of citizenship. From the Rhodesian propaganda perspective, the war continued to be fought against an external enemy. Afro-Asian communists funded by the Soviet Union and China were out to destroy, from the Rhodesian Front perspective, "white civilization" in southern Africa.[25] However, the war and Smith's earlier concessions toward majority rule in 1976 made it difficult to maintain this "othering" of the Zimbabweans fighting for majority rule. Anglo-American support for their efforts – at least diplomatically, but also in terms of humanitarian aid to both ZANU and ZAPU – made it difficult to also maintain a less interventionist policy into 1978.

The Question of Cold War Interventions

On May 19, 1977, the US ambassador to the United Nations, Andrew Young, met with Mugabe at the Nigerian High Commission in Maputo. Accounts of the meeting suggest that Mugabe was tough on Young for not offering anything new, beyond saying the United States would pressure South Africa to put more pressure on Smith and the Rhodesians. According to the account of the US ambassador to

---

[24] "Interview with Mugabe in 'TEMPO'," March 20, 1977, item 60, FCO36/ 1926, BNA.

[25] White, *Unpopular Sovereignty*, 1–36. See also Donal Lowry, "The Impact of Anti-communism on White Rhodesian Political Culture, ca.1920s–1980," *Cold War History* 7, no. 2 (2007), 169–94.

Mozambique, Willard Depree, Mugabe and others in his party "appeared unimpressed, saying this sounded like more of the same." Young and the other Americans then "explained [the] difficulty which [the] U.S. would have in considering military aid." Mugabe and others "objected to what they sensed to be excessive U.S. concern over potential communist influence with [the] liberation movement." After asserting and defending "their right to accept aid from any source", Mugabe added, "It is an insult to our intelligence to believe we will become the pawns of the Russians." Ambassador Depree added his own comment that "Mugabe is an intelligent, articulate person. While firm in his views, he proved willing to listen and to understand U.S. constraints."[26]

Somewhat paradoxically, increased Soviet and Cuban involvement in the Rhodesian war actually became more of a possibility created by Nkomo's growing lack of confidence over his chances to become the first leader of Zimbabwe. The British therefore believed they could bring Nkomo into a direct negotiation with Smith to transfer power to him and the more moderate leaders in Salisbury, thereby circumventing Soviet influence. The British floated strategies in the summer of 1977, such as enlisting the Frontline State presidents and the Nigerians to "ensure that they take a reasonable line towards a settlement in Rhodesia," while at the same time taking a position that "neutralises Cuban and Russian influence."[27] The British were also concerned that Mugabe's position was "under challenge," and that he saw "backing from the Soviet Union and China as essential for carrying on the armed struggle." They did not, however, think he was so committed to "communist ideology," and thought his links were "essentially based on the need for practical support."[28] The Botswana and Zambian governments were pressing Britain to become more involved in negotiations to forestall more extensive Cuban and Soviet involvement.

The British report also noted that the Frontline State presidents had difficulties exerting their influence on the PF leaders. Additionally, the

[26] Ambassador Depree to State, "Meeting with Mugabe," May 21, 1977, Maputo00666, Central Foreign Policy Files, 1973–1976, RG 59, General Records of the Department of State, USNA.
[27] Excerpt from "Minutes of the Gen 12 Meeting of 8 July, 3," 1977, item 231, FCO 36/1929, BNA, in which it is mentioned that "there is a call for a study of ways of reducing Soviet and Cuban influence in the PF, through Kenya and Nigeria."
[28] Ibid.

report cited the difficulties Joseph Garba, a Nigerian brigadier, had communicated in working with Nkomo and Mugabe: "The Nigerians were unhappy about the Nkomo–Mugabe alliance and that they found the leaders difficult people who 'could not be pushed and one had to take their word'."[29] This comment foreshadows the difficulties Garba would face as he tried to force a political unity between Nkomo and Mugabe in 1978. Such a move would ultimately fail, indicating the intractable nature of the divide between ZANU and ZAPU leaders by August 1978.

Nkomo Confronts the West

The minutes from Nkomo's meeting with British prime minister James Callaghan and his foreign secretary, David Owen, on July 27, 1977 at 10 Downing Street show Nkomo taking a tough line with the British. Callaghan opened with the suggestion that the time had arrived when "we had got Smith, and that he would last only for a matter of months." Callaghan went on to say, "What we needed now was African unity if we were to avoid a situation such as had occurred in other parts of Africa." Nkomo replied that he "could not accept this comment." Callaghan responded by arguing "that it was a fact that unity did not at present exist which was necessary to make Zimbabwe a viable country." Nkomo suggested that "nobody could achieve this; the British could not achieve it in their own country." He then argued that the PF had "come a long way" toward unity. Owen said that "if ZANU and ZAPU could work together, that would be fine."[30]

Nkomo replied by expressing his disappointment over "Dr. Owen's recent reference to 'tribalism'. There was no question of this. He knew very well how to handle it." He told Owen that "public references to tribalism were divisive and that we should recognise, publicly if possible, that he had spent his life fighting for unity."[31] The spark for this criticism was a BBC report claiming that the divisions the Frontline State presidents were trying to heal in the PF were "tribal" differences. In a press conference in Lusaka on July 26, Nkomo is reported to have "inferred that in Rhodesia itself, Britain was trying to create a tribal

---

[29] Ibid.
[30] "Note of a Meeting between the Prime Minster and Mr. Joshua Nkomo," July 27, 1977, PREM 15/1171, BNA.
[31] Ibid.

problem that doesn't exist in the country."[32] The discussion at 10 Downing Street turned to the question of integrating PF forces with Rhodesian forces. Callaghan suggested if this could be done, it could constitute "one of the most effective armies and air forces in Africa." Such armed forces would also help to "re-assure those Europeans who might wish to stay behind – many, of course, would leave." Nkomo responded to this idea by stating it was a "very difficult question" because "these were people who had been fighting against each other; many brutalities had been committed. ... The white forces could not imagine themselves working in cooperation with terrorists; the PF forces could not imagine themselves working with fascists."[33]

The meeting's discussion moved on to the question of an internal settlement. Callaghan asked Nkomo how the British should respond "if Smith were to fix up an election on the basis of 'one man, one vote' in collaboration – for example – with Muzorewa and Sithole. Should the British government recognise the outcome?" Nkomo answered, "If people started to play that kind of game, many things could happen; it would be very dangerous. The PF could not simply sit and watch." Callaghan asked Nkomo how they could "fight against 'one man, one vote'." Nkomo responded by saying the fight would not be against "one man, one vote," but against a "puppet government." Callaghan stressed that the British government needed Zimbabwean leaders to help. Callaghan prefaced his next remark by saying "Mr. Nkomo would probably jump down his throat," and then suggested that what might be the "best solution" would be for Nkomo and Muzorewa "to agree to work together." Nkomo responded that this was "not possible," and that "Muzorewa was a liar." Callaghan replied that "he had himself worked with worse liars than Bishop Muzorewa. The fact was that, together, Mr. Nkomo and Muzorewa would sweep the country." Owen interjected that he had told President Carter that "Mr. Nkomo was a true politician." This last comment seemed to get Nkomo off the hook from answering any further questions about the British interest in getting him to compromise, stressing that Muzorewa "amounted to nothing politically." Owen asked if Nkomo could work with Sithole. Nkomo said that he did not know.

[32] American Embassy Lusaka to American Embassy London, "Nkomo Press Conference, Lusaka" July 26, 1977, item 197, PREM 15/1171, BNA.

[33] "Note of a Meeting between the Prime Minster and Mr. Joshua Nkomo," July 27, 1977, PREM 15/1171, BNA.

"He was working with Mugabe. He had told Sithole that he was destroying himself: he had no hope of winning a seat in a free election."[34]

This meeting, without ZANU representatives, shows Nkomo committed above all to the winning of the war and to the transfer of power to the PF. He gave no indication, even after having it raised at the top level of the British government, that he would be willing to break off ties with Mugabe in order to accept a compromised role with Muzorewa, Sithole, or Smith. When asked by Prime Minister Callaghan if there was a role for the others, Nkomo said he had "discussed the problem" with Mugabe. "But there was no basis for discussion with Muzorewa and Sithole: he could not deal with liars. Both Muzorewa and Sithole were incapable of telling the truth. He himself had told his people how things were and they recognised the truth. But Muzorewa was a liar who had been rejected by his party."[35]

Nkomo travelled next to Jamaica at the beginning of August 1977 where he took a very tough line on the British, the Americans, and the internal settlement talks. He emphasized that the Americans should only play an observer role in future negotiations since "Zimbabwe was a British colonial problem." He continued the claim that both the British and Americans were only "looking for an acceptable black face to protect their Rhodesian investments." Nkomo went on to characterize Bishop Muzorewa and Reverend Sithole "as black weaklings with whom there could be no reconciliation." Responding to a question about the role of US ambassador to the United Nations, Andrew Young, in African diplomacy, Nkomo said that he had an "open mind" about this. "But it should be recognised that Young was a black man being used by the Carter Administration and that as an American he was by definition an imperialist."[36] A few days later, the British reported from Georgetown, Guyana, that Nkomo had met with Andrew Young. Nkomo reportedly told Young he wanted "to ensure that there was no joint Anglo-American plan for Zimbabwe" but said the United States could support a British plan. Young apparently explained that "if Americans did not sponsor [the] plan jointly with

---

[34] Ibid.
[35] "Note of a Meeting between the Prime Minster and Mr. Joshua Nkomo," July 27, 1977, PREM 15/1171, BNA.
[36] Kingston to FCO, "telno 364 of 5/8," August 9, 1977, item 216, PREM 15/1171, BNA.

Britain the U.S. Government might have difficulty in providing funds for Zimbabwe."[37]

Nkomo next met with Cyrus Vance, US secretary of state, a week later in Washington, DC, where he repeated his objections to the idea of an external peacekeeping force, especially from the United Nations. According to US reporting of the meeting, Nkomo used the example of the Congo as support for his case against the United Nations presence. "He referred to the alleged partiality of UN forces in the Congo which may have caused Lumumba's fall. He argued that the departure of foreign troops at the time of independence or 'at one minute before midnight' would open a dangerous gap."[38] The Americans were aware of British hopes to separate Nkomo from the PF and were starting to develop doubts about the idea. Briefing notes for Vance's meeting with Owen and the South African foreign minister, "Pik" Botha, state: "The British continue to believe that the Patriotic Front will fall apart and that Nkomo will accept the settlement package and participate in elections. Mugabe could then be isolated and lose Frontline support. This may be the case, but we should not imply to Botha that we are actively encouraging or expecting such an eventuality."[39]

Vance told the British, after meeting with Nkomo on August 15, that he did not believe "Nkomo's acceptance of the UK/US proposals would come easily," because Nkomo opposed the UN force during the interim period. Nkomo also told Vance he opposed a joint Anglo-American proposal. Most importantly, however, the note from this meeting states that "Vance told Nkomo the U.S. would not support an internal settlement."[40] By this stage, both Owen and Vance had assured Nkomo that their governments were not willing to support the "internal settlement" solution. Therefore, both the United States and

---

[37] Georgetown to FCO, "telno 133," August 11, 1977, item 218, PREM 15/1171, BNA.
[38] Bridgetown [sic] for Ambassador Young Only, "Secretary's Meeting with Nkomo," August 16, 1977, STATE194950, Central Foreign Policy Files, 1973–1976, RG 59, General Records of the Department of State, USNA.
[39] Georgetown for Ambassador Young, White House for Brzezinski, "Briefing Memorandum: Vance, Owen, Botha meeting," August 10, 1977, STATE188690, Central Foreign Policy Files, 1973–1976, RG 59, General Records of the Department of State, USNA.
[40] Washington to FCO (telno 3546), "My 3 IPTS," August 15, 1977, item 220, PREM 15/1171, BNA.

the British had given the PF their promise to not support an internal settlement government at the expense of the PF in future negotiations.

ZANU, Mozambique, and the Anglo-American Proposal

Mugabe and ZANU were aware of Nkomo's contacts with David Owen in London and in October 1977, ZANU's Didymus Mutasa, described by the FCO as "an old friend of the Rhodesia Department," relayed this when he paid a visit to the FCO. He said, "Mugabe has [the] impression Secretary of State [Owen] disliked him personally. Mugabe was always reading that other nationalists had met Dr. Owen in London but he had never been invited to London himself."[41] So while Mugabe kept up the public image of the intransigent leader who was not seeking out the British, he did have ways to get the message to London that he did not appreciate the greater attention given to Nkomo. Nor was ZANU immune from letting others know their feelings about ZAPU. An interview with two Zambian journalists in Lusaka revealed that ZANU leaders were telling them they feared civil war with ZAPU, and "accused Nkomo of holding back ZAPU (ZIPRA) until civil war – Russians would help."[42] This was the "zero-hour" theory that ZANU had begun to circulate in 1976. It became a convenient way of painting ZAPU and ZIPRA as secretly waiting to carry out Soviet plans once the war was over. The same journalists told the British on October 5, 1977 that Mugabe had survived "a sticky phase recently," when his leadership was challenged by Hamadziripi, Gumbo, and Mudzi. The story went that "Kangai and Mtende (recently killed in a motor accident in Mozambique) had exposed the plot and at the ensuing meeting held by ZANU in Chimoio in mid-September Mugabe had emerged in a stronger position than ever before." The reporters said that Mugabe was now ZANU's president, and Tongogara was now secretary for defense.[43]

While the threat of a "black civil war" loomed in the future, the immediate threat that heightened the risk of Cuban and Soviet involvement were the continued raids into Mozambique and Zambia by the

---

[41] Hurr to Harrison, October 19, 1977, item 279, FCO36/1929, BNA.

[42] I. C. Ross to Mr. McLoughlin, "Rhodesia: the Aftermath of the Kaunda/Smith talks and the future of the Patriotic Front," October 5, 1977, item 289, FCO36/1929, BNA.

[43] Ibid.

Rhodesians with South African military assistance. Mozambique's foreign minister, Joaquim Chissano, pressed the Americans and the British for military aid to defend against Rhodesian raids. After Chissano's meeting with the British ambassador John Lewen in Mozambique, in December 1977, the problem remained one of weapons. "The military answer was of course for Mozambique to ask for aircraft and other equipment from those friends who were already willing to supply them. They still did not wish to do this, however, since that would mean internationalising the war which was precisely what Smith wanted to happen."[44] Ambassador Lewen also reported a meeting with Samora Machel where Machel chastised the British for "our sluggishness in failing to get rid of Smith, whom he described as our 'nephew', and for failing to solve the Rhodesia problem."[45] Lewen noted that Machel did this with good humor, but that Machel also stressed that he wished the war could be ended as soon as possible.

A key reason for Machel's lack of patience with progress on the Anglo-American proposal was the Rhodesians attacks against ZANU and ZANLA bases and refugee camps in November 1977, as they had done previously in November 1976 during the Geneva talks. British diplomat Charles de Chassiron, based in Maputo at the time, reported to the FCO the serious losses such raids created in terms of loss of life for both ZANLA personnel and for Zimbabwean refugees. While indicating there was confusion over whether the attack on Chimoio had resulted in mostly the deaths of civilian-refugee or guerrilla fighters, it was clear to everyone the losses were substantial. De Chassiron noted the Mozambicans attempted to claim that Chimoio was solely a "civilian refugee transit camp" when updating "a skeptical U.S. Congressional aide." The British understood the camp was a "major ZANLA base, though there were civilians there – the ones for whom ZANU had been diverting UNHCR relief supplies." De Chassiron also noted that ZANU people interviewed after the raid had "thought that Mozambican army was protecting them."[46] De Chassiron described other Rhodesian attacks on November 26 far from the Rhodesian

[44]   Maputo to FCO, "telno 400: Rhodesia," December 7, 1977, item 190, FCO36/2020, BNA.
[45]   From Lagos to FCO "Rhodesia: Possible visit by Field Marshal Carver to Maputo," December 9, 1977, item 194, FCO36/2020, BNA.
[46]   De Chassiron to J. C. Harrison, "Rhodesian attacks in Mozambique," December 14, 1977, item 212, FCO36/2020, BNA.

border, at Tembue, a camp "250 kilometres North West of Tete city." Based on Mozambican intelligence reports, the Rhodesian raids there, which involved "anti-personnel bombs and helicopter-borne troops," resulted in "245 refugees killed and 147 wounded." Even though journalists were allowed to visit only one of the two camps at Tembue, de Chassiron concluded: "There seems little reason to doubt that here too the guerrillas suffered a heavy toll, but there is no doubt either that once again the Rhodesians have killed civilians indiscriminately."[47] Such inability to defend civilians and combatants from air raids made it all the more important for Machel and the Mozambicans to press for a negotiated transfer of power, ideally by 1978.

Smith, the Executive Committee, and the Rhodesian War Effort

Evidence from the SADF archives shows that the SADF Commander was telling Rhodesian general Peter Walls, in no uncertain terms, that the war was unwinnable. The meeting was held on August 17, 1977, at Defense Headquarters, to discuss with the Rhodesians joint plans "to ensure the evacuation of SADF equipment from Rhodesia should the necessity arise." Most importantly, the SADF Commander "emphasised that he saw no military solution to the problem, but only a political one, and that this political settlement was vital for the future of the country." He told Walls that there were three possible future scenarios, one where Ian Smith stays in power, one where Bishop Muzorewa becomes prime minister, and one where Mugabe becomes prime minister. With Mugabe, the SADF Commander, predicted "one could foresee only chaos and a vast outflow of refugees from Rhodesia and a general situation of instability."[48]

While the South Africans were pushing for an accommodation between Smith and Muzorewa, the internal settlement talks moved slowly in Salisbury. Evidence of the meetings among Smith, Muzorewa, Sithole, Chief Chirau, and others demonstrates the difficulties internal settlement leaders were having. One issue that caused

---

[47] Ibid.
[48] "Notes of a Meeting held by C SADF with the Commander Combined Operations, Rhodesia, at 15H00 on 17 August 1977," Rhodesia I, H SAW 3 168, SADF Archives, Pretoria, Defence Intelligence Declassified, 2011.04.04.

lengthy debate was over new franchise rules to continue giving whites what was referred to as "a blocking third" in parliament, to protect white minority interests.[49] An example of the difficulties in the internal settlement talks is contained in the minutes of a meeting in Salisbury on December 23, 1977. Professor Stanlake Samkange argued with Ian Smith; he was critical of Smith for what he called bad negotiations – the one-third reserved for whites and the two-thirds for blacks did not respond to a concept of majority rule. Smith replied that the reason he needed guarantees for whites was he wanted to guarantee whites they would be able to live in a future majority rule country "without recrimination." Samkange replied that the problem with Smith and the Rhodesian Front was they thought only in racial terms. He suggested the United African National Council likely would run white candidates, so it was possible there could be more than thirty-three white representatives in parliament. Samkange added, "So many whites were leaving the country that there might no longer be enough whites to give the 33 seats to." He then criticized Smith: "The government should get away from its racial stand. I appeal to the government, the longer we delay the more perilous the situation gets. If this fails we throw this country into chaos."

Smith's response to Samkange shows the contempt Smith held toward African independent states in the region: "The Professor thinks we think racially. He must know that here in Rhodesia the whites think racially, that is a fact of life here. We live next to Mozambique, Angola and Zambia, what happens there has not helped the racial thinking in this country." Smith then insisted that he had only agreed to the concept of majority rule in his negotiations with Kissinger because he believed that his decision had come with safeguards. He also responded to Samkange's jibe about whites leaving the country in large numbers. Smith argued that this started when he made the announcement based on Kissinger's offer in September 1976. Smith concluded, "The whites tell me that all I have to do is say I no longer accepted majority rule, then we can stop this exflux and start seeing more whites coming here. What I can't do is to accept a settlement which won't solve the problem."[50]

---

[49] For of debates over voting mechanisms during the UDI and the Zimbabwe-Rhodesia state, see Luise White, *Unpopular Sovereignty*, 149–79 and 232–49.

[50] "The minutes of the 9th meeting (Friday December 23rd 1977) of the settlement talks between Smith, Muzorewa, Sithole, and Chirau." SANA DFA 1–151, vol. 2.

At this point, Gibson Magaramombe interjected into the debate: "It is enjoyable to sit at conferences and hear politicians argue." Smith replied, "Speak for yourself." At which point Magaramombe suggested that they all needed to remember that "people lose life by the day while politicians are arguing and drinking tea. We don't want to talk of the past and no one wants to be blamed for the past mistakes. I also want to tell you that the men in the bush are not ours. We may be the first to face the firing squads." This dose of reality may have brought the discussion further, but it would take another four months until the March 3, 1978 internal settlement was finally agreed upon by the major players in what would become known as the "Executive Council" or "Exco."[51]

British and American Attempts to Restart Negotiations

As the news of Smith's and the African leaders' internal settlement talks became more widely known, the British and Americans tried to see how they could best take advantage of this development to push for all-party talks and hopefully bring the PF and Smith back to the negotiating table.[52] The internal settlement talks gave the PF sufficient reasons to break with future negotiations, as they could now argue that Smith was doing what observers had predicted he would do since the failed Geneva talks, thereby using negotiations to buy time while he put together the "puppet" black government. A key Anglo-American goal was therefore to gain the support of the Frontline State presidents in not giving up on negotiations when confronted with the internal settlement. Evidence of the Frontline State presidents' resolve to try to force the PF to negotiations came out one of their meetings in April 1977 in Lusaka. The British had sent long-time Southern African expert Dennis Grennan to interview the PF leaders on the sidelines of the meeting to see where they stood on continued negotiations with the Anglo-American proposal. Grennan met with T. G. Silundika, representing ZAPU, and Mugabe, representing ZANU. He reported that he took Mugabe, Tongogara, Muzenda, and Gumbo "to drinks" as well. Information on what was discussed in the Frontline State presidents' meeting with the nationalists was not easy for Grennan to obtain,

---

[51] Ibid.
[52] Pret WPGR1563 to EXTODD GAA, "Southern African Affairs-Views of South African Sec for Foreign Affairs," November 19, 1976, FCO36/1803.

although he did note that after a three-hour meeting, the Frontline State presidents told Nkomo and Mugabe that while they were willing to "acknowledge the role of the PF as the sole liberation movement they did not endorse the Front's claim to be the sole representative of the people of Zimbabwe in negotiating a political settlement."[53] The Frontline State presidents were taking advantage of the reality of the internal settlement talks to pressure Nkomo and Mugabe by withholding their support for the PF as "sole representatives." As described in Chapter 3, Muzorewa and Sithole had failed to create any meaningful links between themselves and the military leaders in Lusaka and Maputo, making the PF's military role all the more important in terms of leverage. As time went on, the Frontline State presidents would express greater opposition to a role for the internal settlement. In this earlier period, however, while the internal settlement was still not fully developed, they seemed to be using it as leverage to force greater unity among Nkomo and Mugabe, and to increase the level of military engagement with the Smith regime.

ZAPU's George Silundika told Grennan that they objected to American involvement in future negotiations "which would bring the superpowers into the Rhodesia situation." Grennan emphasized that "we were not asking them to stop the armed struggle until an agreement had been concluded." In response, Msika added that "another objection to the British proposals was they would distract the PF's leadership from the prosecution of the armed struggle." Grennan retorted that he "found it an astonishing argument for them to claim that they had the resources to win the war but cannot devote any time or effort to win the peace." According to Grennan, ZAPU's secretary general, Joseph Msika, "laughingly said he thought it was an argument that might go down well with the Presidents!" This was further indication the Frontline State presidents had pushed at the meeting for both parties in the PF to engage in negotiations or find themselves left out.

Grennan was pleased to report to British foreign secretary David Owen that he had got on well with Mugabe, who he found to be "more like the friend I knew 15 years ago than the man at Geneva." Grennan reported Mugabe to be interested in what the British had heard from their meetings in Salisbury and what Owen "really thought" about the

---

[53] Grennan to Sec of State, "Meeting of Front Line Presidents and Patriotic Front Leaders," April 22, 1977, item 98, FCO 36/929.

chances for a peaceful settlement. "At no time did he reject your proposals and indeed made several flattering references to the way you had conducted your discussions during your trip." Mugabe let Grennan know that Owen had "certainly seemed to have impressed" the presidents. At the end of the meeting, Mugabe told Grennan that he expected they would be "seeing a lot of each other in the near future." Grennan characterized Mugabe as a leader who wanted to make sure the British knew he was keen to negotiate, even to the extent of sharing flattering comments about Owen.

Grennan was also aware that ZAPU and ZANU leaders were uneasy about the future of negotiations after meeting with the Frontline State presidents. The inclusion of the United States into future all-party negotiations and its acceptance by the Frontline State presidents gave them reason to worry. Grennan observed they were worried about a future all-party conference without the PF which would "prove an independence constitution to be acceptable to all the other parties including the Presidents." The internal settlement threat had given the Frontline State presidents leverage, as this development left the door open for Bishop Muzorewa and others to negotiate for the "people of Zimbabwe," even as Muzorewa and others lacked any direct link to the liberation forces.

While Mugabe was careful to remain in good books of the British, Nkomo was active diplomatically in this period to build a case for a turnover of power from Smith to the PF. Not only was this done to try to circumvent the internal settlement, it demonstrated Nkomo's hopes to push a negotiated transition that would provide a role for him as the leader of the PF. Since the Geneva talks, Nkomo was aware that in the first independent election, given the strong likelihood that Mugabe would stand separately as the ZANU candidate, that he and ZAPU were unlikely to win a nationwide election. His dealings with the Americans and British in this period show he was eager to move the process along before Mugabe and the ZANLA leaders could consolidate their power in ZANU. Nkomo began to request direct meetings with the British and Americans. Nkomo called a meeting with Stephen Low, the US ambassador to Zambia, in late April 1977 to arrange a face-to-face meeting with Cyrus Vance. Low's assessment of the meeting indicated that Nkomo, while wanting to meet with Vance, was interested in expressing his concerns that the United States should not be part of the next constitutional conference, and that non-PF nationalists should not be invited. In his report of the meeting, Low said there was likely more flexibility in Nkomo's positions on these points and that they were less set in stone than he would like to admit. Low concluded: "One was left with the impression that he [Nkomo] sees no way of coming out of the conference presently proposed as the leader of an independent Zimbabwe and that he is not prepared to accept any process short of this."[54]

Although Nkomo often mentioned that he was following the Frontline States Presidents' firm conditions that he must always negotiate with the British in Mugabe's presence, Nkomo attempted once again to meet independently with Secretary Owen when he was in London to meet with US secretary of state Cyrus Vance on May 6, 1977. The correspondence in the British FCO files concerning this proposed meeting reveals Nkomo's trademark attention to logistics. He wanted the British government to pay for a suite plus four single rooms at the Park Tower Hotel in Knightsbridge. He also wanted immigration to be notified so that he and his entourage could pass quickly through immigration at Heathrow. On the morning of his arrival from Ghana, however, he and his team had to wait more than an hour and a half in immigration because Nkomo refused to have one of his bodyguards surrender his gun, although he eventually did before they were allowed to leave the airport.

Nkomo's May 6 morning meeting with Secretary of State Vance, according to American accounts, show that Vance kept a positive line with Nkomo. It would seem that Nkomo's goal in the meeting with Vance was to receive Vance's promise that the United States would not co-sponsor the next conference, once it was arranged. Nkomo opposed American involvement, arguing that "U.S. participation in a conference would open the door to big power politics." But he diplomatically added, "If the U.S. can assist by means other than getting into a conference, please do so." Vance was willing to concede this demand, saying that he and Owen had discussed what the United States could do, short of co-sponsoring the next conference, and therefore it was not necessary for them to serve as a "co-sponsor." Nkomo and ZAPU's deputy for external affairs, Daniel Madzimbamuto, argued a bit that consultations leading up to a Lancaster House conference would still be

---

[54] Low to State, "Nkomo on the Owen Proposals," April 26, 1977, item 135, FCO 36/1927, BNA.

"internationalized." Nkomo said that he welcomed American assistance but "along the lines of the present meeting": "We cannot have a conference in bits and pieces." Vance warned Nkomo that if the United States were not involved in consultations, "Britain might not be willing to begin the process." In addition, Vance reminded Nkomo and his colleagues that "if a realistic process is not commenced, then there will be no Independence in 1978." In the end, Nkomo seemed to have received Vance's assurance that American "co-sponsorship" had been ruled out. As Vance agreed, he added, "There was too much concern about the word and that our real purpose was to assist the process."[55]

Nkomo did not manage to meet with Owen, who was busy with a Commonwealth heads of government meeting in London that week. Nkomo did meet with John Graham, the FCO's deputy undersecretary of state, in Nkomo's hotel suite on the evening of May 6, after his meeting with Vance. This meeting was also attended by the FCO's assistant undersecretary for Africa, Philip Mansfield. In his report, Graham expressed Owen's "regret" over not meeting Nkomo in London. Nkomo explained that he "intended no disrespect, but he was bound by his agreement with Mr. Mugabe not to have official talks with Britain on his own." He said he " would have been glad to see Dr. Owen 'over a glass of beer' in his hotel, but a call at the Foreign Office or the House of Commons made the thing official." After explaining that the agreement between him and Mugabe did not apply to US secretary of state Vance, Nkomo added, "However the PF was united, one body: it was not a case of ZANU and ZAPU." Getting to matters concerning negotiations, Graham reiterated what Vance had offered in terms of a new joint British and American initiative toward a negotiated settlement. Nkomo said he was delighted to say that Vance had agreed with him earlier in the day to drop the US role as a co-sponsor. Graham said, diplomatically, that it was up to "the US to speak for themselves" but that he had been in a meeting that morning with Vance and Owen where the two "had agreed one again to pursue the approach as a joint endeavour." Graham said there was no interest in calling a new conference now, but when it did happen, "it

55 USDel Secretary in London to Sec State WashDC for Tarnoff and Lake, "Secretary's Meeting with Nkomo," May 6, 1977, 1977SECTO04004, Central Foreign Policy Files, 1973–1976, RG 59, General Records of the Department of State, USNA.

would be co-sponsored by Britain and the U.S." Nkomo repeated the potential problems formal US involvement would create, including a reference to the United Nations Security Council, and potential problems there. Graham related to Nkomo some of the advantages of US involvement, including influence with South Africa, Smith, "and their contribution to the Zimbabwe Development Fund." Graham reported that Nkomo "erupted" at the mention of the development fund. "His country was not to be bought, 'was not to be shackled like Cyprus.' They would need investment, but they would get it for themselves."

Nkomo further complained about British strategy, especially over their decision to include Bishop Muzorewa and Reverend Sithole in future negotiations. "There was a war on and only those who were fighting it should be consulted. There could be no 'peaceful' transfer of power: if there were to be a transfer of power it would be as a result of the end of the war."

Nkomo went on to say that "Britain always tried to complicate things and make difficulties, in Cyprus, in the Middle East, in South Africa, and now in Rhodesia: she tried to set one group against another so as to maintain the troubled waters in which she could fish." Nkomo reportedly characterized Britain as a spider that would come out of its lair and "devour each of the nationalist leaders separately." Graham responded to each of Nkomo's criticisms, and added, as seems typical of diplomats from Britain, his own "ethnic" interpretation of Nkomo's spider analogy. Graham said:

As a Scotsman, the spider stood for me for persistence: if we were thwarted in our search for a settlement in one way, we tried another. What had Mr. Nkomo to lose? We did not want to divide: we were not interested in picking the leaders of an independent Zimbabwe. That was their affair. He should not be so suspicious.[56]

Nkomo's final comments, according to Graham, were his usual welcoming of further talks. "It was not their way to turn people away – and they would receive me." He was, however, "frankly discouraged" by what Graham had said, having been "encouraged" by Vance in what Graham presumes to be a reference to the question of co-sponsorship.[57] So, after a long day of meetings with Vance and then

[56] "Rhodesia: Call on Mr Nkomo," May 6, 1977, FCO 36/1927, BNA.
[57] Ibid.

Graham, it seemed that Nkomo had not gotten as much as he had
hoped from his own shuttle diplomacy to London en route to Paris. He
had not managed to meet directly with Owen, and the major concession of non-US involvement he thought he had obtained from Vance
turned out to be less concrete after talking to Graham. For Nkomo, an
added pressure came from his ties to the Soviets, who were supportive
of negotiations but not if the United States was to take a leading role in
them, hence Nkomo's attempts to gain assurances from Vance that the
United States would play less of a role in future talks. As the next
chapter will argue, the longer negotiations took, and the more nationalists leaders were involved in the negotiations, the greater the difficulties were for Nkomo's goal of becoming leader of the PF in a transition
government before majority rule elections.

Diplomacy Leading Up to the Malta Talks

The Malta talks were an Anglo-American initiative to keep the PF in
negotiations by meeting with Mugabe and Nkomo while Smith and the
internal settlement group continued on their own path. In
November 1977, Owen sent letters to both Nkomo and Mugabe inviting them to London to discuss transitional arrangements. The jointly
signed response from Mugabe and Nkomo is illuminating in terms of
the distain they expressed toward Owen and Britain's position on the
internal settlement talks. The PF leaders' letter stated that they refused
to meet with Owen. Their reasons had to do with the perception that
Owen had changed Britain's intentions for the next talks. Rather than
having a serious discussion of the transition period, according to
Nkomo and Mugabe, Owen was now wishing for the PF to meet
with Ian Smith "to consider with the PF their ideas about the transition
period."[58] Mugabe and Nkomo were dissatisfied: "In a situation of
such grave drain to human lives what time do we have to indulge in
endless processes of trading with ideas when we must urgently reach
agreed decisions to secure the transition towards ending the war and
independence?"[59] They accused Owen of duplicity with Smith, stating
that the "hesitation as to whether to hold the meeting in Malta or not

---

[58] J. N. N. Nkomo and R. G. Mugabe to Dr. Owen, "The Zimbabwe Patriotic
Front," December 8, 1977, item 379, PREM 15/1171, BNA.
[59] Ibid.

coincided with Ian Smith's announcement on 'adult suffrage' and the so-called Internal Settlement as if you [Owen] anticipated this." The letter then quoted Owen's own words, based on his comments made about "Smith's election plans." Owens had said: "The elections must be conducted in a manner which is demonstrably free and fair and all peoples and parties who intend to live in a future Zimbabwe should be free to participate if they wish to do so, whether they are at present living inside or outside Rhodesia."[60]

The two PF leaders interpreted Owen's remarks as indicating he was more concerned with defending Smith than removing him – with the latter a precondition, they declared, for future negotiations. The criticisms of Owen continued, this time in relation to a remark Owen made on the BBC on December 2, 1977, in response to attacks in Mozambique by the Smith regime. The jointly signed Nkomo and Mugabe letter stated the attacks by the "racist regime of Ian Smith" occurred between "23–27th November and massacred scores of Zimbabwean women and children." Critical of Owen, they accused him of not only failing to condemn the attacks, but of demonstrating "a gleeful attitude at them" and lending priority to Owen's "enthusiastic anticipations of the plans of the murderer Ian Smith." They quoted Owen's comment made to the BBC, where he had said that the attacks "also might show the PF, [which] may have some advantages in getting overall compromise, that the Rhodesian defence is not on its back." Nkomo and Mugabe equated this statement with Owen saying Smith's forces had showed "the British colony's armed forces are not weak." They also accused Owen of suggesting that the internal settlement plan offered Smith a way to bring the PF into it "or at least he [Smith] must give them an offer or involve them in an arrangement which they can honourably come inside and be involved in."[61] This latter observation was not far from Owen's intentions, as he would promote such a move in 1978. After accusing Owen of having a "double-faced outlook," they concluded: "We hope you can sort yourself out soon for us to know definitely which direction you are following – that of your 'Proposals' or that of Ian Smith." They concluded that they needed "to know whether or not any meaningful discussions can be held with

---

[60] Ibid.
[61] Maputo to Dr. Owen, "The Zimbabwe Patriotic Front," December 8, 1977, PREM 15/1171, BNA. (Source: Letter to Dr. David Owen from the Zimbabwe PF, December 8, 1977.)

you to secure finally and fully arrangements for an unalterable advent of the independence of Zimbabwe, our motherland. Our armed liberation struggle continues."[62]

In December 1977, Mugabe responded to Owen's invitation for further talks while meeting with Ambassador Lewen in Maputo. Mugabe told Lewen he wanted to know Owen's true intentions, because "some of your [Owen's] recent remarks implied support for those talks, the real aim of which was to keep Smith in power." Mugabe wanted Owen to provide a "denunciation of Smith's internal talks as being contrary to the course of action you had started towards a settlement, and a statement that the conclusion of those talks would not receive the blessing of HM Government."[63] Owen replied to Lewen, telling him, "There can be no question of a denunciation in advance of the kind requested by Mugabe. Alternatively, a refusal to do so might be seized by him as a pretext for advising Nkomo . . . to reject the proposed meeting." Owen instructed Lewen to "do his best to avoid further discussion with Mugabe on this question" and, if Mugabe was to ask about it, Owen told Lewen to tell him that "the Secretary of State is on holiday at present" and that the question could be put to Owen in person if Mugabe and Nkomo agreed to meet.[64]

As 1978 began, the British and Americans felt more confident that the PF leaders would agree to a new round of negotiations even though the conditions discussed above put everyone on edge. A number of factors kept all parties interested in future talks: the internal settlement option; the increased raids into the Front Line States by the Rhodesians; the internal challenges to Mugabe's leadership in ZANU; and Nkomo's own realization that a negotiated settlement might forego the necessity of elections before the transfer of power. Delays in creating the internal settlement government played into the hands of the Anglo-American proposal and the PF, allowing the four actors to meet separately from the Smith regime and the internal settlement nationalists. The result was a series of meetings at the end of January 1978 in Malta organized by the British and Americans. A follow-up meeting in Dar es Salaam in mid-April 1978 attempted to negotiate an agreement on military concerns within the framework of the Anglo-American proposal, with the

---

[62] Ibid.
[63] Maputo to FCO, "telno 423," December 23, 1977, item 360, FCO 36/1930, BNA.
[64] FCO to Maputo, "Telno 244," December 28, 1977, FCO 36/1930, BNA.

British and Americans negotiating with the PF without Smith present. The hope was that such a meeting would move everyone to "all parties" talks with Smith at a Lancaster House–style conference to iron out the new constitution and the transfer of power. At this point, the British, the Americans, and the PF leaders believed majority rule was still possible in 1978, as originally discussed at the Geneva conference. The historical perspective that comes from knowing that the Lancaster House talks would not be convened for almost another year and ten months must not get in the way of appreciating how pressed for time the various parties understood themselves to be in early 1978.

Mugabe's Leadership Challenged Again

Before examining the diplomacy at the Malta talks in Chapter 6, and the ways in which these direct talks with the PF demonstrated the considerable negotiating skills of Nkomo and Mugabe, it is worth reflecting on Mugabe's further consolidation of power in ZANU at the time of the Malta talks. Once again, the long document prepared by those ZANU leaders who were arrested and jailed in January 1978 is useful. Although authorship is listed as "Detained ZANU Leaders, HIGH Command, ZIPA Military Committee and other Senior Commanders in Mozambique," the authorship of the document is attributed to Rugare Gumbo. The nature of the text, twelve single-spaced pages with many typographic errors, seems to indicate that it was typed quickly, which could also reflect that conditions were less than ideal for the prisoners to write and then send out this document to the British high commissioner.

The main theme of the document concerns the breakdown of democratic decision-making in the ZANU central committee and the continued use of arrests and detentions to silence opposition within the central committee. The authors characterize themselves as "progressives" and those who opposed them, and who had them arrested, as "the conservatives." The authors are careful not to list many names of those who arrested them, although they do name Edgar Tekere and blame him for going "about in the camps carrying out a smear campaign against the progressives" and against the four members of the Central committee, Rugare Gumbo, Matuku Hamadziripi, Crispen Mandizvidza, and Ray Musikavanhu, all of whom were arrested on

January 24, 1978, a few days before the Malta talks. The authors claim that "Tekere's campaign sparked off violence [in the] camps exactly seven days after the arrest of the four Central Committee members." Violence in the camps on January 31 reportedly resulted in "the mass arrests and torture of the fighters who supported the line of the progressives." On March 9, the four Central Committee members were turned over to the "conservatives where they were imprisoned [and] severely tortured and stories concted [sic] to the effect [that] they wanted to take the Party and the army to ZAPU."[65]

According to the text, the divide between the "progressives" and the "conservatives" occurred at the September 1977 central committee at Chimoio and at another central committee meeting held in October 1977. According to the account, the September meeting had seen an attempt by the progressives to return to "democratic centralism" as the core of ZANU's decision making. This push had failed, and at the October central committee meeting the progressives were informed of their erroneous thinking. "Our genuine demand to achieve political unity within the PF was interpreted by the conservatives [sic] elements in the Party leadership as efforts to undermine the party and to surrender the party to ZAPU." The report indicated that, in fact, the "formal decision was taken" at the October meeting, "[n]ever genuinely to unite politically with ZAPU" and that "ZANU was to be preserved until independence." What follows is an important confirmation of ZANU's and Mugabe's strategy from late 1977 until independence: "To avoid pressure from frontline states and [the] OAU concerning political unity, the party formulated a strategy and tactic of everything humanly possible to avoid a political merger with ZAPU. The name of the strategy is '*tamba wakachenjera*' literally translated 'play it carefully'." The logic of this strategy would be repeated for many years. "Since ZAPU's thesis was that political unity should come first before military unity, ZANU's strategy would be to start from military unity, so that there is a deadlock and unity would not materialized [sic]."[66]

---

[65] "The Truth about the Recurrent ZANU Crisis and the Emergence of a Two Line Struggle," August 13, 1979, FCO 36/2409, BNA. For Edgar Tekere's perspective, see his autobiography: Edgar Tekere, *A Lifetime of Struggle*, (Harare: SAPES Books, 2007) 85–86; see also Wilfred Mhanda, *Dzino: Memories of a Freedom Fighter* (Harare: Weaver, 2011), 172–200.

[66] "The Truth about the Recurrent ZANU Crisis and the Emergence of a Two Line Struggle," August 13, 1979, FCO 36/2409, BNA.

Interestingly, Blessing-Miles Tendi, in his 2012 interview with Mugabe, was told by Mugabe that *"tamba wakachenjera"* had also applied to ZANU's approach to diplomacy in 1975 around the Lusaka Accords. That is, to remain connected to détente negotiations, while also, at the same time, intensifying the war effort.[67]

This document provides an important foil to the public optimism both PF parties presented to diplomats. The authors suggest the intransigence about possibly unity was explained to them in terms of Chinese Communist Party history. Given that most of the "conservative" leaders in ZANU had studied in China, this is not surprising. The progressives went to some lengths, however, to argue in the document that while the Chinese Communist Party was rightfully wary of unity with the "Kouminta[n]g" based on class differences, they saw no similar differences between ZAPU and ZANU. They argued that "ZANU is not a party in the true sense of a class vanguard. ZANU is composed of different democratic and patriotic forces coming from different strata of society. So also is ZAPU." The authors conclude that the decision to never unify had more to do with the "desire to preserve personal power by the anti-unity elements in the Party." They refer to the dishonesty on this question as "tragic," because "as revolutionaries we should try to be truthful."[68] It was clear to anyone around ZANU and ZANLA that dissent, especially on the question of working with ZAPU, was not to be tolerated.

It is interesting to consider how the British heard of this power move within ZANU. At the end of January 1978, the British were starting to get word that Henry Hamadziripi and Rugare Gumbo had been put under "house arrest" and were "being investigated for alleged links with 'the CIA and British', for having received funds from 'Tiny' Rowland, and for promoting unification with ZAPU in opposition to the rest of the ZANU National Executive."[69] It is worth noting that this leadership crisis, like the ZIPA challenge in 1976 and 1977, showed

---

[67] Blessing-Miles Tendi, *The Army and Politics in Zimbabwe: Mujuru, the Liberation Fighter and Kingmaker* (Cambridge University Press, 2020), 55.

[68] "The Truth about the Recurrent ZANU Crisis and the Emergence of a Two Line Struggle," August 13, 1979, FCO 36/2409, BNA. See Fay Chung, *Re-living the Second Chimurenga: Memories from the Liberation Struggle in Zimbabwe* (Uppsala, Sweden: Nordic Africa Institute 2006), 179–80.

[69] This intel came to the British from "John Borrell, a local freelance journalist." FM Lusaka to FCO, "Rhodesia: ZANU," January 30, 1978, item 125, FCO36/2122, BNA.

again just how much Mugabe relied on his military leaders, particularly Rex Nhongo and Josiah Tongogara, to secure control of the party and enforce discipline among the fighting forces in Mozambique and Tanzania. The British were concerned about the loss of more moderate voices in ZANU given that the arrested leaders had demonstrated their willingness to cooperate with ZAPU in the PF. Keeping with this trend when the British commented on such internal power struggles, they noted that at least Mugabe's faction had handed over the purged leaders to the Mozambicans to imprison rather than the alternative. Hamadziripi, Gumbo, and the others accused of supporting cooperation with ZAPU and ZIPRA would spend most of the remainder of the war held in Mozambican custody, and in mid-1979 they were transferred to join with the ZIPA leaders arrested in 1977.[70]

---

[70] Mhanda notes that many of this group were severely malnourished when they joined the ZIPA prisoners, including Hamadziripi. See Mhanda, *Dzino*, 191–93. For the wider context and details of ZANU's disciplinary actions, see Gerald Mazarire, "Discipline and Punishment in ZANLA: 1964–1979," *Journal of Southern African Studies*, 37, no. 3 (2011), 571–91.

6 | *Negotiating Independently 1978*

With all the efforts at international diplomacy in 1977, the parties were in 1978 still far from the goals of a negotiated ceasefire and transitional government. The Frontline State presidents and the Anglo-Americans had hoped the internal settlement talks would bring the PF to the negotiating table in order to avoid being left out. At this stage, the prospect of "splitting" the PF seemed to be worth a chance from the point of view of British foreign secretary David Owen but not necessarily from the point of view of the Americans or the South Africans. Why Owen would think Nkomo would drop Mugabe and work directly with Ian Smith is an interesting question, which reveals much about how the FCO tended to view Zimbabwean nationalists through the lens of ethnicity. Perhaps it was their detailed knowledge of Zimbabwean nationalist politics, including waves of infighting and intrigues during the mid-1970s that led the British to continue to emphasize ethnic loyalties when forecasting the prospects for Nkomo and Mugabe. This approach led to the view that Nkomo's ambitions to be Zimbabwe's first prime minister, along with his minority ethnic status, were at the heart of the competition between ZANU and ZAPU, rather than personal political rivalries. Nkomo's explosive responses to media reports suggesting the PF could not create unity because of ethnicity shows something about his aversion to analyzing everything through ethnicity. He believed that he had earned the right to be in the top leadership position in the PF because of his seniority to Mugabe and his greater international diplomatic experience over the years. He also believed that ZAPU and ZANU could form a political alliance before the first national elections that could lead to his victory. In a press conference following the Malta meetings on February 1, 1978, Nkomo and Mugabe were "[a]sked whether they would enter the elections as a united party (and) they affirmed that they would."[1] Of course,

---

[1] Fm Valletta to FCO, "Mugabe and Nkomo Press Conference," February 1, 1978, item 144, FCO36/2122, BNA.

Nkomo likely had sufficient reason at this stage to believe Mugabe would not honor this pledge.

Malta Talks: The Americans, the British, and the Patriotic Front

The Malta talks of January 30–31, 1978, were organized primarily in order to reassure the PF that the premise of the Anglo-American proposal was still the foundation for future negotiations, regardless of the internal settlement talks going on in Salisbury. In their approach to Malta, the British were particularly keen to try to use the internal settlement talks as sufficient leverage to get the PF to back off of some of their more adamant pre-settlement demands. An interesting FCO draft briefing for the Malta meeting spelled out the strategy, which was premised on the notion that if the PF remained intransigent, then at some point, they would "have to step back" and would be "unable to prevent Mr. Smith from pursuing his internal settlement initiative to its logical conclusion." This strategy understood that should such an internal settlement materialize, "whether or not it constitutes a genuine handover of power, [it] will exclude the PF and will ensure that the war goes on." The prognosis for such an eventuality was not a positive one. "If this happens, and the PF eventually fought their way to power, the Zimbabwe that they would take over would be economically and politically exhausted and the degree of bitterness between the races and different nationalist factions would have increased immeasurably."[2] It is worth considering how this strategy proposal at this stage in the negotiations reflects a consistent position maintained by the British in terms of race. Because the PF had made it clear that it would not stop fighting once a puppet "black" government were installed and internationally recognized, the pressure on the PF, so this reasoning went, would be that they were now fighting a "civil war" between black Africans and not a "race war" in Rhodesia. The problem with this racialized reasoning is that the PF leaders did not see their fight for power strictly as a racial one. The struggle was now more personal about who would gain the ultimate goal, to obtain and maintain political control of the new state as experienced in Angola, Mozambique, Zambia, Malawi, Botswana, and Tanzania. The nature

[2] Barlow to Graham, "Rhodesia: Talks with PF in Malta: 30–31 January 1978 Steering Brief," January 26, 1978, item 86, FCO 36/2122, BNA.

of the one-party state in southern and central Africa gave the PF the model for a future Zimbabwe.

The same FCO document made a pitch for dividing the PF: "It may be possible, if Mugabe is clearly the hard liner, to separate him from Nkomo. But there is little hope of this. The ideal objective would be to bring Smith and Nkomo together. This is probably only possible for Nkomo within the framework of our proposals."[3] Graham made a similar comment in his pre-Malta briefing, emphasizing "the need to pressure the PF, and if Mugabe continued to remain uncooperative, then to try to form a new party with Nkomo who could step in and accept an offer."[4] As will be shown in the remainder of this chapter, Owen would push for this split, while the Americans remained less convinced of the efficacy of such a plan. So what progress, if any, came from the Malta talks? First, the talks helped to officially bring the PF leaders into formal mediated talks where both ZAPU and ZANU were forced to outline a common position. The talks also permitted Owen and US ambassador to the United Nations, Andrew Young, to take over from the failed Geneva initiative and keep the United States and Britain involved in negotiations. This is an interesting contrast to the Geneva talks period in 1976 where it was Kissinger, the US secretary of state, pushing for talks, and the British ambassador to the United Nations, Ivor Richard, who was not as enthusiastic about Britain's role at the time.

Just before Malta, Owen, learning from the severe criticisms he had received from the PF leaders over his earlier remarks, made two public statements of Britain's support for the Anglo-American proposal and his doubts about the internal settlement. In a press statement provided to the *Daily Express*, Owen remarked that if the internal settlement produced results, that would be a positive note, but as far as they could tell at the time, "the plans proposed in the Salisbury talks would be unlikely to bring about a peaceful settlement and therefore unlikely to be recognized internationally. There must be international acceptance because the UN must recognize a settlement if sanctions are to be lifted."[5] The previous day, January 25, 1978, Owen had addressed

---

[3] Ibid.

[4] J. A. N. Graham, "Rhodesia: Future Policy," January 17, 1978, item 62, FCO 36/2121, BNA.

[5] Owen to Press Officers, "Rhodesia: Pre Malta Scenario," January 26, 1978, item 123, FCO 36/2122, BNA.

parliament on the objectives of the Malta talks. In addition to stressing the "full support of the U.S. Government" for the talks, Owen emphasized the role of elections in determining the legitimacy of the transfer of power in Zimbabwe. Owen was clearly speaking to Mugabe and Nkomo when he emphasized the need for any settlement to include "all parties," and that anything short of this would not be recognized as legitimate. Owen added, "Moreover, a settlement which did not involve all the parties could hardly bring peace to this troubled country."[6] His statement in the House of Commons helped to encourage the PF to meet again in good faith.

Still, even with Owen's concession to Mugabe's demand to publicly state his opposition to the internal settlement, none of the participants entered Malta with much optimism toward a settlement. The British complained that the PF position was too extreme. For example, the British believed the PF leaders were insisting on control of the transitional government in order to block the influence of the "internal" nationalists such as Bishop Muzorewa and to guarantee their control of the post-transition government. The PF leaders were opposed to United Nations observers and peacekeepers, which had to do with a carry-over from the Congo experience, and to how Nkomo and Mugabe remembered the role of the United Nations military intervention there. At this stage, the PF were asking for full control of the police and military security before elections.

Given such formidable differences in starting points for negotiations, the British hoped that at least the Frontline State presidents were going to be more reasonable about a settlement. Owen suggested in his instructions to Frontline State missions before the Malta meeting, "We believe that the desire for a peaceful settlement and a sense of realism exist among the Front Line Presidents, despite President Kaunda's idea, which he is no longer pressing, of postponing elections until after Independence."[7] This last point suggests that Kaunda had floated the idea of a complete transition of power to the PF before any

---

[6] Owen continued, "I must make it clear that the Government, who alone can confer legal independence on Rhodesia, will not lend their authority to any settlement which fails to meet the criteria that I have described." Owen to House of Commons, "Rhodesia: Draft Statement by the Secretary of State in the House of Commons," January 30, 1978, item 127, FCO 36/2122, BNA.

[7] Owen to Immediate Certain Missions and Dependent Territories, "Rhodesia: MALTA Talks with Patriotic Front," January 27, 1978, item 97, FCO 36/2122, BNA.

elections were held, which may have been his way of envisioning Nkomo having any chance of becoming the first leader of Zimbabwe. But the pressure from Nyerere, the United Nations, and the Americans to use the international standard of elections as the necessary means to transfer power would eventually force Kaunda to drop the idea.[8]

The first Malta talks largely failed in moving the PF away from its previous position that it should control the transition period and control security forces during a transition period. Owen's accounts of the meetings, and the memorandums of conversations, show a lack of common ground, as the PF continued to insist that they, as the military forces carrying out the war, were the only Zimbabwean nationalist parties who could take part in a transition. Conversely, the British and Americans used the internal settlement talks to try to push the PF into making some concessions toward a more balanced negotiated transitional government plan. Nkomo reminded Owen at the Malta talks that Owen had previously assured the PF that the only parties qualified to negotiate were those involved in the fighting, therefore ruling out Muzorewa and others. Owen did not agree with this interpretation. Mugabe also pushed Owen to accept the idea that the PF would have to be in charge of the transition. Apparently, the PF's proposal suggested that five individuals serve in the transitional government, four from the PF and one from the Smith regime. The British later commented that they should be careful not to let this proposal leak, as "[i]t would be very damaging if they were thought to be acceptable to ourselves."[9]

Owen and Young challenged Mugabe and Nkomo to step back from their rigid positions. Mugabe told Owen and Young that the PF "would be satisfied with nothing less than a dominant role in the sovereign organ during the transition period. They would not accept a status subordinate to the Resident Commissioner." Owen "stressed that the choice lay between a settlement involving some compromise by the PF and the intensification of the fighting, together with increasingly vigorous efforts by Smith to promote an internal settlement. In the latter event the world would have to stand back." This obvious challenge to the PF to soften their demands was also supported by Andrew Young.[10] He emphasized

---

[8] Ibid.
[9] W. K. Prendergrast, "News Department conversation with Mr Fergusson," January 31, 1978, item 140, FCO 36/2122, BNA.
[10] Valletta to FCO, "My Tel no 44: Rhodesia: Talks with the Patriotic Front," February 1, 1978, item 137, FCO 36/2122, BNA.

the need for the PF to start negotiating directly with the Rhodesian military to pave the way for the removal of Smith. Young argued that "the Rhodesian Front were no longer fighting to preserve white rule but in order to ensure that the transfer of power came about peacefully. The Europeans [white Rhodesians] wanted a guarantee that Zimbabwe would not be torn by civil war over the next decade." Young suggested the introduction of a "UN force" that would guarantee "law and order" and "undermine" the motive whites had for supporting Smith.[11]

As difficult as the first Malta talks were, Owen came away optimistic that his plan to separate Nkomo from Mugabe in the PF remained possible. Owen reported that "Nkomo made no secret of his desire to get into talks with Smith. He also showed himself well aware of the fact that Mugabe, despite his qualities, is a liability to him."[12] As this chapter will argue, Owen had a way of reporting what he thought would be the most beneficial outcome for the Anglo-American proposal. It is therefore difficult to ascribe motive to Nkomo based on Owen's reporting alone.

Soviet Views of the Anglo-American Proposal

While Owen and Vance met with Mugabe and Nkomo in Malta in January 1978, British diplomats in Moscow were analyzing the Soviet's interpretation of the Anglo-American proposal. British diplomat John Holmes once again offered his comments on media coverage from Moscow. This time, he referred to an editorial by Vladimir Kudryavtsev in the January 25 edition of *Izvestia,* where Kudryavtsev's editorials were seen as reflecting Soviet foreign policy positions. Holmes believed this was the first clear expression of what the Soviets wanted to happen in Rhodesia. This included "the idea of handing over power to the PF, disbanding the Rhodesian security forces and leaving the Front to organize election afterwards." Holmes commented "Kudryavtsev's evident hostility to free elections can be left to speak for itself."[13] This Soviet view more or less coalesced with Nkomo's strategy later in 1978 as he

---

[11] Valletta to FCO, "Rhodesia: Talks with the Patriotic Front," January 30, 1978, item 129, FCO36/2122, BNA.

[12] Ibid.

[13] Holmes to FCO, "Nkomo in Moscow," February 2, 1978, item 10, FCO/36/2203, BNA. Kudryavtsev's editorial was also reported in the *New York Times.* "Soviet Bitterly Attacks U.S. Policy," *New York Times,* January 28, 1978, 5.

attempted to negotiate directly with Smith. The goal then would be to obtain a surrender agreement that would turn over power directly to the PF without requiring elections first. Such a strategy would likely have been backed by the Soviets. However, for it to work, Nkomo would have to obtain cooperation from the Frontline State presidents and, most importantly, from Mugabe and ZANU. After Mugabe's consolidating power with those more committed to the *"tamba wakachenjera"* line, cooperation with ZAPU in any bilateral talks with Smith was unlikely to happen.

Holmes also reported information about Joshua Nkomo's visit to Moscow before the Malta talks, when Nkomo had joined a Zambian military delegation looking for military supplies. Holmes' source was a Zambian diplomat in Moscow, only referred to by the name Kunda, who relayed to Holmes what he had seen and heard during Nkomo's visit. Kunda appears to have been a source of intelligence on Zambian and ZAPU relations in Moscow, as the British tried to learn how much military support the Soviets were providing to Zambia and ZAPU. According to Kunda, "Nkomo had come [to Moscow] to put the seal on a promise the Russians had made on his last visit that arms supplies would be increased fairly substantially." Nkomo had apparently "been successful," as "Kunda thought new anti-aircraft missiles (he did not specify a type) were high on Nkomo's shopping list."[14] These Soviet-made anti-aircraft missiles would later be used in September 1978, when ZIPRA would shoot down Rhodesian civilian aircraft. Holmes then describes having joked with Kunda "about it being difficult to fight a guerrilla war with tanks. Kunda took this seriously. Nkomo was very interested in obtaining Soviet tanks, although it was not clear whether the Russians were ready to supply any." According to Kunda, "while tanks clearly could not be used in a guerrilla war, if Nkomo had to fight another kind of war, for example to take over the country, there was an obvious use for them." Kunda added that he "had gained the impression that Nkomo was serious when he said he would fight a Black government in Rhodesia." Kunda told Holmes, "Nkomo felt he had a well-armed, well-disciplined and well-trained force. He was aware of the criticisms levelled at ZAPU for letting ZANU take the brunt of the fighting and had for this reason recently

---

[14]   Holmes to FCO, "Nkomo in Moscow," February 2, 1978, item 10, FCO36/ 2203, BNA.

sent some ZAPU units into Mozambique to mount operations from there (although independently of ZANU)."[15] Such intel might have given the British pause when thinking of Nkomo as their preferred leader for an independent Zimbabwe, but that would assume the British saw these negotiations and potential outcomes strictly through a Cold War lens. In reality, the British were most concerned in early 1978 with managing a transition that would require minimal British commitment in terms of taking formal responsibility for Rhodesia's decolonization process. For this reason, Owen in particular considered working directly with Nkomo outside of the Anglo-American proposal, at least in a scenario that would absolve the British of a longer commitment in terms of overseeing the transitional period as the former colonial power. For Owen and many British Rhodesia experts, Nkomo's connection to the Soviets was less of an issue than the knowledge that he, given his electoral disadvantage to Mugabe, would be more willing to directly work with Smith and the "Exco." This would relieve the British of what seemed the increasing likelihood that they would need to appoint a British governor to oversee elections and the transition to majority rule.

Internal Settlement Stalls Progress on Anglo-American Proposal Talks

Immediately after the Malta talks failed to move the PF position any closer to the Anglo-American proposal, Owen wrote to the British embassies and high commissions in the Frontline States to clarify his position on possible next steps. Owen told his ambassadors and high commissioners that the Americans wanted there to be a message from President Carter to the Frontline State presidents informing them of the results of the Malta talks, and to promise that the United States and Britain were doing everything possible to keep negotiations going. Owen thought it would be better if American and British diplomats did this "by means of oral approaches." He wanted his diplomats to relate that the Malta talks had reached an impasse. Owen told his southern African diplomats, "For us there is now no further room for concessions. It is extremely doubtful, however, whether the Patriotic Front will ever agree to make the compromises necessary to meet us."

[15] Ibid.

Owen emphasized, however, that it was "vitally important that we should give the Front Line Presidents no reason to doubt that we are making every effort, within the framework of our proposals, to meet the legitimate concerns of the Patriotic Front or that our objective remains to secure full agreement on that basis."[16] It would take until mid-March to meet again with Mugabe and Nkomo, this time at the FCO offices in London for two days of talks held on March 13–14, 1978.

Cyrus Vance, the US secretary of state, met with Nkomo and Mugabe on March 11, 1978. After asking the PF leaders for their assessment of the situation, they both complained of the "internal exercise" as being "repugnant" because Smith and the internal settlement represented "a regime not recognized internationally." The PF leaders were upset that given this situation, "the U.K. had pronounced it a step in the right direction and this had been reiterated by the State Department."[17] Vance reportedly replied that "he had said that the Salisbury [agreement] represented a significant step because it had included universal suffrage, an independent judiciary, free elections and a date for Independence." Vance then said that "he and Dr. Owen had expressed serious reservations on other matters." He assured the PF leaders that he "would take the AAP as the yard-stick of propriety." He wanted to know if the PF leaders were willing to meet in New York on March 20, with the intention of bringing the Malta participants (the PF) to meet with the Salisbury Exco (Smith, Muzorewa, Sithole, and Chirau). Nkomo told Vance that he "saw no basis for such a meeting." Vance then "expressed regret" at this news and denied that they "were trying to get the PF to come on the basis of the Salisbury agreement." Vance then called the Salisbury agreement "grossly inadequate," to which Nkomo replied that it was "grossly illegal." Nkomo's position was that they were willing to talk with Smith, but he "did not want 'loyalists' in discussion of the ceasefire."[18]

Mugabe similarly stressed to Vance that there could be no meeting with "civilians" until the military ceasefire had been worked out. Therefore, he did not want to meet again if the plan was to work out

[16]   FCO to Washington, "Telno 300 of 4 February, Rhodesia: Negotiations with the Patriotic Front," February 6, 1978, item 2, FCO 36/2229, BNA.

[17]   Fm Washington to FCO, "My Telno 1025: Rhodesia," March 11, 1978, item 218, FCO36/2124, BNA.

[18]   Ibid.

military and political issues at the same time. He told Vance that he had his "suspicions that the Anglo-Americans were trying to marry the two" (the Anglo-American proposal and Salisbury), and that "there would have to be two stages, first bring the war to an end and then a constitutional conference," with "no illegal marriages." Nkomo added that the United States and Britain "should forget the meeting on the 20th." The meeting was going nowhere for Vance, and he was called out of the meeting to speak on the phone with Nigeria's foreign minister, Joseph Garba, a diplomat who was about to play a more significant role in his attempts at getting the PF to negotiate directly with Smith. When Vance returned from his phone call with Garba, he told the PF leaders that he "understood the PF's position" and that he would be in touch. Mugabe ended the meeting with a criticism of the American position: "Mugabe said that he was puzzled by the U.S. role. They had been brought in by the British but were showing themselves sheepish and supporting the British right or wrong. Vance said that our [Britain and the United States] views had coincided all along."[19] Nancy Mitchell notes that this meeting had been alarming for Vance and his staff and resulted in American pressure on the British to jump start talks around the Anglo-American proposal.[20]

Between the first Malta talks and this mid-March meeting in London, Smith and Muzorewa (along with Sithole and Chirau) had resolved their issues over the internal settlement. Officially announced on March 3, 1978, the internal settlement presented fundamental problems for the Anglo-American proposal negotiations, while causing major problems for Nkomo and Mugabe. Most importantly, the settlement, and Owen's comments that it was "a step in the right direction," caused the PF leaders to "take their gloves off" when Nkomo and Mugabe met with Owen and US ambassador to the United Kingdom, Kingman Brewster Jr., at the FCO on March 13. This two-and-a-half-hour meeting was one of the most contentious between the PF leaders and Owen. The pressure put on the PF by both the Frontline State presidents and the British had the effect of bringing Nkomo and Mugabe closer together, but also helped focus their shared annoyance at Owen and the British. The reason for their sharp criticisms at this

---

[19] Ibid.
[20] Nancy Mitchell, *Jimmy Carter in Africa: Race and The Cold War* (Stanford University Press, 2016), 407–9.

meeting was that Owen, after Malta, had begun to float an idea of a new meeting between the PF and the new internal settlement leaders in New York. Mugabe and Nkomo both strongly objected to Owen on this point, arguing that the PF was still willing to work within the parameters of the Anglo-American proposal, which meant they would meet only with Smith and his military leaders to organize a cease-fire and discuss the mechanics of turning over power to a transitional government. They had no intention of meeting with the three African leaders in the new internal settlement. In fact, they refused to meet with them.

Owen claimed that it would be to the PF's advantage to meet with Muzorewa, Sithole, and Chirau because they were now linked to Smith, which gave the PF a stronger position inside Rhodesia. Nkomo and Mugabe dismissed this logic and were much more concerned that should the British agree to meet with the new "Executive Committee" (Exco), they were getting dangerously close to legitimating the internal settlement. The PF wanted nothing to do with it. The meeting got very heated at times and the minutes display the negotiation skills of Nkomo and Mugabe when they worked together effectively. Based on the meeting's transcript, Owen seems to have been unprepared for the level of mistrust the two leaders conveyed toward him. Owen, for his part, did not help matters by pressing the PF leaders on the possibility that talks with the Exco could happen, perhaps feeling that by being non-committal to their concerns, they would compromise. Nkomo and Mugabe were in no mood to compromise. They wanted the Malta process to continue and Nkomo especially continued to reiterate that the PF would only move forward within the Anglo-American proposal, and that they expected Owen and Britain to not engage with the internal settlement leaders.

Owen met with Nkomo and Mugabe once more on March 13, 1978. At this meeting, Mugabe criticized Owen for his comments that the Salisbury agreement had been a step in the right direction. Owen replied that President Carter had said something similar, but Nkomo interjected that Vance had tried to backtrack from that position. "Mr. Nkomo said that the PF would not abandon the nature of its conference to accommodate 'those people' as the result of an agreement reached in Salisbury. If, as a result of the Salisbury agreement, it was Dr. Owen's intention to abandon his own proposals, he should say so." Owen replied that "one had to live in the real world." Nkomo retorted that "the real world could be anything one chose to make it." This obviously upset Owen, who replied that he had been "much criticised at the outset of his time as a Foreign Secretary for saying publicly that he would have liked to get rid of Mr. Smith straightaway." Owen then directly challenged Mugabe and Nkomo to stop criticizing him personally: "Now the PF spent their whole time having a crack at him. One day he would have a go at them. As a moderate Welshman, he had so far refrained from doing so." Owen responded to criticism by claiming his ethnic difference within Britain, as if to show solidarity. After stating this threat, the conversation became good natured albeit revealing Owen's frustrations, Owen told Mugabe and Nkomo: "The realities of life were that those who had been talking in Salisbury had come up with proposals which we believed to be inadequate and seriously defective but which, in certain areas, were what we and the PF had advocated."[21]

Britain's deputy under-secretary at the FCO, John Graham, provided his handwritten comments on Owen's pessimistic summary of the meeting with the PF leaders. Graham's comments encapsulated the problems the internal settlement had also created for the Anglo-American proposal and for the British in particular: "We have a dilemma. If the Front Line States were successful in putting pressure on the PF to accept our proposals as a package, we shall be asked to deliver, and we cannot." In addition, Graham commented, "A meeting with the PF alone would be severely criticised at home, unless there were a parallel meeting with the Salisbury group. But the harder our position on the Anglo-American proposals, the less likely is it that Mr. Smith and his collaborators will attend a meeting, alone with the PF." Graham then parenthetically suggested, "In fact the major incentive for Mr Smith to attend a meeting is the opportunity it would give to meet Mr Nkomo." Graham was also aware that for the British to stall and do nothing in order to "await developments, though it may well be right, will go down very badly with President Nyerere & Co." He could see "no alternative at the moment" but thought they "need not rush into it."[22] Graham and Owen seemed to have mutually decided to try

---

[21] "Record of a Meeting between the FCO Secretary and the Leaders of the Patriotic Front at the FCO Office," March 28, 1978, item 229, FCO 36/2124, BNA.

[22] Laver to Graham, "Rhodesia: Talks with the Patriotic Front," March 16, 1978, item 224, FCO36/2124, BNA.

to find a way to arrange direct negotiation between Smith and Nkomo. They thought that should the two leaders reach an agreement that would satisfy the international community and the Frontline States, this would find a way out of the dilemma Graham outlined above. Most importantly, a bilateral agreement could potentially relieve the British of having to take extensive control and responsibility for the transition, as emphasized in the Anglo-American proposal.

Owen had already talked with Nkomo about the idea of meeting with Smith directly when they met at the American Ambassador's residence on January 30 in Malta. Owen said that he had "urged Mr Nkomo to consider a meeting with Mr Smith. Mr Nkomo had agreed that this might be a possibility and that, if it were to take place, it could only do so within the framework of the Anglo/U.S. proposals." Owen also reported that Nkomo had been "very realistic about his chances and about Mr. Mugabe, to whom he adopted an attitude mixed between paternal and patronizing. He had made clear that he did not think that he could break from Mr Mugabe."[23] This last point is significant, because as will be shown in this chapter, Nkomo's critics would later characterize his August 1978 private meeting with Smith as an effort by Nkomo to split the PF.

A major pressure on the British, however, that kept them from letting the war take its course and hoping for a settlement between Smith and Nkomo, was that the Frontline State presidents, especially Machel and Kaunda, continued to have their countries attacked by Rhodesian forces targeting ZIPRA and ZANLA forces. This brought a certain urgency to Western diplomacy because the West was unwilling to supply defensive weapons to either Zambia or Mozambique to defend themselves from Rhodesian attacks. There was, therefore, always a possibility that the Soviets and Cubans could provide the more sophisticated weapons and expertise necessary for air defence, or for ZANLA or ZIPRA to take large-scale counter actions against civilian targets in Rhodesia. If the latter were to happen, the fear was that the South Africans and perhaps the Americans would have to join the war to defend Rhodesia. The South Africans were, of course, already pro- viding most of the supplies and even personnel supporting the

---

[23] Graham to Rhodesia Department, "Private Meeting between the Secretary of State and Mr Nkomo on 30 January 1978," February 2, 1978, item 155, FCO 36/2122, BNA.

Rhodesians. Smith and his military commanders would continue to use airstrikes and "hot pursuit" strategies in Mozambique and Zambia to try to weaken ZIPRA and ZANLA through the last years of the war.

Bishop Muzorewa's War of Words with Samora Machel

Given that the internal settlement would soon place Bishop Muzorewa in a position of leadership that involved authorization of military raids against ZIPRA in Zambia and ZANLA in Mozambique, it is important to understand the animosity Muzorewa, Sithole, and others held for Presidents Kaunda and Machel. One dimension of this already existing animosity is found in the claims made by Muzorewa, as described in Chapter 3, that he and the Reverend Sithole had tried to reach the camps in Tanzania and Mozambique in 1976 to assert their leadership as United African National Council leaders, but were blocked by the Mozambicans and the Tanzanians. In March 1978, the Mozambican president, Samora Machel, asked the British and Americans to find someone who could secretly contact Muzorewa and deliver a letter asking him to reconsider his decision to join the internal settlement. The Americans found Dr. William J. Foltz, a Yale University political science professor, who brought the letter to Muzorewa. Professor Foltz, on his way to deliver the Muzorewa's response to Machel, reasoned with the US embassy staff that since Muzorewa didn't seal the envelope, "Muzorewa probably would not object to the U.S.G's [US government's] knowledge of its contents."[24] The full text of Muzorewa's letter was then shared with the British, and is now part of the FCO's record at the British National Archives.

Contained in Muzorewa's reply, dated March 19, 1978, was a very impassioned account accusing Machel and Nyerere of having done all that they could do to keep him and others in the United African National Council from having access to ZIPA forces. Muzorewa complained to Machel that he received an invitation on September 19, 1975 "to go to Mozambique to organize the armed struggle." He claims that he and others in the United African National Council, including its vice president, James Chikerema, were sent along with eight others with five lorries weighing seven tonnes each. "These lorries were filled with all

---

24 Muzorewa to Machel, "Full Text of Letter on United African National Council Stationary," April 3, 1978, item 21, FCO 36/2216, BNA.

the supplies people in the bush need – food, medical supplies and clothing for their cadres. But arriving in Mozambique some of our men were detained, others imprisoned and up to now some are somewhere in Mozambique." Muzorewa complained to Machel that when he arrived he was surprised to discover that he too was under house arrest in Maputo. "I was further surprised to find that a High Command was being developed to take charge of the armed struggle without our knowledge and yet a massive majority of the cadres had been recruited by the UANC." Muzorewa was accusing Machel and Nyerere of taking over the recruits he and the United African National Council had helped send to Mozambique. The Bishop complained that the current request for him to stay out of the internal settlement came too late, given that he had already entered the internal settlement deal with Smith. "I have listened to you and his Excellency President Nyerere's advice in the past and therefore I feel that at this stage and time it was most unfair of you to withhold information of this communication until after I had signed an important agreement with Mr. Smith. Even though your advice has come too late."[25]

Muzorewa then listed the reasons why he did not regret having joined the internal settlement. First, he had succeeded in reaching a negotiated settlement, and, second, there would be real "one-man one vote" elections on December 31, 1978. He asked Machel, "What reason would the geurillas [sic] continue to fight for? Would they continue to wage a war of Liberation or a war to serve a personality?" The actual election would not occur until April 1979. Muzorewa refers to the notion that he and Smith, in the internal settlement, could end the war if only those in the PF were willing to turn in their weapons and join the internal settlement. The chances of this happening were, of course, very slim. At the end of his letter, Muzorewa declared:

I hope that we will never be put in a position whereas an independent Zimbabwe will fight independent Mozambique for the sake of individuals. If you are referring to the Anglo-American proposals which include Mr. Nkomo and Mr. Mugabe, then I would repeat that the door remains open for them to participate with us.[26]

---

[25] Ibid.   [26] Ibid.

He signed off the letter "your brother in struggle ... Abel Tendekayi Muzorewa President United African National Council." Muzorewa's suggestion to Machel about fighting in the future would hold true, as Muzorewa's April 1979 Zimbabwe-Rhodesia government would continue to authorize military attacks on ZANLA forces in Mozambique and ZIPRA forces in Zambia.

The scenario of more war in the future expressed in Muzorewa's letter to Machel pointed to a danger that the Americans and British thought might once again heighten the risk of Cuban and Soviet intervention in Rhodesia. The growing Cold War crisis in the Horn of Africa also influenced new concerns of a possible Cold War conflict over Rhodesia. This threat was discussed in a April 16, 1978 meeting in Pretoria between South African diplomats, Cyrus Vance, Andrew Young, and David Owen. As in previous meetings, the Americans and British wanted the South African's advice on how to proceed, and to assess what levels of pressure the South Africans were willing to assert on Smith to move him to negotiate.[27] Owen started by expressing their concern over what the internal settlement would do to the Anglo-American proposal: "what worried him and Mr. Vance was that what had hitherto been a war between Mr. Smith and the black nationalists could, now that Muzorewa and Sithole were identified with Smith, turn into a fight between the nationalists." Owen noted that should this happen, "it would be difficult to keep the parties in a negotiated posture in that situation." He concluded with a fairly dire warning, "if that happened, each side would fight to the bitter end. The Front Line did not want to internationalise the situation and neither President Kaunda nor President Machel wanted the Cubans in."[28]

---

[27] Sue Onlsow points to a key meeting in 1978 between Pik Botha, Fourie, and Owen in New York where Owen was "convinced ... that the South Africans 'had reverted to their old belief that Nkomo was crucial.'" Sue Onslow, "The South African Factor in Zimbabwe's Transition to Independence," in Sue Onslow, ed., *Cold War in Southern Africa: White Power, Black Liberation* (London: Taylor & Francis, 2009), 118. See also Stephen John J. Stedman, *Peacemaking in Civil War: International Mediation in Zimbabwe, 1974–1980* (Boulder, CO: Lynne Rienner Publishers, 1990), 145–48.

[28] "Record of a Meeting between the FCO Secretary, US Secretary of State and the South African Foreign Minister at the South African Foreign Minister's Residence, Pretoria," April 16, 1978, PREM16/1829, Part 28, BNA.

Owen then referred to Soviet and Cuban interventions in the wars in the Horn of Africa, and worried that the same could occur in southern Africa, although he did add that there could be some value in moving slowly, as "one could argue against bringing the sides together too soon." He added this was possible because "the PF were in no hurry and the Salisbury talkers were buoyant at the moment." Owen did caution, however, that as "the more present attitudes became set in concrete, the greater the danger of a battle between the nationalist groups."[29] Owen had summed up the situation from the Anglo-American perspective with one possible outcome being that the longer the internal settlement took hold, the chances would increase for a civil war between the internal government and the PF, rather than a race war.

Vance's response to Owen's statement showed a slight difference in interpretation. He "agreed with Dr. Owen that if there was breakdown and no settlement then there would be a black civil war. The chances of internationalization and of Cuban and Soviet involvement in such circumstances were very large."[30] While Vance also saw an increased chance for a "black civil war" as an outcome, he saw this as all the more reason to push harder for a negotiated settlement sooner because he believed that odds were greater for the Soviets and Cubans to intervene in such a potential "black civil war." Vance's argument was similar to Kissinger's argument back in 1976. For the Americans, they wanted to move quickly to avoid Soviet and Cuban involvement, but now, a few years later, the need was more to avoid a situation where the United States would have to get involved and take sides in a "black civil war" with Cold War consequences.

Pik Botha, South Africa's foreign minister, not surprisingly, shared the British view that patience was required. Botha had been promoted to foreign minister a year earlier. He was supportive of Muzorewa and the internal settlement, arguing that the new government could succeed in bringing the PF into government. Botha explained "that the PF could come in on an equal basis with no special seats reserved for them but the PF leaders should not be treated as Crown Princes."[31] Such thinking fit well with South African ambitions for a similar internal settlement in Namibia.[32] Botha agreed that a "black civil war" was a real

---

[29] Ibid. [30] Ibid. [31] Ibid.
[32] On South Africa's attempts to gain an advantage in Namibia, see Piero Gleijese, "A Test of Wills: Jimmy Carter, South Africa, and the Independence of Namibia," *Diplomatic History* 34, no. 5 (2010), 853–901; Mitchell, *Jimmy*

possibility, and described to the Americans and the British what this might mean. "If there was a civil war it would be a tribal war. The war would not go through the middle of the country but would be on tribal lines, with Salisbury and Bulawayo at opposite poles. This would be much worse than a civil war."[33] Botha then gave the Americans and British diplomats a brief history lesson about Nkomo and ZAPU: "There had been a time when, in South Africa's view, Mr Nkomo would have been a better leader than the others but he did not seem to realise that there could now be a very terrible civil war if the people did not in fact like him. Mr Nkomo should have allied himself to Rev Sithole or Bishop Muzorewa but he had backed the wrong horse."[34] Botha's implication here was that Nkomo's decision to stay within the PF had now saddled Nkomo to Mugabe, with no way out. Botha was also pushing a "tribalist" trope that already began to blame Nkomo for the future conflicts that he saw threatening in years to come. Interestingly, Botha seemed to be describing a war between Nkomo and Mugabe's parties and armies, not between the PF and the Exco.

Young offered his own insightful comments on what he recognized to be the inability of the PF leaders to work together. "The PF were not a front. He had got the impression that while Mugabe and Nkomo got on well, Mugabe's people thought Nkomo would join the internal settlement." Young explained what he saw ZANU's position: "They were therefore posturing to get Cuban and Russian support almost hoping that Mr Nkomo would sell out. President Machel and President Nyerere were trying to keep Mugabe within the plan."[35] Young's views summed up well the dynamics of the "Nkomo versus Mugabe" politics of the second half of 1978. As demonstrated below, the British would push Nkomo to try to negotiate directly with Smith for a settlement as a way of absolving the British of a more extensive political commitment to a transition under their command. The Americans would disagree with this strategy. As Young predicted, when the news of Nkomo's meeting with Smith became public, ZANU tried to label him as a "sell out" for their own political gains.

Carter in Africa, 229–30; Jamie Miller, *An African Volk: The Apartheid Regime and Its Search for Survival* (Oxford University Press, 2016), 283–85.

[33] "Record of a Meeting between the FCO Secretary, US Secretary of State and the South African Foreign Minister at the South African Foreign Minister's Residence, Pretoria," April 16, 1978 PREM16/1829, Part 28, BNA.

[34] Ibid.   [35] Ibid.

Details from the diplomatic records, however, show that those secret talks were complicated on this point because Nkomo never abandoned Mugabe and the PF during the talks.

Nkomo had independently confirmed Young's perception of the PF relationship when he met with Owen on April 11, 1978, at 1 Carlton Gardens in London. According to minutes of the meeting, "Mr Nkomo admitted the difficulties of negotiating with ZANU but said that he did not want to split with ZANU since this would go down badly with the OAU." Nkomo predicted that a break in the PF would result in continued fighting by ZANLA, "and that even a small amount of fighting could create great problems unless President Machel intervened to cut off help from ZANU." Nkomo thought President Neto of Angola might be able to apply such pressure on Machel. Nkomo also said he was preparing to meet with ZANU in a few weeks. He mentioned "that the people imprisoned were all good people who wanted to bring ZAPU and ZANU together under Mr Nkomo's leadership." He said, "those were the people one could negotiate with whereas those like Tongogara (whom he loathed) ... were hardliners." Nkomo told Owen that he "found Mr Mugabe easy to deal with and reasonable but Mugabe had been forced into the present position by the hardliners." Nkomo concluded that there "might be a moment when ZANU and ZAPU might have to split, but it should be a split of ZANU's making." The notetaker emphasized, "He [Nkomo] kept saying that ZANU were dependent on President Machel and that only he could cut them off." Nkomo also said that the problem with ZANU was that decisions were made by committee.[36]

David Owen on Proposed Secret Talks between Nkomo and Smith

During the run up to the "secret-meeting" between Smith and Nkomo on August 14, 1978, David Owen relayed some of the problems inherent in such a meeting to the British Ambassador in Washington, DC on June 30, 1978: "The presence of [Joe] Garba and [Siteke] Mwale [the Zambian foreign minister] would probably be sufficient cover for Nkomo although, as Kaunda acknowledged, Nigeria is not a safeguard

[36] "Meeting between the Foreign and Commonwealth Secretary and Mr Joshua Nkomo," item 300, April 11, 1978, FCO36/2126, BNA.

vis-à-vis the Tanzanians." Owen indicated his desire to keep the British free of any responsibility for the secret talks: "But it would then be important still for us not to be directly involved in the meeting. ... If the meeting produced results, Kaunda would probably have to consult his colleagues in confidence fairly urgently thereafter."[37] Importantly, and in contrast to the "sell-out" narrative that would follow Nkomo's meeting with Smith, Owen also indicated that he was instructing their representative in Salisbury to tell Smith that he would not likely be able to get away with splitting the PF.

[Redacted] representative will make the point that, in our judgement, an approach by Smith on the basis of splitting the PF and excluding ZANU completely would meet with a rebuff and that Smith will need to make an offer to Nkomo which the latter will regard as enhancing his chances of controlling, or at least neutralizing ZANU but not excluding them.[38]

These instructions reveal Owen's intentions to try to use the talks to give the upper hand to Nkomo, but this indicates his error in judgement that Nkomo was in a strong enough position to "control" or "neutralize" ZANU.

Owen instructed the UK embassy in Washington, and John Graham in Salisbury on June 30, 1978, to convey his "guidance on what might come out of direct talks between Mr Smith and Mr Nkomo and subsequently out of round-table talks." Owen's instructions also expressed his concern that there would be a potential American effort to get in the way. He told Graham, "You should not at this stage show the paper to [Stephen] Low." He instructed that "Washington [the British embassy] should not reveal the existence of the paper to the State Department but I should be grateful for their comments on likely American reaction." From this it would seem that Low, in his close work with Graham, was well aware of the potential secret talks, but that Owen didn't want Low to know the details in order to void him alerting the State Department because of Secretary of State Vance's likely objections.

In the weeks leading up to the secret talks, the British were worried that the OAU meeting on July 7–18 in Khartoum, Sudan, would decide to ignore the Anglo-American proposal and recognize the PF as the sole

---

[37] From FCO to Graham [Salisbury], "Telno 1673," June 30, 1978, item 20, PREM 16/1831, BNA.

[38] Ibid.

Figure 6 Robert Mugabe and Joshua Nkomo at the OAU meeting. Khartoum, Sudan, July 1978. Getty Images.

liberation movement in Zimbabwe. There was some optimism among the FCO's Rhodesia office that such recognition would not happen, given a report from Khartoum, based on the recommendations of the OAU Foreign Ministers, "calling for the involvement of all parties in a conference and stressing that the choice of leaders in Zimbabwe should be up to the people of that country." The advice was to make a statement that the Anglo-American proposal was still on the table, in order to encourage the OAU to continue to support it.[39] The final OAU resolution on Zimbabwe contained wording that "strongly rejects and condemns the March 3, 1978 Salisbury Agreement." The resolution did note that the African participants in the internal settlement were now tied to the racist regime of Ian Smith, stating that these parties "are now an integral part of the resulting treacherous and illegal Salisbury regime." The resolution also referred to the PF as "the sole Liberation Movement of Zimbabwe." But there was nothing directly in the resolution about rejecting the Anglo-American proposal.[40]

[39] P. M. Laver, "Rhodesia: Briefing for Front Line Presidents," July 13, 1978, item 58, FCO 26/2229, BNA.

[40] OAU, "Resolution on Zimbabwe" CM/Res. 680 (xxxi), *Resolutions of The Council of Ministers Adopted at Its Thirty-First Ordinary Session and*

The Nkomo and Smith Meeting and the Subsequent Political Fallout

In Joshua Nkomo's 1984 autobiography, he summarizes the context of his 1978 meeting with Smith, emphasizing that Smith wanted to end the war at this point. "I found Smith a tired man, a battered man. He told me he wanted to surrender power, to hand the whole thing over; I am convinced that he knew the game was up, that the time had come to concede defeat. But I could not on my own accept his offer." Nkomo emphasizes in his autobiography that he refused Smith's offer until he could confer with Mugabe. "I told him that the important thing was his agreement to surrender power. But I also stated that the mechanics of the surrender was not something he could discuss with me alone. I had to bring in Robert Mugabe, my colleague in the PF: it was to the PF that power must surrendered, not to Joshua Nkomo or Zapu." Nkomo even refers to President Kaunda of Zambia as a witness: "Smith was critical of me: he asked President Kaunda why I was acting like that, did I not have the authority to settle? Kenneth, of course, supported my position that I could not finish the conflict on my own; it was the PF that mattered."[41] Nkomo further explained that he and Kaunda enlisted Nigerian president Olusegun Obasanjo and his foreign minister, Joseph Garba, to help convince Nyerere and Mugabe that it was worth following up this first meeting with a second meeting to negotiate directly with Smith. Obasanjo tried to convince Mugabe of the efficacy of this strategy but in the end Mugabe and Nyerere refused to accept the need for any further direct talks with Smith during a Frontline States' summit in Lusaka in early September 1978. The idea that the British and the Nigerians planned the secret Nkomo–Smith talks without Nyerere knowing about them until September's Frontline States' meeting generally comes from British sources. Sources from the United States, however, show that Nyerere knew of the plan in August after the first meeting had taken place and was willing to support a second meeting as long as Mugabe participated.[42]

Approved by The Fifteenth Ordinary Session of The Assembly of Heads of State And Government, 1978, 118.

[41] Joshua Nkomo, *Nkomo, The Story of My Life* (Methuen, 1984),189.

[42] From American Embassy Dar es Salaam to Secretary of State, "Rhodesia: President Nyerere Expresses Concern about Zambia-Nigerian-British Secret Negotiations with Smith," August 22, 1978, STATE215839, Central Foreign

The Rhodesians reported to their South African representatives that they had kept the meeting a secret, saying that "the leaks have come from their side and are highly inaccurate. The meeting was exploratory." The account states that "After much sparring Garba eventually said Nkomo must have the preferential place as permanent chairman of ExCo during interim period." The account says Nkomo agreed to this but "said he would not come in without Mugabe." Smith reportedly "asked whether Mugabe would accept second fiddle to Nkomo." The report states that "Nkomo said several times he would have no problem with Mugabe and was supported by Garba on this." The report indicates Smith's skepticism on this point: "PM expressed doubts and referred to Mugabe's extreme statements re his future intentions." It then goes over the plan to have Mugabe go to Lagos "to be 'persuaded' by Obasanjo, after which PM [Smith] would be invited back to Lusaka to meet Nkomo and Mugabe."[43] This evidence from the Rhodesian archives helps to establish that Nkomo was not trying to make a deal with Smith on his own. However, it also helps to show that Nkomo and Garba, along with the British, clearly wanted to force Mugabe into a secondary role to Nkomo. This part of the deal was not to happen.

President Nyerere held a press conference after the September Frontline States summit in Lusaka to explain why he was against the continuation of the direct talks with Smith. He defended Nkomo's resolve to keep Mugabe in any future equation during his meeting with Smith. "To his credit, Mr. Nkomo said he can't go without his colleague of the PF. . . . Joshua insisted that he cannot go back without Mugabe."[44] Nyerere reported that there had been some discussion at the secret meeting that if Nkomo could bring Mugabe to the next meeting proposed for Lusaka in a week's time, Smith would bring Muzorewa, Sithole, and Chirau. And that if Nkomo was willing, they could reach an agreement without Muzorewa and Sithole, and it would

Policy Files, 1973–1976, RG 59, General Records of the Department of State, USNA.

[43] Secretary Prime Minister Salisbury to Rhodesians Pretoria September 189, 1978. "ADR from Gaylard. Your C. 312 Refers." Smith Papers 4006 (M) 045. pdf.

[44] "Excerpts from President Nyerere's Press Conference in Dar es Salaam Concerning the Lusaka Frontline Summit," September 3, 1978, Doc. 580, in Goswin Baumhögger, *The Struggle for Independence: Documents on the Recent Development of Zimbabwe (1975–1980)*, vol. IV (Hamburg: Institute of African Studies Documentation Centre, 1984), 652.

be a transitional government with Nkomo, Mugabe, Chirau, and Smith. Such public revelations by Nyerere helped to discredit Smith and to demonstrate that the internal settlement leaders were already expendable. Nyerere's objection was that Nkomo, along with the British, Nigerians, and the Zambians, were willing to try direct negotiations without the other Frontline State leaders involved.[45] Mostly, however, Nyerere's strong opposition to these meetings was interpreted at the time as his preference for Mugabe and ZANU within the PF.

Nkomo, for his part, wasted no time in publicly attacking Nyerere for his criticisms brought out against Nkomo. On September 5, 1978, Nkomo's words from a BBC interview, reprinted in the *Zambia Daily Mail,* demonstrated Nkomo's anger with Nyerere for "interfering in the search for a solution to Rhodesia's problems."[46] Nkomo said, in response to Nyerere's statement that the talks had been "worthless," that "Nyerere is not the final authority on what may happen in Zimbabwe." Nkomo also did not rule out future meetings with Smith, saying that it depended on the conditions. "I would go if Smith said he wanted to give up and hand over power to the PF. It is our business to see that he does go. We are not fighting for the sake of fighting, but we want to convince these people that it is futile to continue." The *Zambia Daily Mail* article added, "Nkomo even went as far as to say that Nyerere was no longer one of the Front Line Presidents, since Tanzania had no common border with Rhodesia or Namibia."[47] As Nancy Mitchell argues, the American diplomats in Mozambique and elsewhere took the fallout from this secret meeting as a sign of Mugabe's growing popularity and that despite leadership struggles within ZANU, Mugabe was increasingly looking like the most viable leader for a future Zimbabwe.[48]

Zambia's Mark Chona briefed the Americans on September 10, 1978, on the reasons for the fallout after the first meeting between Smith and Nkomo and gave his reasons why the second meeting never took place. His account is similar to Nkomo's in terms of Nkomo insisting that Mugabe be part of any settlement. Chona added, "Smith was, however, strongly opposed to Mugabe's inclusion.

---

[45] Ibid.
[46] Lusaka to FCO, "Telno 585," September 5, 1978, FCO 36/2127, BNA.
[47] Ibid.   [48] Mitchell, *Jimmy Carter in Africa,* 493–95.

Nkomo said that was the only basis on which the talks could proceed. Smith agreed to meet with Nkomo and Mugabe, and a follow-up meeting was set for August 21 [1978]."[49] Chona is more forthcoming about what happened after the first meeting in terms of Nkomo's behavior toward Mugabe: "Although Nkomo met with Mugabe after his meeting with Smith he did not tell Mugabe about the meeting. Only that the Nigerians wanted to talk to him about matters which he, Nkomo, was already familiar." Chona reported that "Nkomo did not tell Mugabe the purpose of the trip to Lagos was to pressure Mugabe to accept a number two position in the PF prior to the meeting with Smith."[50]

According to Chona, when Mugabe went to Nigeria, Obasanjo put heavy pressure on him to accept a secondary role to Nkomo and to meet with Smith and start a Nigerian brokered settlement. Chona claimed that "although Mugabe told the Nigerians that the Nkomo meeting with Smith was 'a good thing' he resisted Obasanjo's insistence that he subordinate himself to Nkomo and argued that he had to consult his Executive Committee."[51] After this, Garba accompanied Mugabe to Mozambique and to Tanzania to lobby Machel and Nyerere to pressure Mugabe to accept these terms. According to Chona's account of this, "Nyerere was 'enthusiastic' about the report on the meeting with Smith and sent Garba back to see Machel with instructions that Machel must 'send Mugabe to the meeting.'"[52] Chona goes on to say that "Machel agreed and the Front Line Summit meeting was set up at Lusaka in order to coordinate a negotiating strategy for the PF-Smith meeting."

An interesting albeit brief confirmation of Mugabe having temporarily bowed to Nigerian pressures comes from a statement he made before boarding the plane from Lusaka to Maputo. The high commissioner reported the details of the press conference Mugabe held before he left for Maputo, in which Mugabe said that there would shortly be a general congress of the PF to "merge its two wings and elect a single leader." Mugabe said that "the Lusaka meeting had been mainly concerned with the mechanics of a one-party constitution and with

[49] From Secretary of State Washington DC to Ambassador Embassy Lusaka, "Conversation with Mark Chona on Rhodesia," September 10, 1978, STATE235989, Central Foreign Policy Files, 1973–1976, RG 59, General Records of the Department of State, USNA.
[50] Ibid. [51] Ibid. [52] Ibid.

the possibility of joint training in future for ZANU and ZAPU fighters." He was then asked "if he anticipated problems over the leadership of a single party," and replied in his standard way that it would be up to "the forthcoming congress to decide the question of leadership and to choose a Central Committee to lead the single Party." He added that he "would not be bitter if he was not chosen."[53] This brief reference to Mugabe accepting that there would be a merging of the military and political sides of the PF into a single unit only lasted until he was able to make it onto the plane. Once in Maputo, he was able to avoid the problem of having to become Nkomo's second in command.

The public disclosure of the secret meeting between Nkomo and Smith produced a flurry of activity. The British were deeply concerned about what the Frontline State presidents would do at their meeting in Lusaka on September 2. There are a number of accounts of that meeting from foreign ministers that help confirm what Joe Garba had said in his accounts to the Americans. Primarily, Nyerere along with Mugabe were highly critical of Nkomo for having entered into the talks in the first place, even though, according to Kaunda and others, Nyerere was aware of the request to hold a meeting with Mugabe, and Garba had lobbied Nyerere to help make sure Mugabe would participate. The emphasis seemed to be that before the first August 14 meeting had become public knowledge, Nyerere was still supporting continued private talks. However, once the story broke, he became staunchly opposed to any further talks.

Mugabe's ability to wash his hands of any role in the secret meeting was upsetting to the Zambians in particular, but also the Nigerians. Mark Chona described the change in Nyerere's mind at the Lusaka Frontline States summit in early September. Chona told the Americans that Nyerere had pulled Kaunda aside to say that "Nkomo was the leader" and "only Nkomo could lead Rhodesia."[54] He said that Nyerere changed his mind over the course of the meeting as the discussion showed the Nigerian effort was out of step with the Anglo-American proposal, and that once confronted with Mugabe and

---

[53] Lusaka to FCO, "My Telno 524: Rhodesia," August 21, 1978, item 408, FCO 36/2127, BNA.

[54] From Secretary of State Washington DC to Ambassador Embassy Lusaka, "Conversation with Mark Chona on Rhodesia," September 10, 1978, STATE235989, Central Foreign Policy Files, 1973–1976, RG 59, General Records of the Department of State, USNA.

Nkomo, Nyerere was unwilling to push for Nkomo's leadership as a condition for future talks.[55] Again, Chona's account has to be read through his own interests in getting Nkomo the top position in the PF. He told the Americans that privately Nyerere and Machel "both agreed that Nkomo had to be number one," but were "unwilling to take this position when they got into meetings and confronted the two Patriotic Front leaders directly."[56]

George Houser was in Lusaka in early September 1978, and he met with Mr Punabuntu, a press representative at the State House, who was a former editor of the *Times of Zambia*. Punabuntu had also attended the meetings with Smith, Nkomo, Garba, and Kaunda in August. Houser spoke with Punabuntu on Kaunda's direction, as he had been told by Kaunda that Houser was a "trusted friend of Zambia" and that Punabuntu should talk with Houser "frankly" about the "Zimbabwe situation." Punabuntu told Houser that Smith had approached Kaunda and Nkomo to set up the meeting on August 14. Smith wanted Nkomo to join the internal settlement, but only after another Anglo-American conference had concluded. The idea was to obtain enough votes among the parties to elect Nkomo the head of the proposed Council of State that would lead the transition period. "There would be six participants and therefore six votes in such a conference. The idea was that Smith thought he probably could get Chief Chirau to vote for it. Nkomo would have to deliver Mugabe. That would be four votes because Smith would vote for Nkomo." Punabuntu went on: "The idea was to turn power over to the Patriotic Front, but Nkomo was the key to it. Smith had made clear that he really didn't want to deal with Mugabe. If Nkomo wanted to bring Mugabe along with him, that was to be his initiative." Punabuntu explained what happened following the meeting, confirming the account by Garba and others, that Mugabe was sent to Lagos where Obasanjo pressured him to accept a secondary role to Nkomo. Mugabe then went back to Maputo, where he and the ZANU executive decided not to accept the deal. Meanwhile, Nyerere turned against it and faulted Garba for not getting Machel's word, and only accepting Chissano's word.

Punabuntu told Houser that there were many more well-trained and disciplined ZIPRA troops than in 1975. Given this, "Punabuntu made it clear that they saw the only alternative to this kind of settlement as

[55] Ibid.   [56] Ibid.

civil war, eventually between ZAPU and ZANU." He thought the conflict would grow internationally, mostly between the USSR and China, and he asked Houser "to try to do whatever is possible to get the US government to understand the situation in Southern Africa." At this point in the point in their meeting, President Kaunda came to chat briefly with Houser. He and Mainza Chona, the new secretary general of the United National Independence Party, were working out plans for its upcoming conference in Mulungushi, which was to open the next day. Demonstrating the trust Kaunda had in Houser, Kaunda said that at the conference the party was to "choose their candidate for president and to devise a means by which [Simon] Kapwepwe and perhaps Harry Nkumbula would not be able to run."[57]

Houser also met with Robert Mugabe on September 23, 1978. He asked Mugabe about the Nkomo–Smith meeting, and Mugabe verified that "he had heard nothing about the meetings taking place with Smith until after the event." Houser writes in his notes, "Nkomo hadn't the courage to tell Mugabe about the meeting but only told him that it was important for him to go to Lagos." When in Lagos, he was told what took place by Garba.[58]

The US ambassador to Nigeria, Donald Easum, reported to the State Department the heated remarks Garba had for Nyerere once he heard that he had "flip-flopped" on the talks with Smith and the PF. Easum reports how Garba pulled him and British high commissioner, Sir Sam Falle, aside at a reception on September 19 in Lagos. According to Easum, "Garba cut loose a tirade against Nyerere, saying '[t]hat bastard, who does he think he is, playing God? We had it all wrapped up. He told me to go see Machel to get Mugabe on board. It had to be Machel, he said, because he didn't trust Chissano. So I went to Maputo and Machel said he would deliver Mugabe.'" Garba said, "When we were in a hand's grasp of pulling the whole thing off, Nyerere and his boys screw us all up. I am furious – I remain furious – and if I'd been there when Nyerere flip-flopped, so help me I'd have hit him." Garba

---

[57] George Houser Africa Trip 1978 notes, September 7, 1978, 2–4 MSS 294, Houser Papers, MSU Special Collections. For the successful machinations by Kaunda's allies in UNIP to exclude Kapwepwe and Nkumbula from the 1978 UNIP party election, see Miles Larmer, *Rethinking African Politics: A History of Opposition in Zambia* (Farnham, United Kingdom: Ashgate Publishing, 2011), 123–24.

[58] George Houser, "Houser Trip to Africa 1978 – Transcript of Notes," September 9, 1978, Houser Papers, MSU Special Collections.

then told the diplomats that he was done working on Zimbabwe: "I've washed my hands of it, and I'm glad I'm out of it." He then tells Falle and Easum to report to Owen and Vance, and to tell them, "I'm damn sorry – I tried my best and we almost made it – we almost made it."[59] This quote is quite telling of the personal effort Garba put into his own shuttle diplomacy to try to bring the war to an end and to negotiate a settlement between the PF leaders and Smith. It would take another long year of fighting – fighting that became more intensive in terms of the already terrible human toll.

Nyerere told his side of the story to the British high commissioner, Peter Moon, and the US ambassador, James Spain, on September 4 after he summoned the two to his office once he had returned to Dar es Salaam from the Lusaka meeting. Nyerere gave his interpretation of the original secret meeting. He believed the Nigerians were behind the talks, as they had first tried to get Sithole to agree to meet with Nkomo, but he refused so they turned to Chirau, who agreed to meet with Nkomo in London. Garba then brought Mugabe to Lagos to meet with Obasanjo, and Obasanjo told Mugabe of the plan to meet with Smith. Nyerere then told the diplomats that Mugabe "had agreed provided Smith really was willing to surrender and subject to his discussing first with Nkomo and with his Executive." The apparent disagreement between Mugabe and Nkomo, according to Nyerere, was that Nkomo wanted to move forward quickly, and Mugabe wanted to consult first with the ZANU executive in Maputo. Nyerere explains that he did at first think the talks could work but warned Garba "that Smith was slippery: if Smith really was willing to hand over power they could not say 'no' but it was a big if." He was most worried, based on his answer, of the Frontline State presidents losing control over the negotiations. Nyerere had warned Garba that the Frontline State presidents "would not know what they were really advising the PF to get into and there were great dangers of misunderstandings and recriminations." At the Frontline State presidents' summit, Nyerere had heard accounts from Mark Chona and Nkomo of the secret meetings. Nyerere said he was convinced that "Smith had come out to get Nkomo." Nyerere suggested that Smith "wanted Nkomo because he

---

[59] From Ambassador Embassy Lagos to Secretary of State Washington DC, "Garba Lambasts Nyerere on Aborted Smith/PF Meeting," September 20, 1978, 1978LAGOS11686, Central Foreign Policy Files, 1973–1976, RG 59, General Records of the Department of state, USNA.

thought Nkomo could end the war. When Nkomo said he could not come without Mugabe, Smith had initially said that Mugabe was totally unacceptable." Nyerere went on to relate what Garba and others had reported on the crux of the meeting, "that Smith 'had asked Nkomo to persuade Mugabe to come out too, and he put up the proposition that he would deliver Chirau, Nkomo should deliver Mugabe and they could forget about Muzorewa and Sithole.'" Finally, Nyerere related that "Smith had not gone into detail about a handover of power. He had been willing to do so, but Nkomo had refused in the absence of Mugabe."[60] High Commissioner Moon emphasized Nyerere's insistence that the secret meeting had been a ploy by Smith to get Nkomo out of the PF. At the Frontline State presidents' summit the day before, Nyerere said that "the unanimous conclusion of the Front Line leaders (and of Mugabe also) ... had been that there was nothing to be had from secret talks with Smith." Nyerere believed Smith needed Nkomo "to get the fighting stopped, Muzorewa and Sithole having failed to do this." Nyerere emphasized that the Frontline State presidents were now unanimous that there would be no further talk and that "the war should go on."[61]

Nyerere said he believed that the Nkomo/Smith talks had been dangerous because they had "caused some confusion within the PF." Nyerere was also critical of Nkomo for not accepting the Frontline State presidents' judgement during the summit. Nyerere added that should the Rhodesian government collapse, "and there was not one government and one army to replace his regime, there would be civil war (he confirmed specifically that he meant war between ZANU and ZAPU)." Nyerere said that he thought it would then "be impossible for any British Government to avoid intervening and to be drawn into taking sides. The only way to avoid this was through promoting the unity of the PF." However, having said this, Nyerere went on to criticize Nkomo, saying that Nkomo "did not seem to understand that he could not himself end the fighting without Mugabe." There is some inconsistency here in that Nyerere was assuming that Nkomo might think they could end the war without Mugabe, but such an argument would also require downplaying ZANLA's role in the war. As the evidence shows, Nkomo never assumed ZIPRA could go it

---

[60] Dar es Salaam to FCO, "Rhodesia," September 4, 1978, PREM 16/1834, BNA.
[61] Ibid.

alone, without Mugabe and ZANLA, in terms of the transfer of power with Smith.

Nyerere commented that this attempt to "join Smith" had consequences: "If what he has done does not destroy him (Nkomo) politically, he (Nyerere) saw in it at least the beginning of the seeds of his destruction." In response to the diplomats' questions, Nyerere added that the Frontline State presidents' decision not to continue talks with Smith "had been because of their own conviction that Smith's approach was not genuine, and not because of reluctance on Mugabe's part."[62] This again seems to only confirm the obvious, that Mugabe would not accept a secondary role to Nkomo in the PF, hence his refusal to attend a meeting with Smith, and Nyerere's support of this decision.

John Graham was pessimistic about Nyerere's reactions to the Nkomo/Smith talks. He wrote to the FCO that he felt "the great merit of the Nkomo scheme," which he "had thought had been accepted by the Rhodesian Front, was that by achieving complete unity of the PF under Nkomo, the risk of a Mashona/Ndebele (or ZANLA/ZIPRA) war would be greatly reduced." Graham believed that Nyerere, by siding with Mugabe and ZANU in not going forward with future talks, was moving in the wrong direction. "It is sad to see Nyerere, who has always proclaimed his desire to avoid a civil war of the kind that developed in Angola, lending himself to it." Graham went on to criticize those who questioned "Nkomo's ability to unite the Ndebele and the Mashona under his leadership." Graham believed that Nkomo, "with ZAPU, remains the only African political leader who appears genuinely to attempt a national appeal." Soured by Nyerere's response, Graham now predicted a possible "Mugabe/ Muzorewa alliance based on tribalism rather than political affinities, which will tend to increase the risk of a Mashona/Ndebele confrontation."[63] Although Graham may not have been totally aware of Mugabe's animosity toward Muzorewa, Graham was certainly prescient on the future of ZANU–ZAPU relations after independence.

---

[62] Ibid. For Ambassador Spain's account of Nyerere's meeting, see Dar es Salaam to Secretary of State, "Rhodesia: Results of Lusaka Front Line Meeting," September 4, 1978, DAR ES 03769, Central Foreign Policy Files, 1973–1976, RG 59, General Records of the Department of State, USNA.

[63] Graham to FCO, "MIPT: Rhodesia – Negotiated Settlement," September 4, 1978, item 2, PREM 16/1834, BNA.

The Shooting Down of the Air Rhodesian Viscount Plane

Reaction to the "secret meetings" revelation and controversy in early September 1978 likely influenced the decision by ZAPU's military wing, ZIPRA, to shoot down an Air Rhodesia Viscount passenger plane on September 3, 1978 using Soviet-made anti-aircraft missiles. The killing of Rhodesian civilians became international news, especially in Britain, and Nkomo was very tough in his rhetoric justifying the action based on the idea that the Rhodesian government was using civilian planes to transport troops. This act also served to show the Soviets and others that Nkomo was not in the "sell-out" mold painted by ZANU.

Another influence on the escalation of the war after the secret talks were exposed was the competition between Nkomo and Mugabe for Soviet and Cuban support. Mugabe and Nkomo had been in Ethiopia prior to the August 14 secret talks. Nkomo was there from August 6–8. Mugabe had also been there twice before, in May and June. There is an account of these visits to Addis Ababa from the US ambassador to Ethiopia, Frederick Chapin, that is copied in the FCO files. According to Chapin, "ZANU maintains a fulltime publicity and information officer in Addis Ababa, [named] 'Comrade Stalin Mau Mau,' which Nkomo's organization, ZAPU, does not." The report goes on to say that Mengistu treated Nkomo as a "Chief of State." However, a local source in Addis Ababa told the British that Nkomo was increasingly uneasy about the treatment he received there compared to Mugabe. This unnamed source "characterized the ZANU–ZAPU alliance within the PF as an 'unnatural marriage' that cannot in the long run endure." Interestingly, this source noted that it was Mugabe who had gotten himself closer to the Cubans and Soviets than Nkomo: "He went on to say that despite Mugabe's basically African nationalist orientation he was close to being a prisoner of the Cubans and Soviets, something he said was not true of Nkomo." The source also noted, that compared with the way Ethiopian leader Mengistu treated Mugabe, "Nkomo was said to be very unhappy at the results of his visit. Nkomo had apparently come to Addis Ababa hoping to get better treatment than that accorded Mugabe and did not get it." The US ambassador to Ethiopia goes on:

Another reason for Nkomo's visit at this time we are told was his concern over the military advantage which might accrue to Mugabe once the PF soldiers, presently being trained by Cuban advisors in Ethiopia, return to their bases. The large majority of these PF trainees were said to be loyal to Mugabe. Apparently Nkomo did not get whatever he may have asked Mengistu to do in this respect.[64]

According to British observers of the Addis Ababa international solidarity conference, Nkomo and Mugabe "were placed at the top table, but were the only two of the most distinguished guests not to speak. They sat side by side and neither spoke to nor looked at the other throughout the 4 hours of the ceremony."[65]

British accounts of the same event in Addis Ababa gives more details of what Nkomo had said there. Nkomo began by accusing Britain of "trying to bring about a puppet regime in Zimbabwe and Namibia to bolster the South African racist regime. The internal settlement had been set up with the connivance of Britain. An all party conference had not proved possible because 'events of the past two months culminated in stepping up the armed struggle.'"[66] Nkomo then defended the Viscount incident, calling it "the most dramatic event of the armed struggle." The report of his speech notes Nkomo's rebuttal to the accusations that ZIPRA soldiers had killed survivors. "He said 'we did not murder the survivors as they claimed, for we are not like Smith. Contrary to the lie of the Western press, all aboard the plane died when it was shot down and crashed.'" After justifying the shooting-down of the planes because they were thought to be carrying soldiers, "Nkomo described the outcry over 48 white victims, when hundreds of thousands of Africans were killed, jailed, humiliated and deprived of their basic human rights as 'simple racist hypocrisy.' He said, 'We live in an era where racism is religion. This is the legacy of Britain.'"[67] To defend his position as a radical nationalist to the Ethiopian and pan-African audience, Nkomo put the blame squarely on the Western powers for their attempt at splitting the PF and declared his commitment to continued unity with Mugabe in the PF: "Nkomo was described as categorically rejecting the Western-orchestrated split

[64] American Embassy London Incoming Telegram, "Joshua Nkomo visits Addis Ababa," August 10, 1978, item 394, FCO 36/2127, BNA.

[65] Addis Ababa to FCO, "International Solidarity Conference – Nkomo," September 16, 1978, item 2, PREM 16/1835, BNA.

[66] From Addis Ababa to FCO, telno 343, "International Solidarity Conference – Nkomo," September 16, 1978, PREM 16/1835, BNA.

[67] Ibid.

within the PF. He said, 'we agreed with Robert Mugabe that we in the PF will never split over the whole future of our people and our country.' Nkomo and Mugabe shook hands at the conference hall to a standing ovation."[68] Such a show of unity in Addis could not hide the vast differences between the two sides of the PF. The revelation of the Smith–Nkomo meeting was not enough, however, to break the fiction of unity from the perspective of the Frontline States, the Anglo-American diplomats, and most importantly Nkomo and Mugabe themselves.

In discussions following the revelation of the meeting and the condemnation by Nyerere and others, Owen met with the secretary of the Commonwealth, Sir Shridath Ramphal, who would play a major role in future negotiations leading up to, and during, the Lancaster House constitutional conference in 1979. Owen and Ramphal discussed the secret talks and subsequent problems for the PF and future negotiations with the internal settlement government. Owen admitted to Ramphal that he himself had been "involved in the Smith/Nkomo meetings" but he also said, "It was not our fault that Nyerere had not been told earlier what was going on." Mr Ramphal commented that it had been a mistake not to tell Nyerere earlier. Rather than claiming he had hoped to split the PF and have Nkomo reach a deal with Smith, Owen told Ramphal that "there was little doubt that Smith wanted to split the PF. The Nigerians had done well to give the PF cover at the talks with Nkomo. These had a least broken the log-jam." Here is a good example of Owen recalibrating his intentions. Owen told Ramphal that "it was a pity that no further meetings with the PF, including Mugabe, were planned for the moment. It was desirable that direct talks should take place again, including Mugabe; and that Mugabe should accept Nkomo as the leader of the PF."[69]

By September 1978, the prospects of a negotiated end of the war and an Anglo-American proposal settlement were minimal. First, Ian Smith had announced plans for the internal settlement and Bishop Muzorewa's United African National Council had been part of this agreement. David Owen tried his best in a September 12 meeting with Muzorewa to convince Muzorewa to realize how precarious the

---

[68] Ibid.
[69] Meeting with David Owen and Shridath S Ramphal (Commonwealth SG), September 13, 1978, "Namibia/Rhodesia," PREM16/1835, BNA.

situation had become for him. Owen wrote of his meeting with Muzorewa: "I urged him to accept the realities of the situation, stressing that it was obvious that security was deteriorating fast and that there was a real risk of civil war. It was essential to involve the PF leaders in working out a settlement while there was still time for negotiation."[70] Muzorewa, for his part, suggested that the PF was welcome to return to Salisbury and were invited "to join the Salisbury interim administration." He also believed that the British and Americans would not be neutral when it came to appointing a resident commissioner "since it was clear that they were determined to impose Nkomo." He said that the British "would be happy to see the UANC eliminated." Owen claimed to have "firmly rebutted this," but made it clear that the British "did wish them to come together with the other nationalists (and the Front Line states) and be prepared to look again at some of the provisions of the Salisbury agreement." Muzorewa said he was prepared to meet with everyone, including "Nkomo and Mugabe, as well as Presidents Nyerere, Khama and Machel: in no circumstances however would he talk to President Kaunda."[71]

The fallout of the failed direct talks with Smith certainly hurt Nkomo's standing with the Americans. A memorandum to President Carter from the US secretary of defense, Harold Brown, in early October summarized the ways Nkomo's star status was dimming among southern Africa experts in the State Department. Summarizing reports from the State Department, Brown told Carter that Nkomo was increasingly less likely to join an all-party conference, "because he represents a minority ethnic group and is not confident that he could win a free election. He seems more confident of his military option, based on continued military support from the USSR and Cuba, and on the personal loyalty of President Kaunda in Zambia (ZAPU's safe haven)." Brown goes on to report that sources believe that "the other leaders, including Robert Mugabe of ZANU, all of whom represent the ethnic majority, apparently fear [redacted] Nkomo and probably are not anxious to share power with him." Brown suggests that Mugabe, given "his relatively weak political and military positions, might be willing to attend an APC [all-party conference] without Nkomo." He

---

[70] Owen to Salisbury, "Rhodesia: Bishop Muzorewa," September 14, 1978, item 2, PREM 16/1835, BNA.
[71] Ibid.

also thought that it was therefore "possible that Mugabe's chief supporters – Tanzania, Mozambique, and China – might endorse an APC
without Nkomo because they are uncomfortable with the Soviet influence they see in ZAPU." Such analysis is quite different from the overly
confident position Mugabe and ZANU would publicly proclaim, but
not without merit in 1978. Brown then proffered a "Mugabe Option"
to President Carter: "If all of this is true, I think we should consider
a 'Mugabe Option' of supporting an APC despite the possibility that
Nkomo would not come." Brown noted that there was a "disadvantage
of a settlement without Nkomo," as it would likely lead to Nkomo's
"continued pursuit of a military solution with Soviet/Cuban support."
But Brown felt that there would be "a good chance that the prospect of
being left out plus the pressure from the front-line Presidents would
then bring Nkomo to join an APC; if so, so much the better."[72]

Just over a month later, in November 1978, Thomas Thornton
opined in his "Evening Report" for Brzezinski that the US embassy in
London is suggesting that an all-party conference would be useful
"perhaps as a way of moving things slightly off the track of increased
violence that they are now on." The US embassy was also of the
opinion, "that Mugabe may be eclipsing Nkomo as the stronger leader
of the PF."[73] As the Americans were filling in the details to gain a better
sense of the relative strengths of Mugabe and Nkomo in terms of their
abilities to win an election in a post-Rhodesia formation, the British
were also no longer working under illusions that the PF would be able
to unite after the bad blood witnessed between the two parties since the
formation of the PF in October 1976. Writing from Mozambique, the
British ambassador, John Lewen, reported to the FCO a conversation
he had with ZANLA leader Josiah Tongogara. The latter, who was

[72] Memorandum for the President from Harold Brown, Secretary of Defense,
October 7, 1978, "Nkomo, Mugabe, and the All-Parties conference (APC),"
NLC-15-44-4-8-4, Carter Library See also David Martin, "More Doors open
for Mugabe," Observer, October 29, 1978, which links Mugabe to Soviets, as
China cools off on ZANU.
[73] Thornton goes on to make an observation that is relevant for the next chapter:
"Most significant they are very skeptical about the British will to reassert any
authority in Rhodesia. While not excluding the possibility, they believe that the
British would need iron-clad guarantees from everybody in sight that there
would be no violence." Thornton (North-South) writes to Brzezinski,
November 20, 1978, "Evening Report," NLC-24-54-4-4-6 "Rhodesia,"
Carter Library.

held up previously as a leader willing to work with ZAPU and ZIPRA among the ZANU leadership, stated in no uncertain terms the disdain with which Nkomo was held at the end of 1978. Tongogara reportedly told Lewen that "in all earnestness," if Britain were to "impose Nkomo as head of Government in Zimbabwe, ZANU would fight against him." Lewin commented on this threat as follows: "This tends to confirm his reputation as an opponent of unity between ZANU and ZAPU."[74] While this seems to counter the post-independence popular memory of Tongogara as a supporter of cooperation, and he would be more supportive of unity at Lancaster House in October 1979, it more likely refers directly to Tongogara's insistence to the British that ZANU would not stand aside and accept any attempt by the British or the Nigerians to put Nkomo in a leadership position without guaranteeing Mugabe and Tongogara equal footing.

President Nyerere managed to keep his hold on the Frontline State presidents during the Nkomo–Smith talks and the push by Nigeria and Zambia to work without him. In a reflective mood, however, he had told the American chargé at the end of October, "I have always relied on Front Line State unity to get PF unity." He confessed he "sometimes worries about the prospect of a military collapse of Smith's forces because it would put ZANU and ZAPU armed forces in immediate confrontation." Nyerere then reportedly said, "But as long as we have Front Line unity, we can deal with that. Now, however, I have a problem with Zambia – a genuine problem." Nyerere related how he could no longer depend on Zambia, saying, "I think I am losing on FL unity." If unity fails, Nyerere thought that "Smith will get more encouraged to be reckless, he will feel escalation will help him redefine the issue from that of liberation to other ones. – 'All that nonsense about communists and big power interests.'"[75] High Commissioner Moon later reported that President Kaunda had left Dar es Salaam in a hurry, actually not wanting to stay the night. He apparently summoned his private plane from Lusaka, but when it didn't arrive on time, he flew with the Angolan president, Agostinho Neto, in his helicopter.

[74] Lewen to FCO, "My Telno 386: Rhodesia-ZANU (Mugabe)," November 23, 1978, item 522, FCO 36/2128, BNA.

[75] Title states: "Following is (unpolished) draft of telegram which Walker US Chargé, is dispatching about his conversation with Nyerere." Dar es Salaam to FCO and Washington, "My Telno 719: Rhodesia," October 26, 1978, item 79, FCO36/2230, BNA.

Moon concluded that a lot of the disagreements among the Frontline State presidents had to do, supposedly, with Nyerere's failure "to appreciate sufficiently the full extent of the economic and political problems confronting President Kaunda."[76]

Also at the end of 1978, Nkomo made another request for weapons from the Soviets, this time in large amounts. According to Soviet documents, Nkomo "requested the provision of weapons, ammunition, means of transport and communication, uniforms, food, equipment for the medical center and some other equipment in order to provide gratuitous material assistance to this party for 1979." The report notes that "J. Nkomo justifies his request by the need to intensify the armed liberation struggle in order to thwart imperialist maneuvers to resolve the Rhodesian problem on a neo-colonialist basis." Noting the close relationship between the Communist Party of the Soviet Union and ZAPU since 1964, a request was forwarded to the Central Committee of the Communist Party of the Soviet Union for approval. This time, Nkomo could report on a much larger fighting force. "The nature of our revolutionary armed struggle dictates the need for a new for a new organizational structure of army on a battalion basis. These battalions are formed from 10,000 trained fighters, 4,000 people undergoing training and 17,000 recruits which will train over the next 12 months." The list of required equipment called for heavy weapons, including twenty "Strela" anti-aircraft installations, sixty-three 57 mm guns, one hundred and thirty-eight 82 mm mortars, 713 RPG hand-held anti-tank grenade launchers, fifty-four ZGU anti-aircraft installations, 2,700 Kalashnikov assault rifles, 2,800 Simonov SKS carbines, and 1,750 Makarov pistols. The ammunition and supply lists were extensive, including clothing "for 30,000 soldiers and recruits."[77] Nkomo and his generals were preparing for a conventional war against the Rhodesians, and knowledge of this certainly influenced all parties to work toward negotiations later in 1979.

---

[76] Dar es Salaam to FCO, "My Telno 736: Meeting of the Front Line State in Dar es Salaam," October 30, 1978, item 99, FCO36/2230, BNA.

[77] Document CT137/80: On the request of the leadership of the Zimbabwe Patriotic Front (ZAPU), December 12, 1978, Bukovsky Archives, http://bukov sky-archives.net/pdfs/terr-wd/ct137b78.pdf. Thanks to Ben Allison for locating and translating this document for me to use here.

7 | The Big Gamble
The Transition and Pre-election Period

While Nkomo had managed to acquire further financial and military support from the Soviets in 1978, he also returned to Belgrade in Yugoslavia in January 1979 to request further funding and military support from President Tito's government. While there, he described the continued problems he faced in the PF, the inability of Mugabe and the ZANU leadership to accept a political unification, and their insistence on a military unification first, which Nkomo said was impossible. He blamed ZANU for the failure to unite, noting that ZANU's leaders, Mugabe, Tongogara, Muzenda, and Tekere, were "illegal and a group of self-appointed leaders." Having said this, he also went on to stress the importance of ZANU. "Nkomo estimates that it is necessary to preserve the Patriotic Front, because it is 'the only hope for the centralization of the struggle and to preserve the unity of the nation after gaining independence.'"[1] In February 1979, ZIPRA would again use Soviet-supplied surface-to-air missiles to shoot down another Air Rhodesian passenger plane, this one carrying tourists from Victoria Falls to Salisbury. According to accounts historian Nancy Mitchell has found, Ian Smith responded to this attack by contacting President Carter and Prime Minister Callaghan to inform them that the Anglo-Americans were the only ones who could "bring an end to all this inhuman terror."[2] This outcry did not stop the Rhodesians from carrying out air raids on ZIPRA camps in Zambia, as well as raids against a ZIPRA training camp in

---

[1] "Information about the visit of the delegation of the African National Union of Zimbabwe / ZAPU / led President Joshua Nkomo, 7 – 9 January 1979," Savezna Konferencija SSRNJ Sekcija za spoljnu politiku i medunarodne veze [Federal Conference SSRNJ Section for Foreign Policy and International Relations], Broj: 408–19 Beograd, 12.1.1979, Signatura ACKSKJ, IX, 140/53, 5 24, Viii 1978, Arhiv Centralnog Komiteta Saveza Komunista Jugoslavije. Thanks to Sarah Zabic for taking photos of this and other files for me in this archive.
[2] Nancy Mitchell, *Jimmy Carter in Africa: Race and The Cold War* (Stanford University Press, 2016), 506.

Angola in late February. The attack into Angola brought up again the possibility of Cuban and Soviet retaliation.

South African diplomat Piet Van Vuuren in Salisbury reported that he asked the Rhodesians if they were worried about Cuban retaliation after the raid. He pointed out to his Rhodesian contact Mr. Bulls that "there may now be MIG aircraft stationed in Angola that were perhaps three times faster than the Rhodesian planes." He added that Mr. Bulls had "apparently not yet thought of this." Van Vureen stressed that these attacks into Angola "cannot be in the interest of Rhodesia – nor in the general interest of peace in Southern Africa." Van Vureen noted that "since the middle of 1976, there have been 17 airstrikes carried out on bases in Zambia and Mozambique, during which at least 50 camps have been destroyed and between 3,000 and 4,000 terrorists killed."[3] Given the amount of cross-border raids into Mozambique against ZANLA and into Zambia against ZIPRA, 1979 would be a very difficult year. Soviet documents indicate that Nkomo and Mugabe requested Cuban pilots to fly defensive operations against the Rhodesian Air Force, but this request was turned down.[4]

In January 1979, the US ambassador to Tanzania, James Spain, relayed President Nyerere's assessment of the Rhodesia situation. Nyerere was "still clinging" to the Anglo-American plan. "Although he was pessimistic about the future. If civil war is to be prevented in Rhodesia, [the] only alternatives are [the] Anglo-American plan or PF unity. He doubts he can produce the latter. But he also believes that [the] time when success was possible with the AAP is probably past." Ambassador Spain summed up Nyerere's pessimistic prognosis as follows: the "US and UK will do a lot of

---

[3] The South Africans reported air attacks on two ZIPRA camps: Chunga and a camp at Nampundu Mine near Lusaka. The attack on "the ZIPRA camp near Luso in Angola" resulted in the death of "190 terrorists" and "injured 540." Piet Van Vuuren to Secretary of Foreign Affairs, Cape Town, "Rhodesian Aircraft Outside the Country Boundaries," March 6, 1979, 1/156/7, vol. 2, Rhodesia Foreign Policy and Relations, Department of Foreign Affairs, South African National Archives, Pretoria.

[4] Raul Valdes Vivo is recorded to have stated, "I was tasked ... to convey to J. Nkomo and R. Mugabe, that Cuba is unable to satisfy their request to send pilots for the repulsion of air attacks on the training camps for the Patriotic Front armed forces." "Memorandum of Conversation between Minister-counselor of the Soviet Embassy in Havana M. Manasov and Cuban Communist Party CC member Raul Valdes Vivo, 7 May 1979," May 24, 1979, History and Public Policy Program Digital Archive, TsKhSD, f. 5, op. 76, d. 834, ll. 82–84, http://digitalarchive.wilsoncenter.org/document/113031.

talking but with British election coming up, there will be no action. If Labor wins again, and by the time US has possible action arranged, civil war will have begun." Nyerere's own recommendation, according to Ambassador Spain, was a "US-backed British intervention within the next couple of months."[5] Nyerere's pessimism was shared among many other actors in the Rhodesia negotiations. The internal settlement, the failed "secret talks" of August 1978, and the intensification of the war after September 1978 seemed to push the possibility of all-party talks farther off. Plans underway for the 1979 "internal settlement" elections that would create the state of "Zimbabwe-Rhodesia," with Bishop Muzorewa as the first black prime minister, also seemed to confirm Smith's potential success at outmaneuvering the Anglo-American plan.

In February 1979, Sir Anthony Duff, the US assistant secretary of state for African affairs, Richard Moose, and South African secretary of foreign affairs, Brand Fourie, discussed the Anglo-American and South African positions on Rhodesia. Moose and Duff continued to express concerns about the present conditions, especially given the raids by the Rhodesians and South Africans against ZANLA and ZIPRA in Mozambique and Zambia. It was suggested that these raids had even raised incentives for the Tanzanians to consider turning to the Soviets and Cubans to help defend the Frontline States hosting the liberation armies. Duff suggested that Nyerere may have changed his view toward requesting help from the Cubans and Soviets. "Previously Nyerere had believed in Africans solving their own problems but now he seemed to be thinking of using Cubans for the defence of Moçambique, Tanzania and Zambia against Rhodesian attack." Duff summarized his own view of what might be an "undesirable scenario," involving "the creation of a climate receptive to Soviet and Cuban intervention; the departure of the whites; black civil war; and the establishment of a Government subservient to the Soviet Union." There was, according to Duff, evidence of stepped-up contact with Cuban and Soviet advisers in both Zambia and Tanzania.[6]

---

[5] Dar es Salaam to State, "President Nyerere's Views on Namibia and Rhodesia in Meeting with Mayor Bradley," January 6, 1979, DAR ES 00077 060906Z, Central Foreign Policy Files, 1973–1976, RG 59, General Records of the Department of State, USNA.

[6] "Fourie Meeting with Sir Anthony Duff and Mr. Richard Moose, February 21, 1979 at the Verwoerd Building (Office of the Secretary of Foreign Affairs)," DFA 1/156/1, vol. 2.

Moose suggested that President Kaunda was also more inclined to ask for Soviet help to defend against Rhodesian air raids. However, Fourie, given his long experience with Kaunda, replied, "Kaunda has been saying for years that he might have to turn to the Communists. It was true that his position at present was very shaky. If the recent elections in Zambia had been genuine, he might not now have been President."[7] Fourie then presented what he saw as the necessary objectives for Rhodesia: "There cannot be an end to the fighting nor can international recognition be expected and sanctions lifted unless an election is held with all parties' participation and under international – presumably U.N. – supervision. There will also have to be a U.N. Force to hold the ring." Duff responded to Fourie's suggestion with the need for "a cease-fire first." Duff stated that what he would like to accomplish was that "South Africa and the United States and the United Kingdom all accept that this is the basic objective and each of them bring to bear on the parties such influence as they can."[8]

As cooperative as this sounds, the South Africans and the British were not on the same page vis-à-vis the internal settlement, nor were the Americans, but the three nations believed they could influence the negotiations in ways to fit their national interests. The United States wanted Rhodesia to become Zimbabwe without Soviet or Cuban military intervention. The British wanted the same, while also trying to keep their role in the transition to a minimum. The South Africans wanted Muzorewa's government to survive and have sanctions lifted, but they did not necessarily want his government to receive international recognition so that it would remain dependent on South Africa. The South Africans sought first and foremost to have Bishop Muzorewa elected in April 1979, as the first black prime minister, and hoped that if sanctions could be lifted, the Rhodesians could begin to finance more of the war without so much South African assistance.[9]

In June 1979, the US ambassador to Mozambique, Willard Dupree, met with Mugabe in Maputo to go over the latest developments in the US Congress concerning the important vote to delay making a decision about lifting sanctions. Mugabe was quite pleased with this development according to Dupree, who recorded Mugabe's reaction as

---

[7] Ibid.   [8] Ibid.
[9] See Gary Baines, "The Arsenal of Securocracy: Pretoria's Provision of Arms and Aid to Salisbury, c. 1974–1980," *South African Historical Journal* (2019), 1–18.

supporting President Carter, and how continued developments along such lines "would make for excellent relations between the PF and US."[10] Dupree goes on to say that Mugabe characterized the United States "as a great nation," but that it "must not be seen supporting a neo-colonial regime in Zimbabwe. He stressed that PF has never said that US must support [the] PF as such, but that US should support democratic change and progress." Mugabe went on to reassure Dupree that the "PF does not intend to create a dictatorship in Zimbabwe." Mugabe claimed that "he is not anti-US and added that ZANU does not want to be dominated by Soviets or anyone else." He told how the East Germans had asked him to "denounce [the] Chinese in exchange for GDR arms" and his reply had been to say, "ZANU does not accept aid with strings attached." Mugabe is then directly quoted by Dupree as adding "and you know we're not the best friends of the Soviets." As usual, Mugabe could not make this statement without adding a dig at ZAPU. "Mugabe stated that ZANU does not tie its hands on foreign policy. But he didn't know what ZAPU thought on this subject."[11]

By July 1979, British diplomats in Maputo were receiving reassurances from ZANU's Secretary General, Edgar Tekere, that they would participate in any upcoming conferences. Tekere told British diplomat John Doble who had taken over the duties of the British ambassador for Mozambique after the appointed ambassador had suffered a heart attack, that ZANU "were waiting keenly for new proposals from us [Britain]. They would study them carefully. Even if they disliked them, they would come to any meeting we called, even if only to say they could not accept them. ZANU did not like refusing to go to conferences." Doble also noted that Tekere's eldest son "had just joined up" to fight in the war, so Doble felt that while Tekere noted that the war would go on if Britain tried a "'short-circuit' solution," the point was also made that negotiations could bring the war to an end. Asked if Tekere was willing to work with Muzorewa, Tekere said that he could not because "Muzorewa was a traitor" and "even though he had no

---

[10] Fm American Embassy Maputo to Sec State, "Mugabe's Comments on Rhodesian Developments," June 16, 1979, 1979MAPUTO00746, Central Foreign Policy Files, 1973–1976, RG 59, General Records of the Department of State, USNA. For the Carter Administration's decision to not lift sanctions in 1979, see Eddie Michel, *The White House and White Africa: Presidential Policy Toward Rhodesia during the UDI Era, 1965–1979* (New York: Routledge, 2019), 212–24; Mitchell, *Jimmy Carter in Africa*, 460–62, 569–70.

[11] Ibid.

power, they could not talk to traitors." Tekere did note, however, that he had contacts in the Rhodesian Army who "would welcome in a new Zimbabwean army." The bottom line for Doble was "that it seemed ZANU, while maintaining an intransigent line, are not likely to try to prevent further negotiations by seeking to impose impossible pre-conditions."[12]

A few months earlier, Doble had written his interpretation of the Cold War politics at play in the PF following a meeting with Soviet minister-counsellor Arkady Glukhov in March 1979. Glukhov had told Doble that "the situation was ... very difficult for the Soviets," as "they supported Nkomo and the Mozambicans, while the Chinese supported Mugabe and the Mozambicans, and Mozambique and Tanzania supported Mugabe." Glukhov "claimed to be all in favour of a conference to try and get a peaceful settlement."[13] Keith Evetts wrote up an account of Soviet views in Maputo which he sent to Rosemary Spencer in the Rhodesia Department of the FCO. According to Evetts second-hand account, "the Russians are exasperated with the Zimbabweans. They are annoyed that Nkomo has made little progress (and that his reputation is in decline); they do not believe in Mugabe's 'liberated areas'; and they are frustrated by their inability to get PF unity." It is worth noting that both sides in the Cold War were frustrated by this inability. Evetts summarized how the Soviets did not want to give weapons to both sides, "since the two wings of the PF would probably shoot at each other." He also said his source had indicated that the Soviets wanted to avoid "'another Angola' – if only because of the expense."[14]

Just prior to the Lusaka Commonwealth Heads of Government Meeting in early August 1979, Mugabe met with Bulgarian leader Todor Zhivkov in Sofia. Minutes from this meeting demonstrate Mugabe's rhetorical commitment to a communist ideology, as would be expected in his pursuit of military and financial aid from eastern bloc nations. In contrast to his claims of neutrality made to Ambassador

---

[12] Maputo to FCO, "Telno 164," July 21, 1979, item 86–87, PREM 19/109, BNA. John Doble explained his situation in Sue Onslow and Michael Kandiah, eds., *Lancaster House 1979: Part I – The Witness Seminar* (Foreign, Commonwealth and Development Office: London 2019), 65.

[13] To Ambassador from John Doble, "Soviet Views," item 22, FCO 36/2408, BNA.

[14] Evetts to Spencer, "ZANU (Mugabe) Potboiler," March 1, 1979, item 22, FCO36/2408, BNA.

Dupree, Mugabe promised Zhivkov that he and ZANU were committed to "scientific socialism and Marxism-Leninism," and that "[s]hould we establish a socialist zone within the borders of Angola, Zimbabwe, and Mozambique, then success in South Africa will be guaranteed. South Africa is quite aware of this impending danger; that is why it provides assistance to Ian Smith."[15] Zhivkov was straightforward with Mugabe, according to the Bulgarian minutes of their meeting. Zhivkov asked Mugabe: "What is it that separates ZANU and ZAPU? Are there any differences in principle? I don't think there are." He then noted how "[t]he historian of the future will definitely draw the conclusion that there have been no differences in principle. History will give its severe, yet impartial judgment." Zhivkhov then said, "If there are no principal differences, then what can we say? That these differences are unprincipled, which implies that both ZANU and ZAPU will bear the historic responsibility. History will never forgive you. I invited you, and that is why I am frank and straightforward." Mugabe responded with a long discussion of the history of ZANU and ZAPU. He eventually blamed Nkomo for his inability to treat Mugabe and ZANU as equal partners: "I have told him [Nkomo] several times that he must create a realistic idea of the Patriotic Front. People must see us, to see that we are together and have taken up a common struggle against imperialism." Mugabe then gives the usual explanation for the lack of progress in unifying the two parties, utilizing the "*Tamba wakachenjera*" strategy established to avoid unity, "However unity must be achieved at all levels, not only at the top. This is a problem. That is why we insist that military unity be established. Nkomo is unwilling, but we still hope things will change and we won't give up."[16]

Lusaka Commonwealth Heads of Government Meeting Provides the Diplomatic Breakthrough

The Commonwealth Heads of Government Meeting in Lusaka, which was held from 1–7 August, produced the influential Lusaka Accord

---

[15] "Minutes of Todor Zhivkov – Robert Mugabe Conversation, Sofia," July 29, 1979, History and Public Policy Program Digital Archive, Central State Archive, Sofia, Fond 378-B, Record 1, File 523. Translated by Assistant Professor Kalina Bratanova; edited by Dr. Jordan Baev and obtained by the Bulgarian Cold War Research Group. http://digitalarchive.wilsoncenter.org/document/111111.
[16] Ibid.

that articulated the Commonwealth's position on South Africa and Rhodesia/Zimbabwe. In terms of Zimbabwean decolonization, the Lusaka Accord finally confirmed Britain's commitment to overseeing the transition to independence. Given this responsibility, it was necessary for the British to host a formal conference to produce a new constitution to supersede that of the new Zimbabwe-Rhodesia state. Unlike the Geneva talks three years previously, this conference in 1979 had pre-established Britain's role in seeing through the transition to majority rule. The Lusaka Accords also set the stage for Bishop Muzorewa and his EXCO partners to negotiate at Lancaster House. Bishop Muzorewa and the other EXCO leaders had to agree to concede their recently obtained sovereign power as leaders of Zimbabwe-Rhodesia in order to negotiate in all-party talks with the full participation of the PF in the process.[17]

Margaret Thatcher and the Conservative Party came to power after the Conservatives' victory in the May 3, 1979 general election. Prime Minister Thatcher, along with her foreign minister, Peter Carrington, faced an important foreign policy decision early in their administration: whether to push for the Anglo-American proposal negotiated settlement including the PF, and to stand firmly against recognition of Muzorewa's government, or to recognize the Zimbabwe-Rhodesia government and to lift sanctions. While Thatcher and Carrington would later take credit for their decisive foreign policy decisions that led to Lancaster House and the Zimbabwean 1980 elections that included the PF, the backstory involves many others as well. It would be at the Commonwealth Heads of Government Meeting in Lusaka, during the first week of August 1979, where President Kaunda and other Commonwealth leaders famously staged a well-orchestrated plan to convince Thatcher to go against the advice of many of her party's

---

[17] The Text of the Lusaka Accord reached at the Commonwealth Heads of Government Meeting included the following key position: "accepted that independence on the basis of majority rule required the adopting of a democratic constitution, including appropriate safeguards for minorities; –acknowledged that the government formed under such an independence constitution had to be chosen through free and fair elections properly supervised under British Government authority and with Commonwealth observers." Reprinted in SADC Hashim Mbita Project, *Southern African Liberation Struggles: contemporaneous Documents, 1960–1994* edited by Arnold J Temu and Joel das N. Tembe, vol. 9: *Countries and regions outside SADC & International Organisations*, 205–6.

influential leaders. This lobbying was successful, resulting in the British decision to not lift sanctions and, at the same time, to not recognize the new Muzorewa-led government of Zimbabwe-Rhodesia.[18] As Carol Thompson argues in her work on the Frontline State's role in Zimbabwe's independence, the economic pressure from Nigeria, in particular in nationalizing oil production to stop Shell from providing oil to South Africa and Rhodesia, was also a key pressure point to get Thatcher and Carrington to follow the Commonwealth's line of argument.[19]

Just before the meeting in Lusaka commenced, Prime Minister Thatcher met with African Commonwealth leaders to obtain their views of the PF leadership. During a July 31 meeting in Lusaka with Malawi's life president, Hastings Banda, Thatcher listened as Banda praised his old friend, Reverend Ndabaningi Sithole, while also saying, "frankly that only two men could assume power in a democratic Rhodesia: Bishop Muzorewa or Mr. Mugabe. This was because both were Shonas. Dr. Banda said that he did not like Mugabe because he was too close to the Russians; but he was a Shona nevertheless." Banda painted a grim picture of Nkomo's future prospects: "Joshua Nkomo could never rule Rhodesia since he came from a minority tribe and he had no chance of winning." Nor was Banda at all impressed with Muzorewa's chances, at least without the intervention of the British on his behalf. "Bishop Muzorewa commanded a majority, whether one liked him or not." Banda told Thatcher that it was now the "UK's problem." He said that the Bishop wanted "to make his government acceptable to the rest of the world but it was the UK's problem to bring this about."[20] Banda also reassured Thatcher that, in his opinion, there was little chance of the Soviets getting involved in a civil war after

[18] Carrington explains that Britain could not accept the Muzorewa election and recognize his government because everyone else, except the South Africans, were against it. There was even a chance that the Commonwealth would break up over the issue. Carrington evidence provided in Michael Kandiah and Sue Onslow, eds., *Britain and Rhodesia: The Route to Settlement* (London: Institute of Contemporary British History Oral History Programme 2008), 78. See also, Sue Onslow, "'Noises Off': South Africa and the Lancaster House Settlement 1979–1980," *Journal of Southern African Studies* 35, no. 2 (2009), 489–506; A. DeRoche, *Kenneth Kaunda*, 148–50.

[19] Carol Thompson, *Challenge to Imperialism: The Frontline States in the Liberation of Zimbabwe* (Boulder, CO: Westview Press, 1986), 66–67.

[20] "Note of the Prime Minister's Discussion with Life President Banda of Malawi in the Mulungushi Village, Lusaka, on 31 July 1979," PREM 19/10, BNA.

independence. "It was sometimes argued that Nkomo and Mugabe would continue to fight on after independence had been granted. He did not share this view, which assumed that the Russians would intervene openly; there was so far no evidence that they might." Thatcher asked if Mugabe was under Russian control, and Banda said no; nor was President Machel of Mozambique in his opinion. Banda told Thatcher, "Shonas like Robert Mugabe were very individualistic by temperament." The prime minister commented that "this should make them capitalistic as well!"[21]

On Friday, August 3, 1979, during the conference, Thatcher and Carrington met with Botswana president Seretse Khama and his foreign minister, Archibald Mogwe. The two were critical of Thatcher's statement earlier in the day that Bishop Muzorewa was not the same as Ian Smith. Mogwe explained that since no country had recognized the April 1979 election of Muzorewa, the Zimbabwe-Rhodesia state and Muzorewa's position as prime minister remained illegal, so therefore Muzorewa was still representing the same illegal regime led by Smith since the Unilateral Declaration of Independence. Khama was critical of Thatcher and the British for putting too much support behind Muzorewa. Thatcher explained that since coming to power only three months previously, she had been moved by the killings in Rhodesia, and this is why she wanted to move quickly, and added that "there was an expectation back in London that she and her government should support the Bishop."[22]

Mogwe concurred on the need to act quickly, but from his perspective, the need came from another source. "Botswana's great fear was that at the forthcoming Conference of the Non-Aligned [Movement] at Havana, just as at the recent OAU Conference, the PF would be confirmed as the sole legitimate representatives of the Rhodesian people, and this could only encourage and strengthen them."[23] President Khama was less concerned than Mogwe with the OAU. He did not agree with the OAU's assessment of "the PF as the sole legitimate representatives of the people of Rhodesia, and he believed that the resolution should be ignored." For Khama, a direct role for the Commonwealth, with Britain in the lead, was important to intervene before other groups became involved.[24] Foreign Secretary Carrington interjected into the discussion to say that Britain had in fact accepted

[21] Ibid.   [22] Ibid.   [23] Ibid.   [24] Ibid.

responsibility for Rhodesia, but that some member states, notably Nigeria, were trying to push the prime minister and Britain to go further. Carrington argued that "the British Government was on a tightrope over Rhodesia. We had to think not only of the African parties – both inside and outside Rhodesia – to the problem, but we also had to have in mind public opinion in Britain, which was very largely behind Bishop Muzorewa." It is possible that Carrington was in fact expressing his own doubts about Muzorewa in the company of Khama and Mogwe. He concluded by saying "If Britain did anything which appeared in Salisbury to be a sell-out to the PF, there would be no question of getting the whites to agree to change the constitution. Britain was surrounded by different pressures, and we needed all the help we could get if we were not to fall off the tightrope."[25]

President Khama emphasized that he "wanted to keep Britain on the tightrope. He was sure that there was no intention on the part of African people to push the United Kingdom into doing anything which the United Kingdom did not think was right." Khama told Carrington that "it was not only Britain which faced a problem. Some of the Front Line State Presidents had come to realise that they had made a mistake by encouraging the leaders of the PF to think that they were going to be 'top dogs' and they were trying to undo their error. It was, however, a difficult process."[26] Mogwe proffered that the British should not give Muzorewa "precedence ... whatever view they took of him privately."[27]

The result of the Lusaka Commonwealth Heads of Government Meeting was that Thatcher and Carrington had committed Britain to sponsor a Lancaster House constitutional conference and that there would be no recognition of Zimbabwe-Rhodesia, nor any lifting of sanctions. As the meeting's results became known in Zimbabwe-Rhodesia and South Africa, Rhodesian cabinet minister David Smith met with South African diplomats to discuss the next steps. Smith provided an honest assessment of the situation from the perspective of whites and the military. He said that "whites' moral[e] with [the] Lusaka congress was shattered." He also stated, "We are not winning the war, we have to win politically. We are losing military/morale of fighting troops are very low. The will to fight is withering away." Given that the political solution was now all that was left to the Rhodesian

[25] Ibid.   [26] Ibid.   [27] Ibid.

Front, David Smith argued that an all-party conference would offer white Rhodesians a way to negotiate majority rule in which the only discussion will be safeguards for minority groups. Smith also told the South Africans that if elections were held tomorrow, Muzorewa would win.[28] Handwritten notes from the meeting attribute the following to Pik Botha, South African minister of foreign affairs, at this meeting with the Rhodesians, summarizing South Africa's position towards the proposed Lancaster talks: "Mugabe/Nkomo shoot conference down we have made it. Sanctions lifted. Recognition is not important."[29] The last point is a reference to South African hopes that Zimbabwe-Rhodesia would survive without international recognition.

Pik Botha's views corresponded well with an August 10, 1979 South African strategy paper entitled "Guidelines to handle the strategic situation in ZR [Zimbabwe-Rhodesia] following the Commonwealth proposals for a settlement." The document lists the contributing factors to the grave situation in Zimbabwe-Rhodesia, including a "deteriorating" security situation and economy that "is not in a healthy state," the continuation of sanctions, the lack of international recognition for Zimbabwe-Rhodesia while "white emigration is taking place at a steady rate," and the continuation of the PF's "terrorist war" against Zimbabwe-Rhodesia. The document notes, "It is largely due to the RSA's economic, fiscal and military assistance that ZR has not been forced to bow to the military and economic pressures against her."[30]

The strategy paper argued that given the PF's past refusals to negotiate without first having the Zimbabwe-Rhodesia government's "abdication" and the "replacement of the [Security Forces] by forces of the Patriotic Front," it was "unlikely that the so-called PF leaders, especially Mugabe, will in the final instance be prepared to comply with the principles of the settlement initiative as set out in the statement by the Commonwealth Heads of State." In addition to this deduction, the paper believed that the close and public ties between South Africa and Bishop Muzorewa would be "another of the stumbling blocks to

---

[28] "Handnotes, Meeting with David Smith, South African Defense Forces, August 12, 1979," 3 HSAW/3/168, SADF Archives.

[29] Ibid.

[30] "Guidelines to Handle the Strategic Situation in ZR Following the Commonwealth Proposals for a Settlement," HS OPS/DGMS/303/6/3/4, Box H, SAW 168, Group 3, SADF Archives.

international recognition of ZR." Given this, the paper recommended that in order to continue the avoidance of international recognition, strong public recognition of ties between Zimbabwe-Rhodesia and South Africa needed to be maintained.

The Lancaster House Negotiations, September 10 to December 15, 1979

Unlike at the start of the Geneva talks in 1976, at the start of the Lancaster House negotiation in 1979, Joshua Nkomo had little reason to feel confident about his future as leader of an independent Zimbabwe. Frank Wisner, who had led the US diplomatic team at the Geneva talks in 1976, described Nkomo's possible options at Lancaster House in a September 7 telegram he drafted to brief the US ambassador to the United Nations, Andrew Young. Wisner believed that there were too many pressures on Nkomo to allow him to stay within the PF as the conference moved forward.[31] Wisner then described reports of Nkomo's state of mind based on talks with US embassy staff in Lusaka. The general feeling was that Nkomo had become "a perplexed man who in recent months has become increasingly concerned that time is running out on him and his movement." Wisner also summarized the view of the Indian high commissioner in Lusaka, who characterized Nkomo as a "man who thought he was losing control over the course of events in Rhodesia." Aaron Milner, the former Zambian minister who had known Nkomo for years, described to Wisner that Nkomo "believes his Zambian base is eroding as the pressures on Kaunda increase." Milner also relayed to Wisner that Nkomo "apparently is also concerned by ZAPU's younger generation which is pressing for greater authority in the party's councils."

Wisner then gave attention to the many pressures on Nkomo and the "conflicting advice he is receiving from those around him." These divisions are described primarily through ethnicity. "Following the Rhodesian raids into Lusaka last April, Nkomo tended to associate himself more closely with those (mostly Ndebeles and Kalangas in the military wing) who have been pushing for a more activist military

---

[31] From [Wisner] SecState for Ambassador Young, "Rhodesia: Nkomo's Position on the Lancaster House Talks," September 7, 1979, 1979STATE235317, Central Foreign Policy Files, 1973–1976, RG 59, General Records of the Department of State, USNA.

police." In contrast, Wisner said that Nkomo had more recently "begun to pay more attention to his old-time political associates (mostly Shona), who have been supportive of efforts to seek a negotiated solution to the Rhodesian conflict." The reason for their willingness to negotiate, according to Wisner's interpretations, was that "these trusted lieutenants of Nkomo see their positions eroding within ZAPU as the new military generation begins to emerge."[32]

Wisner also noted Nkomo's deep distrust of the Tanzanians, and his belief that the Lusaka Commonwealth Conference Communique had been created to work against Nkomo's position. He noted that even though Kaunda had supported the communique, he would be more supportive of Nkomo at Lancaster. He could not trust the Tanzanians. Wisner then described Nkomo's increasing impatience "with ZAPU's failure to make any significant progress on the political or military fronts." Given Nkomo's age, Wisner believed that this need for a breakthrough was "a major, if not determining factor, behind ZAPU's decision to infiltrate large number of guerrillas into Zimbabwe Rhodesia in recent weeks." This was meant to both put pressure on the Salisbury government, and to put ZAPU in "a much stronger position to demand that its forces play a role in the transition process or the ZAPU 'areas of influence' are recognized under the terms of the ceasefire." Wisner ended by saying that Nkomo, as well as Kaunda, would likely not escalate the war "until it was obvious that the Lancaster talks had broken down and the blame for their collapse could be placed at Salisbury's doorstep." Wisner did note, however that there was pressure on Nkomo to intensify the war: "Nkomo's more radical military advisers, the Soviets, and the Cubans will argue for a settlement that ensures Patriotic Front supremacy in Salisbury and possibly for a major escalation of the fighting." Wisner related that Nkomo told him that he "believes that time is running out on him and his movement and that a solution to the conflict – whether political or military – most come soon."[33]

Patriotic Front Diplomacy at Lancaster House: The Land Issue

There is not enough space to cover the Lancaster House conference here. I would like to instead focus on the debates and diplomacy that

[32] Ibid.   [33] Ibid.

almost scuttled the conference. This had to do with the insistence on protecting white interests in the Constitution, especially the clause that protected white commercial farmers from state appropriation for a ten-year period. Almost a month into the negotiations, on October 11, 1979, Nkomo and Mugabe issued a joint statement, as the PF, listing all of the issues that were still unresolved. The list was long, including issues with "the Declaration of Rights in so far as it affects land and pensions" and "the provisions of the four principal institutions of government (the army, the Police, the Public Service and Judiciary)." The statement did, however, indicate their willingness to cooperate and conceptually agree to the draft constitution. "We are now satisfied that the conference has reached a sufficiently wide measure of agreement on the independence constitution to enable it to proceed to the next item on the agenda."[34] Carrington adjourned the negotiations until the following Monday, which gave the PF time to talk with the Frontline State presidents and others about these objections.

Roderic Lyne, Peter Carrington's secretary, reported on the stalled talks to Prime Minister Thatcher. Lyne indicated that Nkomo and Mugabe were not in total agreement over the impasse. "There were clear signs of strain between ZAPU and ZANU at today's session. Nkomo appears to be looking for a way out, while Mugabe seems determined not to accept the points in the Constitution covering land and pensions, as well as maintaining general reservations about the Army, Police and Public Service." Lyne, all along following the tactics of the British, hoped that this disagreement might lead to a split between Nkomo and Mugabe. "There is a possibility that ZAPU will look for a way out of the dilemma. But, if we have to face a breakdown of the Conference, we will, in Lord Carrington's view, have a fully defensible position, and we would lose the support of Bishop Muzorewa and his delegation if we give way on this issue."[35] Similar to Kissinger's position at Geneva in 1976, Carrington in 1979 was quite willing to have the Lancaster House talks break down, just as long as the British could be seen as having offered Mugabe a compromise that would have allowed him to participate in elections and potentially take over the country through majority rule, and have Mugabe blamed for turning it down.

---

[34] "PF Reply to Chairman's Statement of 11th October 1979," PREM 19/113, BNA (n. d. but likely October 11, 1979), 366.

[35] "Rhodesian Constitutional Conference," October 11, 1979, PREM 19/113, BNA, 338.

Explanations for why the British continued to insist on language in the constitution about compensating whites for agricultural land usually revolve around the "kith and kin" argument, suggesting that it was a functional exercise of looking out for their own. But there was also a negotiating side of it too. Mervyn Brown, who had worked on Rhodesia for many years before becoming the British high commissioner for Nigeria, wrote to Carrington on October 15 to point out how important the land compensation issue was to keep Smith and his supporters at the table. Brown told Carrington that Smith was in Rhodesia "trying to rally white opposition to the constitution." Brown warned Carrington not "to give way on the question of pensions or of expropriation of land without compensation" because "this would rally virtually the whole of white opinion behind Smith and destroy any hope of agreement on the constitution."[36]

The British drafted a response "to use if necessary" in order to address the PF's objections on the land compensation issue. But even in this October 11 draft statement the FCO was clear that the British were not going to commit themselves to an actual amount of compensation. The statement suggested that the British were committed to contributing to "the initial capital" for "an Agricultural Development Bank," or something similar, but then qualified this commitment by stating that "[t]he costs would be very substantial indeed, well beyond the capacity of any individual donor country, and the British Government cannot commit itself at this stage to a specific share in them."[37] There is evidence that this statement was distributed to the PF because letters were prepared to send out to the high commissioners in Lusaka and Dar es Salaam the next day in order to help them explain the standoff at Lancaster regarding land compensation. The letters asked Nyerere and Kaunda to assist in convincing Mugabe and Nkomo to accept the proposed constitution in order to move on to the transitional arrangements. The letter to Nyerere was slightly different, as it referred to Nyerere's earlier advice to the British that they should be sensitive to the PF demands over the land issue. "As you suggested, we have tried to help the PF over the question of land."

---

[36] From Lagos to FCO, "Telno 859," October 15, [1979], "Rhodesia Constitutional Conference," PREM 19/113, BNA, 233.

[37] The draft statement continues: "We should however, be ready to support the efforts of the Government of independent Zimbabwe to obtain international assistance for these purposes." "Statement on Land (For Use if Necessary in Reply to the PF)," October 11, 1979, PREM 19/113, BNA, 341.

The letter described the problems in the negotiations, particularly the PF's opposition to compensating white farmers for land. Nyerere was informed that the Lancaster constitution "does make fully adequate provision for the government to acquire land for settlement. What it also does is to provide for adequate compensation, and that is what the PF are at present unable to accept."[38]

President Nyerere replied that he did not believe the land issue would remain a stumbling block in the negotiations:

Nyerere was grateful for the message, he really did not believe that there was now any major issue between us [Britain] and the PF, and he was seeking to persuade the PF of this. He welcomes the fact that it had come down to the land question and compensation, because he thought this was solvable. "It was not a constitutional issue at all."[39]

Nyerere mentioned that Nkomo had told the BBC that £55 million would be sufficient for land reform. Nyerere told the British high commissioner that he "considered this was very reasonable: in fact rather small. He did not know but he thought that Nkomo, who was very shrewd, might deliberately have named a figure at this juncture with the negotiation in mind." Nyerere expressed his wish that the British should take Nkomo up on this figure. As the high commissioner related, "He was going to say to the PF that they 'should be able to get the kind of money Nkomo was speaking of', and should settle with us [the British] on that basis."[40] This amount was a low amount, as Mugabe would tell a Dutch diplomat a week later that the amount needed for land compensation would be ten times as much. "On the question of land, Mugabe's reluctance to see Zimbabwe begin its independence with 'a debt of £500 million.'"[41] The land compensation impasse at Lancaster would

---

[38] The letter to Nyerere continues: "Peter Carrington made a statement in the Conference on 11 October which was designed to help them even over this hurdle. He promised that we would help, with the limits of our financial resources, with technical assistance for land settlement schemes and capital aid for agricultural development projects and infrastructure. We shall also be ready to help the new government obtain international assistance for these and other purposes." "Draft Letter to Nyerere," October 11, 1979, PREM 19/113, BNA.

[39] "FM FCO to Washington telno 1406 of 14 October 1979," PREM 19/113, BNA, 241.

[40] Ibid.

[41] From Hague to FCO, Telno 323, October 22, 1979, "Reports of Mugabe's meeting on Oct 22 with Van Gorkum, Director General of International Cooperation at the [Dutch] MFA," item 85, FCO 36/2408, BNA.

eventually be resolved, mostly through Commonwealth, American, and British diplomatic interventions with the PF leaders.

The lack of financial commitment from the US government was demonstrated in a comment made by Anthony Lake, Vance's director of policy and planning in the State Department at the time. At a meeting in Washington on October 17, Lake told Robinson from the FCO that the US administration was "very conscious of the need to avoid giving the impression that its purpose was to buy out whites, or that it would compare in size to the old 1977 Zimbabwe development fund." Lake continued to define the American financial role: "The sort of thing that they [Carter Administration] had in mind would be for the whole region, perhaps with a figure nearer to the bottom end of the Zimbabwe Development Fund than to the 55 million pounds attributed to Nkomo in a Speech in Oxford for development purposes generally." Lake concluded, "It would be easier to get money from Congress for a regional fund, and it would certainly be difficult to get money to buy out whites."[42]

But this careful plan to avoid committing funds did not stop the US ambassador to Britain, Kingman Brewster, from helping the PF come to their decision to accept this clause in the new constitution. According to US State Department documents, General Ramphal was the point person in terms of the intervention to assist the PF "out of a corner" and to come up with a "face-saving" response to Carrington's ultimatum over the land compensation language in the constitution. Ambassador Brewster was also instrumental as he and General Ramphal met with Nkomo and Mugabe on October 16 to help the PF with a "face-saving" response. In the afternoon meeting at Ramphal's London home, Brewster told Nkomo and Mugabe that the United States was not in a position to make "a commitment to support a 'land fund' or anything that could be interpreted as a white buy-out." According to Brewster, "both Mugabe and Nkomo indicated that they fully understood the point."[43] Brewster's

---

[42] Washington to FCO, Telno 3234, October 17, 1979, PREM 19/112, BNA, 205.

[43] American Embassy London to Secretary of State, "Lancaster House Conference: Emboff meeting with PF," October 16, 1979, London, 20350, Central Foreign Policy Files, 1973–1976, RG 59, General Records of the Department of State, USNA. The multilateral effort to break the land compensation impasse has been covered in more detail elsewhere, but it is important to understand that the Americans and also the Commonwealth's General Secretary Ramphal intervened to make sure that the land issue would not be the deal breaker at Lancaster. The British may have hoped that Mugabe would have left the talks over this issue. See Timothy Scarnecchia, "Proposed Large-Scale Compensation for White Farmers

account of the meeting is very positive, stating that Nkomo had asked for his help coming up with a response to Carrington, but Brewster apparently indicated that he could not help in this regard. General Ramphal then suggested he would work with the PF on an appropriate response.[44] On the following day, October 17, Brewster explained the hostility he received from Renwick and Spencer over the idea of compensation. "Both Renwick and Spencer reacted very negatively saying HMG was not having any linkage of a 'fund' to [the] Lancaster House package, nor did they envisage any development/land reform 'edifice' arising from Carrington's October 11 statement of British intent."[45]

What comes out of these telegrams is that Carrington had given the PF an ultimatum; either sign onto the British constitution that included compensation for white farmers, or he would proceed to work only with Bishop Muzorewa. Carrington held meetings with Muzorewa without inviting the PF. The Americans believed that the PF wanted some promise of funds to pay for land reform and compensation not only to "save face" but also to help them in the elections, particularly in order to give them the upper hand against Muzorewa. Mugabe had told Brewster that Carrington's decision to meet with the Muzorewa "has wrecked our confidence in Carrington."[46]

George Houser Visits His Patriotic Front Contacts during the Lancaster House Negotiations

American activist George Houser arrived in London at the end of October for a brief visit to check in with the PF leaders. Houser met with Nkomo and Daniel Madzimbamuto on October 29, 1979, in London. Houser recorded that Nkomo was upset with Carrington at

---

as an Anglo-American Negotiating Strategy for Zimbabwe, 1976–1979," in A. Pallotti and C. Tornimbeni, eds., *State, Land and Democracy in Southern Africa* (Burlington, VT: Ashgate 2015), 105–26; Sue Onslow, "Race and Policy: Britain, Zimbabwe and the Lancaster House Land Deal," *The Journal of Imperial and Commonwealth History* 45, no. 5 (2017), 844–67.

[44] Ibid.

[45] From Secretary of State to US Mission to the UN, "Lancaster House Conference," October 17, 1979, State271343, Central Foreign Policy Files, 1973–1976, RG 59, General Records of the Department of State, USNA. See Robin Renwick, *Unconventional Diplomacy in Southern Africa* (New York: St. Martin's Press, 1997), 57–62.

[46] Ibid.

this point in the Lancaster talks as he felt Carrington was pressing "the PF to honor a cease fire and even let Muzorewa remain in his position in the government during the interim period." Houser noted that he later found out that the second point was untrue, that Muzorewa would have to step down. Nkomo then told Houser how he felt that the "PF is in a weakened position because of the Commonwealth conference paving the way for these constitutional talks and making it necessary for the PF to attend." Nkomo confessed that he "didn't know how they are going to resist Carrington in what he refers to as a weakened position at this point." Nkomo said he hadn't given up hope, and that the PF would do its best to seek help from Commonwealth countries to "use their pressure on Carrington to back up the position of the PF."[47] After meeting with Nkomo and Madzimbamuto, Houser met "in quick succession" with Edward Ndlovu, George Silundika, Jane Ngwenya, and Joe Msika, who all agreed that the PF had "held together beautifully," according to Houser. "Apparently, there have been no real differences and there has been a harmonious approach in the discussions."[48]

Having witnessed the acrimonious relations between ZANU and ZAPU in the past, and knowing the details of much of this conflict, Houser wrote how he was impressed by the approach of both ZANU and ZAPU. "For one thing they have a united front which is really working. I have gotten this from all sides. They meet regularly and have frank discussions. There has been no disagreement." Houser's interpretation of the situation also expressed the confidence of the PF that they would be able to get what they wanted. "In addition the PF are really here to seriously negotiate. I think they would like to see an agreement come out of this. But they are not willing to take one which will seriously compromise them."[49] What the PF felt were essentially "deal breakers" at the end of October, according to Houser's notes, included the following: "They are not willing to have their forces disbanded or completely neutralized. They must have a role in both the administration and the defense and the police system during the interim period. If they don't get it, there will just not be any agreement, and the war will go on."[50] As would be decided later in

---

[47] "Houser Trip to London (Lancaster House) and Algeria – notes 1979," MSS 294, Houser Papers, Special Collections, MSU Library.
[48] Ibid.   [49] Ibid.   [50] Ibid.

the ceasefire talks, the PF would not be integrated into the civil, military, or police forces during the transition.

Intelligence gathered by the United States from Lancaster House suggested that while the PF were working together at Lancaster, Mugabe was actually in stronger position in relation to Nkomo than in the past, a reversal in the balance of power that would help to facilitate the PF's ability to stay the course and reach an agreement. On November 15, President Carter's national security advisor, Zbigniew Brzezinski, wrote to Carter to say that although the PF leaders were "not likely to dissolve their PF 'partnership' any time soon," there was evidence that "the balance of power between them is shifting closer toward parity. Mugabe has begun to emerge from under Nkomo's shadow and has become less belligerent publicly." Brzezinski believed that this new strength of Mugabe vis-à-vis Nkomo would help to push both leaders to a settlement.[51] This was a perceptive observation, as much of Mugabe's prior intransigence had been caused, in part, by his lack of firm control over the party and ZANLA due to internal challenges to his leadership of ZANU.

The Americans were also hearing from the South Africans that they were losing confidence in Bishop Muzorewa's chances to win a post-Lancaster House agreement election. Writing from South Africa at a time that would turn out to be only a few weeks from end of the talks, the US ambassador to South Africa, William Edmonson, suggested that the American diplomats at Lancaster House inform the PF and Frontline State representatives that "nothing would please South Africans more than to have [the] PF not participate in [the] Rhodesia elections." He added that American diplomats might "indirectly refer" their Frontline State counterparts "to recent Embassy Pretoria reports that the SAG [South African Government] has doubts about Muzorewa's electoral chances against [the] PF and their statements that the PF is on the verge of winning by the ballot what they could not win by the bullet."[52] Ambassador Stephen Low, who had served as US ambassador to Zambia since 1976 but was now the US ambassador

---

[51] Brzezinski to President Carter, "Information Items: Another Look at the PF," November 15, 1979, NLC-1-8-6-11-4, Carter Presidential Library.

[52] American Embassy Pretoria to Secretary of State, "Rhodesia: Suggested approach to the Front Line," November 23, 1979, Pretoria, 10568, Central Foreign Policy Files, 1973–1976, RG 59, General Records of the Department of State, USNA.

to Nigeria, also commented on the South African view of Lancaster at the end of November, "that a collapse of the negotiations would delight the SAG, which is pessimistic regarding Muzorewa's chances against the PF in an election."[53]

This intel came as the Frontline State presidents were meeting directly with Nkomo and Mugabe to advise them on what direction they should take at the Lancaster House talks. The United States had a new Ambassador in Tanzania, Richard Noyes Viets, who provided an account of his meeting with President Nyerere a few days following the Frontline State presidents meeting with Nkomo and Mugabe. Nyerere had apparently expressed his anger at Lord Carrington for how he was conducting the negotiations with the PF. Ambassador Viets described Nyerere's "emotional and personalized attack" on Carrington. Nyerere reportedly found Mugabe and Nkomo to be "thoroughly irritated 'and damned fed up by his ultimatums.'" Nyerere stressed to Viets that "Carrington must be told that his arrogant and insensitive handling of the PF is resulting not only in an unfortunate personalization of the negotiating process but more dangerously the PF leadership is now openly expressing a loss of trust in him." Notwithstanding Nyerere's complaints, Viets claimed that Nyerere "kept reiterating the need to conclude the negotiation and move on to the election." Nyerere emphasized how he had "warned Nkomo and Mugabe over the weekend not to leave him dangling in the breeze again." Viets' own comment to the State Department indicated that he thought the British were keeping Nyerere out of the loop on the progress made at the Lancaster House negotiations. Viets saw this as a mistake, adding sardonically, "Nyerere is going to be working [in] Southern Africa long after Peter Carrington has returned to till his Buckinghamshire spread. Somebody ought to remind the Brits of this obvious fact."[54]

At the end of November 1979, Pik Botha met in Germany with Vice Chancellor Hans-Dietrich Genscher. According to the South African

---

[53] American Embassy Lagos to Secretary of State, "Lancaster House: Cease Fire Arrangements," November 27, 1979, LAGOS15167, Central Foreign Policy Files, 1973–1976, RG 59, General Records of the Department of State, USNA.

[54] American Embassy Dar Es Salaam to Secretary of State, "Front Line Summit meeting: Conversation with Nyerere," November 27, 1979, Dar Es Salaam, 5712, Central Foreign Policy Files, 1973–1976, RG 59, General Records of the Department of State, USNA.

account of their meeting, Botha was eager to explain South Africa's lack of interest in a continued war in Rhodesia. Botha told Genscher that the German media was incorrect in claiming that South Africa wanted to become even more involved in Rhodesia. Botha explained that South Africa's position was that "only in the event that chaos developed on a large scale" on South Africa's borders would parliament be called together to decide on a course of action. "However, it was a very difficult situation when innocent people were being raped and killed. There was increasing tension and one had the impression that the wood was very dry and merely waiting for a spark."[55] Here Botha references the threat of a "race war," where whites would be victims and therefore requiring South African military intervention. Botha also referenced the shifting futures of "black" and "white" Africa: "Black Africa was sinking and the White man was the stabilising force." Botha's argument was that if the Soviets could be kept out of South West Africa and Rhodesia, then "it would not be long before the African states would see South Africa, with its advanced technological development, in a different light."[56] Most important to Botha was the extreme financial costs the war in Rhodesia had for South Africa. Botha told Genscher that "[a]part from anything else, South Africa was having to supply Rhodesia with credits worth thirty to forty million rand per month."[57]

A telephone conversation between Carrington and Thatcher on November 25, 1979 showed the extent to which the British were still looking for ways to have the PF break the Lancaster House talks. Thatcher told Carrington that she had received news that "the Dar es Salaam people [ZANU] absolutely refuse to congregate in groups inside Rhodesia, because that would be unfair." Carrington replied, "Well in which case there can be no ceasefire." Thatcher ruminated, "In a way I was not displeased because it puts them back into the wrong. So it pleased me quite a lot from the viewpoint of public opinion it looks to me as if they have gone absolutely into the wrong."

---

[55] South African Minister of Foreign Affairs, R. F. "Pik" Botha Meeting Vice Chancellor Hans-Dietrich Genscher Botha Meeting with German Vice Chancellor Hans-Dietrich Genscher, November 29, 1979, 1/156/7, vol. 2, Rhodesia Foreign Policy and Relations, vol. 2, 3 050, DFA Archive, Pretoria.
[56] Ibid.
[57] Ibid. These amounts are equivalent to approximately $24–33.6 million or £16.6–22.2 million in 1979.

Carrington then told Thatcher that he had heard news of another Zimbabwe-Rhodesian bombing raid. Thatcher replied, "Oh no. On Zipra?" Carrington replied, "On Zipra, yes. And it is said to be a camp about 25 miles from Lusaka." Thatcher responded, "Oh Lord it is right inside." To which Carrington offered, "Well you know one despairs of them doesn't one." Thatcher replied, "Yes."[58] As Dumiso Dabengwa and Jeremy Brickhill have described, these air raids were part of the Zimbabwe-Rhodesian effort to destroy roads and bridges that ZIPRA was using to move their forces forward to take more positions inside Rhodesia before the ceasefire was complete. According to Dumisa and Brickhill, these bombing raids meant that much of the "turning point" plans of ZIPRA were unable to be carried out.[59]

---

[58] "Telephone Conversation between the Prime Minister and the Foreign and Commonwealth Secretary in the early evening on Sunday 25 November 1979," PREM 19/115, BNA, f. 87.

[59] See Dumiso Dabengwa, "Relations between ZAPU and the USSR, 1960s–1970s: A Personal View," *Journal of Southern African Studies* 43, no. 1 (2017), 215–24; Jeremy Brickhill, "ZIPRA the People's Army," Center for Innovation and Technology (October 27, 2020), https://cite.org.zw/op-ed-zipra -the-peoples-army. See also Jakkie Cilliers, *Counter-Insurgency in Rhodesia* (London: Croom Helm, 1985), 192–93. See also Pathisa Nyathi, "Lancaster House Talks: Timing, Cold War and Joshua Nkomo," in Sabelo Ndlovu-Gatsheni, ed., *Joshua Mqabuko Nkomo of Zimbabwe: Politics, Power, and Memory* (New York: Palgrave Macmillan, 2017), 149–72.

8 | The 1980 Elections and the First Years of Independence

As news of the Lancaster House constitutional and ceasefire agreements began to spread, the celebratory tone of British correspondences often overlooked the difficulties ahead. The details of the ceasefire and transition period left potential pitfalls for a successful transition. For example, the Tanzanian president, Julius Nyerere, had pointed out to US ambassador Richard Viets that the failure of the British to accept the PF's demands to incorporate their troops into the policing and ceasefire monitoring personnel opened the door for the PF, especially Mugabe's ZANU, to exploit the distribution of forces to their own benefit. Nyerere had told Viets at the end of November that Carrington's unwillingness to negotiate on the sharing of forces during the transition would lead to problems.[1]

The British appointed Lord Soames, then leader of the House of Lords and Winston Churchill's son-in-law, to be the governor of Rhodesia in order to oversee the transitional period, and to organize and monitor the majority rule elections that would determine the first leader of an independent Zimbabwe. A main emphasis in this chapter will be placed on Governor Soames' attempt to balance two main concerns: first, avoiding any major problems with the demobilization of the liberation war armies, and second, the successful staging of an internationally recognized "free and fair" election. The British documents covering this period demonstrate Britain's eagerness to get out of Zimbabwe as soon as possible, while avoiding any conflicts between the South Africans and the Zimbabwean nationalists, as well as between the Rhodesian military and the liberation forces.

Mugabe and ZANU, having felt cornered into accepting the Lancaster House agreement, lashed out almost immediately at the British over the

---

[1] American Embassy Dar es Salaam to Secretary of State, "Front Line Summit meeting: Conversation with Nyerere," November 27, 1979, Dar es Salaam, 5712, Central Foreign Policy Files, 1973–76, RG 59, General Records of the Department of State, USNA.

Figure 7 Signing of the Lancaster House Agreement. London, December 21, 1979. Getty Images.

ceasefire agreements, focusing in particular on the presence of South African troops in Rhodesia in the months leading up to the election. Mugabe sent a letter to Thatcher on January 8, 1980, where he threatened to break the Lancaster House arrangements if the South African military presence was not addressed by the British.[2] From the perspective of the FCO, the presence of the South African troops threatened the transition, mostly because of protests from the OAU and, most importantly, the Nigerians that the South African troops in Zimbabwe-Rhodesia were a violation of the Lancaster House agreement. Discussing how to respond to Mugabe's claims, Charles Powell of the FCO's Rhodesia Department admitted that "there is no alternative to accepting, for the time being, the continued presence of the five South African companies, though wearing Rhodesian uniforms and under Rhodesian command." Powell suggested that the British could split hairs in terms of the language used to describe the situation. "In the meantime we need a new press line – to be agreed with the South Africans – which admits and justifies the existence of the South African unit guarding Beitbridge, but says that the Governor has been assured that there are no other South African forces (as opposed to

[2] Robert Mugabe to Margaret Thatcher, January 8, 1980, FCO 36/2679, BNA.

South African personnel in the Rhodesian force) in Rhodesia."[3] British estimates of South African forces in Rhodesia were quantified in late January as "5 infantry battalions, 3,500 men; 1 parachute battalion, 600 men; 2 artillery regiments, 1,000 men; 6 armored squadrons, 750 men; total 5,850 men."[4]

Powell, who was with Governor Soames in Salisbury to help with the transition, was worried that the much larger South African troop presence in the country would become known to the press and create an international outcry. Powell wrote to the FCO to say that the American representative in Salisbury, Edward Lanpher, had mentioned a larger number of South African troops in Zimbabwe-Rhodesia. Lanpher had told him that Paul Tsongas, a US senator, who had just visited Salisbury, had heard there were some 2,000 South African troops deployed in Rhodesia and "dressed in Rhodesian uniforms." Lanpher had asked Soames about this, but he "had been given a rather ambiguous reply." Lanpher told Powell that the "African lobby" in the United States would put the US administration "under pressure ... to obtain firm assurances" from Britain that "there were no South African forces in Rhodesia."[5]

Later in this same week, the first week of 1980, British diplomats in Maputo requested suggested language from Soames to use in response to Mugabe's letter, which ZANU had turned over to the local Mozambican press. Rather than dwelling on the issue of South African troops in Zimbabwe-Rhodesia, Soames replied that they should reward Machel's help in convincing Mugabe and ZANLA leaders to cooperate with the ceasefire regulations. However, Soames reported of "serious problems" occurring with "ZANLA groups terrorizing the Inyanga/Penhalonga area north of Umtali." Soames recommended that the British diplomats in Mozambique compare ZANLA and ZIPRA: "The point to emphasise is that ZANLA behavior during the ceasefire is in sharp contrast to that of ZIPRA. The latter have been doing their utmost to comply. Of the incidents of violence and lawlessness across the country during this period and confrontations with the

---

[3] C. D. Powell, "Rhodesia: South African Forces," January 2, 1980, item 1F, FCO 36/2790, BNA.

[4] From UK Mission UN New York to FCO, "The Deployment of South African Forces in Zimbabwe," January 30, 1980, item 136, FCO 36/2791, BNA.

[5] C. D. Powell to Mr. Day, "Rhodesia: South African Forces," January 3, 1980 FCO 36/2790, BNA. In 1984, Lanpher would be the US deputy chief of mission at the US Embassy in Zimbabwe, and later the US ambassador to Zimbabwe in the early 1990s.

police the great majority have been attributable to ZANLA." Soames then mentioned important charges against ZANLA: "There is evidence that ZANLA have been given instructions to exploit the assembly process and its aftermath to exert maximum pressure on the population to support ZANU and evidence also of some ZANLA sections being instructed to remain in the field."[6] ZANLA's lack of cooperation created a problem for Soames, but he would eventually gloss over these difficulties in public given the more pressing British concern of making the transitional period as short as possible. The overriding constraint on Soames' powers was to avoid antagonizing ZANU and ZANLA to the point of them rejecting the ceasefire arrangements and breaking from the Lancaster House agreement.

The abuses committed by ZANLA of the agreed upon demobilization and campaign rules were so extensive, however, that Soames at first refused to allow Mugabe, along with hundreds of ZANU political delegates, permission to return to Salisbury to campaign before the election. As leverage to get the ZANLA forces to conform to the rules, Soames used his power to authorize whether or not planes designated to transport ZANU leaders could take off from Maputo. On January 8, Soames informed the British in Maputo that he had approved the arrival of a 20 member ZANU advance party to arrive in Salisbury by the end of the week. Soames did, however, say that he was still not changing his position on "the arrival of large contingents of ZANU members before there has been full compliance by ZANLA with the requirements of the ceasefire. There are still very difficult problems with ZANLA in the Eastern districts."[7]

While the election campaigning got underway, Lord Carrington met in London with US ambassador to Britain, Kingman Brewster, to discuss the situation in Rhodesia. Carrington sent an account of his meeting with Ambassador Brewster to Nicholas Henderson, the British ambassador in Washington. Carrington expressed his concern that Brewster was only preoccupied with actions taken by Lord Soames and the British that would hurt Mugabe's chances of winning the elections. "I observed that all the items in Brewster's catalogue pointed in the same direction. He had not referred to a single matter in which the PF [ZAPU] were to blame."

[6] Soames [Salisbury] to Maputo, "Your Telegram Number 37: Rhodesia ZANU," January 8, 1980, item 27A, FCO 36/2679, BNA.
[7] Ibid.

Carrington elaborated how Brewster "had not taken account of the fact that, for example, there were perhaps up to 6,000 ZANLA guerillas still outside the assembly areas: that Mugabe had failed so far to release 71 political detainees; that daily breaches of the ceasefire by the PF were still occurring."[8] Carrington responded to Brewster with the same "walking a tightrope" idiom he had previously used at the Commonwealth Heads of Government Meeting in Lusaka with President Khama. "I said that the truth was that the Governor was walking a tightrope. He was in the middle of a very difficult situation and being blamed from all sides. This constant sniping was causing us some irritation." Carrington stressed with Brewster that Nkomo in particular had "come good." "We had serious problems with Mugabe .... If Mugabe continued to break the agreement and if he incited his followers to violence, we would face very strong pressure to ban him from the election." All the same, Carrington let Brewster know that Soames would have a "graduated response" to Mugabe's infractions.[9]

By the end of January, the South Africans were, along with others, increasingly willing to accept the reality that Muzorewa would not win the election on his own, and that the best possibility, in their opinion, remained hope of a Nkomo–Muzorewa coalition if none of the parties could win an outright majority. Speaking with German diplomat Wilhelm Haas on January 25, 1980, the South Africans learned that the Germans "shared the British Government's view that no one party could win the election and that the likelihood was that there would be a post-election alliance between Nkomo and Muzorewa." The South Africans were also told that the "German Embassy in South Africa had reported that our government held a similar view and was 'no longer' of the opinion that Bishop Muzorewa would receive an over-all majority."[10] It is important to note that the Germans were not predicting a Mugabe landslide, showing the extent to which Mugabe and ZANU's victory by such large margins was not predicted by the Europeans, nor the Anglo-Americans, nor the South Africans.[11]

[8] Carrington to Ambassador Washington, DC, "Call by U.S. Ambassador: Rhodesia," January 23, 1980, item 1, FCO 36/2874, BNA.
[9] Ibid.
[10] No. K5 Sevret 19h Labushagne, 15.1.1980, 1/156/7, vol. 2, Rhodesia, Foreign Policy and relations with, vol. 3, DFA Archives.
[11] For the discussions between the British and South Africans after Mugabe's victory, see David Moore and Timothy Scarnecchia, "South African Influences in Zimbabwe: From Destablization in the 1980s to Liberation War Solidarity in

South African Strategies before the Zimbabwe Election

A diplomatic problem that resurfaced in January 1980 was the continued presence of South African troops in Rhodesia. The most visible concern was the continued presence of a company of these troops at the Beitbridge crossing, but, as noted above, there were many more South African troops still embedded into Rhodesian Army companies elsewhere in the country. The British mentioned on January 11, for example, that "apart from the company at Beitbridge, the three companies near the south-eastern border are 85 per cent South African."[12] Governor Soames indicated that he and his advisors were working to convince General Walls of "the need to do something about the South Africans," but he also indicated that a higher priority was "our continuing attempt to educate them [Walls and the NJOC] out of their desire to see early action against ZANU(PF)."[13]

Viewed from a South African perspective, South African troop presence can be seen as part of a larger strategy attempting to force the PF to break the ceasefire and pull out of the elections scheduled for February. In January 1980, a detailed discussion was presented on the "total war" strategy in southern Africa.[14] The total war strategy in Rhodesia involved, at this stage in January 1980, working with "the UANC, the Rhodesian Front party, and moderate political parties in Rhodesia and the Rhodesian security forces" to wage "a coordinated total war against the PF, Botswana and Zambia." The document recommended that the South African military needed to remain prepared to intervene should this strategy lead to an escalated conflict.[15]

Their specific plan for Rhodesia also included influencing the British government "to do everything in their power to thwart the PF's efforts to win the election." They also wanted to "encourage and fully exploit" the use of "Bishop Muzorewa's auxiliary forces to politicize the

the 2000s," in Arrigo Pallotti and Ulf Engel, eds., *South Africa after Apartheid: Policies and Challenges of the Democratic Transition* (Leiden: Brill, 2016), 179.
[12]   Soames [Salisbury] to FCO, "Rhodesia: South African Forces," January 11, 1980 FCO 36/2790, BNA.
[13]   Ibid.
[14]   "Die Strategiese implikasies tov Rhodesie in die konteks van Suider-Afrika asook die huidige en verwagte korttetrmyn verwikkelinge" [The Strategic Implications of Rhodesia in the Context of Southern Africa as well as the Current and Expected Short-Term Developments], January 28, 1980, H SAW 168, Group 3, Rhodesia III, SADF Archives, Pretoria.
[15]   Ibid.

population," which could lead to "the boycott of the election by PF parties."[16] In addition, their goal was to do "everything possible . . . to deprive the PF of its political power base by pushing a wedge between the ZAPU and ZANU elements." One other issue familiar to apartheid South African military "special ops" in Southern Africa noted that "criminal military action that cannot be relegated to the RSA must be carried out within Rhodesia at [against] the PF." For the South African soldiers stationed at Beitbridge, the strategy dictated that these troops "must under no circumstances be withdrawn as their presence in Rhodesia may lead to the boycott of the election by the PF. The political implications of an RSA military presence in Rhodesia must be known." This sort of strategy discussion demonstrates the South African hope that they could still derail the Lancaster House agreement by forcing the PF to pull out of the agreement over the issue of South African troops at Beitbridge and elsewhere in Rhodesia leading up to the elections. When the British became aware of just how many South African soldiers were in Rhodesia, Carrington advised that the British "recommend that [General Peter] Walls 'Rhodesianizes' the 3 companies of South African troops present in the country."[17]

In a message to the South African ambassador at the end of January, Soames recounts how, when he met with Walls, he was informed that the South Africans were not willing to cooperate over the issue of South African troops in Rhodesia. However, Soames did note that Walls now understood the importance of working out a compromise with Nkomo. Soames explained that "[t]he difficulties we have had over this issue, reflect, however, the much deeper anxieties of the South Africans and of the Rhodesian establishment about the possibility of a PF victory in the elections." Soames suggested that a solution was still available for the British to influence the South Africans: "We must *inter alia* try to educate the South Africans away from regarding the PF still as a united party and towards the idea – which is now accepted by Walls – that in many ways the best solution would be a coalition involving Muzorewa, Nkomo and the whites."[18]

---

[16] Ibid.
[17] FCO to Cape Town, "MPIT: South African Forces," January 15, 1980, item 98, FCO 36/2791, BNA.
[18] Soames Salisbury to FCO, "Rhodesia: South African forces," January 25, FCO 36/2791, BNA.

The South African Defence Forces Archives contain handwritten notes from a meeting with Britain's Sir Anthony Duff on January 16. Pik Botha is identified as the South African representative at the meeting. The notes reveal interesting perspectives from both sides. Botha seemed to imply that the South African troop presence issue was nonnegotiable, and that it would have in any case have to be decided by Carrington and South African defence minister, Magnus Malan. Botha did, however, ask Duff, "Will we get a SWA advantage out of this?"[19] This implied that perhaps there was room to negotiate troop withdrawals for greater British cooperation over the South West Africa/Namibia negotiations. The problem of the three South African companies in Rhodesia was delicate. As more and more people became aware of their presence, it was only a matter of time before those at the United Nations who were upset about the South African forces at Beitbridge discovered that there were thousands of additional South African soldiers wearing Rhodesian uniforms on the Mozambican border. The notes indicate that Duff suggested "a fuller Rhodesianation [sic] of those forces." But the South Africans responded that this would create a problem among the South African military with "morale" if they had to be led by Rhodesian officers, and also, from the British perspective, if parliament would become aware of this subterfuge, then Carrington and Soames would be called out on it.[20] Despite this South African troop dilemma, Duff also informed the South Africans the news that, although they planned to "take firm action against Mugabe," the British were "not likely to ban Mugabe" from the election: "We are trying to avoid a war before [the] election." The notes also indicate that Duff told the South Africans that whatever actions would be taken against Mugabe for electoral violations were going to be "defer[ed] until after election especially if we can get Nkomo included in ZR government."[21]

A few days later, Malan wrote an official response to Governor Soames detailing why South Africa could not remove their troops from Rhodesia prior to the election, including "the fact that the cease-fire has not been successfully implemented in Rhodesia" and "the continued presence of Mozambican troops in Rhodesia." He told the British that if they were to push the issue of troop withdrawals, South

---

[19] Handnotes Rhodesia meeting January 28, 1980, page 4, 4 H SAW 168, Group 3 Rhodesia III, SADF Archives, Pretoria.
[20] Ibid.   [21] Ibid.

Africa would not only remove their personnel, but also that "their equipment and all equipment on loan to assist with the elections, will be withdrawn." Malan also stated that the "British Government must accept responsibility for any refugees should a situation develop where Rhodesian citizens are forced to seek refuge within the RSA."[22] Malan then reassured the British that South Africa will "continue to provide assistance to the British Governor in Rhodesia in the interest of the safety of the peoples of that country, and in order to ensure that free elections take place." He also stressed that the "South African Government will, however, not tolerate any humiliation whatsoever, whether by means of a United Nations resolution during the following Security Council Debate on 30 January 1980, or otherwise." Malan said if such humiliation occurred, the South Africans "reserved the right to withdraw all troops and equipment forthwith and unconditionally, although their presence had previously been agreed to mutually." The letter ended by stating that the South African government "wishes to give the assurance that it in no way intends to embarrass the British Government."[23] This South African pressure most likely influenced the decision by the United Kingdom's United Nations mission to avoid being present during the United Nations Security Council's unanimous 14–0 vote condemning South Africa's continued military role in Zimbabwe during the election campaign.[24]

Malan had sent to Soames an extensive list of "weapons and accessories." The list corresponds to the one sent to Prime Minister P. W. Botha by Bishop Muzorewa in December 1979. That list, included personnel requests for "six infantry companies with support personnel and equipment; seven fixed wing transport aircraft and eleven helicopters and crew; and, various other personnel attached to

---

[22] Malan, Chief of South African Defense Forces to Governor Soames, January 30, 1980, 2 H SAW 168, Group 3, Rhodesia III, SADF Archives, Pretoria. Appendix listing weapons on loan to Rhodesia is attached to Chief of DA Defence Force to Governor of Rhodesia, "Acknowledgement in Respect of South African Troops and Equipment Present in Rhodesia," January 30, 1980, Rhodesia III, H SAW 3 158, SADF Archives, Pretoria.

[23] Ibid.

[24] UN Security Council, "Question Concerning the Situation in Southern Rhodesia," Resolution 463 (1980) of February 2, 1980. "One member (the United Kingdom of Great Britain and Northern Ireland) did not participate in the voting." Since the resolution was adopted 14–0, this meant that the United States supported the resolution.

ZR units."[25] The extensive amount of guns and ammunition included in the request indicate that Muzorewa and his government were ready to return to war if the transition period did not hold and the war started again.

The Patriotic Front before the Election

One year earlier, in January 1979 and well before the Lancaster House conference was even deemed possible, the US ambassador to Zambia, Stephen Low, had reported that there was a lot of talk amongst observers in Lusaka and Dar es Salaam of "the likelihood of a civil war between ZANU and ZAPU, in the event of a Smith collapse." According to Low's view of the matter, "there seems to be more of a refusal to admit the existence of something for which no answer has been worked out."[26] Almost a year later, at the end of 1979 and after the Lancaster House agreement had been signed, talk of the PF contesting the first election as a coalition of ZAPU and ZANU had quickly evaporated. Nkomo, in his autobiography, says that he was literally left in the cold by Mugabe, as the ZANU team, including Mugabe, had already left for Dar es Salaam when Nkomo turned up at Mugabe's flat for what was to be their first meeting after Lancaster to discuss joint PF election plans.[27]

Mugabe gave a public indication that ZANU would not work with ZAPU for the election during a press conference in Dar es Salaam on

[25] Muzorewa wrote to P. W. Botha: "I therefore on behalf of my government, request that you consider extending the period for both the equipment on loan and the attachment of SADF personnel, as reflected in the attached schedule, to other ZR Security Forces until the end of February 1980." Letter from "Prime Minister of Zimbabwe Rhodesia to Honorable Prime Minister P. W. Botha," dated December 1979 (no day provided), H SAW 168, Group 3, Rhodesia III, SADF Archives, Pretoria. The list of major equipment on loan included "32 Alouette helicopters, 2 Dakota aircraft, 5 Cessna aircraft, 28 Eland armoured cars, 15 Freeret reconnaissance cars, 149 mine protected vehicles, 31 troop carrying vehicles, 8 140 mm guns, 4 88 mm guns, 12 20 mm guns, 270 12.7mm machine guns; 2,261 sub machine guns, 100 .303 Browning machine guns, 766 light machine guns, 4 anti-aircraft guns; 21,200 automatic rifles, 12 air to air missiles." H SAW 168, Group 3, Rhodesia III, SADF Archives, Pretoria.
[26] Fm American Embassy Lusaka to Secretary of State, "Rhodesia: Some Current Zambian Views," January 13, 1979, 1979LUSAKA00129, Central Foreign Policy Files, 1973–76, RG 59, General Records of the Department of State, USNA.
[27] Joshua Nkomo, *Nkomo: The Story of My Life* (London: Methuen, 1984), 200.

December 24. Asked whether the PF would run a joint election campaign as a single ticket, Mugabe said, "The general view within the party was ... perhaps that we pool results rather than try to attempt a merger at this stage which will give rise to several contradictions ... if we feel we can win better by fighting as two separate parties with perhaps some understanding at the end of it we'll do precisely that."[28] The ellipses were in the original text, and the summary says that they had a copy of a tape of Mugabe's press conference. The direct quote above therefore appears to be a fairly accurate account of what Mugabe said, rather than a summary. Interestingly, there was still some hedging in Mugabe's account.

Mugabe's press conference occurred two days before the death of ZANLA's commander Josiah Tongogara. Two months earlier, while in London for the Lancaster House talks, Tongogara had done a long interview with Mozambican journalist Alves Gomes, on October 29, 1979. In that interview, Gomes mentioned that the PF leaders had been saying they would run in the election "as one party." Gomes asked Tongogara how this would look, given that there was still ZANU and ZAPU. Tongogara argued, "The Patriotic Front embraces the 2 companies, ZAPU and ZANU, and we have formed this not because we are going to go to Geneva, or Malta, Dar es Salaam, and London. We formed in order to achieve national unity." Tongogara's position was contrary to what was commonly known; that the PF was formed primarily for diplomacy. Alves asked again, "So you will run the election as only one party[?]" Tongogara said, "Sure, we are seeking an agreement under the Patriotic Front and we will go back as the Patriotic Front. That's all."[29]

Cephas Msipa, an important founding member of ZAPU, describes in his memoir the scene in Salisbury at the end of December when the first ZANLA and ZIPRA leaders returned to organize for the election. Msipa was in charge of escorting both the ZANLA and ZIPRA leaders from the airport to the university where they were to stay. He recalled

---

[28] From Dar es Salaam to FCO, "Press Conference by Mr Mugabe," December 24, 1979, item 108, FCO36/2409, BNA.

[29] "Interview with Comandante Tongogara Alves Gomes," October 29, 1979, item 96, FCO 36/2679, BNA. The accompanying account in the FCO files states that a different version of this interview was published in the *Guardian* on November 3, 1979. This was a translation of the Portuguese version published in *Tempo* magazine in Maputo on November 11, 1979. The description notes, "Surprisingly they are different."

that Enos Nkala failed to show up at the airport to escort the ZANLA leaders. Msipa remembered not seeing Tongogara among the ZANLA leaders who arrived from Mozambique and that was his first knowledge that Tongogara had died a few days before. Msipa told how shocked ZAPU leaders, including Nkomo, were to hear of Tongogara's death. "It was thought that Nkomo's chances as co-leader of the Patriotic Front in the coming election would have been better had Tongogara been alive." According to Msipa, it was soon after this that ZANU's Enos Nkala, Nkomo's arch-rival, announced publicly that ZANU would run in the election separately from ZAPU.[30]

In February 1980, British diplomats at the United Kingdom's United Nations mission in New York, described an interview with ZANU-PF's representative to the United Nations, Tirivafi John Kangai. Kangai was reportedly in good spirits and very optimistic about ZANU's chances in the first election. "He expected 55 seats at worst, 60 at best." This was not a bad prediction, as ZANU would gain fifty-seven seats in the election. A key point was made by Kangai to explain why ZANU decided to run without Nkomo and ZAPU in the Patriotic Front. Kangai emphasized that the decision had been made by Mugabe. "The reason why Mugabe had insisted on fighting the election separately from Nkomo was the need for the electorate to show unequivocally whom they wanted as the leader of an independent Zimbabwe." Kangai added, "But once he had won the election Mugabe would ask Nkomo to form a coalition 'in order to avoid a civil war.'" The FCO's assistant under-secretary for Africa, Philip Mansfield, who interviewed Kangai, asked him if "Mugabe would be prepared to offer Nkomo the job of Prime Minister for a limited period given his seniority." Kangai refused, adding, "It would be impossible to trust Nkomo sufficiently. But he would be offered the Presidency, a prestigious post."[31] Vesta Sithole, in her account of her life and that of her husband Ndabaningi Sithole, mentioned that everyone was surprised to hear Mugabe was going to run alone, especially Joshua Nkomo. She said Mugabe wanted to run with the ZANU party name, but Reverend Sithole went to court to claim ZANU as his party's name, so Mugabe had to accept using the

[30] Cephas Msipa, *In Pursuit of Freedom and Justice: A Memoir* (Harare: Weaver Press, 2015), 90–92.
[31] P. R. A. Mansfield to C. D. Powell, Rhodesia Dept, FCO. "Rhodesia: ZANU (PF)," item 115, FCO 36/2679, BNA.

ZANU-PF name, while ZAPU ran as PF-ZAPU.[32] Therefore, ZAPU was often referred to as the "PF" at this time, although they were, of course, no longer part of a united front with ZANU for the election.

The Elections Observed

On February 25, 1980, Governor Soames circulated a directive to all British ambassadors and high commissioners in the Frontline States to announce his decision not to ban ZANU for election abuses, even though there was clear evidence of ZANU intimidation of voters. A few days before the voting was to begin, Soames instructed British diplomats to share his decision with their counterparts in the Frontline State governments. His instructions stated that it was unlikely he would wish to "make use of the power to disqualify a party in any administrative district: or to decide that the elections cannot be held in any district." Soames added, "It should be made clear that I have taken this decision despite the extensive intimidation by ZANLA, which has rendered it impossible for Nkomo and Muzorewa to campaign in certain areas." Soames explained that his decision was "based on the consideration that any action of this kind is liable to be regarded as arbitrary." He did not wish to "give external critics, and particularly the Front Line Presidents, any excuse to argue that the elections are not free and fair."[33]

This decision infuriated Rhodesian general Peter Walls, who had been complaining to the British throughout the campaign period of ZANU-PF intimidation. General Walls would then try to directly reach out to Thatcher and Carrington in a rather famous letter he wrote on March 1, 1980. Walls claimed that he had been betrayed by Thatcher and Carrington, who had told him at the time of Lancaster House that he would have a final veto if he thought the elections and transition process were not going to plan. In the letter to Thatcher, Walls lambasted Governor Soames for being "incapable of implementing the solemn promise," given by Soames and Carrington, "that he would rely on us for advice on military and other situations, and act in accordance with the interests of survival of a moderate, freedom-loving and anti-marxist

---

[32] Vesta Sithole, *My Life with an Unsung Hero* (Bloomington: Author House, 2006), 119.

[33] Soames [Salisbury] to FCO, "My Telno 804: Rhodesian Elections," February 25, 1980, item 1, FCO 36/2696, BNA.

society." Walls went on to suggest that he would have to make contingency plans if it turned out that Mugabe and ZANU would win the election outright. He asked Thatcher to act in response to this scenario: "it is vital to our survival as a free nation that you declare the election null and void on the grounds of official reports of massive intimidation frustrating the free choice of the bulk of the people." Walls concluded his letter by noting that "it must be without precedent or at least abnormal, for a person like myself to address such a message as this to no less than the Prime Minister of Britain." Walls said, "I do so only in the extremity of our possible emergency, with goodwill, and in the sincere and honest belief that it is my duty in terms of the privileged conversations I had with you and Lord Carrington." Walls signed off his letter to Thatcher with "I don't know how to sign myself, but I hope to remain your obedient servant."[34]

Mugabe did overwhelmingly well in the election, winning fifty-seven seats in parliament. Nkomo received twenty seats in Parliament, but his votes came almost exclusively from populations in the Matabeleland and Midlands provinces. By the end of polling on February 27, Soames called for a meeting with Mugabe. Soames' record of that meeting reflected his impatience with ZANU, although it was clear by this point that the British were not going stand in the way of ZANU's victory no matter how many reports of intimidation and ceasefire violations they received. After Mugabe had complained to Soames "that literally thousands of his men had been picked up lately by the police," Soames disagreed and thought that the 5,000 arrests Mugabe had claimed in a letter to Carrington was a "gross exaggeration."

After "a short disagreement on the subject," Soames told Mugabe that he was "most displeased" with the intimidation by Mugabe's people in eastern and central Zimbabwe. "Though I agreed that things had been done by other people as well, the hard fact was that intimidation by ZANLA was of a totally different order." Soames then let Mugabe know that there would not be any serious efforts by the British to punish ZANU for the many violations recorded before and during the election period, telling Mugabe, "But nevertheless I thought it was in Rhodesia's interest to allow the elections to go on without any move to proscribe any areas, although I could not and would not lightly

---

[34] "General Peter Walls letter to Margaret Thatcher," March 1, 1980, item 216. PREM 19/346, www.margaretthatcher.org/document/120938.

forget what had happened in those areas." Soames summarized Mugabe's response, that "he was glad to hear that I was not going to take any action on proscription. He agreed that there had been intimidation by his people but he thought that the order of intimidation was Muzorewa first, himself second and Nkomo a close third."[35]

Mugabe then discussed some possible coalitions after the elections, stating that "he thought that the most natural coalition for him would be with Nkomo, but his present thinking was that he would be perfectly ready to invite Muzorewa also and some of his people to join the government with him." Mugabe related how it would take time to make a transition, and that he knew "that some people regarded him as an ogre but he wasn't. He did not want anyone to feel that they had to leave the country, but there would need to be, and be seen to be, a growing degree of Africanisation, particularly in the civil service."

Mugabe shared with Soames that he "had many anxieties about how he was going to govern in the immediate future for he realised that he did not have many people of experience or with administrative skills around him." The conversation turned to the timing of independence. Mugabe told Soames, "Independence should not be granted for many months and the British governor and his staff should stay, chiefly in order to give confidence to the people." Soames bluntly replied that this was not in their minds at all, and nor did he see "what role the governor could play once the government had been chosen and was in the saddle." Mugabe then asked Soames how long he thought there would be between the formation of the government and independence. Soames said that "it should be counted in days or perhaps a week, but not much longer. Mugabe said he "hoped it would be at least months."[36] Even though Soames clearly wanted to close up British operations in Zimbabwe, Soames and the British would agree with Mugabe's request for a British team to stay on through May.

Although Soames had told Mugabe earlier that he was aware of a great deal of violations by ZANU, he nevertheless downplayed such news in his public statements during the election. Soames would later report on the first day of polling: "A carnival atmosphere has been reported from many of the polling stations and long queues have

---

[35] Salisbury (Soames) to FCO, "Meeting with Mugabe," February 27, 1980, item 114, FCO36/2679, BNA.
[36] Ibid.

formed. (A queue two and a half kilometers long was reported from Chibi.) The security situation has been very peaceful."[37] Soames conveyed similarly upbeat reports for Mashonaland Central and West, with an emphasis on the "jovial" mood of queuing voters in both important provinces. For Mashonaland East, however, he stated that "[r]eports from Mtoko and Mrewa indicated that intimidation appeared to be building up in the area."[38]

In order to assure a positive stamp of approval from election observers, the FCO put a call out to British diplomats in Europe to help shepherd through the election observer mission's reports written by various European observers. For example, the British obtained a promise from Danish "Ambassador Jeorgensen ... without commitment, to discuss with the foreign minister the possibility that he or the Prime Minister might issue a statement on the lines we requested." The report went further to suggest that the British had requested that such statements would be positive about the electoral process: "Speaking in strict confidence Jeorgensen mentioned that the two Danish election observers were having difficulty in reading [reaching] a joint view. He hinted that the MFA will do its best to ensure that any unhelpful findings will be toned down before release."[39]

On the third and final day of voting, February 29, Soames described reports of intimidation, but framed the reports in terms of a bias inherent in the way Rhodesians complained of observed intimidation. He argued that the main observer groups' acceptance of the election and campaign process as having met the standards of a "free and fair" election was of greater importance: "Voting has ended. The British Parliamentary group have this evening issued a unanimous statement in which they conclude that 'the election results will fairly reflect the general wish of the Zimbabwean electorate.'" After listing a positive response from "an Irish observer ... the leader of the New Zealand team, ... Commonwealth observer group and the Catholic Justice and

[37] From Salisbury (Soames) to FCO, "Your Telno 605 (Not to all): Election Summary," February 27, 1980, item 3, FCO 36/2696, BNA.
[38] Ibid. For the many different perspectives on the elections, see David Caute, *Under the Skin: The Death of White Rhodesia* (Evanston: Northwestern University Press, 1983), 383–426.
[39] From Copenhagen to FCO, "Your Telno 394 to Washington: Rhodesia: Elections," February 27, 1980, item 2, FCO 36/2696, BNA.

Peace Commission," Soames concluded, "We have no reason to believe that any objective observers will report otherwise."[40]

Soames went on to downplay complaints from Zimbabwe-Rhodesia authorities, noting that British election observers stationed in the regions where the Rhodesians had complained the most of intimidation: "With only a few exceptions they have said that the Rhodesian reports are exaggerated."[41] Relieved that the voting had finished without major incident, Soames held a press conference following the closing of the polls and reiterated the need for the international community to remember how the election "has been fought in the aftermath of a cruel war with an imperfect ceasefire and with deep political difficulties and reports of intimidation and other malpractice." Soames admitted that some of the reports were serious but he then pointed out how, for the most part, the election went forward with "a surprising degree of tranquillity and good humour," and that "many countries could be proud to have had elections such as these."[42]

After the election, Soames reiterated British concerns regarding the need to keep whites from continuing to exit the country. Soames seemed satisfied that the British handling of the election had gone a long way to stop the exodus of whites, but more importantly, Mugabe's ability to show himself as a champion of reconciliation and cooperation had gone further in this regard. Soames remarked that he was pleased with Mugabe's decision to retain General Walls to oversee the creation of a new national army and include a few white ministers in his cabinet. "So far – by putting Walls in charge of the integration of the armies, and by appointing David Smith and [Denis] Norman to his cabinet – he [Mugabe] has done enough to encourage most of them to continue to give him the benefit of the doubt." Soames was pleased to

---

[40] From Salisbury (Soames) to FCO, "My Telno 575: Rhodesia: Election Round-up 29 February," February 29, 1980, item 10, FCO 36/2696, BNA.

[41] Soames provided the following information gathered from British observers: "Victoria Province: Not as bad as feared in Bikita but there is strong evidence of intimidation in Gutu. Mashonaland East: In Mtoko and Mrewa *mujibas* are active, the population are relaxed and there is evidence of herding by ZANLA of voters to polling stations further away than necessary. Manicaland: Security force reports are exaggerated in Marenke and Mutasa but voters have appeared sullen (which suggests intimidation) in Inyanga. Midlands: Heavy intimidation in Belingwe and Selukwe. Matabeleland South: Hardly any intimidation." Ibid.

[42] From Salisbury (Soames) to FCO, "Rhodesia: the Elections," February 29, 1980, item 9, FCO 36/2696, BNA.

report that Mugabe still considered him, and the British more generally, as an ally. "At the moment he seems to feel that we are at present the most effective friends he has. We must make the most of the opportunity this offers while the feeling lasts, and before the inevitable communist and third-world diplomatic presence has established itself here and gets to work with him."[43]

The official British statement on the elections was issued from the Paymaster General's office on March 7, 1980. The self-congratulatory statement showed how important the successful transition and election was to the British, and for the Conservative Party more specifically. "The Government has scored a major success in achieving a peaceful solution to the Rhodesia problem, which has defeated efforts of successive Governments over the last 15 years."[44] The statement then addressed Conservative Party members who were rather dismayed by Mugabe's victory. "The landslide victory for Mr Robert Mugabe was not perhaps what some sections of British opinion would have wanted, but we committed ourselves to holding free and fair elections, seeing whom the people of Rhodesia wished to lead them, and handing over power to those people." The statement reassures Conservative Party supporters that Mugabe is not the "afro-communist" he was previously portrayed as, and that the Lancaster House constitution would protect whites in the new Zimbabwe. The statement emphasized that "Mr. Mugabe has everything to gain from proceeding in a measured and careful way, including Nkomo's party and some whites in his Government, and doing everything he can to keep members of the white community in Rhodesia to contribute to the country's economic welfare." Finally, the announcement emphasized that Mugabe and ZANU were no friends of the Soviets. "Mugabe owes no political debts to the Soviet Union: his support during the guerilla war came from China and such countries as Yugoslavia and Romania." The statement added: "The achievement of peace in Rhodesia represents a major defeat for the Russians in that it reduces the opportunities for them to interfere."[45] The above statement reflects just how relieved the British were about the successful elections and Mugabe's victory. They

---

[43] From Salisbury (Soames) to FCO, "Rhodesia: Mugabe and the Whites,"
      March 12, 1980, item 55, FCO 36/2696, BNA.
[44] PMG Note 13/80 Paymaster General's Office Privy Council Office 68 Whitehall,
      "Rhodesia," March 7, 1980, item 43, FCO 36/2696, BNA.
[45] Ibid.

felt that the terms of the Lancaster House constitution would keep
Mugabe and his party committed to the reconciliation project, and,
most importantly, it appeared that in contrast to Nkomo, Mugabe's
victory greatly reduced the possibility of bringing the Soviets and
Cubans into Zimbabwe. The statement closed by expressing how
these election results and this British-led transition would promote
"efforts to achieve peaceful solution to other problems in Southern
Africa and the wider world. It will also greatly enhance Britain's
prestige with our friends among Western and non-aligned
countries."[46]

An example of how willing Mugabe was to demonstrate his anti-
Soviet mindset comes from an exchange with Soames in early April. As
the April 18 Independence Day approached in ten days, Lord Soames
and Prime Minister-elect Mugabe met to discuss the details of the
transition. Soames told Mugabe that the South African government
had agreed to offer two loans, "one of 80 million and one of 85 million
Rands" to his government. Soames described Mugabe as having
"appreciated the favourable terms" that were being offered. "He
gave me [Soames] the impression that he would write a letter confirming that his government will honour these and the other outstanding
loans to the South African Government."[47] Perhaps to show how
grateful he was to the South African government, Soames reported
how,

Mugabe added that he told Van Vuuren [the South African Representative in
Salisbury] in good faith that there were no armed SAANC [South African
ANC] in the country. He had therefore been disturbed to discover on the
following day from the Rhodesian Central Intelligence Organisation that
there were 87 SAANC with ZIPRA in Assembly camp Juliet. 79 were being
returned immediately to Zambia. The other eight are at present in hospital
here.

Mugabe then went further to blame Nkomo for their presence.
"Nkomo had claimed that he did not know about the SAANC in
Juliet, but Mugabe did not believe him. Mugabe made clear that his
own relations with the SAANC were distant and was concerned that

---

[46] Ibid.
[47] To FCO from Salisbury (Soames), "Telegram no. 1286," April 8, 1980, item
      124, FCO 36/2736, BNA. At the time, these amounts would have been worth
      approximately $65 million and $69 million.

Figure 8 Prime Minister Robert Mugabe with Prime Minister Margaret Thatcher and Lord Carrington. May 9, 1980. Getty Images.

the South Africans should not think that he had been misleading them. He genuinely did not know this."[48] Days before the Independence Day ceremonies, Mugabe was positioning himself as the trustful neighbor of South Africa, while castigating Nkomo as the potential problem given his past political and military alliances with the South African ANC.

The Early 1980s

Relations between the United States and Britain and Zimbabwe started out very positively in 1980, particularly given the post-April 1980 independence period and Prime Minister Mugabe's internationally celebrated image as the great reconciler: the African leader who was willing to forgive whites for the crimes committed against him, his liberation army soldiers, and the people of Zimbabwe. Mugabe travelled to Washington, DC, first to visit President Carter in 1980 and then President Reagan in 1983, and to London to meet with Prime Minster

[48] Soames concluded, "There is no harm in Para 2 above being drawn on, in strict confidence, with the South Africans." To FCO from Salisbury (Soames), "Telegram no. 1286," April 8, 1980, item 124, FCO 36/2736, BNA.

Thatcher in 1981 and 1984. Each time he was publicly praised for his politics of racial reconciliation, which was held up as a model for what a post-apartheid South Africa might look like. There was a great hope that with sufficient foreign aid, British military training, and international goodwill, Zimbabwe could rise up to meet all the high expectations held by the Western powers. Importantly, these expectations centered around a sort of hybrid race state, where white capital and expertise would attract new foreign direct investments, and this would insulate the country from the economic and political shocks experienced in many African states in the early 1980s. The ZIMCORD aid conference in 1981 generated large commitments from Western donors ($1.95 billion for 1981–1984),[49] and state-sponsored advances in universal education and medical care began to take off in 1981 and 1982. South African diplomats noted how this compared to earlier promises of aid to help keep white Rhodesians in the country. "At current exchange rates the total aid attracted by Zimbabwe now amounts to US$1.95 billion. This is more than the US$1.5 billion suggested – over 5 years – by Dr. Henry Kissinger as part of the 1976 settlement package. Furthermore, the Zimcord aid refers only to a three-year period."[50]

Early Signs of Tensions in the Zimbabwe National Army

In addition to development aid, the British and Americans were content in this early period to fund integration and training efforts for the Zimbabwean National Army (ZNA) under the guidance of the British Military Advisory and Training Team (BMATT). There were many positive indications of success with the integration process until violence broke out in the ZNA barracks near Bulawayo in November 1980 and February 1981. The violence in February was between ex-ZIPRA and ex-ZANLA in the 12 Battalion. The British high commissioner to Zimbabwe, Robin Byatt, described the situation as still unresolved on February 9, after two days of fighting at Ntabizinduna. According to Byatt, "the trouble began when disabled

---

[49] "The Zimcord Conference," April 6, 1981, SANA DFA 1/156/7, vol. 6 Zimbabwe: Foreign Policy, 10/2/81 to 24/6/81, DFA Archives, Pretoria, South Africa,

[50] "The Zimcord Conference," April 6, 1981, SANA DFA 1/156/7, vol. 6 Zimbabwe: Foreign Policy, DFA Archives.

ex-ZIPRA guerrillas from the nearby Kayisa training centre threw stones at ex ZANLA members of 12 Battalion." After this, the "ex ZIPRA members of the Battalion then joined in and the armouries were broken into." Noting the role of BMATT officers in training the 12 Battalion, Byatt said that they had been disciplined during the earlier Entumbane disturbances, but since the withdrawal of the BMATT co-ordinators six weeks earlier, standards had deteriorated. "The CO is a capable, but young (22) ex-ZIPRA officer."[51] Norma Kriger provides statistics on just how violent these two events were, with 55 people killed in the fighting on November 9–10, 1980 in Entumbane near Bulawayo and in Chitungwiza near Harare. According to Kriger, in the fighting at Entumbane in February 1981, "the understated death toll was 197 – one estimate was that over 300 ex-guerrillas had died – and 1,600 homes were damaged."[52] Many ex-ZIPRA members deserted from the ZNA at this point, as, from their perspective, it did not seem possible that ex-ZIPRA soldiers would be treated fairly and equally in the ZNA. Still, the integration efforts by BMATT were seen as a success, as the bulk of ex-ZIPRA remained in the ZNA and funding continued into the mid-1980s. The British believed it was better to fund and direct the formation of the new ZNA rather than allowing Mugabe to look for future support from the Cubans and Soviets.

Mugabe had, however, accepted a "gift" from North Korea in the form of military advisors and supplies for the training of one brigade of the ZNA, the 5 Brigade, consisting of between 2,500 and 3,500 soldiers. Mugabe told the British that he accepted the North Korean offer to form a sort of "presidential guard," but because the gift came with large amounts of traditional military aid, including tanks and armored vehicles, the decision was made to have the North Korean advisors train the new 5 Brigade for later integration with the four existing ZNA brigades trained by BMATT officers. The British rationalized that at least it was not the Soviets or Cubans who were involved, and therefore did not put up much resistance to the North Korean training. It also let them off the hook in terms of responding to Mugabe's request for training a "presidential guard." The gift had been announced by

---

[51] Salisbury to FCO, "My Telno 44: Internal Situation," February 9, 1981, PREM 19/606, BNA.
[52] Norma Kriger, *Guerrilla Veterans in Post-War Zimbabwe: Symbolic and Violent Politics, 1980–1987* (Cambridge University Press, 2006), 79.

minister of state for national security, Emmerson Mnangagwa, as a North Korean advanced party arrived in Harare on May 21, 1981.[53]

High Commissioner Byatt wrote positively about the political atmosphere in his May 1981 summary report of BMATT's role, noting that the "[t]ensions between Mugabe's and Nkomo's party, and fears that the latter might break the uneasy coalition, have receded." He did, however, question the ZNA's capabilities. He noted that half of ZIPRA and ZANLA had "gone through basic amalgamation training, but the army which is being produced remains insufficiently trained and poorly organised."[54] Commenting on the ex-ZIPRA and ex-ZANLA violence in the Entumbane suburb of Bulawayo in November 1980 and February 1981, Byatt said that "it was notable that the leadership of ZIPRA and ZANLA, who do not see eye to eye over integration policy, did their best to dampen the trouble down and that eleven of the fourteen battalions existing at the time were unaffected." Byatt was optimistic about the reintegration process, although he did hint that there could be difficulties as holdouts for both liberation war armies still had access to weapon caches, specifically "the last ZIPRA and ZANLA redoubts at Gwai Mine and Middle Sabi respectively." Significant to future accusations about arms cachés, Byatt added that "[n]o one believes that units hand over all their weapons when ordered to do so, and there are undoubtedly many secret arms cachés around the country."[55]

On February 27, 1981, BMATT reported on the potential flash point at Gwai Mine where there were still 5,000 to 6,000 demobilized ZIPRA soldiers, and noted that "ZIPRA are thought to be caching arms in this area."[56] A summary of events in 1980 and 1981 from a BMATT perspective mentions that both sides were likely storing weapons, including ex-ZANLA at Middle Sabi.[57] The reporting officer suggested

---

[53]   From Britdefad Salisbury to MoDUK, "FCO/Seoul Tel 41 of 27 Mar. North Korean Military Assistance," May 20, 1981, item 1, FCO106/464, BNA.

[54]   British High Commissioner at Salisbury to the Secretary of State for Foreign and Commonwealth Affairs, "Zimbabwe: The Military Scene and the Role of BMATT," May 14, 1981, DEFE 11/932, BNA.

[55]   Ibid.

[56]   BRITOEFAD Salisbury to MODUK, "Sitrep No 41 (17–26 February 1981)," DEFE 11/932, Zimbabwe, BNA.

[57]   British High Commissioner at Salisbury to the Secretary of State for Foreign and Commonwealth Affairs, "Zimbabwe: the Military Scene and the Role of BMATT," May 14, 1981, DEFE 11/932, BNA.

that the reintegration of Gwai Mine and Middle Sabi would be difficult: "The ZIPRA forces at Gwai now balances to ZANLA forces at mid Sabi. Both are heavily armed."[58] There was, then, sufficient evidence of possible further showdowns between ex-ZIPRA and ex-ZANLA soldiers, which could have been much more significant than the earlier conflicts in 1980 and 1981, given Byatt's suggestion that a standoff among the two former fighters could involve between 5,000 to 6,000 soldiers on both sides. This is important, as the accusations discussed below that would surface in February 1983 to discredit Nkomo and ZAPU would suggest that they were caching arms for about 5,000 soldiers. What is often forgotten as the events of 1982 unfolded, and Mugabe accused Nkomo and ZAPU of hiding arms to use for overthrowing his government, was that ex-ZANLA were also caching arms for a potential showdown. Killings of ex-ZIPRA by ex-ZANLA were a fact of life in 1981, as the same report indicates: "ZIPRA (Gwai Mine) have released 398 men who had absented themselves from ZNA BNS [battalions] before the recent Bulawayo troubles. They include 151 men from 43 BN who went absent following the murder of 3 members of that BN by ZANLA 4 months ago."[59]

Responses to Mugabe's Removal of Nkomo from Office

In February 1982, the US ambassador to Zimbabwe, Robert Keeley, described to the State Department in Washington, DC the details of Mugabe's move against Nkomo and ZAPU surrounding the public revelations of hidden arms cachés on ZAPU-owned properties. On February 17, 1982, Mugabe had announced that he was ordering the removal from office and the cabinet of Joshua Nkomo, Josiah

---

[58] BRITOEFAD Salisbury to MODUK, "Sitrep No 41 (17–26 February 1981)," DEFE 11/932 Zimbabwe, BNA.

[59] Ibid. Kriger notes that Dabengwa, Nkomo, Mnangagwa, and Mugabe had been part of "an ad hoc committee who met in early 1982 to discuss how to handle the arms cachés." Kriger, *Guerrilla Veterans*, 133. Stuart Doran quotes from his 2015 interview with Dumiso Dabengwa that Dabengwa had discussed the arms cachés with Special Branch before it became publicly announced, so it was not such a "discovery" by the government, as portrayed by Mugabe to the press and foreign diplomats. Stuart Doran, *Kingdom, Power, Glory: Mugabe, ZANU and the Quest for Supremacy, 1960–1987* (Midrand, South Africa: Sithatha Media, 2017), n. 89 (location 17097 of the Kindle edition). See also Doran, *Kingdom, Power, Glory* (location 1323).

Chinamano and "two other leaders from the Cabinet" for "alleged connection with secret arms cachés." He would permit other ZAPU members to remain in government. "Nkomo, who had first been Minister of Home Affairs, but demoted to Minister of Public Service in January 1981, was now also charged with secretly and unsuccessfully soliciting South African support for a coup attempt in the months following the 1980 elections."[60] At the press conference, Mugabe blamed Nkomo for planning to work with the South Africans to overthrow Mugabe's government. Mugabe's source for this information was General Walls, who claimed to have evidence that Nkomo had "asked whether the SAG [South African government] would support him if ZAPU staged a coup against Mugabe, and was both times told no." Mugabe also said that he had confronted Nkomo about these meetings, and Nkomo had denied them. "Mugabe lamented the 'dishonesty' of his coalition partner, and said that ZANU felt cheated by the repeated evidence of Nkomo's subversive intentions. 'Now we look foolish, very foolish to have dismissed these rumors, because the man is caught red-handed.'"[61] This is the line that Mugabe would consistently present to diplomats and world leaders over the next few years.

New York Times reporter Joseph Lelyveld covered the expulsion of Nkomo from government in an article entitled "Zimbabwe Showdown," where he perceptively observed that both Mugabe and Nkomo were posturing around the arms caching issue. Describing how former ZIPRA personnel had been "leading army search teams to buried weapons" for the previous few months, Mugabe had made his case on "the discovery of an additional 600 rifles and 200 heavier weapons, including 7 Soviet-made surface-to-air missiles, to the stockpile of arms previously recovered." Lelyveld commented, "It was a sizable caché but hardly enough for a coup." Lelyveld was told by

---

[60] Fm AmEmbassy Salisbury, "Mugabe Announces Cabinet Changes; Nkomo Out," February 18, 1982, Unclassified U.S. Department of State Case No. F-2017–00020, Doc No. C06245987, Date: 05/26/2017, FOIA Reading Room, https://tinyurl.com/y8nfmren. See also Eliakim Sibanda, *The Zimbabwe African People's Union, 1961–87* (Trenton NJ: African World Press, 2005), 250. See Nkomo's rebuttals and account of these events Nkomo, *The Story of My Life*, 224–34.

[61] Fm AmEmbassy Salisbury, "Mugabe Announces Cabinet Changes; Nkomo Out," February 18, 1982, Unclassified U.S. Department of State Case No. F-2017–00020, Doc No. C06245987, Date: 05/26/2017, FOIA Reading Room, https://tinyurl.com/y8nfmren.

former ZIPRA commanders, "that it was buried at the time of last year's fighting for purely defensive purposes, an explanation that sounds plausible to the most detached analysts but the Prime Minister and his supporters seem to reject out of hand." Lelyveld summed up the standoff quite well: "It seems more likely that the Prime Minister's underlying mistrust of Mr. Nkomo, dating back nearly 20 years, merged in some complex fashion with his sense of vulnerability to outside threats and plots, which seem to have been deepening in recent months."[62]

For his part, Joshua Nkomo did not take these charges lightly. Ambassador Keeley reported Nkomo's response: "He [Nkomo] asserted that the PM had never discussed the arms cachés with him (an allegation seemingly supported by an evasive answer Mugabe gave to a question on the same topic at the press conference) nor had he the courtesy to call Nkomo himself and tell him he was out of the Cabinet."[63] At this point in Keeley's tenure in Zimbabwe – he was the first US ambassador to Zimbabwe, officially starting on May 23, 1980 – Keeley was still very much enamored with Mugabe's intelligence and political skills. He ended his report on the events of February 1982 with a rather glowing assessment of Mugabe's skill in handling Nkomo. Keeley wrote how "Mugabe's performance in this touchy situation was one of his most effective . . . . Even while delivering a knockout punch to Nkomo, he did so with velvet gloves, cognizant of the potentially violent reaction of ex-Zipra still loyal to their leader." Keeley saw Mugabe's portrayal of South Africa as a potential ally with Nkomo as a smart move, and by keeping Nkomo out of detention, he avoided making Nkomo "a martyr."[64]

A few weeks later, at the beginning of March 1982, Keeley was still praising Mugabe's political skills in handling his main rival. "He has shot not to kill, but to cripple Nkomo and to further limit the effectiveness of ZAPU as a political force." On the role of the ZIPRA arms cachés, Keeley reflected that they were not likely going to be used

[62] Joseph Lelyveld, "Zimbabwe Showdown: Threat of Conflict Remains," *New York Times*, February 20, 1982.
[63] Fm American Embassy Salisbury, "Mugabe Announces Cabinet Changes; Nkomo Out," February 18, 1982, Unclassified U.S. Department of State Case No. F-2017–00020, Doc No. C06245987, Date: 05/26/2017, FOIA Reading Room, https://tinyurl.com/y8nfmren.
[64] Ibid.

offensively by ZIPRA. "We find no conclusive evidence as yet that the ZAPU arms cachés were anything more than an insurance policy – a fifth Brigade in the ground – to be used in case ZANU pressures were to increase to violent proportions. Nkomo's role in the caching is unclear." Keeley was also starting to see the limits of Mugabe and ZANU-PF's constant attacks on Nkomo and ZAPU. "Mugabe's ultimate design is no doubt the political elimination of ZAPU on the road to a one-party state. Ironically, his pillorying of Nkomo may delay, rather than advance, that day."[65]

ZANU's Determination to Create a One-Party State

In order to fully understand the intensity of ZANU's attacks on Nkomo and ZAPU, it has to be noted that Mugabe and many of his key ministers wanted to "crush" all opposition parties in order to give ZANU complete control of the country.[66] Much of this drive came from the examples of Tanzania, Zambia, Mozambique, and Angola, where Mugabe and others had observed the ways ruling parties had crushed rival politicians and movements in order to dictate the future direction of the country without a meaningful opposition. The Lancaster House agreement had given the white minority a guaranteed number of seats in parliament, but what really added to ZANU's obsession with crushing ZAPU was that ZANU had not been able to break ZAPU's electoral popularity in the Matabeleland provinces and the Midlands. Even ZAPU's showing in the 1980 election had created a threatening

[65] American Embassy to Secretary of State, "Zimbabwe After Nkomo's Sacking," March 4, 1982, Unclassified US Department of State Case No. F-2017–00020, Doc No. C06245984, Date: 05/26/2017, Department of State, FOIA Reading Room, https://tinyurl.com/y64xfkmy.

[66] For detailed evidence of this line of argument, that the violence of Gukurahundi was foremost political in nature in order to force a ZANU-led one-party state, see David Coltart, *The Struggle Continues: 50 Years of Tyranny in Zimbabwe.* (Johannesburg: Jacana Media (Pty), 2016); Doran, *Kingdom, Power, Glory*; Judith Todd, *Through the Darkness: A Life in Zimbabwe* (Cape Town: Struik Publishers, 2007); Lloyd Sachikonye, *When a State Turns on Its Citizens: 60 Years of Institutionalised Violence in Zimbabwe* (United States: Jacana Media, 2011), 15–17; Wendy Urban-Mead, *The Gender of Piety: Family, Faith, and Colonial Rule in Matabeleland, Zimbabwe* (Athens: Ohio University Press, 2015), 203–24; Sabelo Ndlovu-Gatsheni, "Rethinking Chimurenga and Gukurahundi in Zimbabwe: A Critique of Partisan National History," *African Studies Review* 55, no. 3 (2012), 1–26.

response from ZANU. Right from the start, in 1980, Minister Emmerson Mnangagwa was signaling to any opposition that they were not going to experience the sort of democracy they may have envisioned. According to British reports, on June 26, 1980, Mnangagwa had "told the House of Assembly yesterday that parties 'which did not do well in the February [1980] elections' were foolishly allowing themselves to be part of a conspiracy against Zimbabwe." The charges at this stage included "deliberate subversive rumour mongering, collaboration with foreign powers to revert the country's socialist revolution, and external training for sabotage by both military and civilian persons." Mnangagwa spelled out ZANU's expectations: "The State did not seek a nation of 'yes men and women' but there had not yet been a clear commitment by all to the new system of democracy." Mnangagwa cautioned "that all those who sought to undermine the authority of the state would be 'consumed by the fury of the masses and ground to powder by the People's government.'"[67] The other outspoken critic of ZAPU's continued political existence was Enos Nkala, himself an Ndebele, but also a longstanding opponent of Nkomo going back to the days of the ZAPU–ZANU split in 1963. Nkala's hatred for Nkomo was no secret, and the feelings were mutual. From 1980 until the unity accords of 1987 that finally brought ZAPU into ZANU and formed ZANU-PF, Nkala would attack Nkomo personally in his speeches, and was the demagogue who was not afraid to bring his fight with Nkomo to his home area. Historian Enocent Msindo notes that one of Nkala's inflammatory speeches in Bulawayo on July 6, 1980, is still remembered as a turning point in the opposition to ZANU and Mugabe's government for many people. In that speech, Nkala argued "that his duty was now 'to crush Nkomo and forget about him.'"[68] By March 1983, the British gave accounts of Nkala speeches, where he "described Nkomo as public enemy number 1, and said that ZAPU would be 'liquidated.'"[69]

---

[67] From Salisbury to FCO, "Internal Situation," June 26, 1980, PREM 19/606, BNA.

[68] Nkala quoted in Enocent Msindo, *Ethnicity in Zimbabwe: Transformations in Kalanga and Ndebele Societies, 1860–1990* (University of Rochester Press, 2012), 216.

[69] From Harare to FCO, "My Telno 178: Matabeleland," March 7, 1983, item 43/3, DEFE 13/1740, BNA.

Nyerere Visits Bulawayo

An indication of just how bad relations were between the two parties, some nine months after independence, can be found in a press account of Tanzanian president Julius Nyerere's visit to Zimbabwe in December 1980. A South African *Rand Daily Mail* account of his visit takes note of the cold reception Nyerere received when in Bulawayo, given that he was accompanied by government ministers Enos Nkala and Emmerson Mnangagwa. The government reportedly cancelled a rally scheduled for President Nyerere at Barbourfield stadium in Bulawayo after only some 2,000 people turned out for it. The reporter indicated that half of the crowd were school children. The reason given for the lack of attendance was the violence that had occurred three weeks previously, where fifty-eight people were reportedly killed in violence between ZAPU and ZANU supporters. "Supporters of Mr Nkomo's Patriotic Front Party have been angered recently by inflammatory remarks by Zanu-PF Ministers – who have denigrated their role in the armed struggle – and the detention of nine senior PF officials." The cancellation of the rally was all the more embarrassing because Prime Minister Mugabe and then minister of home affairs Joshua Nkomo had both accompanied Nyerere to Bulawayo.

The local population's anger was reportedly directed at the "two Zanu-PF Ministers most despised by PF supporters – Senator Enos Nkala, Minister of Finance, and Mr Emmerson Munangagwa [sic], the Minister of State who ordered the arrest of the PF [ZAPU] officials a fortnight ago." After cancelling the rally, "[a]bout 800 people eventually pitched up at the city hall to hear President Nyerere make an impassioned plea for national unity." In his speech, Nyerere "said unity was essential if Zimbabweans did not want to 'betray Africa' and lose the freedom for which they had fought." Nyerere went on to remind the audience of their nation's potential, "Zimbabwe has an economic base which many of us in Africa envy. You start further along the road to development and prosperity (than many others in Africa)." Finally, Nyerere "went out of his way to mention the role played by Mr. Nkomo and his followers in the armed struggle. He said the time for fighting in Zimbabwe was over and that people should now work to consolidate their independence 'and strengthen the border of Africa's freedom which is now at the

Limpopo River.'"[70] This latter point referred to the need to form a united front against apartheid South Africa. The scene, and Nyerere's words, hint to how Mugabe and ZANU might have used this early transition to build a coalition with ZAPU, but that was not the road Mugabe and ZANU took. The reporter ends the article with Mugabe's reply to Nyerere's appeal to unity. "In reply, Mr Mugabe referred to last month's 'little war' in Bulawayo. He said it was a senseless battle between lawless elements versus the rest – and not between Ndebele and Shona."[71]

This was a much more carefully worded response than the one Mugabe would provide Prime Minister Thatcher in October 1981. When asked about the internal situation in Zimbabwe, Mugabe told Thatcher that "Mr. Nkomo was on the whole now being very helpful." However, he conditioned this by saying, "Immediately after independence relations had not been at all easy." He then went into his often-told story of Nkomo's plans to overthrow his government. Mugabe told Thatcher, "The Soviet Union had continued to give ZAPU weapons and the ZAPU military commanders had tried to overthrow the government. This is why there had been fighting in Bulawayo." Mugabe was consistent in his messaging to Western leaders that Nkomo was still a potential threat in terms of Soviet influence. He did, however, temper his criticisms of Nkomo privately to Thatcher. "But Mr. Nkomo had always been realistic and had not supported his military colleagues." Mugabe said of Nkomo, "He was still not a happy man, and to maintain his credibility with his supporters, he had to attack the Government from time to time. But generally there were no serious problems with him."[72] This was a much softer description of Nkomo than what he would give over the next three years.

The Fifth Brigade as ZANU's Force to Attack ZAPU

Robert Keeley remark that ZIPRA's arms cachés were no more than "an insurance policy – a fifth Brigade in the ground – to be used in case ZANU pressures were to increase to violent proportions" points to the increased

[70] "Nyerere Rally in Bulawayo Is Cancelled," *Rand Daily Mail*, December 5, 1980.
[71] Ibid.
[72] "Call on the Prime Minister by Mr. Robert Mugabe," October 7, 1981, PREM 19/682, BNA. Also at Margaret Thatcher Archive: 811006 1425 MT-Mugabe (682–73).pdf

sense among diplomats in Harare that while Mugabe may have accepted the North Korean "gift" of training and supplying a new ZNA brigade as a way to create a "Presidential Guard," he was also creating a fighting force outside of the British BMATT program to be under direct command of ex-ZANLA officers loyal to Mugabe. For the British officials involved in BMATT, the prospects of a private army loyal to Mugabe and ZANU would remain a concern, but as events in early 1983 unfolded the British were quite willing to make the most of the North Korean responsibility for training of the 5 Brigade. The lack of discipline of the 5 Brigade served as a foil to the other four Brigades that had been trained by BMATT. In some ways then, Mugabe's use of North Korean training and weapons had given the British a way to both remain close and involved with the ZNA while also putting the blame on the North Korean trained brigade for the extreme human rights abuses that were to transpire in 1983.

By September 1982, Ambassador Keeley had now spent sufficient time in Zimbabwe to learn more of the history of the liberation struggle and the years before it. His account to the State Department demonstrates the commonly held ZANU perspective of the struggle between Mugabe and Nkomo, going back to the original 1963 split. Keeley's account still seemed more or less inspired by what he would have likely heard from ZANU intellectuals and politicians. "There were three elements to the split, at least. One was a rejection of Nkomo as leader because he was considered a dishonest, corrupt person who would make deals to assure his own ascendancy, in other words a 'sell-out.'" Keeley then repeated the ethnic explanation for the rivalry, "Secondly, there was the tribal division, with Nkomo being considered a tribalist who was working to advance Ndebele and not 'national' interests (not entirely true)." At least Keeley now recognized the general weakness of this line, although he eventually would also use the ethnicity argument in his assessment of human rights abuses by the Zimbabwe government. His last point was based on a more racial and personal impression of the two movements: "Thirdly, there was a definite ideological or strategic disagreement, with the ZANU people insisting on going for broke, for absolute black rule, with no deals or compromises with the whites, whereas Nkomo was always open to making a deal with almost anyone, to take half a loaf and then work for the remainder."[73]

---

[73] Ambassador Keeley to Secretary of State, "Security Situation in Zimbabwe, Inter-Party Rivalry and Abduction of Amcits," September 22, 1982, Unclassified US Department of State Case No. F-2012–29009, Doc No.

1980 Elections and the First Years of Independence

As previous chapters have shown, this was far from an accurate summary of Nkomo's negotiating style and his commitment to the PF, although ZANU had projected this interpretation since the early détente period in 1974–75. Nkomo had insisted on staying with Mugabe in the PF even when it went against his own personal interests. The problem from Nkomo's perspective, of course, was that Mugabe would never agree to take a secondary role. Having won the majority of seats in the 1980 elections, there was now no longer the need for Mugabe to show respect for Nkomo, or to reciprocate in giving Nkomo the respect Nkomo gave Mugabe during the PF period. Mugabe and his colleagues in ZANU would take matters even further, as they would seek to destroy ZAPU as an opposition party in their attempt to gain total control of the political system in Zimbabwe. Keeley's summary more or less reflects the commonly held diplomatic views of the early 1980s. These views were likely representative of the information obtained from his predominantly ZANU-PF contacts and also from many of the other diplomats he encountered in Harare.

As the months went on, however, and certainly after the deployment of the 5 Brigade and the beginning of the *Gukurahundi* period in late January 1983, Keeley and others began to have a much less rosy view of Mugabe and ZANU's campaigns against Nkomo and ZAPU. Even before the deployment of the 5 Brigade, ZANU had continued to report to the press and international diplomats that Nkomo and ZAPU were involved in treason against the state. On April 2, 1982, Keeley reported on a press conference in Bulawayo by Emmerson Mnangagwa held a few days earlier, where Mnangagwa alleged that the Zimbabwe government had "seized military camps in Matabeleland where people were being trained to overthrow the government and arrested those involved." Mnangagwa claimed evidence "connected the secret camps to Joshua Nkomo's ZAPU and that some leaders of ZAPU knew about them, and that some of those arrested were "former ZIPRA combatants." In parentheses, Keeley reported that Mnangagwa was "very vague about the numbers involved and the potential significance of the secret training."[74] Almost two months later, Keeley was downplaying the threat from dissidents in the country as

C05256499, Date 09/24/2013 DoS, FOIA Reading Room, https://tinyurl.com/yb8m4jzz.

[74] AmEmbassy Salisbury to SecState WashDC, "Munangagwa finds secret ZIPRA Bases," April 2, 1982, Unclassified US Department of State Case No. F-2012–29009, Doc No. C05256453, Date: 09/24/2013 DoS, FOIA Reading Room, https://tinyurl.com/y8hojbz3.

he was beginning to suggest that ZANU's use of Nkomo and ZAPU as the target of their campaign was at risk of making the situation worse:

The dissident problem is not a major military threat, and in fact, the [Zimbabwe government] may be getting on top of it. However, continued pressure on ZAPU, and particularly on Nkomo, and poor handling of ex-Zipra deserters from the national army might help create the Matabeleland Sea in which dissidents could swim … . Militarily, the dissident situation appears to be not a major threat.[75]

Two major events changed the tenor of Keeley's reports on the security situation in Zimbabwe in July 1982. One was the July 23 kidnapping and killing of six foreign tourists, including two Americans, two Britons, and two Australians. The second was the sabotage and destruction of Zimbabwe Air Force fighter jets at the Thornhill Air force base on July 25, 1992. Both events brought the Americans and their diplomatic counterparts into closer and more frequent contact with ZANU and ZAPU leaders.[76] When discussing Nkomo with American diplomats, Mugabe painted a picture of Nkomo as someone unwilling to work to stop the dissidents. Mugabe told Keeley that although "he had tried to involve ZAPU in the government … the situation today is that ZAPU could be doing a lot more to help the situation." Mugabe charged Nkomo with the responsibility of stopping dissidents: "These ZAPU 'youngsters' (the dissidents) had been acting in ZAPU's name. In Nkomo's name. Nkomo could stop it. The truth is, Mugabe said, that some of Nkomo's adherents have been encouraging the banditry."[77] Nkomo, on the other hand, used the

[75] AmEmbassy Harare to SecState WashDC 5870, "Current Security Update: ZAPU, ZIPRA, and the Soviets," May 24, 1982 Unclassified US Department of State Case No. F-2012–29009, Doc No. C05256456, Date: 09/24/2013 DoS, FOIA Reading Room, https://tinyurl.com/y87by8lc.

[76] For a discussion of how these events informed American diplomacy and relations with Mugabe, see Timothy Scarnecchia, "Rationalizing Gukurahundi: Cold War and South African Foreign Relations with Zimbabwe, 1981–1983," *Kronos* 37, no. 1 (2011); Timothy Scarnecchia, "Intransigent Diplomat: Robert Mugabe and His Western Diplomacy, 1963–83", in Sabelo J. Ndlovu-Gatsheni, ed., *Mugabeism? History, Politics, and Power in Zimbabwe* (London: Palgrave Macmillan 2015), 77–92. For an exceptionally detailed account of these events and years, see Doran, *Kingdom, Power, Glory.*

[77] Amb Robert V. Keeley, AmEmbassy Harare to SecState WashDC, "Abduction of Amcits in Zimbabwe: Meeting with PM Mugabe 8.3," August 4, 1982, Unclassified US Dept of State, Case No. F-2012–29009, Doc No C05256470, September 24, 2013, https://tinyurl.com/y87by8lc, as cited in Scarnecchia, "Intransigent Diplomat," 88. For the many complex reasons why dissidents sometimes associated

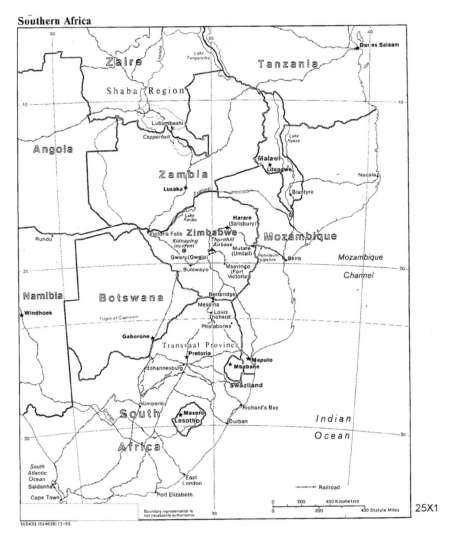

Figure 9 Map of Southern Africa. CIA, "Zimbabwe: Growing Potential for Instability," December 1982.

kidnappings of foreign tourists to demand respect from Mugabe and ZANU in return for his help with trying to locate the kidnapped foreigners.

themselves with ZAPU but without direct connections to Nkomo and other older generation leaders, see Jocelyn Alexander, "Dissident Perspectives on Zimbabwe's Post-Independence War," *Africa* 68, no. 2 (1998), 151–82.

He noted that since he was no longer part of the government, he was unwilling to take a leading role to help the Zimbabwe government that was accusing him of being behind the dissidents and kidnappings.[78]

Mugabe's Meeting with CIA Director William Casey

An example of the closeness between Mugabe and the United States in the first few years of independence is Mugabe's meeting with the head of the CIA, William Casey, who spent a day in Harare on September 28, 1982. Casey met with then CIO director general Derek Robinson and former CIO director general Ken Flowers. Casey discussed with them accusations from South Africa that the Zimbabweans were permitting the South African ANC to enter South Africa. Casey later told Mugabe that he had spoken with both Pik Botha and Magnus Malan the previous day in Pretoria, about the United States "displeasure" over South Africa's "destabilization efforts." Casey told Mugabe, "They didn't deny they were doing that, but said they were retaliating because of operations mounted from Zimbabwe against their country." Robinson denied any such activities. Interestingly, both Casey and Mugabe began the meeting by thanking each other for cooperation on the intelligence front. Mugabe thanked Casey for American "cooperation in developing the Zimbabwean intelligence service."[79] In reply to the question of Zimbabwean assistance to the South African ANC, Mugabe told Casey that "Zimbabwe supports its African brothers in South Africa morally and diplomatically but not militarily," stating, "On that we have been very clean." Casey agreed with this latter point, according to Keeley's account.

Casey asked Mugabe to comment on the internal situation in the country. Mugabe elaborated for Casey the case against Nkomo and ZAPU: "To be sure there are dissident elements, army deserters, the arms cachés, the abduction of foreign tourists. There have been rapes and murders. All this has been directed against the government." Keeley then summarized Mugabe's account of "recent Zimbabwean history." Mugabe told how [h]is party had won the election and had

---

[78] See Scarnecchia, "Intransigent Diplomat."

[79] Secretary of State, 1982, "William Casey's meeting with Prime Minister Mugabe: Namibia, Zimbabwe-South Africa relations, internal situations, CSM article on Civil Rights," From Secretary of State WashDC to US mission USUN, New York, October 2, Unclassified, US Department of State, Case No. F-20212–29009, Doc No. C0525610, Date 09/24/2013, https://tinyurl.com/y9gcpdbe.

taken power. "ZAPU, having been defeated in the election, had asked the USSR for arms and had received them in Zambia – that was after Lancaster house." Mugabe added that "ZAPU had refused to surrender these arms to the national armory. Instead they had cached the arms, some on farms the party had acquired for this purpose." Mugabe said, "We felt we had been cheated by ZAPU."[80]

Later in the meeting, Keeley suggested to Mugabe that the allegations of torture of detained white Air Force officers, as reported by the *Christian Science Monitor* newspaper in the United States, could lead to the United States tying their sizeable foreign aid package for Zimbabwe to human rights. CIA director William Casey, true to form, was less concerned about human rights, and told Mugabe he was only concerned with these issues to the extent that they caused some Republican senators to challenge Zimbabwe's aid levels. Responding to Mugabe's claim that the Western media was making up these stories of atrocities, "Mr. Casey said the aid linkage was not paramount, but stressed that Zimbabwe had what was essentially a public relations problem and they had to understand that we [the United States] don't control what appears in our press."[81] Keeley noted how, at the end of the meeting, Casey presented to Mugabe a leather-bound copy of the book Casey had written on the American revolution, "noting that our countries shared the experience of having had to fight to achieve this goal."[82]

British Concerns prior to *Gukurahundi*

In late September 1982, the British were also expressing concern over potential problems if the ZNA was used to settle scores with ZAPU, given that the British had invested heavily into the BMATT program. The British defence secretary, John Nott, wrote a summary for Thatcher of his one-day trip to Zimbabwe where he met with Mugabe. He said that the Zimbabweans wanted BMATT to focus on training instructors, rather than continuing the role as advisors at the unit level. Nott wrote that this would reduce British "influence with the units themselves" but enable them to "avoid the danger of association with the growing Army thuggery in Matabeleland in particular." Nott was in favor of reducing British contact at the unit level as it would

[80] Ibid.   [81] Ibid.   [82] Ibid.

"make it easier to reduce its [BMATT's] size next year, *and distance us from the nastier side of African behaviour.*" The latter comment is an interesting expression of race state thinking about military discipline in Zimbabwe, and Nott's interest in limiting BMATT's potential liability over future state crimes committed by ZNA soldiers trained and/or led by British soldiers.

Nott's main concern at this point, however, was reports of the torture of white Air Force personnel who were in custody and awaiting trial after being charged with the sabotage of four Hunter fighter jets supplied by the British at the Thornhill base. Nott recommended to Mugabe that the public trials of the arrested Air Force members should be sped up and over soon. If not, given the allegations of torture used to obtain confessions, Britain may choose to withhold training and aid. In response, Mugabe "denied the allegations, and indicated that the officers would be brought to trial: but he also suggested that the British public should be more concerned about the sabotage than about torture." Nott then threatened Mugabe: "we shall have to withhold assistance to the Air Force which the Zimbabweans have asked for."[83] Nott concluded his notes on his meeting with Mugabe, stating, "I was left uneasy by my meeting with Mr. Mugabe." He framed his unease in a way similar to that of other diplomats at the time, writing how Mugabe "either did not know what was going on in his army and on the security front, or that he knew things were not right, but was not disposed or able to do anything about it." This would be the way many diplomats would report on the next period of more intensive state violence against civilians. For Nott, he also noted the consequences of this in a usual racialized trope: "The drift in Zimbabwe towards increasingly unpleasant and extra-constitutional methods must have consequences both for the confidence of white Zimbabweans and for the prospects for Western investment."[84] The British, like the Americans and many other Western diplomats who would be involved in Zimbabwe during the *Gukurahundi* period (1983–87) were mostly concerned to keep their criticisms safely below a level that could

---

[83] Nott does not give the exact date of his meeting with Mugabe. He traveled to five countries between September 10 and 26, and Zimbabwe appears to have been the last place he visited. "Secretary of Defense to Prime Minister," MO 25/2/23/2, October 6, 1982, 821006, Nott to MT, PREM 19/690, Margaret Thatcher Foundation Archive, f. 14. Italics added by author.

[84] Ibid.

possibly push Mugabe toward the Soviet Union. At the same time, most diplomats relied on the reports and sentiments of white Zimbabweans about their own safety and future in Zimbabwe as the key variables to assess what actions Britain should take to try and influence the actions of their supposed "close allies" in ZANU.

Through 1982, Mugabe continued to push back against any criticisms of his government's handling of human rights. Mugabe even made a point of complaining to CIA director William Casey and US ambassador Keeley about Nott's threat to withhold Zimbabwe aid and the BMATT program over human rights issues (e.g., the treatment of the detained Air Force pilots). "Mugabe mentioned that British Defense Secretary Nott had raised the same matter with him last Saturday and had made the same point, that this could jeopardize the British aid program, including BMATT." Keeley wrote that "Mugabe expressed resentment that we [the United States] and the British would tie our aid to such matters and would in effect threaten to cut off aid. That was not the basis on which the Zimbabwe government could accept aid from its friends, he said."[85] This quote from Mugabe captures the attitude Mugabe would take in different diplomatic forums. It was consistent with his messaging to the British and Americans from the meetings at Geneva in 1976 to his meetings with them as prime minister. He was always confident that he should be treated as an equal in a negotiation and not pander to wealthier, more militarily powerful, nations, particularly the British. He genuinely seemed to appreciate the respect he earned from Thatcher and Reagan in these early years, but their respect for him was tied to his delivering what they wanted from a pro-Western African state in southern Africa. Governor Soames had written to Cyrus Vance in March of 1980 warning of the potential break between Mugabe and the West, and the rise of more radical leadership in his place. Soames wrote:

If Zimbabwe does not get sufficient western encouragement and assistance over the next two years, he [Mugabe] could be driven to policies which would lead to a rapid white exodus (so far avoided) on a scale which could lead

---

[85] Secretary of State, 1982. "William Casey's meeting with Prime Minister Mugabe: Namibia, Zimbabwe-South Africa Relations, Internal Situations, CSM Article on Civil Rights," From Secretary of State WashDC to US mission USUN, New York, October 2, Unclassified, US Department of State, Case No. F-20212–29009, Doc No. C0525610 Date 09/24/2013, https://tinyurl.com/y9gcpdbe.

quickly towards the kind of economic problems which have plagued Mozambique; and there could then be a tendency to head towards an early confrontation with South Africa.

According to Soames, the way to avoid this threat was to facilitate "a stable and prosperous Zimbabwe."[86] As the next chapter shows, this balance was to be threatened in 1983 and 1984, but even as evidence pointed toward extreme state crimes against civilians, western diplomats and foreign policy bureaucrats would continue to assess the situation through the lens of race states and Cold War interests.

---

[86] Fm Salisbury to FCO, "For Secretary of State from Governor: Personal Letter to Cy Vance," March 23, 1980, item 56, FCO36/2751, BNA.

9 | Gukurahundi *and Zimbabwe's Place in the 1980s Cold War*

This chapter examines the fundamental shift in thinking among international and regional diplomats over the meaning of a "race state" in Zimbabwe once the settler state had been officially replaced. Zimbabwe's relatively late decolonization process took place during a heightened Cold War competition between the Anglo-Americans and the Soviets, which therefore made Zimbabwe an important addition to the balance sheet of pro-Western allies in Africa. This alliance would allow Mugabe and his colleagues to take advantage of Cold War obsessions in American and British thinking as ZANU carried out a campaign to destroy Nkomo and ZAPU as a political rival. For Nkomo and ZAPU, given their longstanding support from the Soviets, this new dispensation in Zimbabwe would turn out to be disastrous in terms of Nkomo's inability to obtain any sort of external support, and, at times, even an audience, as he and ZAPU were attacked by Mugabe and ZANU in the early 1980s. This state violence carried out against the opposition is increasingly well documented in the literature, so this chapter will continue to focus on how Western diplomats read, interpreted, and rationalized this violence in the context of their own agendas of defending Mugabe and Zimbabwe's policies of racial conciliation as a Cold War success story. There is a large literature on the impact of Operation *Gukurahundi*.[1] What follows in this chapter is a look at the diplomatic responses to events,

---

[1] See Catholic Commission for Justice and Peace and Legal Resources Foundation, *Breaking the Silence, Building True Peace: A Report on the Disturbances in Matabeleland and the Midlands, 1980–1988* (Harare: CCJPZ and LRF, 1999), reprinted in *Gukurahundi in Zimbabwe: A Report on the Disturbances in Matabeleland and the Midlands, 1980–1988* (London: Hurst and Company, 2007); Lloyd M. Sachikonye, *When a State Turns on Its Citizens: 60 Years of Institutionalised Violence in Zimbabwe* (Johannesburg: Jacana, 2011); Shari Eppel, "'Gukurahundi': The Need for Truth and Reparation," in Brian Raftopoulos and Tyrone Savage, eds., *Zimbabwe: Injustice and Political Reconciliation* (Harare: Weaver Press, 2005), 43–62; Stuart Doran, *Kingdom,*

with some new sources from the British archives covering BMATT and Department of Defence files.

A significant dynamic to highlight in this chapter is the often-contradictory Zimbabwe–South Africa relations in the early 1980s. The diplomatic, military, and security archives suggest that while both countries were involved in a competitive rhetorical opposition, there was also a good deal of cooperation on the issue of security. This came about as interests coalesced around Mugabe and ZANU's attempts to destroy ZAPU through claims of "restoring law and order" and ending dissident activity, and South Africa's attempts to secure cooperation from Zimbabwe around issues of the South African ANC's MK operatives (members of its armed wing) entering South African territory. In the sort of "cat and mouse" diplomacy over these two needs, there was a cooperation between the Zimbabwean and South African governments that helped to further marginalize Nkomo and ZAPU. That is, while the Zimbabweans publicly called out South African support for dissidents operating in Zimbabwe, they also understood that the these South African trained and equipped "Super-ZAPU" dissidents were not operating on a scale that would significantly undermine the Zimbabwean state. In some ways, the continued activities by Super ZAPU in 1984 helped the ruling party to justify to Zimbabweans the all-important state-of-emergency powers that permitted detention without trial and indemnity for soldiers and politicians against being held personally responsible for state crimes committed under their leadership. This was useful from the standpoint of consolidating ZANU power, and to potentially move toward the creation of a one-party state.[2]

Power, Glory: Mugabe, ZANU and the Quest for Supremacy, 1960–1987 (Midrand, South Africa: Sithatha Media, 2017); Timothy Scarnecchia, "Rationalizing 'Gukurahundi': Cold War and South African Foreign Relations with Zimbabwe, 1981–1983." *Kronos* (November 2011), 87–103; Jocelyn Alexander, JoAnn McGregor, and Terence Ranger, *Violence and Memory: One Hundred Years in the Dark Forests of Matabeleland, Zimbabwe* (Oxford: James Currey, 2000); David Coltart, *The Struggle Continues: 50 Years of Tyranny in Zimbabwe* (Johannesburg: Jacana Media, 2016).

[2] See John Hatchard, *Individual Freedoms and State Security in the African Context: The Case of Zimbabwe* (London: James Currey 1993); George Karekwaivanane, *The Struggle over State Power in Zimbabwe: Law and Politics since 1950* (Cambridge University Press, 2017), 184–214.

The South African goal with Super ZAPU was to destabilize ZAPU's ability to provide further shelter to the South African ANC, while also causing problems for Mugabe's government. As it would turn out, the ex-ZIPRA dissidents were often unable to maintain supplies themselves, especially guns and ammunition, so the South African–supported "Super ZAPU" stood out due to being relatively well supplied.[3] Therefore, it is important to remember that while South Africa did support "Super ZAPU" dissidents in Zimbabwe, it was not intended as an all-out attempt to destabilize the government as in the cases of Mozambique and Angola. As Stephan Chan describes it, "Zimbabwe was not the main military target. Angola and Mozambique were. The idea was to make Zimbabwe and Zambia feel as if they were caught, west and east, in a pincer – so anxious that the conflict on the borders should not overspill that they dared not look south."[4]

The dissidents in Zimbabwe were also not the same as the ZIPRA army before independence, even though Mugabe and others in ZANU would consistently claim that they were. The treason charges against ZIPRA's generals, Lookout Masuku and Dumiso Dabengwa, had been thrown out in Zimbabwean courts. However, Mugabe and ZANU had both of these ZIPRA leaders immediately detained without charges following their acquittal.[5] Similarly, the Mugabe government secretly cooperated with the South Africans to monitor MK activities in Zimbabwe and met regularly to share intelligence.[6] South Africa had demonstrated clearly in 1981 and 1982, in particular, that it could successfully carry out covert missions in Zimbabwe. The assassination of South African ANC representative Joe Gqabi outside of his home in Harare was a clear message, as was the destruction of ZANU arms

[3] See Phyllis Johnson and David Martin, *Apartheid Terrorism: the Destabilisation Report* (London: James Currey 1989), 68–69.

[4] Stephan Chan, *Southern Africa: Old Treacheries and New Deceits* (New Haven, CT: Yale University Press, 2011), 35–36.

[5] See Karekwaivanane, *Struggle over State Power*, 199; Judith Todd, *Through the Darkness: A Life in Zimbabwe* (Cape Town: Struik Publishers, 2007), 147–66; Eliakim Sibanda, *The Zimbabwe African People's Union, 1961–87: A Political History of Insurgency in Southern Rhodesia* (Trenton, NJ: Africa World Press, 2005), 249–54.

[6] See, for example, exchanges between the Zimbabwean and South African security forces, and records of meetings, in the folder "Zimbabwe: Relations with SA" 1/156/3, vol. 37, DFA Archives, Pretoria.

returned from Mozambique at the Inkomi depot in August 1981, and the Thornhill destruction of the Hunter jets in July 1982.[7] In December 1981, there was an unsuccessful attempt to kill the ZANU-PF Central Committee in their Harare headquarters. The bomb was detonated in a room above where they were due to meet but the Central Committee had postponed the meeting.[8] Such actions, and the threat of greater destabilization, kept Mugabe and Mnangagwa cooperative with the South Africans in periodic mutual security talks between the SADF and the South African Police and Zimbabwean Central Intelligence Organisation and ZNA representatives, which came with a commitment from the Zimbabweans to share intelligence on the MK in Zimbabwe.[9]

1983: Zimbabwe's "Terrible Year"

The previous chapter has set the stage for the tragic events of 1983. With an increase in dissident activities in the Matabeleland North and South provinces and Midlands province in December 1982, and in the midst of British pressure over the detained Air Force personnel, the decision was made by Mugabe and his closest associates to deploy the 5 Brigade, consisting of between 2,500 and 3,500 soldiers, to take over security operations in these three provinces in February 1983. Made up almost entirely of chiShona speaking former ZANLA fighters, the 5

---

[7] Alexander, McGregor, and Ranger, *Violence and Memory*, 189; see also Geoffrey Nyarota, *Against the Grain: Memoirs of a Zimbabwean Newsman* (Cape Town: Struik, 2006), 86–89; Eliakim Sibanda, *The Zimbabwe African People's Union, 1961–87* (Trenton, NJ: African World Press 2005), 249–354.

[8] Stephen Ellis and Tsepo Sechaba, *Comrades against Apartheid: The ANC and the South African Communist Party in Exile* (Bloomington: Indiana University Press, 1992), 108.

[9] See, for example, "Memo to Direkteur General Van Wentzel," 14/3/1983, South African National Archives (SANA), Department of Foreign Affairs (DFA), 1/156/1, vol. 126, Zimbabwe Political Situation and Development, 1/3/83 to 13/3/83. The minutes for the September 6, 1983 meeting between SADF and Central Intelligence Organisation representatives continues to show cooperation, although a detailed summary by the Central Intelligence Organisation of alleged "SADF Assistance to ZPRA and Dissidents in Botswana" is missing from the file, as the paragraph numbers jump from 24 to 32 on consecutively numbered pages in the file, 112–111. "Minutes of Meeting Held on 6 September 1983 at Beit Bridge Zimbabwe Between a Zimbabwe CIO/ZNA Delegation and Representatives of the SADF and the SAP," Foreign Affairs (DFA), 1/156/3, vol. 37, Zimbabwe: Relations with Zimbabwe, DFA Archives.

Brigade's operation was called '*Gukurahundi*', a chiShona term that translates as "the early rain which washes away the chaff before the spring rains." This term had been used by ZANU before, including in the operation to capture and discipline the Nhari rebels in 1974, and Mugabe and ZANU declared 1979 as "*Gore re Gukurahundi*," which was translated as "the year of the people's storm," in a ZANU pamphlet, signifying that it would represent the final push in the liberation war to a ZANU victory.

Evidence shows that there was not unanimous support of the use of the 5 Brigade against civilians, particularly as some of the intelligence officers – including some who had planned the Rhodesian military's counterinsurgency efforts during the war – understood that the use of brutal force to "discipline" civilians was not going to end the dissident problem. There was, therefore, some irony in having former Rhodesian intelligence officers attempt to restrain Mugabe and others in ZANU from using the 5 Brigade in this manner. On the other hand, it is also the case that Mugabe and others wanted to use force not simply to root out dissidents, but to bring Nkomo and ZAPU to their knees with the erroneous belief that ZAPU supporters would capitulate and recognize ZANU as the sole "one-party" government.

A useful survey of ZANU and ZAPU assessments of what should be done about the dissidents comes from a series of interviews carried out by British minister of state Cranley Onslow, who spent four days in Zimbabwe from January 5 to 8, 1983. This trip occurred before the 5 Brigade was deployed, but the British were receiving intelligence of violence against civilians by the ZNA and the special police units already punishing civilians for alleged support of dissidents since 1982. The main concern about Zimbabwe in the British press and from members of parliament in January 1983 remained reports of alleged torture of the white Air Force personnel detained and awaiting trial for their role in the Thornhill Air Force base bombings, some of whom were British citizens. Onslow was sent personally to Zimbabwe to relay the decision of Thatcher and the British military to replace the destroyed Hunter jets. As Onslow made the rounds to inform various Zimbabwean ministers of this decision, he asked if they would try to keep the decision secret, given the current British domestic criticisms of Mugabe's government. Onslow also asked almost everyone he interviewed for an update of the security situation in the Matabeleland provinces. His trip occurred prior to the deployment of the 5 Brigade, but the responses he received are informative of the mindset and opinions of key Zimbabwean politicians just as plans were being made for deploying the 5 Brigade.

Minister Onslow told Minister of State (Defence) Dr. Sidney Sekeramayi "that it would be invaluable to opinion outside (and inside) Zimbabwe if it could be made clear that disciplinary action would be taken against members of the security forces who overstepped the mark."[10] Such a question indicates that the British already had information that the ZNA, police, and Central Intelligence Organisation agents were engaged in violence against civilians prior to the deployment of 5 Brigade. It is also significant that Onslow was willing to bring this up directly with Sekeramayi. Sekeramayi replied that he was convinced the dissident activities could be stopped if Nkomo and ZAPU would give orders to the "ZAPU local infrastructure," who, he claimed, "was involved in what was happening." He also said "that he wasn't too worried about the situation in Matabeleland." He believed that the military could contain it and stop it. His main point was that the Western powers and media would not understand the government's response. "If they [the Zimbabwean government] took a soft line over the situation in Matabeleland, it would be termed 'ineffective,' but if it took the tough action necessary, it would be termed 'brutal.'" Sekeramayi said that "in the long run, people would prefer a strong government to one which allowed itself to be held ransom." He told Onslow that "he therefore hoped for a degree of sympathy from the Western press for tough action to sort out the problem once and for all." Onslow, like his American counterparts, told Sekeramayi that "he had no control over the press." Sekeramayi's responses to Onslow's questions suggests that the ZANU leadership were already contemplating the launch of a much more violent campaign against dissidents and ZAPU supporters than had already transpired in early January.

Minister Onslow also spoke with John Nkomo, a ZAPU politician who remained in government after Joshua Nkomo's expulsion. John Nkomo served as minister of state in the deputy prime minister's office at the time of the meeting. Unlike Sekeramayi, John Nkomo did not

---

[10] "Record of a Meeting between Mr Cranley Onslow MP, Minister of State, FCO and Dr. Sidney Sekeramayi, Minister of State (Defence) Zimbabwe on 6 January," FCO 105/1411, BNA.

agree that ZAPU's leadership could control the dissidents. He believed most of the ex-ZIPRA soldiers who had become dissidents had done so out of jealousy toward ZANU and ex-ZANLA soldiers, and the boredom and lack of employment after demobilization. He said that many were criminals, "but, to acquire credibility among the people, claimed adherence to ZAPU and condemned the 'ZANU' government. Rural people had no access to information and were inclined to believe the dissidents, especially if they backed their claims with arms." Onslow asked John Nkomo whether or not it was "desirable to find a way to meet the political demands which commanded sympathy and thus undermine the dissidents." Nkomo replied how "it was difficult to deal with people who claimed to act in the name of ZAPU but in fact had no connection with them, and indeed did not hesitate to kill ZAPU members." He also argued that ZAPU was hesitant to get involved, "as they would do nothing to create the impression that Zimbabwe was divided into two parts." Like many who spoke to Onslow, John Nkomo suggested that there was evidence of an "external element," meaning South Africa, "seeking to destabilise Zimbabwe under the cover of dissidents."[11]

Perhaps the most interesting meeting Onslow had with ZANU leaders was with the deputy prime minister, Simon Muzenda. Muzenda was a very popular politician in Zimbabwe, as he tended to speak in ways that nonelite Zimbabweans trusted. Most interestingly, when asked by Onslow about the internal situation, he said it was "worrying," and also that "the problem was political." Muzenda placed the emphasis on the political conflict caused by Mugabe's rivalry with Joshua Nkomo, rather than ethnicity. He noted that Mugabe was meeting with Nkomo and trying to work toward a political solution and reconciliation. He also said that "there were doubts whether the dissidents were under central control." Continuing to present a case much different from the harsh messages Mnangagwa, Nkala, and Mugabe would present publicly, Muzenda described how [t]he dissidence was not a tribal conflict. "ZAPU feared they would be permanently excluded from power in a (ZANU) one party state: these fears were being exploited by outside powers. Ex-ZIPRA combatants were also aggrieved about the

---

[11] "Record of Meeting between Mr Cranley Onslow MP, Minister of State, FCO and Mr John Nkomo, Minister of State in the Deputy Prime Minister's Office on 7 January 1983," FCO 105/1411, BNA.

confiscation of farms."[12] Perhaps a voice of reason at the top echelons of ZANU, Muzenda complicated the dominant script coming from ZANU hardliners. That script characterized Nkomo as a "tribalist," seeking revenge for losing the election by secretly controlling the ex-ZIPRA dissidents. John Nkomo and Simon Muzenda had certainly given Onslow a more nuanced way of interpreting the dissident challenge to the Zimbabwean state.

After meeting with Onslow directly, Mugabe would later tell diplomats that he had been bothered by Onlsow's message about the treatment of the Air Force servicemen. Mugabe wrote directly to Thatcher on January 7 to lodge his complaint. He wrote to Thatcher that "I have now, once again, expressed the attitude of my Government to that case." He continued, "At the same time, I have also expressed to him [Onslow] my dismay at the accusation of the violation of human rights levelled at my Government by you and your Government at a time when we are doing our best to make the situation here more peaceful."[13] Mugabe then made the case that given all the efforts to subvert his government by South Africa and those former Rhodesians working with the South Africans, they refused "to be stampeded into hasty actions whose possible effect might be to curtail civil liberties." Mugabe let Thatcher know, "What we need is a little word of encouragement and acknowledgement of what we have managed to achieve so far even with the tremendous odds that faced us at Independence." He then thanked her for agreeing to sell the Hunter jets.[14]

When Onslow returned to London and wrote his report for the secretary of state, a copy of which was later annotated by Thatcher, he characterized the Matabeleland issue as "tribal" in nature, but at least situated the demands of the dissidents in contemporary issues. "In Matabeleland the root cause of the trouble is almost certainly tribal, involving gangs of former ZIPRA men, and closely associated with land tenure problems." Onslow did, however, ascribe some of the blame to Mugabe. "In dealing with this the government scores less well. Mugabe does not disguise his bitterness about the attitude of his old adversary

---

[12] "Record of Meeting between Mr Cranley Onslow MP, Minister of State, FCO and Mr Simon Muzenda, Deputy Prime Minister on 6 January 1983," FCO 105/1411, BNA.

[13] Prime Minister Robert Mugabe to Prime Minister Margaret Thatcher, January 7, 1983, PREM 19/1154, BNA.

[14] Ibid.

Joshua Nkomo." Onslow reported that members of Mugabe's cabinet "spend long hours trying to ensure that the tribal rivalry does not get out of control." And that "as long as Nkomo remains in the wilderness, the potential for friction is there, and Mugabe evidently believes that it is being exploited by South Africa."[15] This last sentence summarizes two ways that Mugabe and his colleagues shaped British diplomatic opinion to fit the idea that Nkomo and South Africa presented a combined threat to Mugabe's government. Onslow's report was done on January 18, before the *Gukurahundi* operations of the 5 Brigade were reported.

There is not sufficient space to discuss in detail the initial 5 Brigade violence of January and February 1983. The report released in 1997 by the Catholic Committee for Justice and Peace and the Bulawayo lawyers working with them remains the most detailed account of the violence by those who survived or witnessed it.[16] It is important, however, to note that the British military and High Commissioner Byatt were well informed of the atrocities. A report from February 1983, addressed to the Ministry of Defence and from S. T. W. Anderson, a British defence advisor based in the high commissioner's office in Harare, is prefaced with "please find attached reports concerning ZNA acts of brutality in Matabeleland." The report contains a great deal of evidence from doctors and from Catholic priests and the Bishop of Matabeleland, Henry Karlen. The first section is Anderson's summary of a conversation he had on February 17 with a medical doctor, who was leaving the country after serving as a mission doctor in Matabeleland since 1969. The doctor's evidence reported how ZNA "soldiers have lists of ex-ZIPRA deserters and these are used in interrogation." The doctor said that if villagers denied knowing the names, they could be killed, "as can equally a report of having seen or heard of him." The soldiers would also at times "make new footprints around a kraal after dark" and if these were not reported the following morning, it would be "used as an excuse to shoot or beat those in the kraal." Another example of the ZNA's deadly behavior was that soldiers would "[s]ometimes ... pretend to be

---

[15] To Secretary of State from Cranley Onslow, January, 18, 1983, PREM 19/ 1154 0.

[16] Catholic Commission for Justice and Peace and Legal Resources Foundation, *Breaking the Silence*.

dissidents and entice the locals to provide assistance. To do so of course then ends in death."[17]

A copy of Bishop Karlen's letter to Mugabe dated February 12, 1983 is included in the materials. Karlen wrote to inform him that he had "been receiving reports of violence perpetrated by the 5th Brigade against civilians in those areas of my Diocese under martial law." Referring to a statement of Sekeramayi made in Parliament, he said, "I was surprised that the Government was not aware of the behaviour and brutal approach of the 5th Brigade who terrorise and intimidate the population through murder of men, women, and children, and beating administered to innocent people of the community." To address Sekeramayi's characterization of the reports as civilians caught in a crossfire, Karlen stated, "At no time has there been a mention of killing innocent people in crossfire. Many cases of rape, even of primary school girls, were brought to our notice." Karlen then referred to motive. "It seems to be the deliberate and indiscriminate revenge on the Matabele people. People have spoken already of a policy of genocide, as this has been expressed by some of the Brigade." Karlen mentioned that people in unaffected areas were fearful that the brigade would be deployed there. "Such deployment would confirm our fears that a policy of genocide is being contemplated."[18]

The file includes Karlen's notes from his travels to different mission hospitals, such as St. Luke's/St. Paul's in Lupane. His notes indicate that in a two-day period, (February 6 to 8), "27 people with gunshot wounds came or were brought to St. Luke's Hospital as well as 31 assault cases. It could not be established how many people were killed, but a number of corpses have been seen. Soldiers do not bother about the injured and the bodies are left lying about." He concluded, "It seems there is indiscriminate shooting and beating up of women, children and men. People have the impression that the Matabele are being crushed."[19]

---

[17] "Meeting Between DA and Dr – 17 Feb 1983," contained in Defence Advisor to Ministry of Defence, "Events in Matabeleland," February 1983 [no day provided], item 40/1, DEFE 13/1740, BNA. A "kraal" is the name for a rural homestead in southern Africa.

[18] Bishop Henry Karlen to Prime Minister Robert Mugabe, February 12, 1983. contained in Defence Advisor to Ministry of Defence, "Events in Matabeleland," February 1983 [no day provided], item 40/1, DEFE 13/1740, BNA.

[19] Ibid. For a detailed account of the *Gukurahundi* in the Nkayi and Lupane Districts, see Alexander, McGregor, and Ranger, *Violence and Memory*, 217–24.

Other materials included in the defence advisor's report included a statement from Father Pius Ncube, who reported that "the Fifth Brigade 'Gukurahundi' are cruel and ruthless on the civilians." He reported that when civilians could not identify dissidents, the soldiers "beat the people mercilessly or shoot them." Among other casualty figures, Father Ncube reported that "[a]t Mlagise North of Gwaai Sdg [Siding] more than 50 were shot dead."[20] A report was provided to Bishop Karlen of an exchange on February 9 between a military commander and one of the people in the audience of survivors outside the clinic arranged to hear from the 5 Brigade officers:

Father of 6 month old baby whose mother was shot and killed with the baby on the back, asks what he should do now. Reply from the soldier next to the Commander: 'You should be dead – you must have run away.' The nurses should not treat the injured but kill them. He was cautioned by the Commander.[21]

These reports were mostly based on observations of only a few days at the beginning of the 5 Brigade activities. It would have certainly been sufficient evidence to raise alarms in London. Journalists thereafter began to present more evidence of killings, beatings, rape, and torture. It was not possible, therefore, for the Zimbabwean government to keep the evidence from the wider world. One of the most perceptive accounts came from the *Guardian's* Nick Davies, who summarized the situation in March of 1983, as follows: "The slaughter of innocent villages in Matabeleland is only the most bloody symptom of a Government clampdown which has seen thousands detained without trial, opponents tortured, the press muzzled, the courts defied and trade unions brought to heel." Davies then identified the core issues at stake. "The Government's response has been equally direct – a deliberate and determined campaign to wipe out the dissidents, to liquidate Joshua Nkomo's Zapu party which is accused of directing them, and to cause

[20] "Report on Incidents involving Atrocities committed by the Government Forces in the Gwaai Siding Area between 30th January and 1st February 1983," contained in Defence Advisor to Ministry of Defence, "Events in Matabeleland," February 1983 [no day provided], item 40/1, DEFE 13/1740, BNA.

[21] "List of Patients Admitted to St. Luke's Hospital from 25.1.83–13.2-83," contained in Defence Advisor to Ministry of Defence, "Events in Matabeleland," February 1983 [no day provided], item 40/1, DEFE 13/1740, BNA.

such terror among ordinary civilians that their popular support will wither."[22] Davies reported of the hope among liberal supporters of Mugabe that perhaps Mugabe was somehow unaware of the 5 Brigade atrocities:

It is a thin hope. ... His own words seem to many to implicate him. In a speech on dissidents to the Zimbabwe Assembly last July, he [Mugabe] warned: 'Some of the measures we shall take are measures which will be extra-legal. ... An eye for an eye and an ear for an ear may not be adequate in our circumstances. We might very well demand two ears for one ear and two eyes for one eye.'"[23]

As Ian Phimister points out, the Western media was surprisingly well informed about the atrocities very early on in 1983, making the lack of international response all the more telling given more powerful Cold War and regional interests.[24]

Nkomo's Temporary Exile to Britain

The entrance of the 5 Brigade into Bulawayo on March 5, 1983 also turned into a search for Joshua Nkomo. As Eliakim Sibanda wrote, "Nkomo's house was searched and ransacked. ... Nkomo beat the military dragnet and fled to Britain via Botswana on March 9, 1983."[25] Nkomo's driver was killed in the attack on his house, and many thought the 5 Brigade were planning to kill Nkomo. After a brief stay in Botswana, Nkomo travelled to Lusaka, Zambia, and then London where a cold reception awaited him from the now pro-ZANU, pro-Mugabe British government. While Nkomo was still in Gaborone, Botswana, the British tried unsuccessfully to pressure Nkomo not to fly to London, with the British high commissioner Wilfred Jones reading Nkomo Britain's "Fugitive Offenders Act," to which Nkomo, according to Jones, "stopped me angrily, saying that this was threatening him and he would not have it." Jones pleaded with Nkomo to reconsider the implications of his traveling to London, telling Nkomo: "He must realise the difficulty of the situation and the

---

[22] Nick Davies, "The Massacre that Misfired," *Guardian* (March 23, 1983), 15.
[23] Ibid.
[24] Ian Phimister, "The Making and Meanings of the Massacres in Matabeleland," *Development Dialogues* 50 (2008), 199–218.
[25] Sibanda, *Zimbabwe African People's Union*, 262.

embarrassment that could be caused all round if he took such a step."
Nkomo replied in his usual style. "He acknowledged the sensitivity of
the situation but said that he had taken many decisions in his life which
were thought unwise at the time but subsequently proved right." Jones
remarked, "Despite further pressure from me he would not budge and
gave no undertaking."[26] Nkomo's flight to London therefore caused
alarm among British officials to the point that Thatcher weighed in on
just how long he should be allowed to stay in Britain. Eager to not upset
Mugabe and ZANU, Thatcher responded to a brief on Nkomo's presence in London by noting in handwriting across the top, "He [Nkomo]
has been given one week only. I see no reason why he should stay here
indefinitely." The brief also mentioned that Zambian president Kaunda
could perhaps receive Nkomo, but it appeared that Kaunda and
Zambia "would try to avoid this. President Kaunda has been at pains
since Zimbabwe's independence to remain neutral in Mr. Nkomo's
quarrel with Mr. Mugabe."[27] British Cabinet notes from March 24,
1983 indicate that Nkomo had "kept a low profile" while in London
for a month, and he had "no formal contacts" with the government.
Thatcher mentioned that she had talked with President Kaunda about
Nkomo's situation. Kaunda had told Thatcher that "there could be no
prospect of reconciliation between the conflicting parties in Zimbabwe
unless Mr. Nkomo returned to the country." Kaunda had told
Thatcher that he was trying to work with the Commonwealth secretary
general to help facilitate Nkomo's return, adding that "[t]here was little
doubt that his life might be in danger if he returned." Thatcher ended
the discussion by noting that "it would be undesirable for the British
Government to have to extend the one month period for which Mr
Nkomo had been given permission to remain in the United
Kingdom."[28]

All of these cold shoulders must have been extremely difficult for
Nkomo to take, especially looking back at his substantial efforts working with David Owen's earlier attempts to negotiate with Smith to put

[26] From Gaborone to FCO, "Your Telno 042: Nkomo," March 11, 1983, PREM
      19/1154, BNA. Thatcher had read this telno, as she initialed it and it has her
      characteristic underlining.
[27] R. B. Bone FCO to A. J. Cole, PM's Office, "Nkomo," March 14, 1983, PREM
      19/1154, BNA.
[28] "Conclusions of a Meeting of the Cabinet held at 10 Downing Street on
      Thursday 24 March 1983," CC(83) 11th Conclusions CAB 2–3, 128/76/11,
      BNA.

Nkomo in charge, not to mention the years of support Nkomo received from Kaunda. The 1980 elections had forced Nkomo into an international political wilderness. A South African intelligence report from this time noted that the Soviet ambassador in Lusaka had scrambled to make sure Nkomo did not head to Moscow, again not wanting to upset their plans to warm up to Mugabe at this time.[29] Nkomo would spend five months in Britain and returned "when the [Zimbabwean] Government tried to deprive him of his Parliamentary seat."[30]

In February 1983, when the first reports of the *Gukurahundi* violence were making it to the international community, the Americans and the British met to discuss what line to take with Mugabe over the situation. The American account of a meeting between the British minister of state, Cranley Onslow, and US assistant secretary of state for Africa, Chester Crocker, indicates that both Britain and the United States wanted to support Mugabe and his government, rather than publicly criticize the Zimbabwean government for the 5 Brigade atrocities. The notes from the meeting state that "when asked whether Garfield Todd's reaction that this was the beginning of the end of reconciliation didn't make sense, Onslow replied that one could make the case that Mugabe no longer believes that Nkomo will contribute to the reconciliation process." Crocker reportedly responded to Onslow "that Mugabe does not appear to have given Nkomo a chance and expressed concern that the present situation could acquire its own dynamic in the United States, negatively affecting both the outcome of the current budget hearings and our ability to handle questions from the press." The Americans reported that "[b]oth sides agreed that while we should not try to make excuses for the GOZ [Government of Zimbabwe], the situation does argue strongly for not turning our back on Mugabe and opening the door for South African destabilization or Soviet intervention."[31] When Onlsow met with Crocker and Wisner a week earlier, Crocker and Wisner were clear that the Cold War implications of Western support for Mugabe meant that the news

---

[29] "Zimbabwe: Uitwyning van Joshua Nkomo" ["Zimbabwe: Expulsion of Joshua Nkomo"], March 16, 1983. DFA 1/156/198.6, South African DFA archives, Pretoria.

[30] High Commissioner Ewans, "Annual Report, 1983," January 3, 1984, item 6, FCO36/1929, BNA.

[31] Secretary of State to American Embassy London, "Crocker meeting with UK Minister of State Cranley Onslow," February 26, 1983, Case No F-2017–0020, https://tinyurl.com/ydh8d4kp.

from Matabeleland should not induce any rash response from the Anglo-Americans. Crocker indicated "that reports of atrocities in Matabeleland by the Fifth Brigade clearly were well-founded. This kind of action, conducted by North Korean trained units, would have an effect on Congress and US opinion generally." Onslow reportedly told Crocker that "we share Crocker's concern, but needed to act in a way which could help and not further complicate the situation." Onslow recommend making their concern clear to the Zimbabwean authorities, but "to the avoidance of dramatic or highly publicised gestures." The British noted that "the prospects of influencing the situation and maintaining Western interests in Zimbabwe" pointed to the need to maintain their assistance there. Lawrence Eagleburger, President Reagan's undersecretary of state for political affairs, is reported to have "agreed that the need in Zimbabwe was to 'stay with it.'"[32] Onslow and Eagleburger met again on March 1, 1983, and they discussed "Zimbabwe Army excesses in Matabeleland." The notes from the meeting indicate that "both sides agreed on the necessity to watch the 'worrying' situation very carefully and to keep in close touch in an effort, as Onslow put it, 'to limit damage.'" Both Eagleburger and Onslow "concurred that the suspension or termination of aid to Mugabe would be unwise."[33]

Rationalizing *Gukurahundi*

It was impossible, really, for diplomats to paint the ex-ZIPRA dissidents in convenient Cold War terms. Even though Mugabe continued to tell the story of continued Soviet supplies of weapons to ZAPU and ZIPRA after the Lancaster House agreement and the elections, diplomats now dismissed this as nothing more than an idle threat, given that the Soviets had shown no indication that they would continue to support Nkomo and instead were trying their best to curry favor with Mugabe and ZANU. The more realistic supporter of ex-ZIPRA dissidents was South Africa in the form of weapons, ammunition, and some

[32] Washington to FCO, "Your Telno 291: Zimbabwe," February 19, item 18, DEFE 24/2801, BNA.
[33] "FCO Minister of State Cranley Onslow's Call on Under Secretary Eagleburger," March 1, 1983, Unclassified US Department of State, Case No. F-2012–29009, Doc No. C05256578, Date: 09/24/2013, DoS FOIA Reading Room, https://tinyurl.com/ydh8d4kp.

training in South Africa. However, as damaging as "Super-ZAPU" may have been, they did not account for those ex-ZIPRA fighters who made up the small but destructive group of dissidents that had left the ZNA on their own or been demobilized from the ZNA and decided to fight the central government.[34] Richard Werbner, who did extensive ethnographical research in the areas affected by the *Gukurahundi*, suggests that this group's motives were a "quasi-nationalism" reflecting the ways dissidents built a defense of primarily the SiNdebele-speaking communities of the southwestern parts of Zimbabwe, and also parts of the Midlands province. Significantly, Werbner makes the point that this quasi-nationalism, and "the polarization of two quasi-nations or super-tribes, the Shona against the Ndebele," was the product of contemporary politics.[35] Werbner notes that the original goals of both liberation movements were to create a unified, nonracial nation state. However, "the recruiting of the armies on a regional basis was itself a process that people who came to be identified by language as Shona or Ndebele."[36] Werbner makes a clear and important statement on what was happening in Zimbabwe: "The catastrophe of quasi-nationalism is that it can capture the might of the nation state and bring authorised violence down ruthlessly against the people who seem to stand in the way of the nation being united and pure as one body."[37] The ability of these dissidents to operate in territories with distinct linguistic and historical differences from the majority chiShona speaking regions of Zimbabwe meant that, ultimately and rather conveniently, diplomats increasingly tended to accept the "tribal" or ethnic explanation for dissident violence presented by Mugabe and others in ZANU.

Rather than emphasizing the political challenges that support for ZAPU presented to Mugabe's party – ZAPU's ability to remain the electoral dominant party in these provinces – diplomats, and more importantly their superiors, tended to accept ZANU's narrative that ZAPU as a party, and Nkomo as a leader, represented a "tribal" threat

---

[34] See Joseph Hanlon, *Beggar Your Neighbours*, 1st ed. (London: Catholic Institute for International Relations, 1986), 180–83.

[35] Richard Werbner, *Tears of the Dead: The Social Biography of an African Family* (Washington DC: Smithsonian Institute 1991), 159.

[36] Ibid.

[37] Ibid. See also the firsthand accounts by those who were victims of the 5 Brigade. Ibid., 160–173.

to the nation state. It was this convenient ability of diplomats to privilege the ethnic explanation that helped them to rationalize the severity of state violence against civilians and ZAPU party members and politicians during the *Gukurahundi* period (1983–1987). This basic idea is fundamental for understanding how diplomats, who should have otherwise been expected to raise serious objections to the reports of violence against civilians, could carry on in 1983 and 1984 as if this violence was something acceptable, or normalized, in an African race state. As Stuart Doran argues, the British, American, Canadian, and Australian diplomats in Harare did not simply "accept" the violence as normalized, but eventually came around to create a collective sense of what could be viewed as "problematic but manageable" in terms of state violence against civilians.[38] I would add to this useful characterization that the diplomatic record also shows that not all foreign diplomats reached a common-sense level of what was manageable, and those that challenged this view found their concerns ignored by higher-level officials in their foreign relations bureaucracies. Those officials in Washington, DC and London tended to justify their overlooking of these civilian deaths and torture by emphasizing African race state themes, such as "tribalism" that, in their minds, such violence could be explained away by precolonial rivalries rather than connecting it to ongoing support for Mugabe and his military. Therefore, the rationalization of Zimbabwean state crimes owed much to a shift toward an African "race state" narrative and trope used by diplomats and foreign affairs bureaucracies reporting on events in Zimbabwe.

One key aspect of this shift is the evidence showing how foreign diplomats relied on white Zimbabweans as their main sources for gauging an acceptable level of state violence. In addition, the relatively small amount of poor treatment of whites in the areas where the 5 Brigade was deployed was also used to contrast accepted levels of African race state violence. A report from March 3, 1983, shows this sort of thinking at work. The BMATT officer reported on the question of whether or not 5 Brigade violence was the consequence of ill-trained soldiers acting beyond their orders, or soldiers following orders to

---

[38] Doran writes, "Articulated or not, most of these countries had made a decision that political violence would not produce a crisis point in bilateral relations unless marked by mass killings over a sustained period. Anything below this threshold would be regarded as problematic but manageable." Doran, *Kingdom, Power, Glory* (Kindle edition, location 10831/20982).

unleash violence against civilians. In a subsection entitled, "5 BDE Modus operandi," the officer explains a racialized logic: "There is now little doubt that the soldiers of 5 Bde have been operating in a controlled manner, carrying out Government policy in their savage treatment of dissidents, potential dissidents and local people who might or might not have given support to the dissidents." The officer argues how, "[o]ne strong indicator to this has been the universally good behaviour in relation to the white people of Matabeleland. Had the killings and beatings been the result of ill discipline, then some whites would almost certainly have been subjected to at least abuse."[39]

British accounts of 5 Brigade action in February 1983 indicate clear orders to avoid engaging with white farmers. High Commissioner Byatt wrote that "Sekeramayi emphasised to me that all commanders had been told to ensure that the white community were treated courteously." As reports of atrocities by the 5 Brigade came in Byatt emphasized that they were ordered not to interfere with whites. Byatt traveled over three days in early February to the Nyamandhlovu and Tjolotjo areas in the Matabeleland North province. He spoke with white farmers and their workers who reported that the operations in Tjolotjo had begun at the beginning of February and were "concentrated on 3 farm compounds where a number of men were beaten or killed." Byatt reported that "[t]he general view amongst the whites and their work force that I spoke to was 'they had some good int [intelligence] because they were the right places [sic].'" Adding to the point that the 5 Brigade were treating whites well, Byatt stated, "Generally the officers have been controlling their soldiers when searching commercial farmers compounds."

Going a bit further, Byatt described some of the information he had heard about how the ZNA hoped to contain the killings of civilians. He related how there had been "excesses including killing and rape in the forest areas and in tribal lands" but that Sekeramayi "dispatched General Sheba Gava [Vitalis Zvinavashe] down to the operational area this week to grip commanders." Byatt's observation after his trip "was that 5 BDE units were under control and operating to a plan." Once again, his test of this was white opinion: "The White community were being courteously treated, were happy that the dissidents had left

[39] "Zimbabwe Situation Report [SITREP] No. 80 - Period 4 Feb to 2 Mar." March 3, 1983, item 20/2, DEFE 24/2801, BNA.

the area but were apprehensive about what would happen if the military withdrew." Byatt reported that Sekeramayi told him the 5 Brigade would not be withdrawn, and that "if necessary barracks will be built for them." Byatt related that in the Tjolotjo area, based on "various reliable reports ... about 30–34 people have been killed of which a number were dissident supporters or active sympathizers."[40]

In another report, Byatt related further evidence from Sekeramayi that the degree of violence was premeditated, down to the region. Sekeramayi had told Byatt on March 3 that "in Matabeleland South (around Gwanda) there has been a marked improvement in the overall situation." Comparatively, "the real trouble had been in Matabeleland North, in Tsholotsho, Nyamandlovu, Nkayi and Lupane." Sekeramayi told Byatt that Matabeleland North was "an area which had seen little fighting during the war and the population had romantic ideas about warfare and their ability to 'deal with the government.' It had been necessary to disabuse them." The "Breaking the Silence" report would later indicate that 5 Brigade was deployed in Matabeleland North in late January 1983. "Within weeks, its troops had murdered more than two thousand civilians, beaten thousands more, and destroyed hundreds of homesteads."[41] Given that this meeting with Sekeramayi took place mid-February, reports of the atrocities were already being discussed.

Sekeramayi told Byatt that he recognized that "harsh action had not helped Zimbabwe's name," arguing similarly as he had to Onslow in early January. "But that, and the government's position, would have suffered as much or more if the increasing dissidence of last year had been allowed to continue." Sekeramayi added, "There had been a risk of a descent towards a Biafra-type situation." Byatt then "reminded him that the Nigerian government had followed up the military phase with a massive unity drive." Sekeramayi "accepted that parallel as valid." Sekeramayi assured Byatt that "the 'current phase' would come to end this weekend. After that the army would be withdrawn but would be told to 'stand still' in its present positions."[42]

---

[40] From BMATT Zimbabwe to MODUK Army, "Operations in Matabeleland," February 17, 1983, DEFE 13/1740, BNA.

[41] Ibid. Catholic Commission for Justice and Peace and Legal Resources Foundation, *Breaking the Silence*, 14.

[42] Harare to FCO, "Your Telno 347 to Washington," March 4, 1983, PREM 19/1154, BNA.

High Commissioner Byatt addressed the question of the Zimbabwe government's role in orchestrating the *Gukurahundi*, and the impact it was having on the many ex-ZIPRA officers in the ZNA in mid-February 1983. He was of the opinion that "[t]he Government's firm policy is certainly having an initial success but much will depend on the future behaviour of soldiers and what sort of follow up action on the civil side is generated." He noted that within the ZNA, "senior ZIPRA officers ... have personally had relatives killed by the army in the last few weeks." Such an observation may have suggested that the killings were much more widespread, and the number killed much higher in this first phase of *Gukurahundi*, than Byatt was reporting. Byatt did indicate that these senior ZIPRA officers "feel powerless to help and are further hindered by the obsessive secrecy that has now developed over all operations which are controlled directly by Nhongo and Gava bypassing both G Branch and Q Branch who are expected to tidy up the resulting nonsenses." Byatt noted that these officers "do not feel trusted and this hurts when they have made sacrifices to support [the] Government and its policy."[43]

The problems for ex-ZIPRA in the ZNA were further exacerbated by Rex Nhongo's announcement that he planned to demobilize 7,000 ex-ZIPRA soldiers from the ZNA. Byatt stated that "the problems that would have created were very apparent to all except Nhongo."[44] The British and others put pressure on Nhongo to rethink such a plan, as it would have immediate impact on the dissident problem and could have potentially led to a rebellion of ex-ZIPRA in the military. Fortunately, after much pressure from ZNA officers and the British advisors, Nhongo walked back this announcement.

Major General Shortis, the leader of BMATT in Zimbabwe, met face to face with Mugabe on March 17, 1983. Shortis's account of the meeting shows he was careful and diplomatic when discussing 5 Brigade with Mugabe. His criticisms were organizational: "I then raised the question of 5 Brigade saying I was not going to talk about Matabeleland but about the importance of improving the command and control and logistic support of 5 Brigade which at present caused them difficulties." Shortis told Mugabe that 5 Brigade's "great asset to

43 From BMATT Zimbabwe to MODUK Army, "Operations in Matabeleland," February 17, 1983, DEFE 13/1740, BNA.
44 Byatt BMATT Zimbabwe to MODUK Army, "ZNA Demobilisation Plan," February 11, 1983, DEFE 13/1740, BNA.

the Government was their loyalty but unless this was controlled and directed they could become a liability." After a detailed recommendation on how command and control could be improved, Shortis described Mugabe's response. According to Shortis, "Mugabe then said that they had no option but to take action in Matabeleland and the use of the 5th Brigade had been 'a humanitarian action to prevent further suffering by the people from the actions of the bandits.'" Mugabe then said this had been "misinterpreted by the press and the world." Shortis replied that he had "been down to the area and quite certainly there had been excesses and innocent people had been killed but also the white commercial farmers felt safer and have been correctly treated." Mugabe blamed ZAPU for not helping to stop the violence and acknowledged that "he now had specific details of some civilians being killed and this would be investigated."[45]

Mugabe then gave Shortis his usual speech about "the intentions of ZAPU," including his rendition of the "Zero Hour" plan from 1976. Mugabe also blamed ZAPU for being "tribal," and for wanting "a government by the Ndebele of the Ndebele whereas his government was a government of Zimbabwe by Zimbabweans not of one tribe or another."[46] Mugabe continued to push his argument that Nkomo and ZAPU were to blame, and that he was justified to act against Nkomo, ZAPU, and by extension, the Ndebele civilian population. To call what he did a "humanitarian action" shows how far Mugabe had convinced himself that he was justified in authorizing the 5 Brigade to act, no matter the cost in human lives and suffering. For Mugabe, this deployment of the military had become a continuation of the war.

A BMATT situation report in early February 1983 provided an account of what the British were hearing about the motivations for the deployment of the 5 Brigade. One such theory was attributed to the "former Deputy Commander of 1 Bde." The theory suggested that "the Security Forces were being launched on a campaign of reprisals etc., aimed at forcing a civil war situation in Matabeleland, in which the Ndebele would be forced to break out weapons from cachés and muster their forces, thereby presenting a proper target for the ZNA." The report went on: "It is too early to say whether this theory has substance,

---

[45] "Record of a Meeting between Mr. Mugabe and Major General Shortis on 17 March 1983," DEFE 24/2864, BNA. Thanks to Allison Shutt for sharing a copy of this file.

[46] Ibid.

but the actions of 5 Bde have more the flavour of pure tribalism, with the Shonas taking it out on the Ndebele. The way in which they are apparently attacking the civilian population as 'supporters' or 'potential supporters' of the dissidents as much as the dissidents themselves, lends evidence to the latter theory."[47] With hindsight, both theories are in some ways plausible explanations without necessarily relying on a "tribalism" causation. Similar to the analysis of many so-called "tribal" wars in postcolonial Africa, the prerequisite for such conflicts is an intelligentsia and leadership willing to mobilize political violence around ethnicity, most often to use state power against a minority group or rival.[48] That was the case in mobilizing 5 Brigade, but it must also be seen as a cynical political calculation by Mugabe and others in ZANU to try to destroy Nkomo and ZAPU and push for a one-party state.

US Cold War Considerations

Likely because he was in Harare and had heard more testimonies of the violence, Ambassador Keeley was adamant about the need to try to influence Mugabe to reverse course. On February 17, 1983, he wrote a memo to the State Department entitled, "Fifth Brigade Behavior in Matabeleland." Keeley started by stating that he was not so concerned with figuring out how much Mugabe knew about the violence:

There can be little doubt that Mugabe went along with or actively supported this mailed fist policy, but the question remains whether he fully comprehended how the Fifth Brigade was going to behave toward innocent civilians. My guess is that he went along with a proposal to use the Fifth Brigade 'to root out and kill or capture the dissidents.'

---

[47] "Zimbabwe Sitrep No 79. Period 7 Jan to 3 Feb 1983," February 3, 1983, DEFE 24/2801, BNA.

[48] One of the clearest presentations of how intelligentsia and politicians mobilize ethnic violence in postcolonial Africa is in Bill Berkeley, *The Graves are Not Yet Full: Race, Tribe and Power in the Heart of Africa* (New York: Basic Books 2002). See also Preben Kaarsholm, *Violence, Political Culture, and Development in Africa* (Oxford: James Currey 2006); and, more recently, Mahmood Mamdani, *Neither Settler nor Native: The Making and Unmaking of Permanent Minorities* (Cambridge, MA: Harvard University Press, 2020) and Achille Mbembe, *Necropolitics* (Durham, NC: Duke University Press, 2019).

Keeley argues that the Zimbabwean Central Intelligence Organisation had presented Mugabe options for responding in January, which "generally recommended a political settlement coupled with increased military/security presence in Matabeleland." However, Keeley said that it had "advised against undertaking military operations because they would be counterproductive." Keeley says it wasn't known what recommendations the military had made, but that "around mid-January" they started to hear about "'Operation Samaritan,' which is what has been happening." Keeley then wrote, "A great deal of damage has already been done. We cannot restore the dead and wounded nor reverse the profound alienation of the Ndebele people that has already transpired. What can be aimed for is a cessation of this disastrous policy." Keeley went on to report that Garfield Todd had presented "a thick packet of testimony to Muzenda, Munagagwa [sic], and Sekeramayi," and that he knew that one or more of them had passed it on immediately to Mugabe. "Now he has no excuse not to act."[49] Judith Todd explained how Henry Karlen, the Catholic Bishop of Matabeleland, worked to make sure the reports of atrocities against civilians reached the highest ZANU leaders. Judith Todd and others also made sure that ZANU leaders received these reports.[50]

Keeley, in his own reporting, discussed why it was difficult to say what the United States should do at this stage to help reverse Zimbabwean government policy. He said that this situation was not just an issue of a bad policy choice, but "the very fundamental issue of relations between the two parties, between the Ndebele and the Shona (a struggle for dominance dating back a century and a half)." Here Keeley begins to put forward the ethnic causation argument, although

[49] Ambassador Harare to SecState WashDC, "Fifth Brigade behavior in Matabeleland," State 061177, March 5, 1983 (contains text of Ambassador Keeley's reply to Crocker dated February 17, 1983), UNCLASSIFIED US Department of State, Case No. F-2012–29009, Doc No. C05256616, Date: 09/24/2013, https://tinyurl.com/ybul89vm.

[50] Todd, *Through the Darkness,* 49–55; for the campaign to pressure government by Catholics and others, see Diana Auret, *Reaching for Justice: The Catholic Commission for Justice and Peace Looks Back at the Past Twenty Years, 1972–1992* (Harare: Catholic Commission for Justice and Peace, 1992); and Michael Auret, *From Liberator to Dictator: An Insider's Account of Robert Mugabe's Descent into Tyranny* (Cape Town: David Philip Publishers, 2009); and Timothy Scarnecchia, "Catholic Voices of the Voiceless: The Politics of Reporting Rhodesian and Zimbabwean State Violence in the 1970s and the Early 1980s," *Acta Academica* 47, no. 1 (2015), 182–207.

he immediately brings it back to the political causation of removing Nkomo and ZAPU, and "in fact the very outcome that everyone involved in the negotiations for a Rhodesian settlement most feared: a post-independence civil war between the two wings of the Patriotic Front liberation movement." Keeley also offered his perspective on Nkomo and ZAPU's position. He said that the "Ndebele/ZAPU side are convinced, from Nkomo on down, that the elections were fraudulent and that they were denied their share of power, despite their major contribution to the successfully concluded liberation struggle." Keeley gave his interpretation of what he saw in the motivations of ZAPU, saying they were "determined to resist Shona domination and Nkomo and his supporters, at least, demand a fifty-fifty power sharing arrangement at a minimum (though they probably secretly believe they should be running the show)." At the same time, Keeley reported that "ZAPU denies it has any responsibility for the dissidents." In terms of future US/Zimbabwe relations, Keeley recommended against the use of US leverage to try to resolve the issue, as he believed ZANU would respond defensively, arguing their military operations were done to make it possible for future development. He ended his report stating how difficult it had become to talk with Mugabe, who had become "unapproachable": "it has only been with the greatest expenditure of energy and ingenuity that we have been able to get people he ought to see in to see him recently. He is reluctant to receive advice, especially when he can guess in advance what it's likely to be."[51]

The State Department itself was, at first, clear about the desired US position. Kenneth Dam, the deputy secretary of state in the Reagan administration, wrote instructions to southern African ambassadors on March 4, 1983. In his instructions, Dam noted that ZANU leaders wanted to put the blame for the violence on the South Africans, which the United States did not believe was wholly accurate. Dam also noted that evidence pointed to Mugabe approving the tactics used "to allow the fifth [brigade] to smoke out the dissidents," but also mentions that Mugabe may not be fully aware of "the methods the unit is employing and is therefore unaware of the ramifications of his decision." Dam noted the difficulty in getting through to Mugabe, and how his

---

[51] Ambassador Harare to SecStateDC, "Fifth Brigade behavior in Matabeleland," State 061177, February 17, 1983, UNCLASSIFIED US Department of State, Case No. F-2012–29009, Doc No. C05256616, Date: 09/24/2013, https://tiny url.com/ybsnphee.

"testiness when confronted on GOZ misbehavior," would make it "difficult to get him to move to reverse the present disastrous course in Matabeleland." Dam strongly concluded, "We are compelled never-theless to try."[52]

In the next few weeks, Keeley put his energy into attempting to ensure that Mugabe was aware of the negative press he and his government were receiving in the United States. He sent a packet of news clippings to Bernard Chidzero, the finance minister, asking him to try to speak with Mugabe about 5 Brigade atrocities. It would later turn out that Chidzero would sit next to Mugabe as they flew to India together. Keeley met Chidzero at the sending-off ceremony in Harare, and Chidzero asked Keeley if he could share the articles with Mugabe. Keeley was pleased to report back to the State Department that his strategy had worked.[53] Underlying the US strategy was a larger preoccupation that continuation of state violence against civilians would undermine the ambitious southern African policy of Chester Crocker, the assistant secretary of state. The larger American interest evolved to focus on keeping Zimbabwe as a model of racial reconciliation and an ally of the West.

The following day, February 18, 1983, Keeley was to report out the coverage of a speech by Mugabe. *The Herald* newspaper covered the speech, with the headline "Bandits Will Be Crushed Says Mugabe." Mugabe told the audience in Chipinge's Gaza stadium, "ZANU(PF) won the country through the barrel of the gun and it will use the gun to destroy dissidents and safeguard the country's independence." Mugabe added, according to the reporter's summary, that "5 Brigade (Gukurahundi) would not leave Matabeleland until every dissident had been routed." Mugabe explained that the "dissidents were fighting a tribal war to put Cde [Comrade] Nkomo into power but this would never happen in Zimbabwe." Mugabe asked the crowd rhetorically, "Who do they think they are? Who does Nkomo think he is? In Zimbabwe there is no important person expect the povo [poor]."

---

[52] Fm SecState WashDC to AmEmbassy Dar es Salaam, Maputo, Harare, "GOZ Decision to send Fifth Brigade into Matabeleland," March 4, 1983, Unclassified US Department of State, Case No. F-2012–29009, Doc No. C05256608, Date: 09/24/2013 https://tinyurl.com/ybsnphee.

[53] American Embassy Harare to SecState Washington, DC, "Zimbabwe: Matabeleland Developments," Harare1572, Unclassified US Department of State, Case No. F-2012–29009, Doc No. C05256606, Date: 09/24/2013 https://tinyurl.com/yxk372qa.

Mugabe added, "The povo elected us and we will rule by the povo's wishes."[54]

Chester Crocker wrote to Secretary of State George Shultz on March 4, 1983, to outline US policy goals for Zimbabwe. After agreeing with Minister Onslow that the United States and Britain should support Mugabe by avoiding public criticisms of him and his government over reports of military brutality and killings of Zimbabwean citizens, Crocker wrote a detailed analysis of the Zimbabwean internal situation for Shultz. Crocker's summary confirms that he and others were now viewing Zimbabwe as an "African race state," and felt it was the responsibility of the United States to use their leverage to keep Mugabe's conflict with Nkomo and the Ndebele from influencing Cold War politics. Part of this strategy involved keeping whites in Zimbabwe. Crocker began his historical background by stating that "like African leaders since the wave of Independence began in 1957, he [Mugabe] wants to consolidate his power. In practice this means the suppression of the rival, minority Ndebele tribe by the Shona, who triumphed through Mugabe's ZANU party in the 1980 independence elections." Crocker added, "This comes against a background of centuries of tribal rivalry, characterized in the past as well by violence." Crocker coupled this "African state" trope with Mugabe's "need ... to maintain a climate of law and order in Zimbabwe that encourages the still economically necessary white minority to stay." Here Crocker invoked a common contrast in this trope, the perceived tensions between a "tribal" versus "modern" state.

Crocker suggested to Shultz that Mugabe's gamble may likely result in even greater violence. "From Mugabe's perspective, the key question is whether turning the Fifth Brigade loose on the Ndebele will succeed in crushing dissidence and restoring law and order, or whether, in fact, it will drive the Ndebeles – *a warrior people historically*, into an even more violent, organized and disruptive alienation." Crocker said although it was still not clear what would happen, they suspected that "the latter will be the result, with various serious consequences for Zimbabwe's own future prospects." Such thinking ignored the political reality of the moment: that ZAPU and ex-ZIPRA soldiers

[54] American Embassy Harare to SecState WashDC, "Mugabe on Dissidents," Harare01194, Unclassified US Department of State, Case No. F-2012–29009, Doc No. C05256569, Date: 09/24/2013, https://tinyurl.com/yyycjnyb.

were in no position to organize and mount an effective counter offensive against the Zimbabwean government and the ZNA.

Crocker clarified his argument to get at his real preoccupation that "ironically, this course could play right into the hands of Mugabe's least favored foreigners – the Soviets and the South Africans." At this point, Crocker argued that there were two different positions among South Africans. First, there was the position of those who stand to benefit from a stable and economically successful Zimbabwe, "as a multiracial society would have fed a hope that there is a viable alternative to racial separation as the basis for society." He went on to outline the other position: "That was exactly what some other white South Africans were worried about; for them, it was a good thing that it be seen that blacks were not able to run a multiracial nation successfully." Crocker argued that South Africa had therefore "played a game of economic cat-and-mouse with Zimbabwe and provided clandestine military assistance to the ZAPU dissidents and other opponents of Mugabe's government, fanning the already existing sparks of Ndebele and white resentment of the ZANU/Shona triumph in the elections."[55]

Crocker's main concern revolved around avoiding the evidence of Zimbabwean government's state crimes interfering with his plans for southern Africa. His main worry was that two strongly opposed groups in the United States could both argue for a reduction in US foreign aid to Zimbabwe. Crocker understood that the "Human Rights constituency sees the Fifth Brigade's actions as the US associated with yet another brutal government." He also identified in the United States, "the people who wanted Ian Smith to rule forever in Rhodesia," who would wish to "see cutting off aid to Zimbabwe despite the fact that one reason for Mugabe's action is to preserve a stable climate for whites in Zimbabwe." For Crocker, the risk was that both groups could do harm by "zeroing in on aid and possible Peace Corps programs in Zimbabwe, ... thus stripping us of the tools to influence Zimbabwe and to continue to build good relations."[56] It was, therefore, the threat

---

[55] To the Secretary from AF- Chester A Crocker, "Information Memorandum: A Strategy to Deal with the Zimbabwe Problem," March 4, 1983, FOIA Virtual Reading Room, US Department of State, Case No. F-2012–29009, Doc No. C05256585, Date: 09/24/2013, https://tinyurl.com/ycu6ngb2. Italics added by author.

[56] Ibid.

of future American domestic pressure caused by the coverage of the violence that was the most damaging to Crocker's wider southern African Cold War strategy.

Keeley and Crocker had an illuminating exchange on March 11, 1983, after receiving the news of the attack on Nkomo's home in Bulawayo and Nkomo's subsequent exit from Zimbabwe to Botswana. Crocker replied to Keeley's account of the recent events with a clear understanding that these events were a political crackdown that was "discouraging prospects for return to stability and reconciliation." Crocker summarized the situation as a political debacle: the Zimbabwean government's "readiness to use brutal force, distortions, smear tactics, and scapegoating to destroy ZAPU, eliminate Nkomo politically, and intimidate the Ndebele under cover of anti-dissident operations are all disheartening."[57] Having outlined the serious political issues facing Zimbabwe, Crocker then instructed Keeley that they "must keep in mind several broader issues and themes that are central in Washington thinking." These included his belief that it was "logical and historical" that Britain should take the lead. Another theme was the issue of the US assistance program to Zimbabwe, and how it would come under pressure from the media, the public, and "Congressional criticism."[58]

Crocker's third point was the most significant in terms of Cold War perceptions of Zimbabwe. Crocker wrote that "it is clear beyond question that GOZ 'strategy' plays directly into Soviet and certainly SAG [South African government] hands." The rest of the memo to Keeley indicated that new signs of Mugabe trying to "at least explore more 'normal' relations with Moscow" were "troubling in several respects." Crocker said that such a decision suggested "basic lack of realism about Zimbabwe's margin of maneuver." Crocker then suggested two possible rationales for this move: one might be "to smoke out definitively Soviet intentions toward ZAPU," the other to "reflect a view that Harare will need eastern support to do things that western friends might shrink from."[59] In Crocker's Cold War logic, it was thus

---

[57] S Harare 1726 sent FM SecState WashDC to AmEmbassy London for AF Assistant Secretary Crocker from Keeley, "Nkomo," March, 1983, Unclassified US Department of State, Case No. F-2012–29009, Doc No. C05256614, Date: 09/24/2013, https://tinyurl.com/y89bb9b9.
[58] Ibid.   [59] Ibid.

better to not criticize Mugabe, should that criticism push him closer to the Soviets.

Keeley replied to Crocker's instructions the same day, and his reply included his own criticisms of the standard US line of following Britain's lead in this situation. At first Keeley agreed with the idea that Britain should take the lead. He then quickly goes "off the record" to say, "We don't entirely share the FCO's confidence about how much of a lead their representatives here are willing and eager to take." He asks Crocker parenthetically "to protect our relations with our British colleagues, with whom we have always worked closely," but then provides a fairly stark and critical impression of his British counterparts, starting with High Commissioner Byatt. "The UK High Commission has always, since Independence, cared more about the UK's bilateral relations with the GOZ and has not been inclined to participate in demarchés that might cause them damage." Keeley stated that Byatt is scheduled to leave Harare "after nearly a three-year tour and a decade of involvement with the Rhodesian problem." He suggested, therefore, that Byatt "doesn't want to go out on a low note. That is, a GOZ–UK confrontation over the GOZ's strategy for Nkomo, ZAPU, and the Ndebele and Matabeleland." Keeley also had some off the record criticisms of General Shortis of BMATT, with whom he had spoken with "ten days ago, before he'd received his instructions on what to say about Matabeleland." Keeley said that he found him "excessively defensive about what has been going on in Matabeleland," and that he was "almost an apologist for the GOZ." However, Keeley then stepped back from overtly criticizing General Shortis, noting his obvious "vested interest in the success of BMATT's armed forces integration exercise," and stating that Shortis "tends to downplay the dangers of a blow-up which would scuttle that long and arduous effort." In the end, Keeley rationalized Shortis's blinders because, "[b]y all accounts it has been successful to the degree BMATT could make it so, in the face of a long-standing political and tribal conflict BMATT were powerless to affect." By referencing the "tribal conflict," Keeley was expressing the standard response in which "tribalism" was used to distance Western interests from any responsibility or culpability over the behavior of the Zimbabwean military and intelligence organizations, even when these same interests were supplying funding and training to these institutions.

Keeley then turned back "on the record" in his telegram to Crocker: stating, "We are as perplexed as you about Mugabe's role in the whole affair." Keeley stated that he "gets the sense that he has allowed others to 'do the necessary,' that is, whatever they think is necessary to bring the dissident problem under control, while wishing to keep his hands clean as far as possible, so that it doesn't appear he has abandoned his much-admired policy of national reconciliation." Keeley repeated a phrase that was often used by Western diplomats since Mugabe returned to the scene in 1975: "To some extent he has become a captive of events beyond his control. He has to maintain control over the faction-ridden and fractious ZANU party, which requires that he bend to the wishes and impulses of his more militant colleagues when the pressure from that quarter becomes too great."[60] Keeley added, "I am not trying to apologize for his recent behavior but rather to understand and explain it." He thought that Nkomo leaving Zimbabwe had "in a way ... lifted a great burden from his [Mugabe's] shoulders." Keeley went on, "He has not liked or trusted Nkomo for the past twenty years and could no longer work with him. There are others in ZAPU he can work with." Keeley would learn more about the state crimes committed against citizens during the *Gukurahundi* and become more critical and also supportive of more critical voices in Zimbabwe.

On March 25, 1983, the CIA presented a "Warning Report: Sub-Saharan Africa" based on feedback from Vice President Bush's trip to Africa in November 1982. The report outlined the trouble spots in Africa for Cold War conflicts, which included Zimbabwe. The report warned that the officials accompanying Bush had heard of "considerable concern ... over the potentially serious internal security problems that are developing in the wake of the government's often heavy-handed military efforts to suppress dissidence in Matabeleland, the base of opposition leader Joshua Nkomo's popular support." It suggested that "most analysts feared that there would be a continued and perhaps rising level of violence there in the next few months – possibly involving white civilians – even though the government's military operations appear to be winding down."[61]

An additional CIA report, dated March 23, 1983, argued that the crackdown on ZAPU had led Mugabe to become "substantially more

---

[60] Ibid.

[61] Acting National Intelligence Officer for Africa, "Warning Report: Sub-Saharan Africa," NIC #2209–83/1, March 25, 1983, CIA-RDP91B00776R000100010030-7, Approved for Release 2008/11/14.

25X1

Figure 10 Map of Zimbabwe. CIA, "Zimbabwe: ZANU-ZAPU Rivalry and Intelligence Assessment," April 1983.

strident" in his rhetoric, "blaming his problems on South Africa and its alleged Western backers." The report noted that Mugabe "clearly resents the criticism of the Western press has made of his handling of Ndebele dissidence, and he has accused US and other Western media of following a double standard in the coverage of violence in Matabeleland." The report suggested that this "deepening cycle of repression and violence in Zimbabwe already has undermined an important Western goal: the creation of a moderate, democratic, multi-racial society in Zimbabwe to serve as an example for South Africa." The intelligence report did not see a threat from any possible Soviet and South African role in the conflict. That was first because the CIA saw the Soviets as courting Mugabe, even providing the Zimbabwean government with the first Soviet weapon shipments in March 1983. Secondly, the CIA doubted South Africa would intervene in Zimbabwe as they were in Angola or Mozambique, "in part because ZAPU's tribal base is too small – the Ndebele are about 16 percent of the population – and geographically localized to support a viable insurgency."[62] A few weeks later, on April 5, 1983, the CIA issued a special analysis entitled, "Zimbabwe: More Instability Ahead," where the same points were made as to why there was little chance of a ZAPU insurgency, and little incentive for South Africa to become more involved. But the "Outlook" section reiterated the concerns about what the repression in Matabeleland meant for relations between the Zimbabwean government and whites. "Mugabe's abandonment of a moderate course toward the Ndebele may encourage ZANU hardliners to push for more radical approaches toward the whites or the economy. Such moves could destroy Zimbabwe's reasonably successful economic and political relations with the West." The report concluded that "if the cycle of dissident terrorism and government repression continues, relations probably will deteriorate further. As a result, Western governments will find it harder to justify their aid programs to Zimbabwe."[63] This latter point reiterated Crocker's big worry as well, that the violence jeopardized US aid programs to Zimbabwe, without which it was difficult to keep Mugabe part of the Western alliance to assist with Namibia and Crocker's plans for southern Africa.

British Responses to Initial *Gukurahundi* Reports

For all of Ambassador Keeley's criticism of Byatt, there is archival evidence that Byatt did provide his government a more critical assessment of Mugabe and the 5 Brigade violence. For example, in a confidential "Short Assessment of the Situation and Prospects in Zimbabwe," dated April 7, 1983, Byatt wrote that while "[s]tatesman-like in many of his policies, Mugabe has made repeated mistakes over ZAPU and the Matabele." Byatt stated that Mugabe "overestimates both the threat they pose and the efficacy of his own weapons (army, police, etc) in confronting it." He argued that "it is almost impossible to deal with a guerrilla/terrorist situation of this kind by military means alone, not backed by a careful political and intelligence effort."[64] Here

---

[62] CIA Director of Intelligence, "Zimbabwe: The ZANU-ZAPU Rivalry: an Intelligence Assessment, March 23, 1983, CIA-RDP84S00552R000200030002 -4, Sanitized Copy Approved for Release 2011/07/05.

[63] CIA Special Analysis, "Zimbabwe: More Instability Ahead," April 5, 1983, CIA-RDP85T01094R000200010065-3, Approved for Release 2008/06/10.

[64] Byatt to Secretary of State [Onslow], "Zimbabwe," April 7, 1983, E28 DEFE 24/2788, BNA.

though, he puts much of the blame for civilian deaths on the 5 Brigade: "General Shortis tells me that the Brigade's operational command is a shambles. That may explain why much of the killing of civilians happened." He also thought this may explain why dissidents were able to kill white farmers in areas the 5 Brigade was deployed. Byatt noted, "The farmers are an attractive target because they draw international attention and maximise embarrassment to the government."[65] Most importantly, Byatt claimed that the "dissidents do not pose a threat to the existence of Mugabe's government. Nor do the conditions exist for a regular civil war." He then made an important point: "But the behaviour of the Fifth Brigade in January and February has left a deep scar." He compared the situation to Ulster in Northern Ireland, as "although the Matabele minority mostly dislike what the 'boys in the bush' are doing, they condone it because they share the frustrations which provoke it." Byatt stated that unless there were to be outside support from the South Africans or the Soviets, "Mugabe's forces will be able to contain the dissidence but not eradicate it."[66]

One interesting note in Byatt's report was his observation that white farmers in Matabeleland would likely leave the country. The white farmers "will go ... . But their numbers are small. It is a marginal area for farming." He related that white farmers elsewhere in the country "draw such comfort from the fact that ours [Britain] is seen as the dominant external influence on Mugabe's government, and from the presence of our military training team." Byatt essentially concluded that the Zimbabwean government was facing a "very difficult security problem on their hands (albeit partly of their own making)."[67] This sort of write-off of an entire region of the country, given the positive relations between the British and white farmers elsewhere in Zimbabwe, also indicates a race state view of the situation. On a wider scale, the British were also writing off the Ndebele civilians that suffered under the state-sponsored violence of the 5 Brigade. Although not articulated, Byatt's support for Mugabe made clear that these Zimbabweans were unfortunate victims, but not important enough to press Mugabe too hard regarding their treatment. As Ambassador Keeley had noted about Byatt as he left his high commissioner position, he was not going to protest to Mugabe on the issue of state crimes, and he could still continue to downplay the number of

[65] Ibid.   [66] Ibid.   [67] Ibid.

victims in March 1983. He believed it was better to maintain the close relations between Britain and Zimbabwe built up over the first three years of Zimbabwe's existence than publicly criticize Britain's man in Zimbabwe.

Thatcher and Mugabe Meet in New Delhi

On November 24, 1983, British prime minister Margaret Thatcher met with Mugabe and Mnangagwa in New Delhi. While summarizing the political climate in his country, Mugabe provided Thatcher his own version of the first three years of independence, noting that 1980 and 1981 had been largely successful in terms of his reconciliation policies. He then noted that Ian Smith was "bitter that the cause for which he had fought was lost. Others had similar feelings." This statement was followed by a long description of Joshua Nkomo, who Mugabe described as "very bitter." Mugabe explained that Nkomo had wanted to "enter a pact with Mr. Mugabe's party for electoral purposes" after the Lancaster House Conference had ended. "But Zanu had wanted the leadership question to be settled and believed that it was for the people to choose their leader." Mugabe claimed that his party "had pledged themselves to coalition with Zapu whether they won or lost." But, he argued, ZAPU "had broken ranks" by seeking out "an alliance with Muzorewa and even with Ian Smith." After stating that Nkomo "wanted to be leader and wanted his party to have a Parliamentary majority," and that his "bitterness continued to simmer," he made the claim that ZAPU received weapons from the Soviet Union "after the elections," including "56 Sam 7 missiles," and that these weapons "had now come into the possession of the Zimbabwe Government."[68] Earlier Mugabe had claimed that ZIPRA moved weapons into the country after Lancaster House, and now he was claiming they had done so after the 1980 elections. Similar to the way Mugabe appealed to Governor Soames after the elections, he was clear to indicate to Thatcher that he and his ruling party were able to block any potential links between Nkomo and the Soviet Union.

---

[68] Record of a Conversation between the Prime Minister and the Prime Minister of Zimbabwe, 24 November 1983 at the British High Commissioner's Residence in New Delhi," item 2, PREM 19/2004, BNA.

President Mugabe then told Thatcher about ZAPU's "'zero hour' strategy," which Mugabe linked back to 1976 and 1977, when "[t]hey [ZAPU] had decided to leave the fighting to Zanu in the expectation that the latter would become exhausted and would not in the end be able to resist Zapu." Mugabe claimed that once this moment was reached, "[t]hen Zapu would have moved in with an army well equipped with Soviet weapons." Mugabe explained that ZAPU went against orders and did not turn in many of these weapons, caching them instead, as "[t]hey had acquired over 25 large farms for storing these weapons and also for retraining cadres." Mugabe claimed that ZAPU "deliberately ... had not integrated their crack forces." He then confided to Thatcher that "his confidence in Nkomo was immediately dashed" once the arms cachés were found. He then described the removal of Nkomo, and two other ZAPU ministers from the Cabinet, but was quick to point out that he kept some ZAPU Cabinet members. Mugabe concluded, "The situation was now under control but pockets existed e.g. isolated farms where people felt unsafe."[69]

Mugabe also discussed the continued detention of three of the seven white Air Force officers, who were detained after the Zimbabwean courts had dismissed their cases due to evidence of torture. Mugabe mentioned the loss of $36 million in weapons destroyed at the Inkomo barracks outside of Harare in August 1981. He believed that South Africa was responsible for blowing up the arms depot and claimed that it had been the work of a South African agent working in the ZNA. The agent had confessed, but according to Mugabe, he was released by a policeman with "an Afrikaans name."[70] Mugabe told Thatcher this story to further his argument that the media and politicians in Britain and United States were unfairly critical of the continued detention of the accused Air Force officers involved in the sabotage of Thornhill. Mugabe claimed that "orchestration was apparent" in the United States, Britain, the British press, and the Conservative Party's accusations that he was "infringing human rights."

[69] Ibid.
[70] Ibid. Others estimate the value of the weapons destroyed at Inkomo Barracks to be worth Z$50 million. See John Dzimba, *South Africa's Destabilization of Zimbabwe, 1980–89* (London: Macmillan 1998), 55. The destruction of these former ZANLA weapons was another indicator of South Africa's ability to carry out attacks in Zimbabwe.

Thatcher interjected on this point: "there was no orchestration – look at what the press said about her." She told Mugabe that he "was entitled to complain," and went on: "We know about preventive detention from our experience in Northern Ireland where many British soldiers had lost their lives." She did, however, relate that the "allegations of torture" were what had "really provoked criticism in Britain," adding, "of which she thought Mr. Mugabe had no knowledge." In reply, Mugabe stated "that no government would ever instruct that torture be used. But security people had their methods." Mugabe added how "Mr Mnungagwa [sic] was deaf in one ear as a result of torture. Other members of the present Cabinet had suffered similarly." He further qualified that torture was not carried out on government orders, and that the three remaining white officers in detention would not be harmed and would be released soon.[71] When two of the Air Force personnel were freed, they were debriefed in Britain where one of them "wished to make clear that they had discovered from other prisoners in jail that torture was widespread in Zimbabwe. Victims were both white and black, but especially Ndebele." The released airman said, "Torture appeared to be applied to anyone who obstructed the authorities."[72]

Mugabe concluded his talk with Thatcher with a criticism of both whites in Zimbabwe and the disapproval of his government by whites in Britain. "Did these critics recognize the good that he had tried to do? Did the good vanish because of one or two isolated acts?" He then related how the majority of whites in Zimbabwe were content. "They still had their privileges, except the privilege of ruling." He noted that they still "had a far higher standard of living and occupied prominent posts. Firms had not been nationalised and had even been encouraged to expand." Thatcher told Mugabe that she faced many questions about Zimbabwe in the House of Commons, and that she "had been asked to cut off all aid to Zimbabwe." She said that she would not do so as this "would not be conducive to helping those whom we wished to help." At one point, Thatcher interjected that "it was true that critics did not take into account the fact that Mr. Mugabe and his people had suffered and had experienced preventive detention." Mugabe replied

[71] Ibid.
[72] "Record of a Call on Mr Rifkind . . . Thursday 15 September 1983," PREM 19/ 1154, BNA. For a discussion of the use of torture by the Zimbabwean state in the early 1980s, see Karekwaivanane, *Struggle Over State Power*, 199–207.

that he "would never claim that the fact that he had been detained entitled him to detain others. But did people in Britain really expect the situation in Zimbabwe would have been normalised so soon?" Mugabe added, rhetorically, as if he had read CIA director Casey's book, "What was the state of America four years after independence?"[73]

While Thatcher was still keeping up the appearance of collegiality with Mugabe in late 1983, the growing distance between the Anglo-American diplomats in Harare and Mugabe was best articulated in the annual review prepared by High Commissioner Martin Ewans for 1983, the first year of Ewans's tenure in Harare. Ewans was an experienced member of the Foreign Service, having previously served in Karachi, Ottawa, Lagos, Kabul, Dar es Salaam, and New Delhi, before arriving as high commissioner in Harare. Ewans's review of 1983 was so critical of Mugabe that Tessa Solesby of the FCO's Rhodesia Department tried to play down some of his criticisms, stating in her cover letter to the report that Ewans "may paint some of the shadows rather too black, for example in his description of Mugabe who, for all his weaknesses, still has a strong strain of pragmatism and realism and remains (as the South Africans seem to accept) the best leaders available from our point of view."[74] Ewans's opening lines for his review demonstrated his disdain for what had transpired, and his penchant to frame events in a race state framework, where Mugabe and his ruling party are assessed in comparison with "black Africa." Ewans started his report stating: "Not to put too fine a point on it, Zimbabwe has had a rotten year, even worse than 1982, which I see that my predecessor [Byatt] described as 'bad.'" Ewans noted that a "crippling drought and world recession" were partly to blame, but noted that there had been "no lack of self-inflicted wounds" as well. "*The country has by no means sunk to the depths of incompetence and dissolution which are a feature of so much of the rest of black Africa.* But she has finished the year in markedly worse shape than when it began."[75]

---

[73] "Record of a Conversation between the Prime Minister and the Prime Minister of Zimbabwe, 24 November 1983 at the British High Commissioner's Residence in New Delhi," item 2, PREM 19/2004, BNA.

[74] Solesby does say, however, that "nevertheless Mr Ewans's impressions of having a "rotten" year behind him will be shared by many of us at this end."
T. A. H. Solesby Central African Department to Mr. Squire, "Zimbabwe: Annual Review 1983," January 26, 1984, item 6, FCO36/1929, BNA.

[75] High Commissioner Ewans, "Annual Report, 1983." January 3, 1984, item 6, FCO36/1929, BNA. Italics added by author.

Ewans placed the blame for this squarely on Mugabe's autocratic obsession with defeating Nkomo and ZAPU. "The root of much of the trouble has lain in the combination of arrogance and arbitrariness which has characterised Mugabe's increasingly autocratic style of leadership." Here Ewans again compared Mugabe to other leaders in black Africa. "As so often in Africa too much has come to depend on the instincts, good or bad, of one man, and Mugabe's instincts, when allied to inexperience and isolation, have simply been too wrong too often."[76] Ewans specifically placed the *Gukurahundi* on Mugabe's shoulders. "Early in the year he was faced with growing armed dissidence in Matabeleland, caused largely by his own ineptitude the previous year in precipitating an unnecessary showdown with Joshua Nkomo's largely Matabeleland-based ZAPU." Ewans then criticized Mugabe's use of the 5 Brigade: "His response was to send in the 5th Brigade, a cowardly and ill-disciplined Shona unit 'trained' by the North Koreans." High Commissioner Ewans, unlike other British diplomats that may have been less willing to put the blame on Mugabe, continued to describe the disastrous outcome of this use of the 5 Brigade by Mugabe: "Instead of engaging the dissidents, they tried to re-establish governmental authority through a campaign of murderous intimidation of local villagers." He did, however, suggest that the 5 Brigade had been brought into line by the beginning of 1984: "The error was admitted and the 5th Brigade brought to heel more quickly than some outside observers have been prepared to concede, but not before hundreds, or, if some accounts are to be believed, thousands, had lost their lives."[77]

1984

There is not sufficient space here to cover diplomacy in 1984 in detail, nor space to cover the remaining years of violence before the 1987 Unity Accords brokered between Mugabe and Nkomo.[78] Therefore, I will close out this chapter by presenting some evidence from the British and American archives to demonstrate that state violence and crimes did not end with the initial retreat and retraining of the 5

[76] Ibid. [77] Ibid.
[78] See Doran, *Kingdom, Power, Glory*, for in-depth coverage of the remaining years of the *Gukurahundi* period before the Unity Accords, from the perspectives of Commonwealth and South African diplomats.

Brigade in 1983. However, the Anglo-American diplomats, while not actually making use of any serious political leverage to protest the violence, tended to compare subsequent years of violence to 1983, and rationalized that since in their eyes it was not getting worse, there was little more that could be done. In many ways, there was a tendency to accept the claims that the South Africans were trying to use the dissidents to attack Mugabe and his government, and therefore the violence against dissidents, and the civilians who allegedly supplied them, was somehow justified. All the while, Britain's BMATT program was still operational, so there still remained the concern that they could be held accountable for crimes committed by the ZNA, including the 5 Brigade.

The notes from a meeting in London on November 14, 1983 between the FCO's Zimbabwe experts and BMATT Commander, Brigadier Edward Jones, indicated that both groups believed "that the current political climate was more receptive to a continuing role for BMATT and less inclined to believe that cessation of aid was imminent." The topic turned to the 5 Brigade, where "certain reservations were expressed about future behaviour of 5th Brigade in Matabeleland," which would suggest that there was intelligence that they were still operating there. "It was understood that the ZNA felt that they had made a mistake in requesting Korean training assistance and were now actively seeking ways to retrain both 5th Brigade and the Presidential Guard along British military lines." The minutes noted that "[i]t was emphasised that BMATT would not be involved in this retraining apart from the occasional officer coming through on normal courses."[79]

By May 1984, journalists were reporting that BMATT was involved in the retraining of the 5 Brigade. Brigadier Edward Jones of BMATT wrote to London to complain about these stories and denied any BMATT role in retraining 5 Brigade soldiers. He did note, however, that BMATT took in five Brigade officers for training, amounting to eight officers since August 1983. He went on to give his assessment of the 5 Brigade: "For the future there may be some cause to be very cautiously optimistic – though I would not like to be held to this." He said "Brigadier Shiri (Commander 5 Brigade) is currently attending the

---

[79] "Minutes of a Meeting to Consider Policy Regarding Future of BMATT Zimbabwe Held on Monday 14 November 1983," item 11/1, DEFE 24/2865, BNA.

Staff College. He has been heard to be openly critical of the training his Brigade received from the [North] Koreans." Still talking of Shiri and the 5 Brigade, Brigadier Jones added, "On the other side of the coin his Brigade is seen to be 'politically reliable' and very experienced. They have been undoubtedly deployed operationally far too long and are physically and mentally exhausted (they are not the only people in this boat)." Jones ended his letter, "I am very aware of the sensitivities surrounding 5 Brigade and will do nothing to tarnish BMATT's position by unnecessary association with them."[80]

In January 1984, US ambassador Keeley reported to the State Department, based on a front-page *Sunday Mail* story, that Minister Nathan Shamuyarira had, in a speech given in London, described that there was now a new, "second phase of terrorism" in Zimbabwe. Shamuyarira said that South Africa and their "Super-ZAPU" were now mostly responsible for dissident violence and for the killing of whites. Most important, from Keeley's reading of this, was a quote from Shamuyarira saying "ZIPRA elements are no longer in the field as bandits, nor are Joshua Nkomo and other ZAPU leaders involved in the second phase of terrorism." Keeley noted this was "the first time a GOZ minister has said Nkomo and ZAPU are not involved in 'Super-ZAPU activities'; indeed Prime Minister Mugabe said the contrary only last Wednesday in Parliament."[81] The clearing of Nkomo and ZAPU was potentially good news, but the allegations and incriminations from Mugabe, Nkala, and other ZANU elites were not to stop in 1984. Nor, sadly, were the attacks on civilians charged with supporting dissidents. The tactics shifted from the 1983 direct attacks on villages, schools, and clinics. The new pattern was to bring individuals to military camps in Matabeleland. In addition, 1984 would see a new curfew and food supplies cut off to certain areas. The *Gukurahundi* was not over.

In February 1984, the US Embassy in Harare would report back to Washington, DC with the news of numerous additional casualties related to Operation *Gukurahundi*. The source of this information was a team of foreign journalists who visited Matabeleland for three

---

80 Brigadier C. E. W Jones to Major General A W Dennis, May 15, 1984, item 39/1 DEFE 24/2789, BNA.
81 From American Embassy to Secretary of State, "Shamuyarira Says ZAPU Not Involved in Second State Terrorism," Washington, DC, January 30,1984, Unclassified US Department of State Case No. F-2012–29009, Doc No. C05256750, Date: 09/24/2013, https://tinyurl.com/y369pzsb.

days in late February 1984. The accounts of their visit that they shared with Western diplomats reflected new Zimbabwean government and 5 Brigade campaigns in the affected provinces, with the withholding of food aid being deployed as a weapon. In their interviews with "Catholic Church sources," they learned that there was "no food entering the curfew area," and that "the GOZ had been systematically slowing the distribution of maize meal supplies to Matabeleland for some months. Now, however, it was denying it to some areas." Journalists "were shown a letter by senior officials from several churches in Bulawayo dated February 13 to Prime Minister Mugabe. It asked them to take steps to alleviate the food shortages and to curb government forces' excesses against the Ndebele. So far, the church leaders have received no reply."[82]

One of the reporters briefing the Americans had obtained an interview with a retired ZNA general, Mike Shute, a member of the commission established by Mugabe in June 1983 to investigate the 5 Brigade atrocities. Shute told the reporter that "he believed that approximately 30,000 Ndebele have been either abused or killed by the government forces in the past year. Shute stated that the inquiry Commission was so overwhelmed with reports of atrocities during the brief period of time its members held interviews in Bulawayo that the Commission had closed down for the time being." For the Americans, the most significant point of this reporting was the new number of 30,000 victims. In response, the US State Department sent requests to Ambassador Keeley in Harare for further confirmation of these numbers, as these numbers would likely put Zimbabwe's substantial US foreign aid at risk. Of note, these numbers were based on evidence collected internally by the Zimbabwean government's Chihambakwe Commission, on which Shute had served. Shute also expressed doubt that the findings of the Commission "will ever be made public – as promised by Mugabe – because of their controversial nature."[83] In January 1984, ZAPU leader Josiah Chinamano also gave the Americans his prediction that "the Commission won't amount to much, since the GOZ had stacked the cards against a fair report." He explained that four of the five members were "ZANU loyalists," and

---

[82] US Embassy, Harare to State Department "Atrocities and Food Shortages in
     Matabeleland," February 28, 1984, Declassified Case No. F-2012–29009, Doc
     No. C05256769. https://tinyurl.com/y93knhaz
[83] Ibid.

were never sworn in. He also criticized the process used to collect testimonies: "The Commission had refused to interview people in the rural areas, instead requiring them to travel to Bulawayo. Once these people return to their villages, their lives are in serious danger, and no letter of immunity from prosecution will protect them from a bullet."[84]

The deputy chief of mission at the US Embassy in Harare, Edward Lanpher, who had a spent many years working on Zimbabwe during the Carter administration, replied to the questions asked about Shute's number of 30,000 victims, saying that it referred to 1983 numbers, although he added, "But the beatings experienced last year are very much a part of what we are hearing now – how many or how it compares in magnitude with last year we can't say at this point." Lanpher added, "The allegations of withholding of food, if proven, represent an 'abuse' affecting far more than 30,000 people." With respect to a question about how the ZNA was behaving in 1984, Lanpher replied that "this year's offensive against the dissidents is better organized and disciplined than was the case last year. ... Last year the ZAPU political infrastructure was as much a target of the army as the dissidents."[85] There is no indication from the available US files that the large number of alleged victims provided by Shute resulted in any new US approach to Zimbabwe.

A summary of Mugabe's Independence Day speech on April 17, 1984 was sent to the FCO from Harare and indicated the extent to which Mugabe continued to stress the need for a one-party state, as well as his belief that a one-party state was now attainable after the violence of the previous two years. The summary reinforced that the *Gukurahundi* violence was intended to pave the way for a constitutionally recognized one-party state. Mugabe confidently claimed, "Matabeleland was now under control. The security forces were to be commended: disparagement of their methods would be ignored." The summary noted that "[i]n other speeches Mugabe also laid into the churches for, as he put it, allowing themselves to be

---

[84] Embassy, Harare to State Department, "Staffdel Christenson and Stetson had met with Josiah Chinamano," January 25, 1984, Declassified Case No F-2012–29009, Doc No CO5256748, https://tinyurl.com/y6wfxtc6.

[85] American Embassy Harare to Secretary of State, "Reports of Atrocities and Food Shortages in Matabeleland," March 5, 1984, Unclassified US Department of State Case No. F-2012–29009, Doc No. C05256775, Date: 09/24/2013, https://tinyurl.com/y3vx6zse.

ventriloquized by ZAPU over Matabeleland. This was echoed in a nasty editorial in the *Herald*. The Catholics have issued a pained denial."[86]

Deputy Chief of Mission Lanpher, who had personally negotiated with Mugabe and Nkomo during crucial moments of the Lancaster House negotiations, described the depths of Mugabe's rhetorical violence toward Nkomo and the Catholic bishops in Matabeleland. Bishop Karlen was reporting of new 5 Brigade violence in 1984, and Mugabe was asked about this when he made his first trip to Bulawayo in over a year, on April 13 and 14, 1984, under heavy military protection. At the press conference, Mugabe reportedly "rejected allegations of brutality made in a document prepared by Catholic Bishop Karlen . . . which was leaked to the press."[87] The next day, he addressed similarly small crowds in Gwanda. Lanpher described the scene based on reports from journalists. "Helicopters, spotter planes, and armored cars with anti-aircraft guns provided security for the PM's visit to Gwanda." In contrast, "School children, brought in by army truck, under the supervision of armed soldiers who were 'protecting them from dissidents,' listlessly applauded the PM's arrival." Mugabe gave his speech in chiShona with government minister Enos Nkala translating into SiNdebele.

Mugabe held a press conference after his Gwanda speech where he defended the curfew and responded to claims that the Zimbabwean government was promoting "mass starvation," claiming that "this was normal in a 'war-like operation.'" However, "when pressed about allegations of brutality by troops, particularly five brigade, against civilians rather than dissidents, the Prime Minister became very defensive." Mugabe reportedly "said civilians who supported dissidents are dissidents themselves, 'and they all pray to the super-God Nkomo.'"

---

[86] From R. P. Ralph Harare to R.H. Brown, FCO, "Independence Day Celebrations," April 18, 1984, item 11, FCO105/1742 1984, BNA. For more on the response of the Catholic Church and the Catholic Commission for Justice and Peace, see Catholic Commission for Justice and Peace and Legal Resources Foundation, *Breaking the Silence*; Timothy Scarnecchia, "Catholic Voices of the Voiceless: The Politics of Reporting Rhodesian and Zimbabwean State Violence in the 1970s and the Early 1980s," *Acta Academica* 47, no. 1 (2015), 182–207.

[87] American Embassy to Secretary of State, "Mugabe Visited Matabeleland: Rejects Allegation of Atrocities and Slams Nkomo's Book," Unclassified US Department of State Case No. F-2012–29009, Doc No. C05256815, Date: 09/25/2013, https://tinyurl.com/yya8te5y.

He went on to charge the Catholic Church in Matabeleland and Bishop Karlen "of erecting 'a Mammon of their own in the nature of Joshua Nkomo.'" Mugabe told reporters that "others did not question the allegations because they were made by 'A Man of God.' But this man of God was 'worshipping Mammon instead of the real God.'"[88]

Lanpher reported that Mugabe also took questions at the press conference about Joshua Nkomo's new autobiography, which had just been published in Harare. Interestingly, besides having said, "most of the book is 'lies,'" Mugabe brought up two points from the book. The first was a denial that "he had agreed to meet Ian Smith in Lusaka in 1978," which Nkomo claimed Mugabe had agreed to before consulting Nyerere. The second was Nkomo's claims that Mugabe had met with the South Africans in Maputo before the 1980 elections. Lanpher ended the telegram by noting that "the PM was characterized as being withdrawn and ill at ease, a description we have heard frequently in recent years."[89]

The day before Zimbabwe's Independence Day, 1984, the American Ambassador to the UK, Charles H. Price, reported from London on the large number of "horror stories on Robert Mugabe's treatment of the people of Matabeleland" appearing in the British Press, including feature stories in the London *Sunday Times* and the *Observer*. What this new reporting revealed was the continued abuses by the 5 Brigade. The editor of the Observer, Donald Trelford, is reported to have been in Bulawayo the week before, "where he claims he was contacted in the middle of the night at his hotel and taken to see victims of the Zimbabwe Army depredations." The story included a description of "the Brigade Major of the Fifth," who allegedly held up a dead baby to show a village rally, and said, "'This is a dissident baby. This is what will happen to your babies if you help dissidents.' He then dropped the tiny corpse to the dust."[90]

---

[88] Ibid.
[89] Ibid. Nkomo claimed that Mugabe was prepared to meet Smith in the second meeting before Nyerere and the other Frontline State presidents put a stop to direct talks. See Joshua Nkomo, *Nkomo, The Story of My Life* (London: Methuen, 1984), 90.
[90] American Embassy London to State, "Zimbabwe: Tales of Terror from Matabeleland," April 17, 1984, Unclassified US Department of State Case No. F-2012–29009, Doc No. C05256813, Date: 09/24/2013, https://tinyurl.com /y4o4aae2.

The report also described Peter Godwin's story for the *Sunday Times,* Godwin had also travelled to speak with witnesses. Both Trelford and Godwin were hearing reports of the "horrors of Bhalagwe camp, near Antelope mine, an abandoned gold mine where many people died from beatings and electric shock treatment." Godwin reported on a mine shaft he visited, "five miles from a Zimbabwe army camp in Southern Matabeleland." Godwin wrote, "According to eyewitnesses every night for 'many weeks' trucks arrived at the shaft from the direction of the army camp at Balaghwe [sic]. Corpses were unloaded and thrown in."[91] There were additional stories, and a report that Tiny Rowland, the director of Lonrho and owner of the *Standard,* wrote a letter to Mugabe apologizing for Trelford's story. The embassy also reported that Nkomo was in London to promote his new autobiography. An Nkomo interview with BBC is paraphrased to say, "that Since February he [Nkomo] has repeatedly warned Government ministers that atrocities were being committed; he produced witnesses; and it was all ignored."[92]

In addition to reporting the continued use of the ZNA and 5 Brigade to carry out acts of terror and torture, Ambassador Price commented on the difference between British and American thinking about Zimbabwe since 1980. Price said that "we sense that the cup of goodwill for the country in this town [London] is pretty well drained." Price observes that "the British never shared the facile euphoria found in Washington in 1980 that somehow Zimbabwe would serve as a model for peaceful change in Southern Africa." Price said that "British pundits felt the bitterness and divisions would seep through the benign façade of peace and unity exemplified by white school children singing independence songs in Shona at Rufare [sic] stadium." Price reflected on how the "spiral downwards – especially in the crucial Shona/Ndebele relationship – has now gone beyond what was predicted by the cynics here." Price has, in what may seem a sympathetic statement, once again restated the premise of Cold War race state thinking. He

---

[91] Ibid. For a recent discussion of the significance of the Bhalagwe camp in local collective memory, see Shari Eppel, "How Shall We Talk of Bhalagwe? Remembering the Gukuranhundi Era in Matabeleland, Zimbabwe," in Kim Wale, Pumla Gobodo-Madikizela, and Jeffrey Prager, eds, *Post-Conflict Hauntings: Transforming Memories of Historical Trauma* (New York: Springer, 2020), 259–84.

[92] Ibid.

concluded with an observation of British FCO opinion. "We find our FCO contacts benumbed by the current situation and certain of only one thing – there is little they can do to influence events in Zimbabwe for the better."[93]

A few months later, in June 1984, The FCO's Tessa Solesby had the opportunity to visit Harare and Bulawayo. After her visit, her criticisms of Mugabe grew closer to those of High Commissioner Ewans, but she still remained more diplomatic in her approach around the topic of blame. One important exception in her report involved Mugabe's alleged admission that he was responsible for the "starvation curfew" of 1984. Addressing her own question, "But who is giving what orders?", Solesby related how she "found no disagreement with our assessment that Mugabe has the dual aim of containing the dissidents and breaking ZAPU political power and believes tough military suppression can achieve both objectives." Solesby noted that Mugabe "admits to having ordered the 'starvation' curfew and must have realized that the innocent would suffer (though there is happily no evidence of deaths)." Such a claim does not coalesce with the reports the Americans received regarding the extent of the starvations in early 1984.[94] Solesby took a step back, suggesting that "local opinion differs on whether Mugabe can be held responsible for the beatings and killings. He claims that he is not and our High Commission and BMATT tend to give him the benefit of the doubt." She concluded, however, with reports of local talk arguing that Mugabe could have stopped the killings: "On the other hand others with whom I spoke believe that had Mugabe really wished to avoid atrocities he could have ensured that clear orders were given down the line."[95] As careful as Solesby was to not comport total responsibility to Mugabe, she was nonetheless critical, as she included the following summary: "All of this is consistent with at least a readiness by Mugabe to turn a blind eye to a level of violence which we would consider unacceptable."[96] For

---

[93] Ibid.

[94] For the larger context and more details on this phase of the *Gukurahundi*, see Hazel Cameron, "State-Organized Starvation: A Weapon of Extreme Mass Violence in Matabeleland South, 1984," *Genocide Studies International* 12, no. 1 (2018), 26–47.

[95] Miss T A H Solesby, "Zimbabwe: Visit to Harare and Bulawayo," June 12, 1984, item 17, FCO36/1929, BNA.

[96] Ibid.

Solesby, this was a fairly serious criticism, but this point was not accompanied by any suggestion of public criticisms of Mugabe.

On August 15, 1984, the US Embassy reported the following from a response during Mugabe's prime minister's question time concerning his stated goal of establishing a one-party state in Zimbabwe: "Cde [Comrade] Mugabe said a one-party state was a 'desirable state of affairs' as it made for greater democracy. A one-party state was a way of life in Africa, and in Zimbabwe it should be established 'as soon as possible' after the next general election." Mugabe added, amid laughter, "There can be only one cock – we cannot have two cocks. There was only one Mzilikazi, and not two. There was only one Lobengula and not two."[97] As insulting this sort of language was to Ndebele and Zimbabwean history, Mugabe certainly knew it was the sort of "joke" that was meant to ridicule and humiliate Nkomo.

British high commissioner Martin Ewans would report in November 1984 on Mugabe's speech at the funeral of a ZANU-PF senator and Central Committee member. Senator Moven Ndlovu's murder started a new cycle of violence against ZAPU politicians and supporters.[98] Mugabe, according to Ewans, "made a forceful speech castigating ZAPU, whose 'underground armed bandits' he held responsible, saying the time had come to declare ZAPU an enemy of the people and to show them that ZANU (PF) could 'bite.'" The report stated that "Nkomo had denied ZAPU's involvement, but Mugabe has sacked the remaining ZAPU members of his government."[99] The two remaining ZAPU members were John Nkomo and Cephias Msika. This started another phase of anti-ZAPU violence in the *Gukurahundi* leading up to the 1985 elections. The violence continued after, as Norma Kriger notes: "Mugabe was disappointed that ZAPU had retained 15 of the

---

[97] Fm AmEmbassy Harare to SecState WashDC, "Mugabe's Question Time in Parliament," August 17, 1984, Unclassified US Department of State Case No. F-2012–29009, Doc No. C05256850, Date: 09/24/2013, https://tinyurl.com/y c7vhj68. The quote does not appear in the Hansard transcript of this question time, although its appearance in the pro-ZANU *Herald* newspaper makes it likely that Mugabe did say this, but it was not included in the Hansard.

[98] David Coltart describes the crackdown on ZAPU members after the murder and the questionable circumstances of the Senator's murder. No one was ever charged for the murder but this did not stop the abuses of ZAPU members in the area. Coltart, *The Struggle continues*, 160–63.

[99] From Harare to FCO. "Security Situation," November 12, 1984, FCO 105/ 1742, BNA.

16 Matabeleland seats. Almost immediately after the polls closed, violence flared up again, spurred on by Mugabe's advice to his supporters to 'go and uproot the weeds from your garden.'" Once again, Mugabe labelled Nkomo and ZAPU as "enemies of the country."[100]

In February 1985, the US Embassy was reporting "that ZANU, in one way or another, has been going after ZAPU/the Ndebele in a targeted manner." Reports included "beatings administered by bussed-in ZANU youth league groups, and CIO/5 Brigade hit squads taking ZAPU people from their homes in the middle of the night." This hit squad was said to be terrorizing the Beitbridge area to "put ZAPU on notice that the Beitbridge killing of Senator Ndlovu last November would not go unpunished."[101]

The last two chapters have demonstrated the shift in Western diplomatic approaches to the government of Zimbabwe, as well as the competition between Mugabe and Nkomo that had caused much preoccupation in the years preceding the transfer to majority rule in 1980. The key elements of this transition were, on the one hand, the preoccupation with keeping Zimbabwe a pro-Western ally in the Cold War context of the early 1980s, and on the other hand, the shift toward viewing Mugabe and his government as a black African race state as news of brutal state crimes against civilians became well known. The first two years of the transition involved monitoring the treatment of white Zimbabweans, and criticisms from Britain over the torture of white Air Force servicemen, which created a debate over the future of the British BMATT program in Zimbabwe. Once reports of mass killings began to surface in February and March of 1983, Western diplomats attempted to put some pressure on Mugabe and others to stop the killings, usually couched in terms of what these killings were doing to Zimbabwe's international reputation, rather than in terms of direct threats to cut off development and military assistance. Mugabe, however, understood that this localized diplomatic pressure was not likely to result in serious consequences for him or his government in terms of foreign aid and

---

[100] Norma Kriger, "ZANU(PF) Strategies in General Elections, 1980–2000: Discourse and Coercion," *African Affairs* 104, no. 414 (2005), 10. See pp. 7–13 for a fuller discussion of the 1985 violence. See also Coltart, *The Struggle Continues*, 155–59; Doran, *Kingdom Power, Glory* (Kindle edition, location 10206 of 20982).

[101] American Embassy Harare to Secretary State Washington, DC, "Matabeleland 'on Boil' Again," Unclassified US Department of State Case No. F-2012–29009, Doc No. C05256903, Date: 09/30/2013, https://tinyurl.com/y2ut34o8.

continued cooperation with the West. He was, after all, still the Cold
War ally the United States and Britain wanted to support. Even if he was
uncooperative on a number of issues.

While this chapter focused on diplomatic responses to the mass
killings committed during Operation *Gukurahundi*, it is important to
remember that diplomats were not the only pressure groups in
Zimbabwe. As the noted evidence shows, the religious community,
the doctors, and the legal community in Zimbabwe did much of the
actual work to call attention to the killings. Journalists also had
a crucial role in getting the story out, which, in turn, was used by
diplomats to put "soft" pressure on Mugabe and others to "rein in"
the 5 Brigade in 1983. This was not enough to stop the violence.
Another important role in publicizing the evidence of *Gukurahundi*
violence came from Joshua Nkomo himself. He effectively used his
Parliamentary privileges to publicize the accounts of victims in 1983
and in 1984. He also publicized the killings while in London. As Shari
Eppel has pointed out, "what you saw was 5 Brigade on a learning
curve of how to get more clandestine with each passing year." The
public pressure from groups inside Zimbabwe, and international media
coverage, and pressures about media coverage from diplomats meant
that the *Gukurahundi* tactics shifted from the 5 Brigade atrocities of
early 1983, to the use of military bases for killings and torture in 1984,
to the use of "hit squads" and disappearances in 1985.[102]

This chapter, therefore, provides a crucial counterpoint for the "race
state" thesis put forth in previous chapters. The question to consider,
from a race state perspective, then, is how the ways in which diplomats
and entire foreign relations bureaucracies framed Zimbabwean politics
before 1980 allowed them to confidently shift their perspective to fit
a new concept of Zimbabwe as an "African state," where political
violence, lack of rights for citizens, and autocracy was viewed as the
norm. This rationalization would then allow the international community to overlook human rights abuses carried out by the state under the
direction of its highest leaders.

[102] Personal communications with the author, October 23, 2014. For full quote,
see Timothy Scarnecchia, "Catholic Voices of the Voiceless," 202–3. See
Shari Eppel, "Repairing a Fractured Nation: Challenges and Opportunities in
Post-GPA Zimbabwe," in Brian Raftopoulos, ed., *The Hard Road to Reform:
The Politics of Zimbabwe's Global Political Agreement* (Harare: Weaver Press,
2013), 211–50; Eppel, "Gukurahundi."

Conclusion

To step back and assess the entire period covered in this book it is possible to reflect on unintended consequences of this diplomatic history. First, the preoccupation with creating mechanisms to keep whites in Zimbabwe that began with the plans for the Geneva talks was of a much higher priority for Western powers than finding ways to avert a potential civil war between ZAPU and ZANU after independence. From a Cold War and domestic political perspective in Britain and the United States, avoiding a potential "race war" was a greater priority than avoiding a potential "civil war" between ZAPU and ZANU. For many Western diplomats who understood the core political nature of the *Gukurahundi* campaign in 1983, which in its extreme form was an attempt to "wipe out" the opposition once and for all, it became convenient to express this fundamentally political violence as a "tribal" conflict. The use by diplomats and experts of "tribal" or ethnic violence as the central rationalization of state violence allowed them to speak in a shorthand language with other bureaucrats, as well as to their own leadership, that increasingly categorized Zimbabwe and Mugabe as working within a presumably familiar mode of operation that was assumed to be similar to the rest of Africa. In this way, falling back on "tribal" or ethnic difference as the assumed and unquestioned African source of political violence allowed Europeans and Americans to detach themselves from their own nation's responsibilities in creating the context for such postcolonial violence.

This book has looked at the archival records left by those involved in the creation of Zimbabwe as a postcolonial state. The main theme of the book has been to demonstrate a fundamental aspect of twentieth century global diplomacy, the racializing of states during the Cold War. Rather than ascribing racist ideas solely to diplomats from the West as they interacted with African diplomats, it is fundamentally more significant to consider how entire state bureaucracies collectively fell back on ideas of race and ethnicity (tribalism) to rationalize actions and

315

inactions in specific chapters of Zimbabwe's decolonization. An add-itional contribution of this study has been to demonstrate the ways in which Zimbabwean and other African diplomats took advantage of how not only American and British diplomats, but also South African and Commonwealth diplomats, saw their demands through racial lenses.

The diplomatic efforts of Joshua Nkomo and Robert Mugabe in particular, as well as many of their comrades and African diplomats from the Frontline States and Nigeria, help to demonstrate both the limits and opportunities the Cold War offered African leaders and diplomats. The situation created in the mid-1970s by the Portuguese dismantling of the colonies of Angola and Mozambique and the Cuban and Soviet support for the victorious MPLA in Angola dramatically changed the opportunities available to Zimbabwean nationalists. The previous chapters have demonstrated how Nkomo's ZAPU and Mugabe's ZANU took full advantage of this opportunity to negotiate on a much larger stage than previously thought possible. These two leaders, along with other diplomats, demonstrated many important characteristics of African diplomacy when confronted with ultimatums from more powerful Cold War powers. Their ability to use techniques of intransigence at times and cooperation at other times to try to build their own personal political and military power is to be expected. What is likely less expected, and less appreciated, is how well Nkomo and Mugabe worked together in the years from Geneva in 1976 through the Lancaster House talks in 1979.

Even though British diplomats were well aware of the long history of rivalry between Nkomo and Mugabe, they held a positive assessment of the way Nkomo and Mugabe negotiated together as the PF. Lord Carrington's private secretary, Roderic Lyne, would sum up the effectiveness of Nkomo and Mugabe's teamwork at the Lancaster talks. In a 1999 interview, Lyne recalled the "stormy" bilateral meet-ings held with the PF in Carrington's office. He recalls how Nkomo would pound angrily on the coffee table, so much so that those present expected it to eventually break. Lyne also recalled the successful chemistry between Nkomo and Mugabe during these heated talks. "Nkomo would do a lot of talking and shouting and ranting. He was a big powerful man and he'd bring his fists crashing down on the coffee table." Meanwhile, as Nkomo "ranted" on, Lyne remembers, "Mugabe would sit there saying very little, but he was an extremely clever, very astute man. Then he would come in at a certain point with a rapier thrust. He would make some killer point, a point that was really difficult to answer." Lyne summed up the nature of the PF relations at Lancaster: "Nkomo and Mugabe didn't like each other; they were rivals for power. They were very suspicious of each other, but they were also a pretty clever double act and tough to negotiate with; a very wearing process."[1]

There are a number of reasons why this close cooperation between Nkomo and Mugabe as diplomats has not been fully acknowledged in the Zimbabwean historiography. This book has demonstrated that while Nkomo was definitely trying to find a way to become Zimbabwe's first leader, he never betrayed the promise made to Nyerere and the Frontline State presidents to remain in the PF. The preceding chapters show that this was not necessarily a loyalty emanating from Nkomo's personal "character," but rather the pressures he faced to maintain Soviet, Eastern bloc, and OAU military and financial support. The details of the multilateral diplomacy carried out over years in order to get the PF to the negotiating table also reveal an alternative explanation of Robert Mugabe's characterization as an intransigent politician. For many, this pattern is seen as a sign of his strength. In reality, his inflexibility was often linked to his relatively weak position as the outright leader of ZANU. The historical record, at least as can be reconstructed from the sources available from archives to date, demonstrates that Nkomo was often in a better position to be intransigent and more radical than Mugabe. At other times, particularly during August and September 1978, it was Mugabe's confidence that he and ZANU would ultimately come to power that helps to explain his unwillingness to work with Nkomo toward a ceasefire and transfer of power negotiated by the Nigerians, the Zambians, and the British. The continuation of the war, and the escalation of the war after September 1978, led to extensive loss of life among combatants and civilians. This was an unfortunate escalation of the war at a point when the South Africans and the Rhodesians recognized that the liberation war was "unwinnable" from the Rhodesian and SADF perspective, as the South Africans had made clear to the Rhodesians since 1977.

[1] BDOHP Biographical Details and Interview Index, Lyne, Sir Roderic Michael John (Born 31 March 1948), 26.

The ways Nkomo was portrayed at the time and subsequently has unfairly presented him as a leader who would "sell-out" the nationalist interest to cut a deal to make himself the leader. He may have had the chance to do so a few times, but in each case, he insisted on remaining with Mugabe in the PF. It is important to reiterate, however, that his consistent commitment to stay in the PF was done because he understood that to split the PF would amount to political suicide for him and his party. He knew that the military aid received from the Soviets, the Eastern bloc, the OAU, and many European sources would transfer to Mugabe and ZANU if he was seen as initiating the break in the PF to join the internal settlement.[2] In addition, Nkomo's personal rivalry with Bishop Muzorewa meant that he was not going to try and form an alliance with Muzorewa and the United African National Council, even as Western diplomats tried to make this alliance happen.

There are many historical lessons to be learned from the diplomacy conducted to create Zimbabwe. The significant intervention of the Americans in 1975 and 1976 had a large impact on the outcomes of Zimbabwe's decolonization process. Historian Jeremi Suri, in the introduction to his political biography of Henry Kissinger, notes that Kissinger's career saw him "work feverishly to make the world a better place. His actions, however, did not always contribute to a world of greater freedom and justice." Suri diplomatically remarks that Kissinger "contends with his own complicity in unintended consequences."[3] Based on the evidence presented in Chapters 3 and 4, Kissinger in southern Africa seemed to gain personal satisfaction from his complicity with the South Africans and Rhodesians. It seems that Kissinger in particular, was determined to try for the outcome he wanted (i.e., Smith's announcement that he accepted majority rule in two years), and he really "didn't give a damn about Rhodesia" beyond that goal.[4] Kissinger's attempt to "solve" the Rhodesian problem certainly forced the British to get more involved in Rhodesia, something they were generally doing their best to avoid. But Kissinger's insistence on

---

[2] See Gorden Moyo, "Mugabe's Neo-sultanist Rule: Beyond the Veil of Pan-Africanism," in Sabelo J. Ndlovu-Gatsheni, ed., *Mugabeism? History, Politics, and Power in Zimbabwe* (London: Palgrave Macmillan, 2015), 61–74.

[3] Jeremi Suri, *Henry Kissinger and the American Century* (Cambridge, MA: Belknap Press of Harvard University Press, 2007), 15.

[4] This point is made in Stephen Stedman, *Peacemaking in Civil War: International Mediation in Zimbabwe, 1974–1980* (Boulder, CO: Lynne Rienner Publishers, 1990), 119–23.

pressuring the Frontline State presidents and South Africa to bring the PF and Smith's government to Geneva certainly changed the dynamics of the negotiations in the Cold War race state context.

As shown in Chapters 5 and 6, the British were in no hurry in 1977 and 1978 to reach a settlement, nor, it would seem, were the Frontline State presidents. It seemed that the liberation war had turned in favor of the liberation war armies, so there was no need to move too quickly. However, into this void entered Ian Smith and his "EXCO" who were bent upon reaching an internal settlement that would result in a black prime minister, but most importantly the lifting of sanctions and the return to international recognition. The pressures from the Frontline State presidents and pressure groups in Africa, the United States, and the Commonwealth nations did not allow the internal settlement and "Zimbabwe-Rhodesia" to work as planned, resulting in the dramatic results of the Lancaster House negotiations in 1979. The Americans wanted to avoid another "Horn of Africa" Cold War conflict by 1978–79, so they put greater pressure on the parties to negotiate. In the end, it was South African and Rhodesian raids into Zambia and Mozambique that forced the Frontline State presidents – Presidents Kaunda and Machel in particular – to put the ultimate pressure on Nkomo and Mugabe to negotiate in earnest.

As emphasized from the outset of this book, the use of diplomatic files as sources of history presents potential problems regarding how power relations are presented, and how voices are mediated. However mediated and biased these sources are, I believe that these files offer a valuable window into the world of power negotiations and reveal, in historical time, the ways in which leaders such as Nkomo and Mugabe confronted the offers of the Cold War powers and Frontline State presidents to try to achieve the goal of African sovereignty, as well as compete with each other in order to become the first leader of the new state. These files have also shown that the more powerful states involved, particularly the United States, Britain, and South Africa, were not as capable of managing the decolonization process as they sometimes believed. In the end, South African support for the internal settlement did help to force the PF to accept the Lancaster House agreements, but the weaknesses of Muzorewa's Zimbabwe-Rhodesia state coalesced with Cold War pressures from the United States and Britain to insist that the PF be the main power brokers at Lancaster House.

A major tragedy of Cold War conflicts in Africa is that the continued funding of ZANLA and ZIPRA by so many outside forces meant that Mugabe and Nkomo were never forced by material circumstances to combine their militaries. As much as they succeeded in combining their diplomatic talents to navigate and negotiate a decolonization process, the recognized problems of two separate liberation armies would lead to a major tragedy after independence. As discussed earlier in Chapter 9, Richard Werbner's important argument that the "quasi-nationalisms" and ethnic political violence that tore apart the vision of a united Zimbabwe was fundamentally a product of the two liberation armies that were, with some important exceptions, recruited on ethnic lines. Attempts to force real unity on the PF, and the Frontline State presidents' attempt to use the OAU Liberation Committee to do so, all failed given that there remained other options for Nkomo and Mugabe to fund the war.

As this book has attempted to demonstrate, the development of ethnicity as an operating factor within the factionalism of Zimbabwean nationalists also contributed to the Anglo-Americans' consistent interpretation of almost every new development, or most often setback, in the liberation struggle through the lens of ethnicity. What these chapters have hopefully demonstrated, is that the personal rivalries and political struggles between ZAPU and ZANU were more significant than the ethnic differences. In the end, however, the election campaigning and the post-independence violence that culminated in the *Gukurahundi*, while politically driven, was to be rationalized by many different international actors and diplomats as primarily an ethnic conflict – one that the foreign powers could conveniently wash their hands of, using tropes of supposed typical African state behavior, even while they remained intimately involved in the restructuring and day-to-day practices of the ZNA.

Once Mugabe and ZANU had taken power, the ability of the United States and Britain to influence behaviors were limited, particularly in terms of the ability to curb the abuse of state power in Mugabe's goal of destroying Nkomo and ZAPU and creating a one-party state. The diplomatic record demonstrates that British and American diplomats did more to try to stop the excesses of 5 Brigade violence than is often believed, but it also shows that no matter the amount of leverage they had, the decision was made by their superiors in the FCO and US Department of State to avoid antagonizing the goodwill and anti-Soviet stance of Mugabe's government over the *Gukurahundi*. South Africa, after failing to keep

Mugabe from coming to power, and who had responded with immediate acts of sabotage and assassination attempts on Mugabe's life, eventually worked out a relationship involving the two countries' mutual security interest in weakening ZAPU and also weakened the ability of the South African ANC to operate freely from Zimbabwe. This cooperation was far from being "successful," as both sides worked to undermine it, but the existence of this cooperation suggests that the longstanding relationship between Rhodesian military and intelligence and South African counterparts did not end in 1980. That is, despite Mugabe and ZANU's strong anti-apartheid rhetoric and international reputation, when it came to compromising with South Africa on economic and security issues, they understood well that they could not push too hard against South Africa. In a perverse way, South Africa's destabilization efforts with "Super-ZAPU" allowed the Zimbabwean state to continue renewing the state-of-emergency measures that, in turn, permitted state agents and the military to act with impunity against ZAPU. International knowledge of South African involvement also offered Mugabe and others in ZANU the ability to justify the use of state violence against its own citizens.

Finally, it is worth pointing out the obvious, that the institutional racialization of "white states" and "black states" in Africa did not end with the decolonization of Zimbabwe. It remains part of the culture of diplomacy, media coverage, and public opinion some forty years later. These sorts of underlying rhetorical devices are infused in much of the debates and multilateral and bilateral negotiations of today. Hopefully, the evidence presented here can allow students of history to reflect on the power of such belief systems and help to understand how they remain extremely detrimental to ending the cycles of violence and brutality still evident today. It is important to emphasize that the historical narrative presented in this book has tried to make the case that this violence was never only an "African problem," but rather the continuation of many historical strains of violence. It is also impossible and dangerous, therefore, to place all the responsibility for the political violence of the 1980s only on the shoulders of Robert Mugabe. The tendency to do so only perpetuates the personification of history, missing out on how such large-scale state crimes are not just done because of one individual. It is also worth remembering that it was not just one or two Anglo-American leaders who were responsible for the hypocrisies and hubris of Western leaders and bureaucracies in this history. It would take entire foreign relations bureaucracies in the

United States and Britain to achieve this. They had congratulated themselves in 1980 for their role in creating a client state in a Cold War sense, but they were also relieved that the new Zimbabwe was no longer viewed as their responsibility. By 1983 and 1984, the Zimbabwean government and its state crimes could be defined and classified as outside the responsibility of those powers who only a few years earlier celebrated their role in creating a new type of Cold War race state.

Select Bibliography

Alexander, Jocelyn. "Dissident Perspectives on Zimbabwe's Post-Independence War." *Africa* 68, no. 2 (1998), 151–82.

"Legacies of Violence in Matabeleland, Zimbabwe." In Preben Kaarsholm, ed. *Violence Political Culture & Development in Africa: Legacies of Violence in Matabeleland, Zimbabwe*. Athens, OH: Ohio University Press, 2006, 105–19.

"Nationalism and Self-Government in Rhodesian Detention: Gonakudzingwa, 1964–1974." *Journal of Southern African Studies* 37, no. 3 (2011), 551–69.

The Unsettled Land: State-Making & The Politics of Land in Zimbabwe, 1893–2003, 1st ed. London: James Currey, 2006.

Alexander, Jocelyn and JoAnn McGregor. "*Adelante!* Military Imaginaries, the Cold War, and Southern Africa's Liberation Armies." *Comparative Studies in Society and History* 62, no. 3 (2020), 619–50.

"War Stories: Guerrilla Narratives of Zimbabwe's Liberation War." *History Workshop Journal* 57, no. 1 (March 2004), 79–100.

Alexander, Jocelyn, JoAnn McGregor, and Terence O. Ranger. *Violence and Memory: One Hundred Years in the Dark Forests of Matabeleland, Zimbabwe*. Oxford: James Currey, 2000.

Auret, Diana. *Reaching for Justice: The Catholic Commission for Justice and Peace Looks Back at the Past Twenty Years, 1972–1992*. Harare: Catholic Commission for Justice and Peace, 1992.

Auret, Michael. *From Liberator to Dictator: An Insider's Account of Robert Mugabe's Descent into Tyranny*. Cape Town: David Philip Publishers, 2009.

Baines, Gary. "The Arsenal of Securocracy: Pretoria's Provision of Arms and Aid to Salisbury, c. 1974–1980." *South African Historical Journal* 71, no. 3 (2019), 1–18.

Barber, James P. and John Barratt. *South Africa's Foreign Policy: The Search for Status and Security, 1945–1988*. Cambridge: Cambridge University Press, 1990.

Baumhögger, Goswin. *The Struggle for Independence: Documents on the Recent Development of Zimbabwe (1975–1980)*. Hamburg: Institute of African Studies Documentation Centre, 1984.

Bhebe, Ngwabi and Terence O. Ranger. *The Historical Dimensions of Democracy and Human Rights in Zimbabwe*. Harare: Zimbabwe University Publications, 2001.

Borstelmann, Thomas. *The Cold War and the Color Line: American Race Relations in the Global Arena*. Cambridge, MA: Harvard University Press, 2001.

Brickhill, Jeremy. "Making Peace with the Past: War Victims and the Work of the Mafela Trust." In Ngwabi Bhebe and Terence Ranger, eds. *Soldiers in Zimbabwe's Liberation War*. London: James Currey, 1995, 163–73.

Campbell, Horace. *Reclaiming Zimbabwe: The Exhaustion of the Patriarchal Model of Liberation*. Trenton, NJ: Africa World Press, 2003.

Catholic Commission for Justice and Peace and Legal Resources Foundation. *Breaking the Silence, Building True Peace: A Report on the Disturbances in Matabeleland and the Midlands, 1980–1988*. Harare: CCJPZ and LRF, 1999. Reprinted as *Gukurahundi in Zimbabwe: A Report on the Disturbances in Matabeleland and the Midlands, 1980–1988*. London: Hurst & Company, 2007.

Caute, David. *Under the Skin: The Death of White Rhodesia*. Evanston: Northwestern University Press, 1983.

Chan, Stephen. *Robert Mugabe: A Life of Power and Violence*. Ann Arbor, MI: University of Michigan Press, 2003.

Charlton, Michael. *The Last Colony in Africa: Diplomacy and the Independence of Rhodesia*. London: Blackwell, 1990.

Cilliers, Jakkie. *Counter-Insurgency in Rhodesia*. London: Croom Helm, 1985.

Coltart, David. *The Struggle Continues: 50 Years of Tyranny in Zimbabwe*. Johannesburg: Jacana Media (Pty), 2016.

Crocker, Chester A. *High Noon in Southern Africa: Making Peace in a Rough Neighborhood*. New York: WW Norton & Co, 1993.

Dabengwa, Dumiso. "Relations between ZAPU and the USSR, 1960s–1970s: A Personal View." *Journal of Southern African Studies* 43, no. 1 (2017), 215–24.

"ZIPRA in the Zimbabwe War of National Liberation." In Ngwabi Bhebe and Terence O. Ranger, eds. *Soldiers in Zimbabwe's Liberation War*. London: James Currey, 1995, 24–35.

Davidow, Jeffrey. *A Peace in Southern Africa: The Lancaster House Conference on Rhodesia, 1979*. Boulder, CO: Westview Press, 1984.

Davis, Stephen M. *Apartheid's Rebels: Inside South Africa's Hidden War.* New Haven, CT: Yale University Press, 1987.

DeRoche, Andrew. *Andrew Young: Civil Rights Ambassador.* Wilmington, DE: Scholarly Resources, 2003.

Black, White, and Chrome: The United States and Zimbabwe, 1953–1998. Trenton, NJ: Africa World Press, 2001.

Kenneth Kaunda, the United States and Southern Africa. London: Bloomsbury Academic, 2016.

Doran, Stuart. *Kingdom, Power, Glory: Mugabe, ZANU and the Quest for Supremacy, 1960–1987.* Midrand, South Africa: Sithatha Media, 2017.

Dorman, Sarah Rich. *Understanding Zimbabwe: From Liberation to Authoritarianism.* London: Hurst, 2016.

Dzimba, John. *South Africa's Destabilization of Zimbabwe, 1980–89.* London: St. Martin's Press, 1998.

Eppel. Shari. "Gukurahundi: The Need for Truth and Reparation." In Brian Raftopoulos and Tyrone Savage, eds. *Zimbabwe: Injustice and Political Reconciliation.* Harare: Weaver Press, 2005, 43–62.

"How Shall We Talk of Bhalagwe? Remembering the Gukurahundi Era in Matabeleland, Zimbabwe." In Kim Wale, Pumla Gobodo-Madikizela, and Jeffrey Prager, eds. *Post-Conflict Hauntings: Transforming Memories of Historical Trauma.* Cham, Switzerland: Palgrave Macmillan, 2020, 259–84.

"Repairing a Fractured Nation: Challenges and Opportunities in Post-GPA Zimbabwe." In Brian Raftopoulos, ed. *The Hard Road to Reform: The Politics of Zimbabwe's Global Political Agreement.* Harare: Weaver Press, 2013, 211–50.

Garba, Joe. *Diplomatic Soldiering: The Conduct of Nigerian Foreign Policy, 1975–1979.* Ibadan: Spectrum Books Limited, 1987.

Gleijeses, Piero. *Conflicting Missions: Havana, Washington, and Africa, 1959–1976.* Chapel Hill, NC: University of North Carolina Press, 2002.

Visions of Freedom: Havana, Washington, Pretoria, and the Struggle for Southern Africa 1976–1991. Chapel Hill, NC: University of North Carolina Press, 2013.

Hanlon, Joseph. *Beggar Your Neighbours,* 1st ed. London: Catholic Institute for International Relations, 1986.

Hatchard, John. *Individual Freedoms and State Security in the African Context: The Case of Zimbabwe.* London: James Currey, 1993.

Horne, Gerald. *From the Barrel of a Gun: The United States and the War against Zimbabwe, 1965–1980.* Chapel Hill, NC: University of North Carolina Press, 2001.

Houser, George M. *No One Can Stop the Rain: Glimpses of Africa's Liberation Struggle*. Somerville, MA: Pilgrim Press, 1989.

Irwin, Ryan M. *Gordian Knot: Apartheid and the Unmaking of the Liberal World Order*. Oxford: Oxford University Press, 2012.

Johnson, Phyllis and David Martin. *Apartheid Terrorism: The Destabilization Report; [a Report for the Commonwealth Committee of Foreign Ministers on Southern Africa]*. London: J. Currey, 1989.

Kandiah, Michael and Sue Onslow, eds. *Britain and Rhodesia: The Route to Settlement*. London: Institute of Contemporary British History Oral History Programme, 2008.

Karekwaivanane, George. *The Struggle over State Power in Zimbabwe: Law and Politics since 1950*. Cambridge University Press, 2017.

Khadiagala, Gilbert M. *Allies in Adversity: The Frontline States in Southern African Security, 1975–1993*. Athens: Ohio University Press, 1994.

Kissinger, Henry. *Years of Renewal*. 1st ed. London: Simon & Schuster, 1999.

Kitchen, Helen. *Angola, Mozambique, and the West*. 1st ed. Westport, CT: Praeger, 1987.

Kriger, Norma J. *Guerrilla Veterans in Post-War Zimbabwe: Symbolic and Violent Politics, 1980–1987*. Cambridge University Press, 2006.

"ZANU(PF) Strategies in General Elections, 1980–2000: Discourse and Coercion." *African Affairs* 104, no. 414 (2005), 1–34.

Laïdi, Zaki. *The Super-Powers and Africa: The Constraints of a Rivalry: 1960–1990*. Translated by Patricia Baudoin. University of Chicago Press, 1990.

Larmer, Miles. *Rethinking African Politics: A History of Opposition in Zambia*. Farnham, United Kingdom: Ashgate Publishing, 2011.

Lowry, Donal. "The Impact of Anti-communism on White Rhodesian Political Culture, ca. 1920s–1980." *Cold War History* 7, no. 2 (2007), 169–94.

Martin, David, and Phyllis Johnson. *The Struggle for Zimbabwe, The Chimurenga War*. 1st ed. London: Faber And Faber, 1981.

Masunungure, Eldred V. and Jabusile M. Shumba. *Zimbabwe: Mired in Transition*. 1st ed. Harare: Weaver Press, 2012.

Mazarire, Gerald. "Discipline and Punishment in ZANLA: 1964–1979." *Journal of Southern African Studies* 37, no. 3 (2011), 571–91.

"ZANU's External Networks 1963–1979: An Appraisal." *Journal of Southern African Studies* 43, no. 1 (2017), 83–106.

Mazov, Sergey V. *A Distant Front in the Cold War: The USSR in West Africa and the Congo, 1956–1964*. Washington, DC and Stanford: Woodrow Wilson Center & Stanford University Press, 2010.

Mbembé, Achille and Libby Meintjes. "Necropolitics." *Public Culture* 15, no. 1 (Winter 2003), 11–40.

Meredith, Martin. *Our Votes, Our Guns: Robert Mugabe and the Tragedy of Zimbabwe*. New York: Public Affairs, 2002.

Mhanda, Wilfred. *Dzino: Memories of a Freedom Fighter*. Harare: Weaver Press, 2011.

Michel, Eddie. *The White House and White Africa: Presidential Policy Toward Rhodesia during the UDI Era, 1965–1979*. New York: Routledge, 2019.

Miller, Jamie. *An African Volk: The Apartheid Regime and Its Search for Survival*. Oxford University Press, 2016.

Mitchell, Nancy. *Jimmy Carter in Africa: Race and the Cold War*. Stanford University Press, 2016.

Mlambo, Alois S. *A History of Zimbabwe*. Cambridge University Press, 2014.

Moore, David. "ZANU-PF and the Ghosts of Foreign Funding." *Review of African Political Economy* 103 (March 2005), 156–62.

Mugabe's Legacy: Coups, Conspiracies and the Conceits of Power in Zimbabwe. London: Hurst, 2021.

"The Zimbabwean People's Army Moment in Zimbabwean History, 1975–1977: Mugabe's Rise and Democracy's Demise." In Carolyn Bassett and Marlea Clarke, eds. *Post-colonial Struggles for a Democratic Southern Africa: Legacies of Liberation*. London: Palgrave Macmillan, 2016, 22–39.

Moyo, Gorden. "Mugabe's Neo-sultanist Rule: Beyond the Veil of Pan-Africanism." In Sabelo J. Ndlovu-Gatsheni, ed. *Mugabeism?: History, Politics, and Power in Zimbabwe*. London: Palgrave Macmillan, 2015, 61–74.

Msindo, Enocent. *Ethnicity in Zimbabwe: Transformations in Kalanga and Ndebele Societies, 1860–1990*. University of Rochester Press, 2012.

Msipa, Cephas. *In Pursuit of Freedom and Justice: A Memoir*. Harare: Weaver Press, 2015.

Muehlenbeck, Philip E., ed. *Race, Ethnicity, and the Cold War: A Global Perspective*. Nashville, TN: Vanderbilt University Press, 2012.

Munguambe, Clinarete Victoria Luis. "Nationalism and Exile in the Age of Solidarity: Frelimo-ZANU Relations in Mozambique (1975–1980)." *Journal of Southern African Studies* 43, no. 1 (2017), 161–78.

Muzondidya, James and Sabelo Ndlovu-Gatsheni. "'Echoing Silences': Ethnicity in Postcolonial Zimbabwe, 1980–2007." *African Journal on Conflict Resolution* 7, no. 2 (2007), 257–97.

Muzorewa, Abel Tendekayi and Norman E. Thomas. *Rise Up and Walk: An Autobiography*. London: Evans Books, 1978.

Ndlovu-Gatsheni, Sabelo. "Introduction: Mugabeism and Entanglements of History, Politics, and Power in the Making of Zimbabwe." In Sabelo Ndlovu-Gatsheni, ed. *Mugabeism?: History, Politics and Power in Zimbabwe*. New York: Palgrave Macmillan, 2015, 1–25.

"Introduction: Writing Joshua Nkomo into History and Narration of the Nation." In S. Ndlovu-Gatsheni, ed. *Joshua Mqabuko Nkomo of Zimbabwe: Politics, Power, and Memory*. New York: Palgrave Macmillan, 2017, 1–49.

"Rethinking Chimurenga and Gukurahundi in Zimbabwe: A Critique of Partisan National History." *African Studies Review*, 55, no. 3 (2012), 1–26.

Ndlovu-Gatsheni, Sabelo and Finex Ndhlovu, eds. *Nationalism and the National Projects in Southern Africa: New Critical Reflections*. 1st ed. Pretoria: Africa Institute of South Africa, 2013.

Nkomo, Joshua. *Nkomo: The Story of My Life*. London: Methuen, 1984.

Noer, Thomas J. *Cold War and Black Liberation: The United States and White Rule in Africa, 1948–1968*. Columbia: University of Missouri Press, 1985.

Nyarota, Geoff. *Against the Grain: Memoirs of a Zimbabwean Newsman*. Cape Town: Zebra, 2006.

Nyathi, Pathisa, "Lancaster House Talks: Timing, Cold War and Joshua Nkomo." In Sabelo Ndlovu-Gatsheni, ed. *Joshua Mqabuko Nkomo of Zimbabwe: Politics, Power, and Memory*. New York: Palgrave Macmillan, 2017, 149–72.

Onslow, Sue, ed. *Cold War in Southern Africa: White Power, Black Liberation*. Abingdon: Taylor & Francis, 2012.

"'Noises Off': South Africa and the Lancaster House Settlement 1979–1980." *Journal of Southern African Studies* 35, no. 2 (2009), 489–506.

"Race and Policy: Britain, Zimbabwe and the Lancaster House Land Deal," *The Journal of Imperial and Commonwealth History* 45, no. 5 (2017), 844–67.

Owen, David. *Time to Declare*. London: Michael Joseph, 1991.

Pallotti, Arrigo. *Nyerere e la decolonizzazione dell'Africa australe (1961–1980)* [Nyerere and the Decolonization of Southern Africa (1961–1980)]. Firenze: Le Monnier – Mondadori, 2021.

"Tanzania and the 1976 Anglo-American Initiative for Rhodesia." *The Journal of Commonwealth History* 45, no. 5 (2017), 800–22

Phimister, Ian "The Making and Meanings of the Massacres in Matabeleland." *Development Dialogues* 50 (2008), 199–218.

Preston, Matthew. *Ending Civil War: Rhodesia and Lebanon in Perspective*. London: Tauris Academic Studies, 2004.

Raftopoulos, Brian and Alois Mlambo, eds. *Becoming Zimbabwe: A History from the Pre-colonial Period to 2008.* Harare: Weaver Press, 2009.

Ranger, Terence O. and Ngwabi Bhebe. *Soldiers in Zimbabwe's Liberation War.* Harare: University of Zimbabwe Publications, 1995.

Renwick, Robin. *Unconventional Diplomacy in Southern Africa.* New York: St. Martin's Press, 1997.

Sachikonye, Lloyd M. *When a State Turns on Its Citizens: 60 Years of Institutionalised Violence in Zimbabwe.* Johannesburg: Jacana Media, 2011.

Sadomba, Zvakanyorwa Wilbert. *War Veterans in Zimbabwe's Revolution: Challenging Neo-colonialism and Settler and International Capital.* Oxford: Boydell & Brewer, 2011.

Scarnecchia, Timothy. "Catholic Voices of the Voiceless: The Politics of Reporting Rhodesian and Zimbabwean State Violence in the 1970s and the Early 1980s." *Acta Academica* 47, no. 1 (2015), 182–207

"The Congo Crisis, the United Nations, and Zimbabwean Nationalism, 1960–1963." *African Journal on Conflict Resolution* 11, no. 1 (2011), 63–86.

"Front Line Diplomats: African Diplomatic Representations of the Zimbabwean Patriotic Front, 1976–1978." *Journal of Southern African Studies* 43, no. 1 (2017), 107–24.

"Joshua Nkomo: Nationalist Diplomat: 'Father of the Nation' or 'Enemy of the State.'" In Sabelo Ndlovu-Gatsheni, ed. *Joshua Mqabuko Nkomo of Zimbabwe: Politics, Power, and Memory.* London: Palgrave Macmillan, 2017, 173–92.

"Intransigent Diplomat: Robert Mugabe and His Western Diplomacy, 1963–1983." In Sabelo Ndlovu-Gatsheni, ed. *Mugabeism? History, Politics and Power in Zimbabwe.* New York: Palgrave Macmillan, 2015, 77–92.

"Proposed Large-Scale Compensation for White Farmers as an Anglo-American Negotiating Strategy for Zimbabwe, 1976–1979." In Arrigo Pallotti and Corrado Tornimbeni, eds. *State, Land and Democracy in Southern Africa.* Burlington, VT: Ashgate, 2015, 105–26.

"Rationalizing 'Gukurahundi': Cold War and South African Foreign Relations with Zimbabwe, 1981–1983." *Kronos* (November 2011), 87–103.

The Urban Roots of Democracy and Political Violence in Zimbabwe: Harare and Highfield, 1940–1964. University of Rochester Press, 2008.

Scarnecchia, Timothy and David Moore. "South African Influences in Zimbabwe: From Destabilization in the 1980s to Liberation War Solidarity in the 2000s." In Arrigo Pallotti and Ulf Engel, eds. *South*

Africa after Apartheid: Policies and Challenges of the Democratic Transition. Leiden: Brill, 2016, 175–202.

Schmidt, Elizabeth and William Minter. *Foreign Intervention in Africa: From the Cold War to the War on Terror.* New York, NY: Cambridge University Press, 2013.

Sellstrom, Tor. *Sweden and National Liberation in Southern Africa.* 1st ed. Uppsala, Sweden: Nordiska Afrikainstitutet, 2003.

Shamuyarira, Nathan M. *Crisis in Rhodesia.* 1st ed. Andre Deutsch, 1965.

Shaw, Agnus. *Mutoko Madness.* Harare: Boundary Books, 2013.

Shubin, Vladimir. *The Hot "Cold War": The USSR in Southern Africa.* London: Pluto Press, 2008.

Sibanda, Eliakim. *The Zimbabwe African People's Union, 1961–87.* Trenton, NJ: African World Press, 2005.

Sithole, Masipula. *Struggle within the Struggle.* Salisbury: Rujecko Publishers, 1979.

Sithole, Vesta. *My Life with an Unsung Hero.* Bloomington: Author House, 2006.

Smith, Ian Douglas. *The Great Betrayal: The Memoirs of Africa's Most Controversial Leader.* London: Blake Publishing, 1997.

Southall, Roger. *Liberation Movements in Power: Party and State in Southern Africa.* Pietermaritzburg: KwaZulu-Natal Press, 2013.

Stedman, Stephen John J. *Peacemaking in Civil War: International Mediation in Zimbabwe, 1974–1980.* Boulder, CO: Lynne Rienner Publishers, 1990.

Stiff, Peter. *Warfare by Other Means.* 1st ed. Alberton, South Africa: Galago, 2002.

Suri, Jeremi. *Henry Kissinger and the American Century.* 1st ed. Cambridge, MA: Belknap Press of Harvard University Press, 2007.

Tamarkin, Mordechai. *The Making of Zimbabwe: Decolonization in Regional and International Politics.* London: Frank Cass, 1990.

Temu, Arnold J. and Joel das Neves Tembe, eds. *Southern African Liberation Struggles: Contemporaneous Documents, 1960–1994.* Tanzania: Mkuki na Nyota, 2014.

Tendi, Blessing-Miles. *The Army and Politics in Zimbabwe: Mujuru, the Liberation Fighter and Kingmaker.* Cambridge University Press, 2020.

"Transnationalism, Contingency and Loyalty in African Liberation Armies: The Case of ZANU's 1974–1975 Nhari Mutiny." *Journal of Southern African Studies* 43, no. 1 (2017), 143–59.

Thatcher, Margaret. *The Downing Street Years.* London: Harper Collins, 1993.

Thompson, Carol B. *Challenge to Imperialism: The Frontline States in the Liberation of Zimbabwe.* Boulder, CO: Westview Press, 1986.

Todd, Judith. *Through the Darkness: A Life in Zimbabwe*. Cape Town: Struik Publishers, 2007.

Vance, Cyrus. *Hard Choices: Critical Years in America's Foreign Policy*. London: Simon and Schuster, 1983.

Verrier, Anthony. *The Road to Zimbabwe, 1890–1980*. London: Jonathan Cape, 1986.

Watts, Carl Peter. *Rhodesia's Unilateral Declaration of Independence: A Study in International Crisis*. Basingstoke: Palgrave Macmillan, 2008.

Werbner, Richard. *Tears of the Dead: The Social Biography of an African Family*. Washington, DC: Smithsonian Institute, 1991.

White, Luise. *The Assassination of Herbert Chitepo: Texts and Politics in Zimbabwe*. Bloomington: Indiana University Press, 2003.

Unpopular Sovereignty: Rhodesian Independence and African Decolonization. University of Chicago Press, 2015.

Windrich, Elaine. *Britain and the Politics of Rhodesian Independence*. New York: Africana Pub. Co, 1978.

Index

African Studies Series

For EU product safety concerns, contact us at Calle de José Abascal, 56–1°,
28003 Madrid, Spain or eugpsr@cambridge.org.

www.ingramcontent.com/pod-product-compliance
Ingram Content Group UK Ltd.
Pitfield, Milton Keynes, MK11 3LW, UK
UKHW020402140625
459647UK00020B/2597